MANAGING OPERATIONAL RISK IN A CHANGING WORLD

MANAGING OPERATIONAL RISK IN A CHANGING WORLD

PENNY CAGAN

WILEY

Published by John Wiley & Sons, Inc., Hoboken, New Jersey.

For general information on our other products and services or for technical support, please contact our Customer Care Department within the United States at (800) 762-2974, outside the United States at (317) 572-3993 or fax (317) 572-4002.

Wiley also publishes its books in a variety of electronic formats. Some content that appears in print may not be available in electronic formats. For more information about Wiley products, visit our web site at www.wiley.com.

Library of Congress Cataloging-in-Publication Data has been applied for:

Hardback ISBN: 9781394421619
ePDF ISBN: 9781394421633
ePub ISBN: 9781394421626

Cover Design: Wiley
Cover Image: © TechSolution/stock.adobe.com

Typesetting: Set in 11.5/14 Bembo Std by Lumina Datamatics

SKY10149649_031726

For my mother, Diane Cagan, who has been my lifetime role model, and my brother Ross Cagan, who has supported me through some challenging times.

For all my present and former colleagues who have suited up and wrestled the risk battles with me and my students who I continue to learn risk lessons from.

Contents

Acknowledgments

Thank you to the John Wiley team who accepted my manuscript with so much grace and enthusiasm. And a special thank-you to Sherri-Anne Forde and Judith Newlin who helped steer me through the process with their patience and good advice and Gemma Valler who first introduced me to the Wiley community, where my book found a home.

Michael Grimwade was instrumental with steering me to a publisher. I would like to thank him for his generosity in offering to read a few chapters of my book and for helping me to find my way to the Wiley community. His operational risk book and enthusiasm for the operational risk discipline continue to inspire me.

I would like to thank the interviewees whose insight, professional experience, and in some instances risk battle scars contributed greatly to this book, including Mike Silva, Aarona Chou, Craig Spielman, Maureen Day, Tom Balogh, Jae King, Alicja Cade, Jeannie Pumphrey, and Evan Sekeris. I have worked over the years alongside many of these amazing risk professionals who have been my partners, coaches, and friends in the risk journey.

I would like to also thank Charles Fishkin who did a careful reading of my early chapters and provided strong feedback that allowed me to restructure the book and my overall approach. I would also like to thank Philippa Girling who I first discussed the book with and challenged me to forge ahead with the project. Her operational risk management book was an important foundation for my own.

Sim Segal provided me with the initial opportunity to teach as an adjunct lecturer in Columbia University's Enterprise Risk Management program, and I am deeply grateful for his support and the exposure the program has provided to so many future risk leaders, who are our future.

I am deeply grateful to Roland Kennett from ORX, Mike Finlay from Risk Business, and Rajeev Sethi from IBM, who were generous in their provision of data and case studies. We go back decades and grew up together in the operational risk discipline and have a shared history together.

Finally, I would like to thank my dear friend, Mary Hall Mayer, who helped steer me through the book writing process and has always been there for me during some of the greatest challenges of my life.

Introduction to Operational Risk Book

Operational Risk at a Crossroads

Managing the many complex risks of our time has brought the management of operational risk to a crossroads. When I first entered the discipline in the late 1990s, the mandate was simple: collect, aggregate, and analyze the firm's operational risk losses. This was the moment on the heels of the monumental Barings PLC operational risk event when the global banking community was debating what the first operational risk capital charge would look like and how to best quantify the discipline. The industry looked to insurance methodologies of estimating losses for guidance and adopted in the early days a loss distribution approach. At this time, I brought to market the first database of external losses, which was based on public accounts (from the press, company statements and reports, public regulatory censures) of operational risk events. I built this database to include case studies with focus on the breakdown of controls, because I knew deep down that there had to be more than counting internal losses numerically and there was a trove of lessons to be learned from industry peers.

Today, we have come a long way since those early days of counting loss events and through a complicated thicket of advanced measurement approaches and modeling and the split-off of certain operational risk disciplines, such as third-party and cyber, into stand-alone functions. The Office of the Comptroller of the Currency's (OCC) Heightened Standards was a game changer in the banking industry regarding expectations of the roles and responsibilities of the front-line businesses (first line of defense) and risk management functions (second line of defense) in the management of operational risk. This ultimately placed more responsibility for the direct management of operational risk on the front line and significantly altered the definition of the role of risk management in the second line. It also led to a definition of the audit function (the third line) and a three lines of defense model that is widely accepted today in financial institutions, while present but more loosely implemented in other industries.

Operational risk departments defined their role after the passage of Heightened Standards as one that is independent of the business and focused on review and challenge and oversight. The frontline business, as the first line of defense, became responsible for directly managing operational risk, while the independent risk management function in many institutions took a step away from direct management and focused on the documentation of their oversight and review and challenge activities. The quality of the documentation became important, and I have sat through industry discussions on how to document ongoing review and challenge, including developing home-grown databases.

We are now at a point in the evolution of operational risk where management in some institutions is questioning the value of the function, beyond the expectation that you need one to meet regulatory requirements. The world has become more complicated, as have the risk issues, and management is not always seeing the active engagement of operational risk professionals in the ongoing management of risk. In some ways, this is the result of the interpretation of the three lines of defense model and the emphasis on "independent" risk management. But, in my opinion, as someone who managed operational risk before there was so much emphasis on independence, there is nothing that precludes solving operational risk challenges together with the frontline business and providing advisory support in the "flow of business activity" rather than after the fact. And ultimately, to add value, the function needs to be aligned with the firm's priorities and strategies and have the stature necessary to have a seat at the table with senior management.

This book is my attempt to provide the long view of operational risk, from its origins as a named discipline to a discipline with several critical subspecialties, including cyber, technology, data, model, business continuity, resiliency, third-party, and transaction processing risk management. It is designed to provide a base of knowledge for risk professionals newly entering the operational risk or nonfinancial risk discipline and for those with more experience that would benefit from a reference source.

I have supplemented foundational concepts with my personal experience coming from 40 years of working in the field and interviews with industry veterans. Managing operational risk or nonfinancial risk in the real world can only truly be learned by rolling up your sleeves and solving risk challenges. I have incorporated interviews with industry veterans who share their perspective and strategy for managing operational risk. It is hoped that our collective experience can assist with this learning process.

Chapter 1

The History and Importance of Operational Risk

The Definition of Operational Risk

The place to start understanding the operational risk discipline is with the definition. The Basel Committee on Banking Supervision (BCBS) solicited feedback from the industry on the definition of *operational risk* in the late 1990s, and there was a lot of discussion in forums on what it was and how to define it. Before the industry settled on a definition, which continues to be the standard today, the discipline was referred to as "all other risks." If it was not credit or market risk, which were undergoing quantification in the 1990s, then it was "all other risks."

The definition that the industry settled on through the Basel forums is this:

> *The risk of loss resulting from inadequate or failed internal processes, people and systems, or from external events. This definition includes legal risk but excludes strategic and reputational risk.*

The key components of the definition are processes, people, systems, and external events. This definition has served as a touchstone and mantra over the years when I tried to determine if an operational risk event had occurred. The definition was designed originally to put a box around what could be quantified as distinct operational risk events. For this reason, legal risk was included, because it could be quantified by fines, penalties, or punitive damages resulting from supervisory actions, as well as private settlements.

Reputational risk, which I consider an "outcome" or "impact" of an operational risk, was excluded, as was strategic risk.

Here are the key components of the definition:

- **Internal processes:** Failures or inadequacies in the institution's processes, such as procedural errors, incorrect data entry, or flaws in the design of a process
- **People:** Human errors, misconduct, lack of training, or other issues related to personnel that can lead to operational failures
- **Systems:** Failures or inadequacies in technology systems, such as software bugs, hardware failures, or cybersecurity breaches
- **External events:** Events outside the institution's control, including natural disasters, terrorism, regulatory changes, or external fraud

The Office of the Comptroller of the Currency (OCC) has a slightly different definition from what was put forward by the Basel Committee, with more emphasis on resiliency:

> *Operational risk is the risk to current or projected financial condition and **resilience** arising from inadequate or failed internal processes or systems, human errors or misconduct, or adverse external events.*

Most global banking institutions have adopted the Basel definition directly or adopted it for their own organization. Several nonbanking financial institutions crafted definitions that reflect their more monoline business models.

Here are a few examples, with specific exposures relevant for their business model called out, such as fraud, cyber, data security, and compliance:

A Credit Card and Payments Company:

"Operational risk includes fraud, data breaches, cyber threats, technology failures, and compliance lapses that could impact Visa's global payments ecosystem."

A Wealth Management Company:

"Operational risk encompasses technology failures, process inefficiencies, regulatory compliance issues, fraud, and customer service breakdowns that can lead to financial or reputational damage."

A Fintech and Payments Company:

"Operational risk is the risk of direct or indirect loss due to failures in processes, human error, technology disruptions, fraud, cyber threats, or third-party service providers."

An Insurance Company:

"Operational risk arises from failures in people, processes, and systems, as well as external events, including legal and compliance risks, underwriting errors, and claims processing failures."

An Asset Management Firm:

"Operational risk is the risk of loss or adverse impact resulting from inadequate or failed internal processes, people, systems, or from external events, including legal, regulatory, and reputational risks."

The Impact of the Barings PLC Unauthorized Trading Event

Before there was a clear articulation of the definition and the development of a framework, operational risk was managed and quantified under the credit risk umbrella. Banks mostly believed they had operational risk covered under their credit risk frameworks. And then the landmark Barings PLC event happened, which changed everything. The Barings event was a wake-up call that operational risk could be large and that it was more than back-office inconsequential errors that had little impact on a financial institution's viability.

The Barings event crystallized the call for a definition, framework, and most importantly capital charge associated with managing operational risk. A rogue trader by the name of Nick Leeson literally brought down a 200-year-old institution in 1995 through a series of unauthorized trades in the bank's Singapore office. Veteran operational risk managers have internalized the facts of the Barings case because it was so foundational to establishing a formal discipline; it is worth reviewing the event for newer managers who might not have lived through the shock that the event created.

Nick Leeson worked as a derivatives trader at Barings Bank in Singapore. He primarily traded futures contracts on the Singapore International Monetary Exchange (SIMEX). He was viewed as a star trader by his management, who had the stomach to make speculative bets that resulted in impressive profits. Those profits, however, were imaginary. He was accumulating losses that eventually grew to approximately USD $1.3 billion. He hid the losses from his management in an unused account, which infamously became known as 88888. As the losses accumulated and he tried to trade out of his hole, he continued to double-down on bad trades.

Barings Bank declared bankruptcy in February 1995 after the losses came to light. This event shocked the industry into realizing how large and impactful an operational risk event could be. The equivalent today would be if a solid UK bank like Barclays went under because of a single operational risk event. The likelihood of an unauthorized trading event taking down a bank today is lessened because of all the frameworks, controls, and capital coverage that are in place as guardrails to mitigate unauthorized trades. But I would never say that it could not happen because clever people can always find new ways to skirt compliance policies.

The collapse of Barings brought to light the lack of operational risk controls and frameworks in the industry. It became clear that managing the risk as part of a credit framework was not adequate. The discipline needed its own tools, methodologies, controls, risk management practices, dedicated professionals, and a name and definition. It also brought to light how the actions of a single person could jeopardize the entire firm.

The Introduction of Basel II and Operational Risk Capital Adequacy

The Barings event and other operational mishaps at the time prompted a significant regulatory response, which was managed globally through the Basel Committee on

Banking Supervision with input from each of the jurisdictional regulatory supervisors around the world. Industry working groups convened to provide feedback on what a global operational risk framework would look like. This was the genesis for the drafting and implementation of the Basel II framework by the Basel Committee on Banking Supervision (commonly known as BCBS), which for the first time would introduce requirements and guidelines for managing operational risk.

The first order of the Basel II framework was to put in place capital adequacy requirements for operational risk. This was highly contentious with the industry arguing that since they were already covering operational risk through their credit risk capital frameworks, it would be double counting. This required a distinct definition for operational risk that distinguished it from credit risk. To this day, if an operational risk event results in a credit loss (known as a *credit boundary event*), such as poor operational processes that lead to a credit exposure, it is included in credit capital calculations (although tracked in operational risk databases for awareness).

Basel II was not only about capital, and there was a lot of industry debate on whether operational risk could be quantified like credit and market risk. Basel II also included requirements for the management and supervision of operational risk. The industry was divided between quantitative and qualitative factions (I fell in the later), with the arc of the discipline ultimately pulling away from an Advanced Modeling Approach (AMA) through the recent refinement of Basel III.

Basel II introduced the first foray into modeling operational risk and determining regulatory capital, which included a menu of three approaches:

1. Basic Indicator Approach (BIA): Calculated capital based on a fixed percentage of 15% of the bank's average gross income over a three-year period.
2. The Standardized Approach (TSA): Introduced basic indictors for eight standard business lines, which were multiplied by gross income.
3. Advanced Measurement Approach (AMA): Banks developed their own internal models to calculate capital that were believed to be most sensitive to their operating environment. The models required approval by regulators and relied on four factors:
    - Internal Loss Data: Banks' repositories of historical operational risk loss events
    - External Loss Data: Events that occurred to peer institutions
    - Scenarios: Hypothetical but plausible operational risk scenarios
    - Business Environment and Internal Control Factors (BEICFs): Assessment of risks and controls

The largest and most sophisticated of banks were expected to develop AMA models for determining regulatory capital. Quantitative analysts who were hired from other disciplines to model operational risk quickly discovered that it was not an easy task, because operational risk is inherently different from credit or market risk, which have a baseline of potential exposure that can be more predictable. The 20-year experience in quantifying operational risk has led to a massive pull-back under the revised rules of Basel III (known as Basel III Endgame), which has put forward a single standardized approach for calculating capital.

The components of the AMA models are foundational to the management of operational risk and are here to stay as is the ongoing effort to quantify the discipline along with improving its management controls:

- Collecting, tracking, and analyzing internal loss events is critical for identifying patterns of exposure to operational risk and prioritizing controls.
- External loss events allow for a proactive appraisal of an institution's own control environment based on what peer institutions have experienced.
- Scenario analysis provides a forward-look into what severe but plausible operational risks can occur within an institution and inform resiliency plans.
- Business environment and internal control factor assessments have mostly been implemented through risk and control self-assessment (RCSA) programs, which identify risks and assess the efficacy of mitigating controls.

After years of negotiation and industry feedback throughout the later part of the 1990s and early 2000s, the BCBS released the Basel II framework in June 2004, which included the definition of operational risk and the approaches for quantifying and managing operational risk. It was a ground-breaking time for the discipline, because for the first time there was an industry-wide definition and framework that banking institutions needed to adhere to. However, this was not the end of breath-taking unauthorized trading events.

The passage in 2004 of the Basel II Framework was the beginning of a long journey in the maturation of the operational risk discipline. Financial institutions around the world, with rules and regulations passed by global regulations in support of Basel II, were expected to put operational risk programs in place that included the hiring of operational risk officers and personnel and the development of core frameworks across the industry. These core components included internal processes and controls that identified, assessed, and mitigated operational risks. A 2006 Basel document titled "Basel II: International Convergence of Capital Measurement and Capital Standards: A Revised Framework" further and comprehensively refined the standards for allocating operational risk capital.

While financial institutions were busy building out their regulatory capital teams, there was a lot of growth happening on the management side of operational risk. The Basel Committee published groundbreaking guidance in June 2011, in a paper titled "Principles for the Sound Management of Operational Risk," which was an update of a much earlier paper published in 2003. The paper addressed the evolution of operational risk over the past decade and outlined its view of strong industry practices based on governance, risk management, and disclosure. The document acknowledged that the range of practices had evolved since the initial adoption of formal operational risk frameworks.

Foundational to all the regulatory documents was the concept of strong risk governance, including the role of the board of directors, that sets the tone, approves risk frameworks, and establishes from the top of the house the enterprise's capacity and willingness to accept risk through an expression of risk appetite. Strong governance relies on a three lines of defense model, which includes managing risks through the front-line ownership of its risk and control environment; second-line risk management in its independent oversight role; and audit as an independent assurance function. In theory, with this belts and suspenders approach, an enterprise should be fortified in its management of operational risks.

The Language of Operational Risk

What was remarkable about Basel II, in addition to its introduction of an operational risk framework and methodology, was the focus on establishing an operational risk taxonomy, which essentially became the language of operational risk. This was the first time that a group of bank risk professionals came together through industry forums to establish an operational risk taxonomy that was designed to allow banks to collect internal loss data in a consistent manner with the goal of allowing any one institution to compare itself with its peers. Ultimately, a global consortium called ORX was established to enable the sharing of loss data among member institutions.

The following are the seven operational risk event types that the industry developed and that Basel II adopted. It is a generic list that most institutions have used as a base for their more precise and detailed taxonomies, but it serves as a good starting point for discussing the types of operational risk and for determining what is and is not an operational risk event. The taxonomy was originally developed more than 20 years ago to be able to put rails around distinct operational risk events for the purposes of capital calculation under Basel II, but over time it has grown to become the standard (if basic) language of operational risk.

The Basel II framework, established by the Basel Committee on Banking Supervision, defines seven categories of operational risk events to standardize the classification and management of operational risk across financial institutions. These categories are detailed in the Basel II documentation, particularly in Annexes 8 and 9 of the 2006 Basel II document per the Bank for International Settlements.

Here are the seven operational risk event types as defined by Basel II, with examples that I have experienced through my work in senior operational risk roles:

1. **Internal fraud:** Losses due to acts of a type intended to defraud, misappropriate property, or circumvent regulations, the law, or company policy, excluding diversity/discrimination events, which involve at least one internal party.

   Example: A banker transferred funds out of a senior client's account into their own.
2. **External fraud**: Losses due to acts of a type intended to defraud, misappropriate property, or circumvent the law by a third party.

   Example: Funds were transferred into a fraudster's account through a business email compromise (BEC) scheme.
3. **Employment practices and workplace safety:** Losses arising from acts inconsistent with employment, health or safety laws or agreements, from payment of personal injury claims, or from diversity/discrimination events.

   Example: A bank is sued by a fired control executive for alleged retaliation related to escalating control issues.

4. **Clients, products, and business practices:** Losses arising from an unintentional or negligent failure to meet a professional obligation to specific clients (including fiduciary and suitability requirements), or from the nature or design of a product.

   Example: A wealth manager sells an annuity product to an 85-year-old, which is unsuitable for their stage of life.
5. **Damage to physical assets:** Losses arising from natural disasters or other events.

   Example: A bank branch is burned down during protests in California.
6. **Business disruption and system failures:** Losses arising from disruption of business or system failures.

   Example: A trading department halts derivatives trading after a third-party vendor is the victim of a ransomware attack.
7. **Execution, delivery, and process management:** Losses from failed transaction processing or process management, from relations with trade counterparties and vendors.

   Example: A bank suffers $7 million loss after wrong currency is entered into FX trading system. Refer to Table 1.1.

Basel III Endgame

The global banking regulatory committee continues to iterate the requirements for managing operational risk in response to industry events, changing operating environments and emerging risks. The 2008 Financial Crisis, also known as the Great Financial Crisis, resulted in a rethinking of the financial industry's capability to manage risk. It was a frightening time for those who lived through the demise of financial institutions that appeared as reinforced as the fortress buildings that they occupied. In the month of September 2008, Lehman Brothers, Washington Mutual, Merrill Lynch, and AIG all collapsed in the United States. In a demonstration of how interconnected the global markets are and how quickly a contagion can occur, several European and UK banks failed during this same month, including Halifax Bank (HBOS), Dexia, and Fortis.

In response to the Great Financial Crisis, the global banking community and regulators undertook a soul-searching exercise to determine what went wrong and why all the controls implemented under Basel II had not offered appropriate protection. There was a lot of discussion at the time that risk taking had become in effect "too risky," especially with the overheated mortgage markets where documentation and income requirements were severely compromised in the years leading up to the crisis. The offering of subprime mortgages at low initial rates expanded the availability of housing, but when these loans reset, they were no longer affordable to many homeowners.

The investment and fees earned from these securitized securities brought in significant profits for financial institutions across the industry. Many of these institutions took on substantial debt to finance their securitized businesses and found themselves over-leveraged when the value of their mortgage-related assets plummeted and access to wholesale funding disappeared. But when the interest rates on the underlying subprime loans reset, many homeowners—who in many cases had not undergone proper income verification—could no longer afford their mortgage payments and defaulted. As a result, the most exposed banks were left with hefty losses, with several experiencing runs by their depositors who were terrified that their funds may not be properly safeguarded. There were other factors that led to the financial crisis, including a severe pullback by the banks to lend across their credit products because of the losses that were building up. Although the crisis started in the United States, the contagion spread across the global markets. The US Federal Reserve and their counterparts across the world stepped in to bailout the banks that were deemed "too big to fail."

The events of this traumatic time for the markets ultimately led to the revision of Basel II and the introduction of Basel III. The global regulatory community responded with additional regulations in their jurisdictions, including in the United States the introduction of the Dodd-Frank Act, to provide more oversight over risk taking by the financial institutions that they supervised, especially those that were considered "too big to fail" or "systemically important."

After a period of soul-searching and dissecting what went wrong, the Basel Committee introduced Basel III in 2010. Basel III was drafted with the goal of uplifting the management, oversight, and regulation of risk taking in the banking community. The goal was to fully implement Basel III by 2019, but there have been significant delays with some aspects, including those that impact operational risk in the United States. The most current iteration can be found in the Basel Committee on Banking Supervision's document titled "Basel III: A global regulatory framework for more resilient banks and banking systems."

The revised standards for calculating capital requirements for operational risk have been controversial. Basel II established a standard that offered a menu option of three approaches including the Basic Indicator Approach, the Standardized Approach, and the Advanced Measurement Approach. The largest and most systemically important banks were expected to adopt the Advanced Measurement Approach, which allowed them to tailor their calculation of operational risk capital for their own institutions. Many spent more than 10 years building these models, hiring teams, and developing quantitative talent.

Basel III has essentially removed the menu approach and offers just what has become known as the New Standardized Approach for measuring operational risk capital. From the perspective of the Basel Committee, this allows for more standardization and comparability among banks. From the perspective of quantitative-bent practitioners, it represents a massive retreat from the ability to properly quantify and tailor their institution's operational risk capital.

At the time of drafting of this chapter, Basel III in the United States has been put on hold perhaps indefinitely, following a great deal of industry pushback on the new approach for operational risk capital, which by some estimates would have resulted in significantly higher charges for the large global banks. This is the culmination of a 20-year dance between the banks and the global regulators on capital charges, with the regulators pushing for larger charges and the banks balking at the anti-competitive spirit of the proposals.

Figure 1.1 demonstrates the trajectory of the Basel Committee's focus on operational risk.

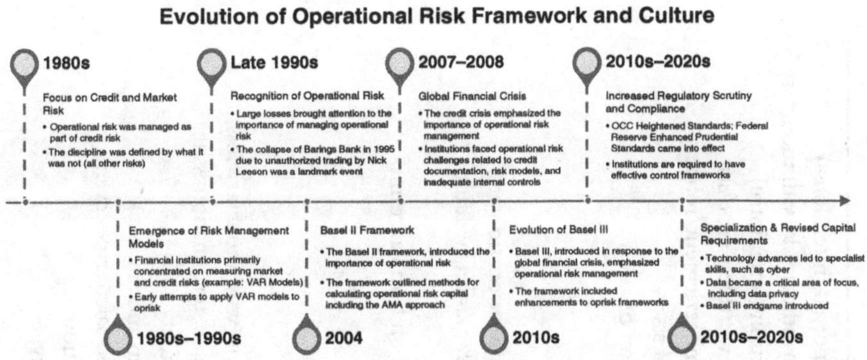

Figure 1.1 Basel Committee's focus on operational risk

Significant Unauthorized Trading Events

The following unauthorized trading events have similarities in common. The traders were viewed as "superstars" by their management because they were seen as being highly profitable; in many cases, they were operating outside the firm's controls that were not robust enough to prevent these events. The rogue traders doubled down as they accumulated losses in failed attempts to recover, which resulted in even larger losses. They hid their losses using secret accounts and falsifying records. The risk management frameworks and oversight controls were insufficient to prevent these events.

In many cases, the rogue traders exhibited behavioral clues that were ignored by their senior management because they were viewed as "high-flyers" who were responsible for impressive earnings. They pushed back on compliance requests for information and, in general, flouted the bank's rules while they acted above such mundane restrictions.

1. **Barings Bank (1995):** Nick Leeson was responsible for approximately USD $1.3 billion in unauthorized trading losses related to speculative trades on the Singapore Exchange.
2. **Daiwa Bank (1995):** Bond trader Toshihide Iguchi concealed losses over an 11-year period by falsifying records that resulted in a USD $1.1 billion loss.
3. **Societe Generale (2008):** Jerome Kerviel was responsible for a USD $7.2 billion in losses related to risk trades in European stock index futures.
4. **UBS (2011):** Kweku Adoboli was responsible for USD $2.4 billion in losses in the bank's London Office, resulting from unauthorized trades that he had concealed through the creation of false documents.
5. **JPMorgan Chase (2012):** Bruno Iksil, who came to be known as the London Whale due to outsized trades, was responsible for a $6.2 billion loss resulting from credit derivative trades. Although this was not a classic unauthorized trading event, it had many characteristics of one.

Table 1.1 from the Basel Committee demonstrates the level 2 breakdown of the seven event types.

Table 1.1 Detailed Loss Event Type Classification

Event-Type Category (Level 1)	Definition	Categories (Level 2)	Activity Examples (Level 3)
Internal fraud	Losses due to acts of a type intended to defraud, misappropriate property or circumvent regulations, the law or company policy, excluding diversity/discrimination events, which involves at least one internal party	Unauthorized activity	Transactions not reported (intentional) Transaction type unauthorized (with monetary loss) Mismarking of position (intentional)
		Theft and fraud	Fraud/credit fraud/worthless deposits Theft/extortion/embezzlement/robbery Misappropriation of assets Malicious destruction of assets Forgery Check kiting Smuggling Account takeover/impersonation etc. Tax noncompliance/evasion (willful) Bribes/kickbacks Insider trading (not on firm's account)
External fraud	Losses due to acts of a type intended to defraud, misappropriate property or circumvent the law, by a third party	Theft and fraud	Theft/robbery Forgery Check kiting
		Systems security	Hacking damage Theft of information (with monetary loss)
Employment practices and workplace safety	Losses arising from acts inconsistent with employment, health or safety laws or agreements, from payment of personal injury claims, or from diversity/discrimination events	Employee relations	Compensation, benefit, termination issues Organized labor activity
		Safe environment	General liability (slip and fall, etc.) Employee health and safety rules events Workers' compensation
		Diversity and discrimination	All discrimination types

Clients, products and business practices	Losses arising from an unintentional or negligent failure to meet a professional obligation to specific clients (including fiduciary and suitability requirements), or from the nature or design of a product	Suitability, disclosure and fiduciary	Fiduciary breaches/guideline violations Suitability/disclosure issues (know-your-customer, etc.) Retail customer disclosure violations Breach of privacy Aggressive sales Account churning Misuse of confidential information Lender liability
		Improper business or market practices	Antitrust Improper trade/market practices Market manipulation Insider trading (on firm's account) Unlicensed activity Money laundering
		Product flaws	Product defects (unauthorized, etc.) Model errors
		Selection, sponsorship and exposure	Failure to investigate client per guidelines Exceeding client exposure limits
		Advisory activities	Disputes over performance of advisory activities
Damage to physical assets	Losses arising from loss or damage to physical assets from natural disaster or other events	Disasters and other events	Natural disaster losses Human losses from external sources (terrorism, vandalism)
Business disruption and system failures	Losses arising from disruption of business or system failures	Systems	Hardware Software Telecommunications Utility outage/disruptions

(*Continued*)

Table 1.1 Continued

Event-Type Category (Level 1)	Definition	Categories (Level 2)	Activity Examples (Level 3)
Execution, delivery and process management	Losses from failed transaction processing or process management, from relations with trade counterparties and vendors	Transaction capture, execution and maintenance	Miscommunication
			Data entry, maintenance or loading error
			Missed deadline or responsibility
			Model/system misoperation
			Accounting error/entity attribution error
			Other task misperformance
			Delivery failure
			Collateral management failure
			Reference data maintenance
		Monitoring and reporting	Failed mandatory reporting obligation
			Inaccurate external report (loss incurred)
		Customer intake and documentation	Client permissions/disclaimers missing
			Legal documents missing/incomplete
		Customer/client account management	Unapproved access given to accounts
			Incorrect client records (loss incurred)
			Negligent loss or damage of client assets

Source: Bank for International Settlements / https://www.bis.org/basel_framework/chapter/OPE/25.htm / Last accessed by Nov 07, 2025

Table 1.2 is the taxonomy from ORX, which has set global standards for collecting, analyzing, and reporting on operational risk loss data through its consortium model (see Chapter 6 for background on ORX). It demonstrates how the industry has further developed the Basel event types.

Table 1.2 The ORX Reference Taxonomy

Level 1 Risks	Level 2 Risks
People	
	Breach of employment legislation or regulatory requirements
	Ineffective employment relations
	Inadequate workplace safety
External Fraud	
	Third-party/vendor fraud
	Agent/broker/intermediary fraud
	First-party fraud
Internal Fraud	
	Internal fraud committed against the organization
	Internal fraud committed against customers/clients, or third/fourth parties
Physical Security & Safety	
	Damage to organization's physical asset
	Damage to organization's physical asset
	Injury to employee or affiliates outside the workplace
	Damage or injury to public asset
Business Continuity	
	Inadequate business continuity planning/event management
	Processing/execution failure relating to clients and products
	Processing/execution failure relating to securities and collateral
Transaction Processing & Execution	
	Processing/execution failure relating to a third party
	Processing/execution failure relating to internal operations
	Change execution failure
Technology	
	Hardware failure
	Software failure
	Network failure
Conduct	
	Insider trading
	Anti-trust/anti-competition
	Improper market practices
	Pre-sales service failure
	Post-sales service failure
	Client mistreatment/failure to fulfill duties to customers
	Client account mismanagement
	Improper distribution/marketing

(*Continued*)

Table 1.2 Continued

Level 1 Risks	Level 2 Risks
	Improper product/service design
	Whistleblowing
	Breach of code of conduct and employee misbehavior
Legal	
	Mishandling of legal processes
	Contractual rights/obligation failures
	Noncontractual rights/obligation failures
Financial Crime	
	Money laundering and terrorism financing
	Sanctions violation
	Bribery and corruption
	KYC and transaction monitoring control failure
Regulatory Compliance	
	Ineffective relationship with regulators
	Inadequate response to regulatory change
	Improper licensing/certification/registration
	Breach of cross-border activities/extra-territorial regulations
	Prudential risk
Third Party	
	Third-party management control failure
	Third-party criminality/noncompliance with rules and regulations
	Inadequate intragroup agreements/SLAs
Information Security (including Cyber)	
	Data theft/malicious manipulation of data
	Data loss
	Cyber risk events
	Data privacy breach/confidentiality mismanagement
	Improper access to data
Statutory Reporting and Tax	
	External financial and regulatory reporting failure
	Tax payment/filing failure
	Trade/transaction reporting failure
Data Management	
	Unavailability of data
	Poor data quality
	Inadequate data architecture/IT infrastructure
	Inadequate data storage/retention and destruction management
Model	
	Model/methodology design error
	Model implementation error
	Model application error

Source: Courtesy of O.R.X

Bibliography

Basel Committee on Banking Supervision. *OPE. Calculation of RWA for Operational Risk. OPE 25. Standardized Approach.* July 5, 2024. https://www.bis.org/basel_framework/chapter/OPE/25.htm.

Basel Committee on Banking Supervision. *Revisions of the Principles for the Sound Management of Operational Risk.* August 2020. https://www.bis.org/bcbs/publ/d508.pdf.

Basel Committee on Banking Supervision. *Basel III: A Global Regulatory Framework for More Resilient Banks and Banking Systems – Revised Version.* June 2011. https://www.bis.org/publ/bcbs189.htm.

Basel Committee on Banking Supervision. *Basel III: Finalising Post-Crisis Reforms.* December 7, 2017. https://www.bis.org/bcbs/publ/d424.htm.

Basel Committee on Banking Supervision. *Basel II: International Convergence of Capital Measurement and Capital Standards: A Revised Framework – Comprehensive Version.* June 30, 2006. https://www.bis.org/publ/bcbs128.htm.

Basel Committee on Banking Supervision. *Revisions to the Principles for the Sound Management of Operational Risk.* March 31, 2021. https://www.bis.org/bcbs/publ/d515.htm.

Basel Committee on Banking Supervision. *Principles for the Sound Management of Operational Risk.* June 2011. https://www.bis.org/publ/bcbs195.htm.

Basel Committee on Banking Supervision. *International Convergence of Capital Measurement and Capital Standards: A Revised Comprehensive Version* (annex 9). June 2006. https://www.bis.org/publ/bcbs128.pdf.

European Banking Authority. *The EBA Publishes Key Regulatory Products on Operational Risk Losses Under the EU Banking Package Implementation.* August 4, 2025. https://www.eba.europa.eu/publications-and-media/press-releases/eba-publishes-key-regulatory-products-operational-risk-losses-under-eu-banking-package.

Francisco Covas, Gonzalo Fernandez Dionis, Katie Collard, Brett Waxman, and Jose Maria Tapia. *A Modification to the Basel Committee's Standardized Approach to Operational Risk.* Bank Policy Institute, May 4, 2022. https://bpi.com/a-modification-to-the-basel-committees-standardized-approach-to-operational-risk/.

Chapter 2

Managing Operational Risk in the New World Order

Managing Through the Great Challenges of Our Time

We are living through tumultuous times that present great challenges for operational risk managers. I am drafting this book at a time when the world literally seems on fire. Devastating wildfires engulfed parts of Europe and North America. The smoke from wildfires drifted down from Canada to where I live in New York City and during the darkest day turned the sky at midday first black and then an unsettling shade of yellow.

I traveled to France in September, where the temperature was in the 90s (Fahrenheit) without the promise of early autumn relief. NASA declared the summer of 2024 the hottest on record for the earth. The World Meteorological Organization announced that 2004 was in fact the hottest year on record globally. It previously called 2023 the hottest year on record and added, "It's a deafening cacophony of broken records." We continue to break these records year after year. As I write this, the State of Texas is recovering from catastrophic floods in Hill Country that left 134 dead and 101 people still missing.

At the same time, as we are experiencing the impact of an earth that is heating up, we are barely recovered as a society emotionally from the disruption caused by the global COVID pandemic, which posed challenges for business operations across the globe. There are recent reports on the uptick of COVID, although no one is predicting that it will be as virulent as it was in the days before vaccines and immunity. Bill Gates has warned that we are not properly prepared for the next pandemic, which the World Health Organization has warned can be more virulent than the last one.

For the most part, operational risk departments were able to think quickly on their feet during the early days of COVID, dust off old pandemic playbooks if they had them, and rise to the occasion of managing the operational risks associated with sending teams home, working remotely, dealing with the impact of their people getting ill, rewriting policies that relied on office presence, and executing risk acceptances for what could not be dealt with remotely. A friend who is the chief technology officer of a large healthcare organization commented that if he knew he had to send the whole company home to work remotely, he would have asked for a year to plan. And yet, most organizations coped surprisingly well with their entire workforce working remotely.

But will we be ready for the next pandemic that might occur at the same time as many other disruptions? We live in a world where severe risks and events are occurring simultaneously, and we appear to be in a near constant state of, if not crisis, turmoil. We will spend quite a lot of time in future chapters examining how to manage the confluence of risks as they occur concurrently.

We have also lived through a time of instability in the banking sector as demonstrated by the failure of Credit Suisse and Silicon Valley Bank. Silicon Valley Bank (SVB), which received extensive press in the United States, suffered from concentrated loan portfolios that were vulnerable to interest rate hikes, which resulted in significant losses in its portfolio. This was attributed to the failure to manage credit risk and to diversify the client and funding portfolio. But there was operational risk failures associated with how SVB operated.

A review of the SVB's MRAs, which was published posthumously by the Federal Reserve, indicates that there were deficiencies with the bank's governance and controls across its second-line technology and systems, cyber, information security, data governance and protection, vendor management, financial crime monitoring, and sanctions programs. There were also outstanding findings associated with the bank's board effectiveness and overall risk management. These are, in essence, operational risk issues.

Credit Suisse experienced numerous reputational and financial events before its final death knell, including exposure to two failed investment funds, a spying scandal, and instability at its senior ranks. The final straw in its ability to remain viable was an announcement that it had found material weaknesses in its financial reporting for 2022 and 2023. This came on the heels of the SVB collapse, where there was already a lack of trust in the transparency of bank financials. Reporting issues are at their heart operational risk, and in this case, the notice to the markets that it was going to restate two years of financials led to a further lack of faith that the bank could continue and a weakening of its available liquidity.

Another challenging aspect of operational risk management is managing the risks associated with artificial intelligence (AI). AI and especially generative AI are very much front and center in the popular and business consciousness these days. There are fears that it will restructure work that is performed today by knowledge workers in the same way factory automation changed the work landscape during the Industrial Revolution. The last thing anyone wants to be is a "luddite" who smashed factory machines in the nineteenth century in revolt. AI is here to stay and over time will change not just how we work but how we live our lives. It is time for operational risk professionals to embrace its capabilities while developing controls to manage its risks.

Operational risk professionals must be at the center of the efforts to develop risk management frameworks and controls to manage AI risks and use its capabilities to identify emerging risks. AI can be used to identify and assess risks, through the analysis of control and other data to determine the risk profile of an institution. Its use in RCSA, risk appetite, and other risk assessments (including compliance, financial crime, fraud, data governance, fair lending risk assessments) will not only create efficiencies but will also assist with identifying emerging risks and in time lead to stronger risk management. It can be powerful in monitoring transactions, processes, communications, pattern irregularities, anomalous behavior, and control breaks.

At the same time, AI poses new risks that operational risk professionals need to address head on. There are unique risks associated with using AI, including bias, data privacy, aggregation of data, hallucinations, transparency and black-box risks, models, third parties, and information security, that should be specified in governance frameworks. Standard operational risk methodologies and tools are not sufficient to manage these risks today and require an industry response to the development of adequate frameworks. Operational risk professionals, assisted through participation in industry forums, have the skills and knowledge to bring this work forward.

Operational risk managers need to be at the center of the great challenges of our time:

- Climate risk
- Pandemics
- Financial dislocation
- Social issues
- Artificial intelligence
- Geopolitical issues

Managing Operational Risks Associated with Geopolitical Events

While the world is coping with the impact of global warming, financial instability, pandemics, and AI, we are faced with serious geopolitical risks that present additional challenges for operational risk managers, including tensions in the Middle East and Eastern Europe. We entered 2023 with significant risks associated with the ongoing Russia-Ukraine conflict, which escalated the tensions between Russia and the NATO membership countries. As the war grinded on, there has been the risk that it could spill over into NATO countries, either intentionally or through accidental mishaps. Western companies that had significant operations in Russia, such as BP and Citi, have seen their operations locked in Russia since the country's invasion of Ukraine, which has created operational challenges for the firms.

Geopolitical tensions are impacting trade and the global supply chain. In addition to the impact on wheat supply emanating from Russia's invasion of Ukraine, the global supply chain could be fundamentally affected by the increasing complexity of relations between China and the West. The World Trade Organization has identified a shift in trade relations resulting from what it calls "friendshoring" as countries move trade relations to friendlier countries and away from China. The organization warns that in the long run this will lead to higher costs, destabilization, and protectionism. The United States has taken measures to reduce its trade exposure to China of what it has identified as strategically important goods and services, including placing prohibitions on the type of semi-conductors the United States can sell to China.

While institutions were dealing with the consequences of the Russia-Ukraine conflict and the complicated implementation of sanctions and getting their arms around the implication of supply chain issues on their operations and those of their clients, a catastrophic event occurred in the Middle East. On October 7, 2023, Hamas invaded the state of Israel in a surprise and brutal attack. This has resulted in a massive military operation by the state of Israel. The British Foreign Policy Group characterized the conflict as one that has "rewired key geopolitical relationships and with growing concern that the conflict may spread across the Middle East." The conflict has indeed spread to Iran and its proxies. The US military sent military warships to the Middle East early on and later supported Israel in an attack on Iran's nuclear reactors.

Operational risk professionals need to be at the center of the great challenges of our time, and geopolitical risk is one of the primary ones we face today. I have asked about the prospect of global instability at every operational risk conference and roundtable that I have attended recently because, in general, the topic has not been on the agenda. I received mostly silence in return. For the most part, the sense I have gleaned from operational risk professionals is that although they acknowledge that these are critical events, they are dealt with elsewhere in their organizations.

I would argue that the operational risk manager of today and tomorrow needs to have their pulse on the critical issues happening in the world and how they impact their organizations and communities. This includes having contingency plans in place for what the implications would be if their countries are pulled directly into conflicts for their people, operations, and clients and working directly with their risk and compliance colleagues to understand the interconnectedness among risk types when these catastrophic events occur. Operational risk can often be a driver for other risks, such as compliance risk. An example is the operational processes associated with monitoring transactions for sanctions that required implementing in the early days of the Ukraine War.

The place to start is to have a nimble process for constructing forward-looking scenarios that account for the broad implications of escalating tensions in the world, including wars, civil unrest, and the impact of physical risks associated with climate change. These scenarios can be used to create or update resiliency playbooks, assess, and plan for emerging risks, create awareness among senior management and the board, and for financial institutions, in the estimation of the impact on regulatory capital.

Geopolitical scenarios should account for risks associated with people, process, technology, and physical events. Potential risks include the loss of bandwidth if one's home country is pulled into a military incursion and military reservists are called into action; additional factors to consider are employee fear, depression, and anxiety in the face of uncertainty of war and especially among those who have connections with the warring countries, which can impact productivity and effectiveness.

Geopolitical risks impact the supply chain. This involves risks related to China-US relations and the movement of goods through countries that are affected by geopolitical issues, including neighboring trade partners, as exemplified by the impact to the movement of grain from Ukraine to Africa and the restriction of sending certain technologies to China.

We experienced elevated cyber risks on the heels of the Russian invasion of Ukraine. In the early days of the Israeli War, there were reports of cyberattacks on the military and government, in addition to media websites. There has also been a concern with the risk of fake news and misleading posts on social media, with AI credited for exasperating the problem.

Wars result in the destruction of physical property and assets, which can have impact not just on the residents and employees in the impacted location but on the investments and clients of exposed parties. This can spill over to other locations through protests that can lead to the destruction of properties. Global cities, including London and New York, have experienced mass protests in the days following the Israeli War, which create disruptions to business operations, transportation, and logistics.

These scenarios do not require a leap of imagination, and they mostly deal with risks we know could happen but perhaps at one time did not consider probable. These risks should be built into our scenarios and resiliency plans. I will discuss how to build resiliency associated with risks we may not know about later in Chapter 17.

The following is an overview of the operational risks associated with geopolitical events that should be considered when developing scenarios:

People:
- Mobilization of critical employees for military reserve duty
- Political instability and divisiveness that can lead to social instability
- Significant impact on the emotional well-being of employees

Process:
- Disruptions in the supply chain, including neighboring countries and trade partners
- Impact to third-party relationships, especially if reliant on vendors situated in a war zone

Technology:
- Escalation in cyberattacks, akin to those witnessed following Russia's invasion of Ukraine and the subsequent attacks during the Israeli War
- Proliferation of fake news and misleading social media posts

External:

- Social unrest associated with geopolitical events can result in damage to physical assets, such as corporate properties being vandalized or set ablaze
- Swift changes in laws and regulations that are process intensive in their implementation

Managing Change

With all the technological, societal, and geopolitical shifts that we are experiencing in society today, it is equally important that organizations manage the risks associated with change. Operational risk functions in the first and second lines are positioned (or should be) to oversee the risks associated with change in their organizations. This includes managing technological change, including risks associated with managing large transformation projects.

Organizations have mostly shifted away from the "waterfall" approach that breaks down projects into distinct phases and have adopted "agile" approaches, which are iterative and run project phases concurrently. Both approaches require effective governance and oversight, and operational risk professionals should have active roles monitoring progress and identifying risks and mitigants. These risks can include system issues that compromise the ability to transact when they are implemented. In financial institutions, if monitoring systems are not properly implemented, the result could be the failure to properly monitor transactions with regulatory compliance impact.

I have experienced more than once in my career the discovery years after a system was implemented issues involving some type of calculation that was embedded into a system that negatively impacted clients, such as overcharging for mortgage fees or interest rates. I have also experienced feeds that were not properly implemented, and years later it was discovered that transactions were not properly monitored. This resulted in regulatory compliance issues and the failure to identify in a timely basis the potential for bad actors entering or transacting at the bank. Ultimately, these issues were discovered through testing, but it happened years after the implementation and testing of controls were not conducted regularly or at a granular enough level to identify these issues.

Poor systems implementation can lead to data issues. Data is a key asset of all institutions and central to most (if not every) activity. Incomplete, inaccurate, or untimely data can impact financial reporting, which we have seen was a key factor in Credit Suisse's liquidity crisis when it announced material financial reporting weaknesses. Poor data management practices can have dire consequences for clients. If a financial institution provides incorrect information to a credit organization that affects a client's credit rating, this can impact their ability to acquire a car, a home, or even a job.

Banking institutions have been on a journey for more than a decade implementing the requirements outlined by the Basel Committee on risk data aggregation and risk data, which is known in the industry as "BCBS 239." This focused effort on risk data establishes governance principles that can provide guideposts for data management more broadly.

The data problem in institutions with complicated data feeds that have developed organically and often through mergers is infinitely more complex than the governance principles that BCBS 239 established. This has resulted in complicated and often convoluted data routines that require significant overhaul of an organization's data architecture and significant budget and resource commitments to streamlining the entire data lifecycle, from creation to production. The data challenge is especially complicated in larger organizations.

Operational Risk at a Cross-roads

Managing the many complex risks of our time has brought the management of operational risk to crossroads. When I first entered the discipline in the late 1990s, the mandate was simple: collect, aggregate, and analyze the firm's operational risk losses. This was the moment on the heels of the monumental Barings PLC operational risk event when the global banking community was debating what the first operational risk capital charge would look like and how to best quantify the discipline. The industry looked to insurance methodologies of estimating losses for guidance and adopted in the early days a loss distribution approach. At this time, I brought to market the first database of external losses, which was based on public accounts (from the press, company statements and reports, public regulatory censures) of operational risk events. I built this database to include case studies with focus on the breakdown of controls, because I knew deep down that there had to be more than counting internal losses numerically and there was a trove of lessons to be learned from industry peers.

Today, we have come a long way since those early days of counting loss events, and through a complicated thicket of advanced measurement approaches and modeling, and the split-off of certain operational risk disciplines, such as third-party and cyber, into stand-alone functions. The Office of the Comptroller of the Currency's (OCC) Heightened Standards was a game changer in the banking industry regarding expectations of the roles and responsibilities of the frontline businesses (first line of defense) and risk management functions (second line of defense) in the management of operational risk. This ultimately placed more responsibility for the direct management of operational risk on the front line and significantly altered the definition of the role of risk management in the second line. It also led to a definition of the audit function (the third line) and a three lines of defense model that is widely accepted today in financial institutions, while present but more loosely implemented in other industries.

Operational risk departments defined their role after the passage of Heightened Standards as one that is independent of the business and focused on review and challenge and oversight. The first-line business, as the first line of defense, became responsible for directly managing operational risk, while the independent risk management function in some (not all) institutions took a step away from direct management and focused on the documentation of their oversight and review and challenge activities. The quality of the documentation became important, and I have sat through industry discussions on how to document ongoing review and challenge, including developing homegrown databases.

We are now at a point in the evolution of operational risk, where management in some institutions is questioning the value of the function, beyond the expectation that you need one to meet regulatory requirements. The world has become more complicated, as have the risk issues, and management is not always seeing the active engagement of operational risk professionals in the ongoing management of risk. In some ways, this is the result of the interpretation of the three lines of defense model and the emphasis on "independent" risk management. But in my opinion, as someone who managed operational risk before there was so much emphasis on independence, there is nothing that precludes solving operational risk challenges together with the frontline business and providing advisory support in the "flow of business activity" rather than after the fact. Ultimately, to add value, the function needs to be aligned with the firm's priorities and strategies and have the stature necessary to have a seat at the table with senior management.

It is critical to set up the operational risk team in the second line of defense (i.e., independent risk management) for success in both today's complicated world and the future. A successful team requires people who have specific expertise in the subtypes of operational risk, including third-party, cyber, technology, data risk management, model, fraud, and transaction processing. Often, it is helpful to hire people from the business and first line of defense who have direct experience with managing these risks. For instance, hiring someone on the team from operations will be invaluable in understanding how processes within the firm work and where the vulnerabilities are. The same can be true for hiring a technologist to oversee technology risk and someone who has directly managed vendors to oversee third-party risk.

A team of specialists should be balanced by professionals who understand the portfolio of risks across the organization and the interconnectiveness among risk types. These are individuals who can articulate the overall risk profile and level of accepted risk, as determined by the expressed operational risk appetite. It is critical that the interplay of risks is assessed and their impact on the overall operational risk profile is understood. For instance, third-party arrangements expose an organization to almost every operational risk in its risk taxonomy, including cyber, data, technology, and fraud risks.

When an event happens at a third-party vendor that impacts one's organization, such as a cyber breach, it is important to have the people with the wherewithal to look across the risk spectrum and determine the overall exposure. If the third party has access to the organization's systems, customer and personal data, processes, payment portals, and confidential reports, it will be necessary to look across all these risk types to determine the amount of harm that has been done and the remediation. The person on the team in charge of operational resiliency is often the right person to pull together the report on the exposure and develop the remediation plan.

Ultimately, it is important to get the balance right between specialists and generalists, between people who can go deep and people who can go broad. The head of the operational risk department will need to be capable of traveling both paths and going deep into the details (with reliance on the team) and understand the end-to-end exposure of operational risk within the organization. This requires someone who has deep experience, has lived through many events, understands the organization's processes, and knows what works.

In addition to a diversity of skills, an effective operational risk department should have the value of inclusion embedded in its very bones. This means the hiring not just of a diversity associated with skills but also a diversity in age, experience, ethnicity, perspective, and geography in a global organization. I have heard more than one senior manager say that they hire the best person for the job or the person with the best skills for the job. I never know what that means in reality, except for the fact that I think it's a red flag because often the "best" means "someone just like me." The "best" should be considered in terms of the make-up of the group in its entirety. A successful operational risk department is one that listens to all voices.

The second line of defense provides oversight, establishes policy and frameworks, and defines and monitors operational risk appetite levels (which is set in either the first or second line depending on the institution). The first line of defense owns the risk and, ultimately, is responsible for managing operational risk and the control environment. As mentioned, there was a fundamental shift in the banking industry in roles and responsibilities when the OCC passed Heightened Standards. This requires the first line to give some thought to who is responsible for executing the operational risk framework and controls for the firm.

While the second-line operational risk department most typically (but not always) resides within an independent risk function and reports to the chief risk officer (CRO), first-line operational risk or control functions most typically (but not always) report into the chief operating officer (COO) or chief administrative officer (CAO). They also report in some organizations into the chief financial officer (CFO). It is important for the first line to give the same consideration to the diversity of its team setup as the second line and ensure people with diverse skills are in place to manage specific risks, such as fraud, and to understand the broad risk profile of the interaction among all the operational risks.

Communicating Operational Risks

Communication is one of the most important skills an operational risk professional can have. Risk management is (or should be) tied to the firm's strategy at every level. It starts with the board of director's expression of risk appetite and is interpreted throughout the organization at each level. A risk professional plays an important role in shaping, communicating, assessing, and monitoring the firm's risk appetite and requires strong written and verbal skills to do this effectively.

The worse outcome for an operational risk professional is to identify risks but not be able to communicate the hazards effectively to the board and senior management. This includes synthesizing complicated risk themes into concise messages that can be understood by senior management and the board. It also requires the ability to verbally present these risks to senior and board-level committees. At the heart of communication is the ability of an operational risk professional to exude confidence, credibility, and knowledge. These are learned skills that the manager of an operational risk function should work tirelessly to develop in the team.

It is through communication that the management of all the operational risks we discussed in this chapter come together. The operational risk manager needs to consider how these risks impact the operational risk profile of the firm from a portfolio view and how they interact with each other. At the end of the day, it is not just about identifying and assessing the level of the risks but working to get the necessary management attention and resources for managing and mitigating them.

Interview with Industry Veteran on Managing Operational Risk and Compliance: Mike Silva

Mike Silva is a seasoned compliance executive, with extensive experience leading compliance functions in large and complex financial institutions. He is currently at the forefront of applying new technologies to solve compliance issues and serves on the board of an advanced technology nationally chartered bank. He is also a member of the Bretton Woods Committee and serves on the Future of Finance Working Group. Mike previously served as a senior executive at the New York Federal Reserve Bank where his roles included serving as the chief of staff during the financial crisis and as lead examiner for Goldman Sachs. Mike started his career in the US Navy where he served as a naval flight officer. Mike credits his time in the Navy conducting flight operations for the perspective he gained on operational risk, which emphasized the hazards of not managing the discipline well.

1. **Question**

   These are complicated times in terms of managing operational risk and compliance, especially with so much change in the operating environment. What are some of the qualities, skills, and experience an operational risk manager needs today to be effective?

   Answer

   First and foremost, a deep understanding of whatever business operations you are supporting is critical. You need to know the business you are covering to effectively mitigate operational risk. Equally important, you need to understand the business to have credibility with your business partners.

   Second, you need to be well versed in regulatory requirements, including those that are related to your primary regulators, such as the OCC, Federal Reserve, FINRA, FDIC, FCA, and equally important, you need to understand operational risk frameworks, such as Basel II/III, COSO, and RCSA.

   It is also important to stay grounded in current and emerging technologies, and emerging technology-based risks, such as cybersecurity.

   Strong interpersonal skills and especially emotionally intelligent persistence is critical to success, as business leaders are often reluctant to spend time and money on reducing operational risk, and you need to have the stamina, patience and persistence to keep pushing through roadblocks.

   I would be remiss if I did not mention imagination. You need to be able to imagine not just what could happen in terms of risk exposures, but also how creative solutions can be developed to manage those risks.

2. **Question**

   As someone who has served as a chief compliance officer, which included operational risk in your remit, what were some of your challenges in managing the discipline?

   Answer

   First of all, while it is true that one of my tenures as a chief compliance officer included operational risk as part of my remit, I have to say that I am not at all sure placing the discipline under the remit of the CCO is the optimal reporting structure, as I see the two as different disciplines that require different skill sets. Consider the compliance mandate, which is ensuring compliance with all applicable laws, rules and regulations. Now consider the operational risk mandate, which is to mitigate the risk of loss resulting from inadequate or failed internal processes, people and systems, or from external events. The operational risk mandate covers a much wider range of activities. If anything, I would argue that compliance is a form of operational risk, and therefore compliance should be under it.

   Second, to more directly answer your question, I would say that my biggest challenge was that I had no operational risk experience! By virtue of my Federal Reserve tenure, I had some basic understanding of regulatory expectations for the discipline. But literally, I had no experience at all with operational risk frameworks (e.g., Basel II/III, COSO, RCSA). So, my biggest challenge was making sure there was someone in charge of it who knew what they were doing.

3. **Question**

   From your industry perspective, what do you think financial institutions can do better today in managing operational risk?

   Answer

   There are two things: first raise the stature. The discipline is about ensuring operational excellence. Operational excellence contributes directly to the bottom line. Therefore, operational risk should have the same stature as any business. Second, invest! Get the right people and systems in place. In my experience, financial firms are extremely focused on short-term results and therefore tend to be penny-wise and pound foolish when it comes to investing in something like operational risk.

   Not spending money on something like operational risk may improve your bottom line for the next quarter, but, especially for larger firms, I guarantee you that if you fail to adequately invest in managing it, you will eventually have a mishap of some kind that costs you much more than it would have cost to mitigate that risk.

4. **Question**

   What would the operational risk department of the future look like? And how do you think AI will change the management of operational risk, both in terms of an enablement technology and as a creator of new risks?

   Answer

   My experience with the advanced technology bank I am associated with suggests that the ops risk departments of the future are going to be much more technology and AI based. AI is changing and will continue to change the management of operational risk in just about every way you can imagine.

As data sets and large language models grow over time, I think AI will be able to perform just about every ops risk role there is, and the function of the ops risk staff will be much more about setting standards, performing quality assurance, interpreting the actions and recommendations of AI to senior management, and most of all, understanding and remaining in charge of the AI.

The way I think about the risks of AI is that they are very similar to the risks posed by any employee, but with exponentially greater consequences because of how fast it can operate. The way to manage that risk is like managing the risk of any employee: Do they have the right training? Do they reliably produce desired results? Do they receive constructive feedback on a timely basis when their performance is deficient? Do they operate with integrity?

5. **Question**

When you look back on your career, what lessons learned would you like to share with the profession?

Answer

The biggest lesson is that working as a risk manager of any kind is a noble endeavor. For me personally, it was very satisfying. People are wired in different ways. I am wired for service, and I found the second line of defense to be a great form of service. You are working to protect customers, shareholders, your fellow employees, and the broader public. That is a job worth doing.

My next lesson learned is that doing the noble work of risk management will likely at some point call for courage. I am not talking about the more typical day-to-day disagreements with the first line where you utilize your understanding of the business, interpersonal skills and emotional intelligence to agree on a control that is a bit of a compromise but is ultimately acceptable to you and the business. I am talking about an occasion when a very powerful person is determined to do something you consider seriously ill-advised and you have to stand-up to that person and say, "No, not on my watch." Such moments can pose serious career and financial risks. Hopefully such moments will be few, but they will come, and you should be prepared for them. I consider myself fortunate to have started my career in the Navy because that was an environment that emphasized doing the right thing no matter the cost and was laser focused on managing risk. That was an excellent foundation for building a second-line career in finance.

6. **Question**

What advice would you give an operational risk manager early in their career?

Answer

My first piece of advice would be to become very knowledgeable about AI because the future is going to be all about working with and managing AI. My second piece of advice is one that I give to everyone early in their career regardless of their field: be prepared to roll with the punches. I had a plan for every moment of my career and that plan never worked even once! But by rolling with the circumstances and making the best of whatever opportunities that came my way, I ended up having an overall career that was more enjoyable, satisfying, and successful than anything I planned on.

Bibliography

Andy Bounds. WTO Warns about Fragmentation of Global Trade into Allied Blocs. *Financial Times*, September 12, 2023.

Banking Committee on Banking Supervision. *Principles for Effective Risk Data Aggregation and Risk Data*. January 2013.

Bill Gates. I Worry We're Making the Same Mistakes Again. *New York Times*, March 19, 2023.

Board of Governors of the Federal Reserve. *Review of the Federal Reserve's Supervision and Regulation of Silicon Valley Bank*. April 28, 2023.

British Foreign Policy Group. *The Geopolitical Consequences of the Israel-Hamas War*. October 27, 2023. https://bfpg.co.uk/2023/10/geopolitics-of-israel-hamas-.

CNN. *US Escalates Tech Battle by Cutting China off from AI Chips*. October 18, 2023.

Darren Dodd. Ukraine War and the West's Relations with China Reshape Global Trade. *Financial Times*, September 18, 2023.

NASA.Gov. *NASA Announces Summer 2023 Hottest on Record*. September 14, 2023.

Ryan Gallagher. *War Tests Israeli Cyber Defenses as Hack Attempts Soar*. Bloomberg. October 18, 2023.

Sean Fleming. A Short History of Jobs and Automation. *World Economic Forum*. September 30, 2020.

S&P Global. *Top Geopolitical Risks of 2025*. https://www.spglobal.com/en/research-insights/market-insights/geopolitical-risk.

Steven Lee Myers. Fact or Fiction? In This War, It Is Hard to Tell. *New York Times*, October 13, 2023.

Tiffany Hsu and Stuart A. Thompson. A.I. Muddies Israel-Hamas War in Unexpected Way. *New York Times*, October 28, 2023.

World Meteorological Organization. *Provisional State of the World Climate in 2023*. November 30, 2023. https://wmo.int/resources/publications/provisional-state-of-global-climate-2023#:~:text=The%20WMO%20provisional%20State%20of,%2Dindustrial%201850%2D1900%20baseline.

World Trade Organization. *Global Trade Outlook and Statistics*. April 2025. https://www.wto.org/english/res_e/booksp_e/trade_outlook25_e.pdf.

Zolan Kanno-Youngs, Judson Jwos, and Derrick Bryson Taylor. Nightmare Scenario Hurricane Batters Mexico's Western Coast. *New York Times*, October 25, 2023.

Chapter 3

Building the Team for Today and Tomorrow Across the Lines of Defense

Managing Operational Risk Across the Lines of Defense

When asked the basic question on how to set up an operational risk practice, the first answer that most professionals will offer is the "three lines of defense." The model is dependent on three layers of risk management, where the first line (the business) is the risk taker and owns its risk and control environment, the second line (risk and compliance) is responsible for oversight and the primary owner of the risk framework and methodology, and the third line (audit) is responsible for overall assurance that the framework is properly designed and implemented to mitigate and manage risks. When a notable operational risk event occurs, often it represents a failure by all three lines of defense. It should be noted that some have advocated for a "four lines of defense model" with the fourth dimension encompassing bank regulators and internal auditors.

The financial crisis of 2008 was the catalyst for the wide adoption of a three lines of defense model in the banking industry. The watershed moment was the passage of the Office of the Comptroller of the Currency (OCC)'s "Guidelines Establishing Heightened Standards for Certain Large Insured National Banks, Insured Federal Savings Associations, and Insured Federal Branches" in September 2014. Heightened

Standards and the passage of the Federal Reserve's Enhanced Prudential Standards that same year were game changers. They solidified the dialogue on the role of the first- and second-line functions. I was working at a large US bank at the time and witnessed many second-line operational risk activities move to the first line, including myself. I thought of this as a great migration of the lines of defense.

It was unclear as the banking industry emerged from the Great Credit Crisis if the first-line functions truly understood that they owned their risks. I was told by one former regulator that when questioned what went wrong, senior executives pointed to failures in their risk and compliance departments. It is unclear how widespread that perspective was, but it represented at least for some a lack of understanding that when things go wrong, the first line of defense needs to bear the primary responsibility (although it does not preclude the second and third lines from doing their jobs and from accountability).

The best-managed institutions always understood that their business operations owned their risks from front to back, but still the industry was posed for a major shift in how it executed the management of its risk environment. Heightened Standards, on the heels of all the issues identified coming out of the Great Credit Crisis, was somewhat responsible for the emergence of the formal first-line operational risk and control functions that in some circles came to be known as the *one-and-a-half line* or an in-business risk and control function. If the business was to fully and completely own the implementation of risk frameworks, they needed in-business expertise to fulfill their responsibilities.

The adoption of Heightened Standards has led to many years of dialogue on the roles and responsibilities among the lines of defense for ensuring an organization is resilient and fosters a strong risk culture. Lack of role clarity and redundancy of roles have been some of the most debated topics among risk professionals in their attempt to implement efficient and effective operational risk frameworks. If the roles are not clearly defined, there is confusion among who is responsible for what, and at the same time, this can lead to a lack of responsibility by anyone for a specific activity or function. For this reason, it is important to have a very clear and specific defined chart of roles and responsibilities across the lines of defense, which is customarily incorporated into an operational risk policy and standard and is updated according to a published schedule (usually annually when the governing document is updated).

The formation over the last few years of a robust first line of defense control or business risk functions led to a dialogue on the role of the second-line operational risk function. If the first line now fully and completely owned its operational risks and associated operational risk practices, questions emerged as to the role of the second line. The industry predominantly landed on a framework that requires the first line to own the implementation of risk and control activities, while the second line owns the methodology, oversight, and credible challenge. The second line is also responsible for "risk advisory," which is an important activity and one where the second line can provide great value in assisting the first line with designing implementation programs and remediations. See Table 3.1.

Implementing a three lines of defense framework does not mean that an independent second line should operate at arm's length, as the risk advisory role is a critical

Table 3.1 Operational Risk Three Lines of Defense Model

First Line: Business	Second Line: Risk	Third Line: Audit
Risk owner	Oversees operational risk mitigation efforts and challenges implementation of the framework	Provides independent assurance on the adequacy and effectiveness of risk management
Control owner	Monitors internal controls and confirms and challenges results of control effectiveness assessment processes	Ensures that controls are sufficient from a design and implementation perspective
Implements operational risk management framework (RCSA, issue management, risk appetite, risk metrics, scenario analysis, loss data)	Responsible for development and rollout of operational risk framework and methodologies, including policies and training	Assesses adequacy of firm's assessment of risks and provides assurance they are well articulated and mitigated; assesses adequacy of operational risk framework
Remediates loss events	Provides advisory support and review and challenge of remediation activities	Assesses adequacy of remediations
Develops and reports on business specific risks, controls, issues and metrics through business level committees and business management	Aggregates metrics and risks and provides reporting at the enterprise level to senior management and the board	Reports to the audit committee of the board on operational risks and the quality of the mitigation program

one, and ultimately, it is about achieving the right balance between independence and assisting the first line with solving risk problems. The second line has been criticized for being too bureaucratic and simply checking boxes on predesigned forms indicating that the first line has carried out its duties. At the end of the day, the partnership among the lines of defense in solving critical problems together is the most effective approach, and it is not precluded by the three lines of defense model. The first line needs to trust that the second line is a partner that, although independent, has the knowledge and expertise to assist with implementing the operational risk framework.

It should also be mentioned that the second line should not operate in isolation when it designs the operational risk framework, policy, and standards. A framework is only as good as its ability to be implemented, and the first line's perspective and input are critical. There is no worse strategy than for the second line to develop a framework and validate it through second-line committees and then release it fully baked to the first line with a required implementation date. This is a solution for only cursory acceptance and implementation by the first line, rather than full ownership. There is no room in our complicated ever-evolving risk environment for any one risk function to stand back and be an independent observer.

General vs. Specialist Roles

It is worth repeating that we are living through complex times, with the complexity of the risks that we face mirroring the operating environment. Emerging risks associated with geopolitics, artificial intelligence and large language models, quantum computing, cybersecurity, climate change, and market volatility require deep specialist knowledge to effectively assess and manage. These are skills that may not always reside in the second line, where traditional operational risk specialists have focused on frameworks and program implementation.

It is important when managing and building an operational risk team in the second line to have experts in framework, taxonomies, regulations, and policies; it is also important to balance the team with specialist skills. These skills include experts in third-party, cyber, business continuity, model management, and data risk management. Some organizations have split out some of these operational risk specialties, with separate reporting lines into risk leadership in the second line or business leadership in the first line.

There are benefits of having a cohesive operational risk function where the owners of the framework and methodologies sit side by side with the specialists. There are many interconnections between these risks, and the true value that an operational risk team can bring is to be able to understand these interconnections. For instance, it is difficult to discuss risks associated with cyber without considering third parties, data, and resiliency. It is also difficult to discuss risks associated with AI without considering model and data risk management. Third-party arrangements expose an organization to almost every operational risk in its risk taxonomy, including cyber, data, technology, and fraud risks. And all these risks require a strong knowledge of the framework and current and emerging rules and regulations.

The first-line corporate functions, such as the technology and chief operating teams, have people who specialize in cyber, business continuity, resiliency, and third-party risks. These are critical roles that reside closely with the business where the risks emanate and are very much in the spirit of Heightened Standards and first-line ownership of risk. The value a second-line operational risk team can bring as a risk partner is the ability to connect the dots and assess the interplay among these risks.

A successful team in the second line requires people who have specific expertise in the subtypes of operational risk, including third-party risk, cyber risk, technology risk, data risk management risk, model risk, fraud risk, and transaction processing risk and who are equipped to work holistically with the first line. Often, it is helpful to hire people from the business and first line of defense who have direct experience with managing these risks. For instance, hiring someone on the team from operations will be invaluable in understanding how processes within the firm work and where the vulnerabilities are. The same can be true for hiring a technologist to oversee technology risk and someone who has directly managed vendors to oversee third-party risk.

A team of specialists should be balanced by professionals who understand the portfolio of risks across the organization and the interconnectiveness among risk types. These are individuals who can articulate the overall risk profile and level of accepted risk, as determined by the expressed operational risk appetite. It is critical that the interplay of risks is assessed and their impact on the overall operational risk profile is understood.

When an event happens at a third-party vendor that impacts one's organization, such as a cyber breach, it is important to have the people with the wherewithal to look across the risk spectrum and determine the overall exposure. If the third party has access to the organization's systems, customer and personal data, processes, payment portals, and confidential reports, it will be necessary to look across all these risk types to determine the amount of harm that has been done and the remediation. The person on the team in charge of operational resiliency is often the right person to pull together the report on the exposure and develop the remediation plan.

Ultimately, it is important to get the balance right between specialists and generalists, between people who can go deep and people who can go broad. The head of the operational risk department will need to be capable of traveling both paths and going deep into the details (with reliance on the team) and understand the end-to-end exposure of operational risk within the organization. This requires someone who has deep experience, has lived through many events, understands the organization's processes, and knows what works.

The second line of defense provides oversight, establishes policy and frameworks, and defines and monitors operational risk appetite levels (which is set in either the first or second line depending on the institution and risk type). The first line of defense owns the risk and, ultimately, is responsible for managing operational risk and the control environment. There was a fundamental shift in the banking industry in the roles and responsibilities when the OCC passed Heightened Standards. This requires the first line to give some thought to who is responsible for executing the operational risk framework and controls for the firm.

The Composition of Operational Risk Teams

Ultimately, the lines of defense need to be constituted in a way that reflects the structure of the organization they are designed to serve. Reporting lines matter, and in a mature operating structure, the first and second lines must tree up to separate and independent functions. While the second-line operational risk department typically resides within an independent risk function and reports to the chief risk officer (CRO), the first-line operational risk or control functions most typically (but not always) report into the chief operating officer (COO) or chief administrative officer (CAO). They also report in some organizations into the chief financial officer (CFO). It is important for both lines of defense to consider the diversity of its team and as mentioned, to ensure people with diverse and complementary skills are in place to manage specific risks, such as fraud, third party, and resiliency, and to understand the broad risk profile of the interaction among all the operational risks.

It is also important to consider the diversity of a team, including gender, ethnicity, age, personality style (introvert versus extrovert), and neurodiversity. I have heard more than one senior risk leader say that they hire "the best person for the job," but often their

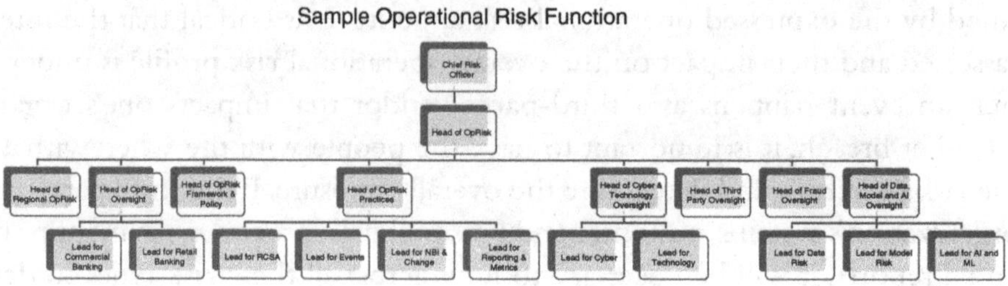

Figure 3.1 Global risk function

definition of the "best person" is someone who looks like everyone else on their team or their skill set fits the structure of the firm's taxonomy or framework.

This is a complicated and diverse world that requires a diversity of thought, approach, experiences, and personal styles to manage an organization's operational risks. The senior people with deep experience who have been around the block a few times and know what works and what doesn't are critical members of a team. It is also important to recruit a cadre of people with potential, who may come from different industries and bring new perspectives to the team. Seasoned professionals bring deep experience from having managed through issues in the past, while hiring for potential brings a diversity that will help the team think through newly emerging issues. And hiring someone who is neurodiverse may bring a different skill set to the team, such as finding patterns of risks in complicated data sets. It is also important that the team is as interconnected as the risks they manage.

Figure 3.1 shows an example of how a large global operational risk department might be organized, with dedicated positions for framework, policy, regional, business, and functional oversight. A smaller or less global organization will have a flatter structure, with more combined functions.

Interview with Industry Veteran on First-Line Risk Management: Aarona Chou

Aarona started her career as a management consultant with a big four firm, where she worked with a variety of financial institutions assisting with solving their risk and control issues. She subsequently was head of first-line control organizations of the wealth management divisions of two Global Systemically Important Banks (G-SIBs). This included providing oversight of financial advisors.

1. **Question**
   What has your relationship been with the second line from your first-line perspective?
   Answer
   In my experience, the relationship between first- and second-line partners has been very collaborative and productive with healthy tensions. I rely on my second-line colleagues to provide advice and constructive challenge to topics we wrestle with. Their expertise and objectivity are critical to help me avoid blind spots and biases.

In the meantime, my second-line colleagues look to me for in-business practitioner's feedback to the frameworks and methodology they designed. I see myself as the conduit between the second-line oversight function and the business front-line risk takers. I help the two sides see different perspectives and come to pragmatic solutions that balance risk and rewards. The key to a successful relationship is to understand the end goal, which is to advance the organization's commercial interest without unacceptable risks and with the roles both lines play to achieve that end goal. When asked by the regulators about the first- and second-line relationship, I answered, "We keep it hot, not hostile." There is a real independence of views and robust discourse between the two lines, and at the end of the day, we come to common ground as responsible risk stewards of the organization.

2. **Question**

How do you balance being in a risk and control oversight function with being a business partner?

Answer

I believe the first-line risk control role is pivotal to sustainable commercial success, with the emphasis on "sustainable." Therefore, my personal objectives, which are cascaded to my staff, are these dual mandates: *enabling (not spoiling) business while meaningfully reducing (not eliminating) risks.* Achieving the dual mandates requires constant calibration of business imperatives and risk drivers as well as healthy skepticism. I regularly challenge business partners and my staff with "What if …," "How do peers approach this," and "What precedence or parallel exists as a cautionary tale?" My business risk-taking partners trust me in safeguarding the firm's future with their pursuit of growth and profitability because I can articulate to them the trade-offs of risk and rewards with facts and analytics. On the other hand, I earned my second-line partners' confidence in my rigor and vigilance in risk mitigation and management. This is how I know I have struck a good balance in being a helpful business partner and a strong risk steward.

3. **Question**

How do you manage business challenges and pushbacks on operational risk concerns?

Answer

Managing business challenges and pushbacks on operational risk concerns is hard, certainly harder than managing compliance risk concerns because you don't always have the regulatory stick as the justification. It is also hard because the cost to remedy operational risk concerns can be significant and is often perceived as nice-to-have or discretionary rather than must-have or mandatory as is the case of remediating compliance risk concerns. Therefore, it is helpful to draw upon press coverage of financial or reputational impact resulting from operational risk events. People like stories and need to have context. I read a lot of business news and books to use these lessons learned to help business understand what could happen and what did happen.

4. **Question**

What regulatory expectations are most relevant to operational risk management in the first line?

Answer

There are heightened operational risk management regulatory expectations on data and model governance, third-party risk management, and process automation. While regulators have paid attention to cyber risk management, the focus tends to be on technological and preventive measures, all of which are important. There is not enough focus on resilience as in what to do when the firewall is breached, data is leaked, and systems are disrupted. UK PRA and FCA are more advanced in requiring firms to contemplate cyber resilience as an eventuality. I believe this is one area where US regulators can be more prescriptive as the industry, and candidly regulators themselves and federal government agencies are struggling with how to manage this fast-evolving risk considering escalating geopolitical conflicts and accelerating technological advances. We need to move beyond just solving yesterday's problems (i.e., process automation).

5. **Question**

How do you help embed a strong risk culture in a business unit that is commercially focused?

Answer

Plain and simple, you need to embed risk management in everything you do and in every business process. This includes automating controls and embedding escalation protocols into processes. A strong escalation framework is one that is embedded in business processes, including defining dollar values when you need to escalate to senior management and requiring lessons learned and deep dives when events occur. It needs to be part of how you do business, rather than a stand-alone activity. Tone from the top is key; employees need to know that we are in the business of taking and managing risk. Everybody is a risk manager, and blind pursuit of commercial interests without understanding and properly mitigating risks will not yield long-term success.

6. **Question**

What are some examples of operational risks you've identified in your previous role(s)? How did you mitigate them?

Answer

Resiliency is a critical risk. With the COVID experience, various natural disasters, and the risk of cyber-related disruptions, resiliency is more important than ever. To manage this risk, it is important to have strong disaster recovery, business continuity, and third-party risk management controls in place. A firm needs to understand its vulnerabilities, its critical processes, and how it will come back online in the event of a business disruption.

Data privacy has also been top of my risk agenda. It is important to understand the points of vulnerability and how data can be compromised across firewalls and by the firm's own employees. A large control issue has been recently identified by regulators related to off-network devices, which can compromise data security, in addition to records retention regulations. Some firms have provided their employees with very locked-down devices to monitor their data usage.

I am always concerned about processing errors. Many firms operate with a lot of legacy manual processes, which also contributes to poor data quality. It's important to understand how this can impact a firm's ability to transact during volatile periods and to make sure any new business initiatives that rely on manual processes also do this analysis. For instance, it's a strong control to subject a new business initiative that relies on manual processes to operating limits while an automated solution is under development.

Bibliography

Board of Governors of the Federal Reserve System. Enhanced Prudential Standards for Bank Holding Companies and Foreign Banking Organizations. *Federal Register* 79, no. 59 (March 27, 2014): 17239–17403. https://www.federalregister.gov/documents/2014/03/27/2014-05699/enhanced-prudential-standards-for-bank-holding-companies-and-foreign-banking-organizations.

Committee of Sponsoring Organizations of the Treadway Commission (COSO). *Enterprise Risk Management Framework*. Accessed April 13, 2025. https://www.coso.org/.

The Institute of Internal Auditors / https://www.theiia.org/globalassets/documents/resources/the-iias-three-lines-model-an-update-of-the-three-lines-of-defense-july-2020/three-lines-model-updated-english.pdf / Last accessed by Nov 6, 2025.

Institute of Internal Auditors (IIA). *The IIA's Three Lines Model (2020 Update)*. Accessed April 13, 2025. https://www.theiia.org/en/content/3-lines-model/.

Office of the Comptroller of the Currency (OCC). OCC Guidelines Establishing Heightened Standards for Certain Large Insured National Banks, Insured Federal Savings Associations, and Insured Federal Branches; Integration of Regulations. *Federal Register* 79, no. 176 (September 11, 2014): 54518–54547. https://www.occ.gov/news-issuances/federal-register/2014/79fr54518.pdf.

Chapter 4

Making It Real: Developing a Framework for the Real World

I am at heart a framework geek. I love the elegance and structure of frameworks and believe they are necessary for managing all risk types and are an important driver for the maturity of risk disciplines. Operational risk frameworks provide the guardrails for managing risk and understanding the necessary commensurate controls, but they are only as effective as their ability to be implemented by the front line and to identify emerging risks.

A very senior executive at a bank I was interviewing with many years ago referred to the firm's current operational risk team as "ivy tower ***" (an inappropriate curse word was used that I will not repeat). This stuck with me, because as much as I love frameworks, I have been on the outlook during my career for when they are perceived as too much "in the tower." This is a hazard when they are designed and managed by corporate risk teams that are removed from the front line. The front line should be involved in their design and evolution and accept "ownership" of the frameworks.

Frameworks should not be implemented through a "paint by numbers approach" where a team just needs to follow each element through to understand their risks and document the results. Instead, they should be malleable and able to be revised as change presents itself. They should also be flexible so that they can be applied across all operational risk types, and the core elements of the framework should be integrated, along with the teams that implement them.

One of the challenges with frameworks is that they take some time to design and can be structured to manage yesterday's risks. For instance, there is a danger if the framework is heavily dependent on a taxonomy (which most operational risk frameworks are) that emerging and converging risks or risks that cannot be easily defined are overlooked.

Incorporating scenario analysis into the core elements of a framework, which allows for the identification of the convergence of risks and newly emerging ones, allows for a more forward-looking approach than simply leveraging a risk assessment organized by a taxonomy. Most financial institutions have scenario programs in place for modeling and regulatory capital purposes, but they are not always integrated into risk appetite and risk assessments.

The Operational Risk Framework Is Only as Effective as Its Implementation

In large institutions, the requirement on the first line to implement the operational risk framework is significant. As an example, the Risk and Control Self-Assessment (RCSA) process requires teams that are knowledgeable about their business and how to assess risk and controls to determine the level of risk currently in the organization and the efficacy of controls. This is not an exercise in any size institution that can be relegated to a junior analyst without proper oversight and management engagement. The process requires an understanding of the data that goes into assessing the level of risk and expert qualitative judgment in making the final determination, as well as an ability to properly assess the effectiveness of the controls both individually and from the perspective of the overall control environment and establish remediation plans where they are not operating effectively.

I experienced firsthand at an institution how ineffective the RCSA program can be if it does not have the right level of attention. I was hired earlier in my career to transform a large bank's RCSA program after it experienced a very public risk event that resulted in a significant monetary loss and reputational damage. I pulled the RCSAs for the business unit that was at the center of the loss, and all the underlying issues that led to the event were spelled out clearly in the documentation. A junior analyst had executed the RCSA for the function and implemented some limited remediations. But no one involved in the process paid enough attention to understand how critical the identified control issues were and how much harm they could ultimately do to the bank. One of the first changes I made to the program was involving senior management in the process, including the kick-off and assessment of the results.

I have experienced first-line organizations that were very effective in managing operational risk and others that were less so. In one organization that I worked in, there was a mismatch in the skills and capacity of the first and second lines, with the later more senior, experienced, and well-staffed. This resulted in the second line assigning more issues to the first line than they were able to remediate and a significant backlog. As a remedy, to help the first line climb out of the hole it found itself in, people from the second line and third line (internal audit) were moved into the first line to assist with the remediation.

At the heart of managing operational risk and remediating issues is the framework. It provides the guidepost for how we manage operational risk. From my experience, the framework is only as useful as its implementation. The second line can design a beautiful framework that meets all regulatory, industry, and management expectations, but if the first line struggles with its implementation, an analysis among the lines of defense is necessary. The drivers for this struggle might be a first line that does not have the right risk skills or capacity or a framework that is too complicated to be implemented. The first scenario requires a look across the lines of defense for the right operating model and rules of engagement, and the second scenario requires a simplification exercise.

Operational risk frameworks have become complicated in larger institutions that have mature programs in place, and there has been an industry effort to simplify key components. This may include simplifying the complexity of requirements related to the implementation of risk assessments, including RCSA, reducing the number of risk assessments, stripping complexity out of how risk is assessed and making its determination more intuitive, and considering leveraging advanced techniques such as AI, to aggregate data and assist with analysis. It might also require a reduction in the amount of documentation that is required.

I have heard throughout my career complaints from the first line that they are so busy executing the operational risk framework that they do not have the bandwidth to manage their business. This might reflect the lack of understanding by the first line that managing operational risk is very much part of managing the business, but it might also indicate that the framework is too complicated. It is important for all lines of defense to hold regular workshops to discuss the framework and the operational risk operating model so that it is effective but not overwhelming.

At the end of the day, the framework needs to be robust so that the material operational risks are identified, is forward looking to identify emerging risks, has a process for assessing controls associated with those risks and protocols for remediating ineffective or missing controls, provides for the ability to articulate the end-to-end risk profile, and monitors the level of risk against the stated risk appetite. If it adds on layers of first- and second-line risk assessments, requires extensive documentation that no one reads, and cannot articulate the overall level of operational risk clearly and simply, then it is a candidate for simplification.

The operational risk framework is also part of a risk ecosystem in a bank and should be connected to other risk disciplines, including market and credit. Some organizations have single enterprise frameworks that establish the core components for all risk disciplines, which include risk assessment, control management, issue and remediation management, compliance and regulations and tracking of changes, regulatory management, monitoring, metrics, reporting, product governance, and risk appetite. There is a trend for organizations to center their frameworks on risk appetite and use it as the baseline for risk assessments and monitoring. It is an elegant approach that allows for the determination of the overall risk profile across the organization.

A unified enterprise framework incorporates the interplay among the risk types, allowing for an understanding of how operational risk can be a driver for other risk types. A credit event can occur if the underlying processes, such as documentation, tracking collateral, and conducting research on the client or counterparty, are not performed properly. This was one of the lessons of the credit crisis in 2008, when there was a massive issue with the determination of credit worthiness of mortgage applicants and a lax attitude toward documentation.

The failure of operational risk processes, such as poor documentation, ineffective monitoring of transactions, incomplete due diligence of customers and incoming employees, systems issues with transaction monitoring, failure to capture and monitor regulatory mandated communications, and documentation storage deficiencies, can result in compliance issues. For this reason, there is a great deal of synergies among compliance and operational risk functions, and there has been some movement in large financial institutions to manage them together under the banner of "nonfinancial risk."

Elements of the Framework

Alas, we come to the framework itself, which has lately come under a lot of criticism. Much of the criticism is that many of its elements result in check-the-box exercises. It is worth noting that of all the elements, the RCSA program comes under the most scrutiny, with some calling for its demise. It is also worth noting that some of the loudest RCSA critics are those who never had the responsibility of managing an operational risk program and tend to strike at its efficacy from the sidelines. However, having said that, if the RCSA program is not executed with care and the appropriate level of senior level oversight and it is not used as a tool in the actual management of operational risk, it can feel like a perfunctory but not very meaningful exercise. It is up to the people who create the framework and implement it to make each element meaningful.

There are many graphical views of operational risk frameworks in the industry, but the one I like best is what I think of as the "virtuous feedback loop" where the program components are interconnected and inform each other. Figure 4.1 demonstrates how this should work in practice. For instance, developing risk appetite statements and key risk indicators (which should be aligned) should inform the determination of how the firm rates its risks and controls. Internal and external loss events should be key inputs into the risk and control assessment process, along with any open issues and identified control gaps. The risk assessment process should also result in opening issues and action plans when it identifies control gaps and determines that residual risk is out of appetite. Monitoring and reporting should be prioritized by the identified most critical exposures and control issues, and all of this should inform cultural awareness and training programs.

Governance

Creating, modifying, or implementing an operational risk program starts with clearly defining how it will be governed and answering a few foundational questions:

- What function owns the program, including the framework, policy, and procedures?
- What is the role of the respective lines of defense?

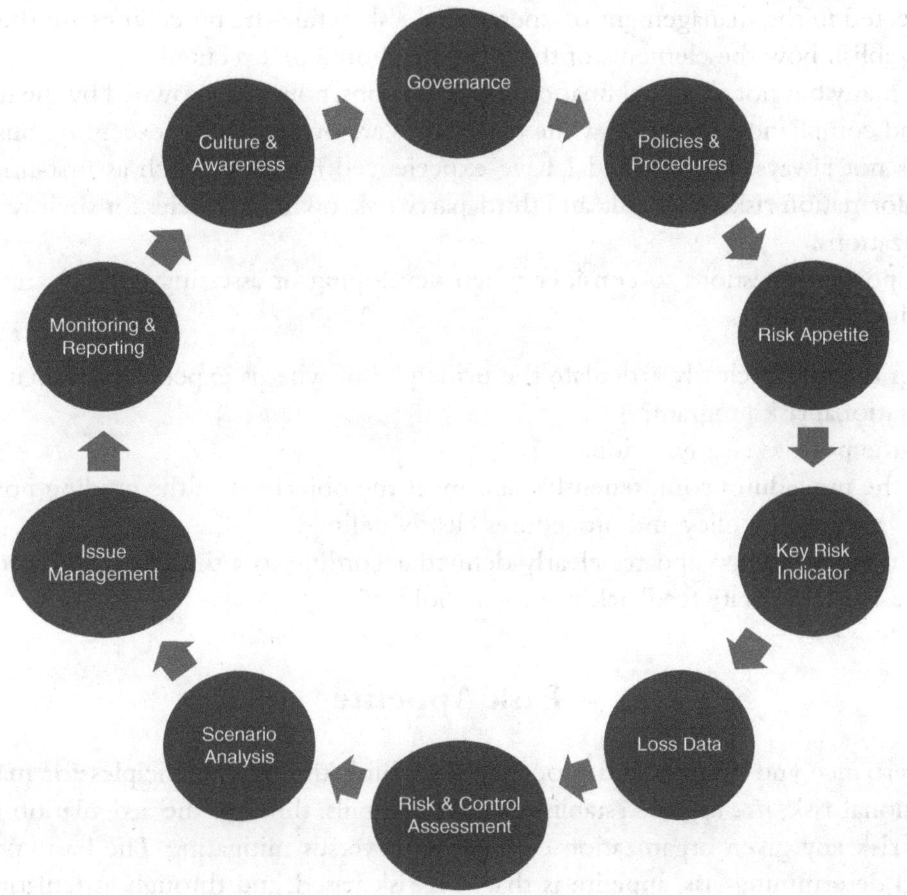

Figure 4.1 Operational risk framework

- What is the role of the board and senior management?
- What are the escalation paths when issues arise, and who is the final decider?
- What will the committee structure be for reporting and reviewing operational risk matters?

An important consideration is determining a governance construct that is appropriate for the size and complexity of any given organization. A large global organization will have clearly defined roles and responsibilities across the lines of defense, while a small or midsize one may have more of the responsibilities sitting in either the first or second line.

There is no one-size-fits-all for determining governance, as long as the basic questions listed earlier are answered and the roles and responsibilities are clearly defined.

Policies and Procedures

Following the considerations of governance is the ownership of policies and procedures. The rule of thumb is that policies are the "what" and set out the basic principles of what is expected in the management of operational risk, while the procedures are the "how" and establish how the elements of the program should be executed.

In many but not all global financial organizations, policies are owned by the first-line risk and compliance functions, while procedures are owned by the executing businesses. This is not always the case, and I have experienced functions, such as first-line cyber and information risk, fraud risk, and third-party risk, owning policies for their respective organizations.

Important questions to consider when developing or assessing policies and procedures include these:

- Does the policy clearly articulate the principles of what is expected in executing the operational risk program?
- Are the policies clearly actionable?
- Are the procedures comprehensive and meet the objectives of the guiding policy?
- Is ownership of policy and procedures clearly defined?
- Are required policy updates clearly defined according to a timeline and a process in place to incorporate feedback from stakeholders?

Risk Appetite

If governance and policies and procedures establish the basic principles for managing operational risk, *risk appetite* establishes the guardrails, through the articulation of how much risk any given organization can live with versus mitigating. The basic principle behind determining risk appetite is that it is risk based, and through articulating how much risk is acceptable, the firm can focus on managing where it has the largest and most critical exposures. Determining operational risk and nonfinancial risk appetite is more nuanced than determining it for the financial risk disciplines, such as market and credit risk, which are easier to quantify based on how much risk a firm is willing to take and what the ultimate reward or pay-off is. The critical consideration for operational risk is how much it is willing to invest in controls to mitigate identified risks.

Many years ago, an industry colleague who headed the operational risk department at a monoline credit card company told me that he figured out how to get rid of all operational risk in his firm. I was curious to find out how he did this, as he seemed to have come upon some type of miracle mitigant. His answer was to "shut down the firm!" That, of course, is not a viable solution, but the underlying message is clear: the "reward" or "upside" to accepting operational risk is to be in business.

Developing a risk appetite program starts with the drafting of clear, well-articulated risk appetite statements that include the determination of how much risk for operational risk as a whole and for each of its subtypes (fraud, cyber, third party, business resiliency, technology risk) an organization is willing to accept. The statements should be linked to metrics that are monitored to determine if the pre-defined operational risk level is breached or nearing so (the ubiquitous red breach level and yellow warning level).

It is not acceptable to manage all operational risks down to a zero base through the development of controls, as this would be untenable and likely put the firm out of business. Managing the control environment is among the most critical operational risk activities, but it requires fine-tuning. The classic example is fraud as no financial institution will manage its fraud down to zero. It is through risk appetite statements that it is possible to articulate how much fraud an organization is willing to accept and, consequently, where it should focus its control resources.

Questions to consider when developing a risk appetite program include the following:

- How much risk is the organization willing to accept for operational risk overall, and for each operational risk subtype (such as fraud, cyber, third-party, business continuity)?
- What function is responsible for developing and monitoring risk appetite statements?
- What is the process for developing risk appetite metrics?
- How granular will the organization approach the development of risk appetite statements and metrics?
- What is the strategy for monitoring risk appetite?
- What is the aggregation methodology for understanding risk appetite across all operational risk disciplines?
- How do new business initiatives impact existing risk appetite?
- What are the escalation channels when risk appetite is breached?

Key Risk Indicators

Everyone who has ever worked in operational risk knows the drill when it comes to key risk indicators: they should be actionable, forward-looking, measurable, and timely. The "forward-looking" attribute is the one that most operational risk professionals struggle with. Ideally, they should tell us more than what has happened in the past and should be predictive of something.

When I was working at a big four bank, I received feedback from a regulator that our key risk indicators were not forward looking. This was a number of years ago when the industry was grappling with how to develop KRIs and what they actually told us. The interesting coda to this story is that the same regulator took a job in a bank after he left the agency, and when I ran into him at a conference, he told me he was struggling with developing predictive KRIs.

Returning to the initial thesis that the framework elements should be interconnected, KRIs should ideally be developed as part of the risk appetite program and tracked against the articulated risk appetite statements. Many firms have sets of distinct operational risk appetite metrics and key risk indicators and report both to their executive committees and boards. That approach never made sense to me, as I always believed that the most elegant solution is to have one set of risk appetite metrics. (It should be noted that each business will have its own set of operating metrics, often known as *key performance indicators*, that are not risk metrics).

These are questions to consider when developing KRIs:

- What function owns the development, reporting, and monitoring of KRIs?
- Are they aligned with the firm's risk appetite statements?

- Have they been back-tested against internal and external loss events to determine if they are predictive?
- How granular should they be?
- What are the escalation channels for breached KRIs?
- Are thresholds (breach and near breach) defined and back-tested?
- Are you able to articulate risk appetite for each operational risk "subtype" (i.e., third-party, cyber, resiliency, data, model, fraud, transaction processing).

Loss Data

As mentioned earlier in this book, operational risk data is where it all began for the formalization of the operational risk discipline. When the industry first got together to define the operational risk framework ahead of Basel II, the first task was to define an industry-standard operational risk taxonomy that would assist with the consistent collection of operational risk loss events.

The early Basel II framework was focused on four key elements: internal loss data, external loss data, scenario analysis, and business environment and internal control factors. This is the space where I started my operational risk career when I brought the first operational risk database to market. I had spent the first half of my career working in an investment banking research function and took a job at an operational risk start-up ahead of the passage of Basel II called Operationalrisk.com where I could use my research skills. It was during the heady dot-com days of the late 1990s, and it became clear as the industry was discussing approaches to managing operational risk in the aftermath of the devastating Barings event that every global bank would need operational risk loss data.

Operationalrisk.com was a Deutsche Bank venture that had recently acquired Bankers Trust. Douglas Hoffman, who was my early mentor in the discipline, managed the insurance department at Bankers Trust and had collected the bank's loss event data for many years and before most banks had put such programs in place. Doug hired me to make something out of the spreadsheet he had developed of Bankers Trust's losses, which was the beginning of the first external loss database. We named the database Financial Institution Risk Scenario Trends (FIRST), and it was truly a first of its kind. It went through several different owners and today is part of the IBM Open Pages suite.

Most financial institutions today of any size have historical loss databases that contain their internal loss events, and many subscribe to FIRST or one of its competitors. The databases are all organized around standard operational risk taxonomies, with many being formed from the basis of the seven operational risk event categories discussed in Chapter 1 of this book.

Internal loss data provides important inputs into a global banking organization's regulatory capital models; informs its risk appetite statements and metrics, risk, and control self-assessments; and provides an understanding of a firm's exposures. External loss events, which are events experienced by a firm's peers, when analyzed for control failures, provide content and context for proactively assessing a firm's exposures and putting plans in place to remediate any control issues ahead of an actual event occurring.

The premise is that if an event can happen to a peer institution, it can happen to your own organization. External events also provide important inputs into scenario analysis.

In another example of how interconnected the operational risk framework must be to be effective, operational risk internal loss events are an important input into an organization's risk appetite framework. Many banks track risk appetite metrics against their loss database. A standard metric is loss events that are 1% of the organization's total revenue on a quarterly basis or 2% on a rolling 12-month basis.

It should be mentioned that managing an operational risk database is a big undertaking and requires professional oversight. AI is emerging as an accelerator to assist with the management of the repositories of operational risk data. AI can be used to identify duplicate entries, reconcile against the general ledger, look for anomalies and incomplete records, and assist with reporting on trends. Until recently and even today for most institutions, many of these activities still rely on manual crunching of data and pain-staking reading through events to understand trends.

These are questions to consider when developing a loss data program, or assessing an existing one:

- What function owns the development, oversight, and monitoring of the operational risk loss program?
- Is the loss data collected and indexed against a structured taxonomy?
- How is the loss data used to manage operational risk?
- Are trends tracked and actions defined when loss events occur over a certain threshold?
- Are loss event thresholds aligned with the firm's risk appetite statements?
- What are the escalation paths for large loss events?
- What are the regular reporting paths for reporting aggregate operational risk losses and trends?
- How are external loss events used to proactively manage operational risk?
- Is the operational risk taxonomy appropriate for the size and complexity of this program and the other components of the framework?

Risk and Control Assessment

A risk and control self-assessment, affectionately known in the industry as RCSA, has become the headline activity in organizations of all sizes. RCSA is designed to identify and rate inherent risks, assess the efficacy of controls, and determine residual risk. The level of residual risk should be assessed against the firm's risk appetite for operational risk overall or for any given operational risk subtype, such as fraud or cybersecurity. It is a strong practice to put a remediation plan in place if residual risk is determined through the RCSA program to be outside the firm's appetite. (See Chapter 5 for a different view on assessing risk.)

RCSA is foundational to managing operational risk following a risk-based approach by determining inherent risk (i.e., the risks inherent in a business, function, or process without the consideration of controls) and assessing the effectiveness of controls against the level of inherent risk. Assessing inherent risk is not easy for everyone, and some struggle with how to assess risk without the benefit of controls. The reason it is important is because the level of inherent risk should determine where resources should be prioritized in the implementation and management of controls. I once worked in an organization that focused on control testing rather than assessing risks, and the program became wildly out of control without the focus on risk that allowed for the prioritization of control work.

As previously mentioned, RCSA comes under frequent criticism for being a check-the-box exercise. I introduced top-down workshops in one large banking organization that hired me to restructure its RCSA program into a risk-based approach. It was a journey, but by involving the management teams of each business that was assessed, the exercise was informed by meaningful risk and control discussions. Ultimately, it is how the RCSA is used to manage an organization's risk and control environment that makes it worthwhile.

These are questions to consider when developing or managing an RCSA program:

- What function owns the development of the RCSA framework?
- What function owns the implementation of the RCSA program?
- Are roles and responsibilities for all RCSA activities clearly defined?
- Is the risk assessment unit structure clearly defined (i.e., is the risk assessment performed by business unit, legal entity, or process?)
- Is the taxonomy clearly defined, including the level of the taxonomy that the risk assessment will be conducted at?
- Has a methodology been developed for rating risks and controls, and aggregating the final results?
- Is a process defined for closing any identified control gaps, or residual risks that are above appetite?
- Are the data sets that inform RCSA, including operational risk losses, peer events, open issues, regulatory and audit findings, clearly defined?
- Is the RCSA designed to align with the firm's strategy?
- How are the results of the RCSA used to make business decisions, including critical investments in systems, processes, and controls?

Scenario Analysis

If loss data is backward looking and RCSA is a point in time and should also be predictive and forward looking, scenarios are truly forward looking and are designed to incorporate large events into the operational risk framework. They should be plausible but represent rare, high-severity losses. They are an important tool for predicting emerging risks and rely heavily on a risk manager's imagination. (See Chapter 2 for the importance of imagination.)

Scenarios are important for financial institutions that are required to calculate capital for regulatory purposes and are a critical input into the operational risk comprehensive capital review and analysis (CCAR) process, which in many organizations relies on operational risk scenarios and models to calculate the amount of capital that is required to cover future high-severity losses under stressed conditions. But the plot is lost if scenarios are limited to capital exercises. They are an important tool for identifying future risks and enhancing risk awareness among senior management, the board, and the first-line business. Institutions that are not required to estimate capital and conduct regulatory stress tests should develop their own libraries of operational risk scenarios. They should be considered as inputs into RCSA and risk appetite.

Scenarios can be developed through workshops or surveys. I have relied on workshops when developing scenarios because there is something powerful about bringing a group of people together across disciplines to discuss potential risks. It is important depending on the type of scenarios under development to include the appropriate subject-matter experts in the workshops. I have experienced very senior-level interest and involvement in selecting and estimating scenarios, because of their impact on capital in institutions that rely on them for that purpose.

These are questions to consider when developing or managing operational risk scenarios:

- How will the scenarios be used (CCAR, models, RCSA, risk appetite, emerging risks)?
- Have the right subject-matter experts been identified for each topical scenario?
- Has a library of scenarios been created that include qualitative and quantitative components?
- Is there a process for vetting the scenarios with senior management?
- Has an approach been developed for executing the scenarios?
- Has the process been properly documented?
- Is the process designed to be repeatable and consistent?

Issue Management

Issue management is how organizations get better every day. I once heard someone refer to it as the "little engine that could" of risk management, because it is how an organization issue by issue and action plan by action plan improves its control environment. It is a critical element of an operational risk framework, and it is how control gaps that are identified through RCSA, control testing, risk appetite breaches, scenario analysis, and operational risk events are mitigated. It is an important connection point to all the other framework elements.

Designing and managing an issue management program should be a first- and second-line joint project, with the second line often (but not always) responsible for the policy and framework, while the first line is responsible for its implementation. The third line (audit) is often responsible for validating that an issue and its action plan is designed to mitigate the risk and is implemented as designed. This is especially true for higher risk issues or issues assigned by regulators or audit. This is where good cooperation among the lines of defense is critical for success (see the interview with Aarona Chou in Chapter 3).

These are questions to consider when developing or managing an issue management program:

- Are the roles and responsibilities clearly delineated among the lines of defense? Is this spelled out clearly in the policy?

- Do the roles and responsibilities include ownership of the issue by an executive at the right level of seniority (often called the accountable executive), and is each action plan associated with an issue assigned to an appropriate person?
- Is there an escalation process if the action plans associated with an issue fail to meet deadlines on time?
- Is a governance process in place that includes committee or forum reporting on the status of issues and action plans?
- Has an issue rating scale been developed that reflects the level of risk impact that the issue is designed to mitigate?
- Has an impact matrix been developed and published that provides guidance on issue ratings by impact?
- Are resource plans required as part of the scoping process for action plans?

Monitoring and Reporting

The important role of reporting is often overlooked and relegated to junior people on a team. But it is one of the most critical activities that an operational risk manager can engage in because it allows for communication with senior management and the board on present and emerging operational risks. In essence, it is how an operational risk department communicates with the most senior people in an organization, and it is important to hone a message that is concise and understandable.

A risk manager must focus on honing that message and ensuring that it is communicated in plain language that is devoid of jargon. The worst mistake an operational risk manager can make is communicating in "risk speak" to senior management and the board. They need to know what they should be concerned about, what is being done about it, and what they can do to assist with the issue. It is especially important when communicating with this audience to be clear if you are informing versus asking for something. The guidance I was given earlier in my career is when creating a report for senior management or the board, you should be able to answer the question, "So what?" There should be a call to action.

It is also important to get the level of reporting correct, with more detail offered in business-specific risk and control forums and less when the report is created for a board package. The reporting structure for risk committees and the board should include an overview of the current state of operational risk, and any material loss events, including those that have happened to industry peers that are relevant.

Key risk indicators are important monitoring tools and should be developed to reflect the level of critical risks. A strong practice is to tie KRIs to risk appetite.

These are questions to consider when developing or managing operational risk reporting and monitoring:

- Have standard report templates been developed for each forum and committee that is at the appropriate level?
- Are roles and responsibilities clearly defined and documented, with proper level of senior oversight?

- Are key risk indicators developed that track through metrics, with defined thresholds, an organization's critical risks?
- Are KRIs aligned with risk appetite?
- Are operational risks monitored against the firm's risk appetite?
- Are escalation protocols in place when key risk indicator thresholds are breached?
- Are data aggregation methodologies in place to report on trends and themes?
- Are you able to articulate your firm's (or business) risk profile through the development of a methodology?
- Can you articulate the top 10 operational risks for your firm, and how they are being mitigated?

Culture and Awareness

Culture and awareness provide the foundation for a strong risk management program. The risk management principles start with "tone from the top" and the messaging that senior management pushes through the organization on the importance of risk management. It is bolstered through "echo from the middle" where middle management is incentivized to do the right thing. I have witnessed true disconnects between what senior management says (*manage risk prudently*) and how middle management is incentivized to bring in revenue, which may only be possible if they assume excessive risk.

The tone from the top can feel perfunctory if it starts and ends with email communications from senior management on the importance of risk management. What is most important is senior management's actions and openness to fixing an organization's control issues. I have seen CEOs roll up their sleeves and help solve risk and control issues and essentially "walk the talk." I have seen other CEOs keep far away from anything related to control management as if it had a bad smell.

Building an organization that values its risk culture can be reinforced through many strategies, including regular culture, risk, and compliance training. I have witnessed several organizations implement "operational excellence" programs, where they tracked compliance and control metrics and highlighted the good work of their organization's culture bearers.

These are questions to consider when developing or managing a risk culture awareness program:

- Do you have clear messaging about the important of a risk culture crafted and socialized with key stakeholders, including senior management?
- Is the message pushed down from senior management to the entire organization?
- Does the firm's compensation structure support the message?
- Are the firm's risk takers identified and assessed for their risk mitigation strategies?
- Are the risk culture values integrated into the firm's performance management system?
- Have lessons learned from internal and external events been communicated widely to continuously enhance the risk culture?
- Is the launching of a culture awareness and operational excellence campaign feasible?

The following chart demonstrates where the elements of the framework are most interconnected:

	Governance	Policies & Procedures	Risk Appetite	Key Risk Indicator	Loss Data	Risk & Control Assessment	Scenario Analysis	Issue Management	Monitoring & Reporting	Culture & Awareness
Governance		X	X			X		X	X	X
Policies & Procedures	X		X	X	X	X	X	X	X	X
Risk Appetite				X	X	X	X	X	X	X
Key Risk Indicator			X		X	X	X	X	X	X
Loss Data			X	X		X	X	X	X	X
Risk & Control Assessment			X	X			X	X	X	X
Scenario Analysis			X	X		X		X	X	X
Issue Management			X	X	X	X	X		X	X
Monitoring & Reporting			X	X	X	X	X	X		X
Culture & Awareness	X	X	X	X	X	X	X	X	X	

Bibliography

Basel Committee on Banking Supervision. *International Convergence of Capital Measurement and Capital Standards: A Revised Framework.* June 2006. https://www.bis.org/publ/bcbs128.pdf.

Basel Committee on Banking Supervision. *Revision to the Principles for the Sound Management of Operational Risk.* March 2021. https://www.bis.org/bcbs/publ/d515.htm.

Craig Spielman. *Risk and Control Self Assessment – This time it's personal.* Cefpro Connect, January 27, 2025.

Penny Cagan. *RCSA: The Changing Dynamics of Self-Policing Risk.* Cefpro Connect, January 27, 2025.

Chapter 5

Managing Operational Risk Appetite and Key Risk Indicators

Managing operational risk, or any risk discipline, without a risk appetite framework is like flying a plane without a flight plan. Although you can still fly the plane, you may not know if you are within appropriate altitude and flying at an appropriate speed. You could enter dangerous airspace and be at risk of escorted by fighter jets, if for instance you are above protected airspace or, worse, enter enemy airspace. The flight plan, like the risk appetite framework, defines the risk thresholds, or altitude limits; has checkpoints that function like risk appetite metrics; and warns of hazards that require diversions.

Maintaining a risk appetite is a requirement of global prudential regulators. The US OCC's Heightened Standards and Federal Reserve Enhanced Prudential Standards require formal, board-approved written risk appetite statements, including operational risk. This includes qualitative statements and quantitative limits, with thresholds, that are tracked through defined metrics. The European Central Bank (ECB) and the Prudential Regulation Authority (PRA) require board-approved risk appetite frameworks that incorporate operational risk.

Although a regulated banking organization almost anywhere in the world is required to have a fit-for-purpose risk appetite framework in place, it is a strong practice for institutions in other industries to develop risk appetite frameworks, which can serve as their risk flight plans. It allows an organization to first articulate how much risk they are willing to take and to monitor against that level on an ongoing basis, through metrics and predetermined thresholds. It assists with decision-making when strategic opportunities arise, such as the decision to acquire or divest a business, enter a new arrangement with a partner, go to market with a new or expanded business initiative, enter new markets, invest in new technologies, or take on additional debt. It also assists with operational resilience, as risk appetite can be defined in terms of acceptable disruptions (see Chapter 17). Finally, it allows for an organization to be on the same page from the board downward on what is acceptable risk taking.

Definitions

The OCC defines risk appetite accordingly:

> *The bank's risk appetite is the aggregate level and types of risk that the board and management are willing to assume to achieve the bank's goals, objectives, and operating plan, consistent with applicable capital, liquidity, and other requirements. The development of a risk appetite should be driven by both top-down board leadership and bottom-up management involvement. Successful implementation depends on effective interactions among the board, senior management, IRM, and frontline units.*
>
> Source: https://www.occ.treas.gov/publications-and-resources/publications/comptrollers-handbook/files/corporate-risk-governance/pub-ch-corporate-risk.pdf?utm_source=chatgpt.com

There can be some confusion between what is meant by risk appetite, risk capacity, and risk limits. The Financial Stability Board (FSB) provides the following definitions:

Risk Appetite: *The aggregate level and types of risk a financial institution is willing to assume within its risk capacity to achieve its strategic objectives and business plan*

Risk Capacity: *The maximum level of risk the financial institution can assume given its current level of resources before breaching constraints determined by regulatory capital and liquidity needs, the operational environment (e.g., technical infrastructure, risk management capabilities, expertise) and obligations, also from a conduct perspective, to depositors, policyholders, shareholders, fixed income investors, as well as other customers and stakeholders.*

Risk Limits: *Quantitative measures based on forward looking assumptions that allocate the financial institution's aggregate risk appetite statement (e.g., measure of loss or negative events) to business lines, legal entities as relevant, specific risk categories, concentrations, and as appropriate, other levels.*

https://www.fsb.org/uploads/r_131118.pdf

Considerations When Managing Risk Appetite

The following are considerations when managing an operational risk management framework:

Strategy: Risk appetite must be aligned with a firm's strategic plan, and business decisions must consider risk appetite and how much incremental risk they would add to the organization. For instance, if a risk appetite statement indicates that the firm has low tolerance for doing business with high-risk individuals and the high (red) level threshold of the metric tied to this statement is 5% (high-risk individuals as percentage of total), the entrance into a new business will require an analysis of how many high-risk individuals it will result in onboarding, or an assessment of whether the level of acceptance of these customers should be higher.

Top-down: Risk appetite statements and thresholds must be approved by the board from a top-down perspective for the enterprise. The board must ensure it aligns with the firm's strategic plan and provide oversight that the aggregate level of risk appetite is not breached. At the board and enterprise level, the risk appetite for operational risk will be for the overall level of operational risk and for each of the operational risk types, including cyber, technology, fraud, business continuity, and third-party.

Bottom-up: Each business must determine risk appetite for their operational risk exposure, which should be aligned with the top-level risk appetite statements that the board approved. For instance, if the board states that it has no appetite for violations of law, each business will adopt the same zero-tolerance statement. The bottom-up view is also expressed by metrics that are consistent across the enterprise and able to measure the risk for each of the major business units. Ultimately, the metrics will require aggregation across the businesses, which is why consistency is important.

Risk limits and metrics: Operational risk appetite limits are typically established by operational risk management in partnership with subject-matter experts and senior management through the development of thresholds that track risk appetite through high, medium, and low levels (or red, amber, and green). These risk limits are approved by the chief risk officer, senior management, and the board, and applied to each of the major businesses. It is worth noting that metrics that are expressed in terms of percentages work well across all businesses, while absolute numbers require consideration of size and complexity.

Thresholds: Risk appetite metrics should have thresholds that allow for reporting upward through the organization, downward through to the businesses, and sideways for operational risk and its types (cyber, fraud, third-party, technology). Thresholds should be back-tested against internal and external events to determine if they function as early warnings that risk levels are rising. They should be reviewed regularly and adjusted according to feedback and lessons learned from the operating environment. It is a red flag that a threshold may require adjustment if an event occurs that was not reflected in the metrics.

Key risk indicators (KRIs): It is a strong practice to align KRIs with risk appetite. I have experienced firms that had multiple sets of operational risk metrics that are reported to the board and risk committees, which led to confusion and a presentation of different views of risk. If the risk appetite framework is set up in a way that metrics can be aggregated and disaggregated at an enterprise, business, and operational risk type level, one set of consistent metrics can provide a single view of operational risk. Additional key performance metrics provide a different view and allow a business to measure their performance against standard benchmarks.

Realistic versus aspirational: Risk appetite metrics should not be aspirational. They should reflect the current level of acceptable risk. As an example, if the thresholds for operational risk are at the moderate level for successive quarters, the acceptable operating level for operational risk is moderate. Some organizations believe that it's a strong practice to set aspirational risk appetite levels such as low risk when the actual KRI level is moderate for some length of time, to demonstrate a strong culture to regulators and stakeholders. In the end, however, it will lead to scrutiny as to why the organization has operated at breach levels for an extended period.

Monitoring: Risk appetite metrics provide a view into the current risk profile of operational risk for the enterprise, each of the risk types (fraud, third party, cyber, technology), and each business. Second-line operational risk typically aggregates risk appetite metrics quarterly for the enterprise and reports through risk committee and the board, although the enterprise risk management function may do this for all risk stripes.

Remediation: It is a strong practice to consider remediation before the top level (or red) threshold of the aggregate or individual risk appetite metric is crossed. This may occur when a rising metric hits the amber level for more than one quarter. Remediation includes a review of the metric to determine the level of risk it reflects and if an issue and action plan is required to be opened. It is important to consider cyclical factors and overall patterns, such as seasonality, which impacts fraud, when considering remediation.

Flexibility: Risk appetite statements and metrics should be flexible and reviewed and challenged on a regular basis and preferably at least quarterly, as the operating environment is increasingly dynamic. The reviews should also occur when there are material changes within the organization that might impact the overall appetite for operational risk. This could include regulatory changes, reorganizations, mergers and acquisitions, geopolitical events, and market volatility.

RCSA: In addition to risk appetite metrics, RCSA provides a point-in-time view of a firm's risk profile. Final residual risk ratings should be reviewed alongside risk appetite levels to determine if they are within appetite. It's a strong practice for an issue and action plan to be opened if the final level of operational risk in aggregate or for an individual operational risk type is above appetite.

Risk Appetite Framework

Governance

Risk appetite governance starts with the board's approval and review and challenge of the firm's risk appetite statements and thresholds. Each party in the pyramid in Figure 5.1 has an important role to play in managing operational risk, and governance must flow down from the board but also up from the business and functions so that a comprehensive view of operational risk across the enterprise can be obtained and also so that the pockets in the organization that are above the risk appetite can be targeted and remediated if necessary.

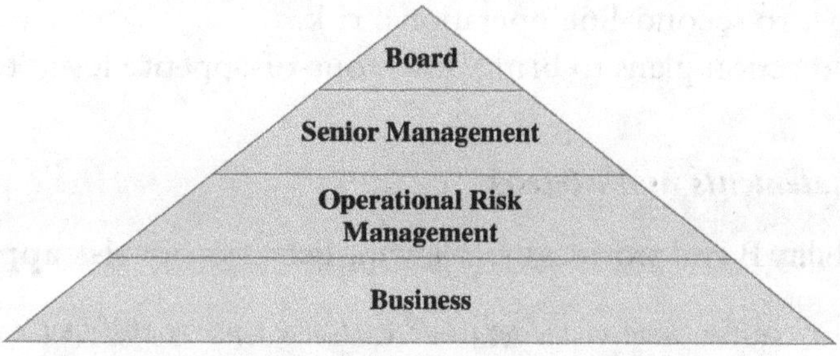

Figure 5.1 An overview of the roles and responsibilities associated with managing operational risk appetite

The board's responsibilities include the following:

- Approve operational risk appetite at the top of the house and for the enterprise.
- Ensure alignment with the firm's strategy and annual business plans.
- Align business decisions with RA, including mergers, partnerships, and reorganizations.
- Ongoing monitoring of actual risk limits versus agreed-on levels.
- Ensure appropriate resources are in place to manage RA.

Senior management's responsibilities include the following:

- Establish operational risk appetite for the enterprise from a top-down perspective.
- Ensure operational risk appetite is aligned with strategy and annual business plans.
- Monitor risk appetite levels and be accountable for breaches.
- Explain material breaches to the board, including root cause and any remediations.
- Ensure RA framework is implemented across the firm and translated for specific businesses and functions.
- Allocate appropriate resources to manage risk appetite.

Operational risk management's responsibilities include the following:

- Develop the operational risk appetite framework across the enterprise that incorporates risk appetite statements and metrics and thresholds for all operational risk types (cyber, third-party, fraud, technology, business continuity).
- Review and challenge first-line risk appetite statements and reported metrics.
- Monitor adherence to risk appetite at an enterprise and operational risk type level.
- Escalate breaches to CRO, senior management, and the board.
- Aggregate and report on operational risk appetite metrics to the risk committee and the board.

Business responsibilities include the following:

- Establish an operational risk appetite for each business and function from a bottom-up perspective that is aligned with the strategy and annual business plans.
- Monitor adherence to the risk appetite within the business and function.

- Escalate breaches to second-line operational risk.
- Open issues and action plans to bring down out-of-appetite levels to within appetite.

Risk Appetite Statements and Metrics

The Financial Stability Board provides the following definition for **risk appetite statements**:

> *The articulation in written form of the aggregate level and types of risk that a financial institution is willing to accept, or to avoid, in order to achieve its business objectives. It includes qualitative statements as well as quantitative measures expressed relative to earnings, capital, risk measures, liquidity and other relevant measures as appropriate. It should also address more difficult to quantify risks such as reputation and conduct risks as well as money laundering and unethical practices.*
> Source: `https://www.fsb.org/uploads/r_130717.pdf`

Risk appetite statements are often purposefully broad so that they can apply across the organization at the enterprise, business, risk stripe, and operational risk type level. The details are expressed through the metrics that translate the statements into articulated thresholds and, ultimately, make them actionable.

The following are examples of risk appetite statements.

Operational Risk

The firm has a low tolerance for operational risk losses and will manage its operational risk exposure to protect its financial position, regulatory capital, and reputation. Total annual operational risk losses will not exceed 1% of revenue on a quarterly basis and 2% on a rolling 12-month basis.

Metrics:

Metric	Green	Amber	Red
Total Operational Risk Losses (Rolling 12-Month Basis)	<1% of revenue	1–2% of revenue	>2% of revenue
Total Operational Risk Losses (Quarterly Basis)	<0.5% of revenue	0.5–1% of revenue	>1% of revenue

Compliance and Regulatory Risk

The firm has no tolerance for violations of laws and regulations, anti-money laundering laws, and sanctions requirements.

Metric:

Metric	Green	Amber	Red
Number of Regulatory Breaches per year	0–5 minor breaches (self-reported, minor fines)	6–10 significant breaches (repeat issues, single MRA, moderate fine < $25M)	>10 major breaches (multiple MRAs, consent orders, fine > $25M)

Financial Crime Risk

The firm has low tolerance for conducting business with high-risk customers who pose heightened money laundering and sanctions risk.

Metric:

Metric	Green	Amber	Red
Percentage of High-Risk Clients vs. Total Client Base	<3% of revenue	3–5% of revenue	>5% of revenue

Cybersecurity and Data Protection

The firm has no tolerance for cybersecurity incidents that compromise customer data, financial records, or critical banking systems.

Metric:

Metric	Green	Amber	Red
Number of Cybersecurity Incidents per Quarter	0–2 minor incidents (low impact)	3–5 incidents (medium impact, isolated data exposure)	>5 incidents or any major breach (customer data compromised)

Fraud

The firm has zero tolerance for internal fraud or unethical behavior that violates legal and ethical standards.

Metric:

Metric	Green	Amber	Red
Internal Fraud Losses as % of Total Quarterly Revenue	<0.01%	0.01–0.05%	>0.05%

Business Continuity and Operational Resilience

The firm has low appetite for disruptions to critical banking services (e.g., payments processing, core banking operations), with robust contingency planning.

Metric:

Metric	Green	Amber	Red
System Downtime for Critical Banking Services (Hours per Year)	<4 hours	4–12 hours	>12 hours

Integration with Operational Risk Program Components

Risk appetite is an important input into several components of the operational risk framework, including RCSA, issue management, KRIs, governance, and awareness and training. It serves as not just the guardrails for managing operational risk across the enterprise but also as the measurement of how much risk is allowable across the enterprise and for each business and risk stripe, and where on the measuring scale the current risk profile resides. The associated risk appetite metrics allow for monitoring the level of risk and allow for proactive remediation if the thresholds start to hit unacceptable levels. It is truly a proactive risk management tool if the metrics are calibrated at the correct levels and reflect the risk properly that they are designed to monitor.

The following is a mapping of certain components of the Operational Risk framework to risk appetite:

Operational Risk Framework Component	Integration with Risk Appetite
Governance & Policy	The second-line OpRisk function incorporates the importance of managing the risk appetite into the operational risk policy, drafts an operational risk standard or procedure, an overall RAS and metrics, and works with functions and subject-matter experts (cyber, third-party, technology, resilience) to draft RAS and metrics for OpRisk types. The board approves the OpRisk RAS and thresholds. The standard includes defined roles and responsibilities. The second-line OpRisk reports on risk appetite metrics to risk committee and the board. The first line reports to business risk and control committees.
RCSA	The final residual risk levels for OpRisk overall and OpRisk types are aligned with risk appetite levels to determine if the risk profile is within the appetite.
Issue Management	The residual risk levels that are above risk appetite and risk appetite metric breaches are reviewed and considered for remediation through the opening of issues and action plans. It is a strong practice to consider remediation when rising threshold levels cross the amber threshold.
KRIs	Risk appetite defines the thresholds for KRIs, with the reporting of a single set of metrics as a strong practice. Risk appetite metrics and KRIs (if reported as a single set or separately) should be designed to be forward looking and to serve as early warning indicators of risk levels that are approaching or breaching appetite.
Monitoring & Reporting	Risk appetite metrics and threshold levels are monitored closely for rising risk levels and reported to risk committee and the board. Thresholds and metrics are modified if events occur that were not reflected in the metrics. Risk appetite levels should be monitored for change in operating environment and risk profile and modified if necessary.

Operational Risk Framework Component	Integration with Risk Appetite
Culture & Awareness	Risk appetite provides an opportunity to communicate the importance of managing risk within appetite and not assuming more risk than is articulated. The message that risk is managed within acceptable levels must be reinforced through training and messaging from senior management.

Key Risk Indicators

Key risk indicators (KRIs) are ideally linked to risk appetite statements and can be structured to meet the requirements of having a set of risk appetite metrics that measure and monitor the risk level that the organization is undertaking and a set of metrics that are ideally forward looking and allow for proactive risk mitigation. Some organizations manage a short list of risk appetite metrics and a much longer and more granular list of KRIs. The list of KRIs should be well-honed, actionable, and back-tested to determine that they tell you something. A short list of KRIs (no more than one-page) should be included in risk committee and board packages. Providing multiple pages of KRIs is counter-productive, as senior management and the board will not know what to react to.

The generally accepted definition of KRIs is that they provide early warning of an increase in risk levels or emerging issues. Here is the Basel Committee definition:

Key Risk Indicators: *Key Risk Indicators are statistics and/or metrics, often financial, which can provide insight into a bank's risk position. These indicators should be reviewed on a periodic basis (often monthly or quarterly) to alert banks to changes that may be indicative of risk concerns. Such indicators may include for example the number of failed trades, staff turnover rates and the frequency and/or severity of errors and omissions.* `https://www.bis.org/publ/bcbs86.pdf`

Embedded in the Basel Definition is the concept that KRIs must provide insight into a *bank's risk position.*

There are three other types of indicators that should not be confused with KRIs, that are performance and control based:

Key performance indictors: These indicators are generally used by a business or function to measure how they are doing against business objectives. This can include metrics related to business revenue or growth rate, customer satisfaction scores, or average time to complete a process.

Key control indicators: Key control indicators measure how effectively a control is working. Examples include percentage of know-your-client reviews completed on time, percentage of control tests completed according to plan, and percentage of remediation plans closed on time.

Objectives and key results (OKR): OKRs are used by organizations to define and track objectives and measure progress through quantifiable key results. It helps align teams, improve focus, and track success. Examples include increased sales growth by a specified dollar amount, improving customer retention, or expanding the sales pipeline by a predetermined percentage.

The following are considerations for managing KRIs:

Leading indicators: A true KRI will be a leading indicator that serves as a forward-looking indicator of an emerging risk issue. It should be designed for preventative measures to be taken to manage the level of risk to acceptable levels.

Lagging indicators: Lagging indicators track past activity and are useful to understand trends and themes attached to past activity and events. They are backward looking and can provide a false sense of security because they may miss current and emerging trends and themes.

Ownership: KRIs should be tagged to owners, who are responsible for monitoring the level of risk. The KRI owner should ideally be the risk owner. For instance, the chief technology officer or someone within their team would be the likely owner of the KRI related to system capacity. The second-line operational risk function will often have a person assigned to work with the KRI owner on determining the appropriate threshold and provide review and challenge of the threshold levels and any necessary remediations. This might be the second-line information risk manager.

Thresholds: Determining a meaningful threshold is critical. They should be based on real data and experience and back tested. For instance, if a system becomes unstable at 90% capacity, the 90% level is where the high (red) threshold should be set, and the medium (amber) level determined where there should be additional scrutiny before the system becomes unstable—perhaps at the 80% level. If hard data is not available, management experience and subject matter expertise should be tapped into.

RCSA: RCSA can provide significant inputs into KRIs. RCSAs that result in residual risk above appetite at a business, function, or enterprise level should be reviewed to determine if additional KRIs require development or if the risk is already monitored by an existing KRI. Some institutions develop KRIs for all RCSA residual risks above (red) or (amber) and monitor their levels until they are back within acceptable levels. At the same time, KRIs provide important inputs into the RCSA risk ratings.

Back testing: Back testing indicators against events that have occurred or known control breakdowns is a strong practice that allows for a determination of if indictors are leading and predictive.

Percentages: Reporting in percentages is preferable to actual numbers because they normalize data, place the data within context, and allow for reporting across businesses and functions.

Trends and themes: KRIs should be reported within the context of trends and compared against prior quarter and 12-month period. Comparing against prior period a year ago allows for understanding the impact of seasonality if relevant and for understanding the direction (up, down, or stable) of the KRI's current value.

Root cause: The underlying driver and root cause should be included in the KRI dashboard comments along with the remediation plan for bringing amber and red thresholds back within appetite. This should include an explanation for why the KRI is above or approaching appetite. For instance, if the percentage of software patches is in the red category, the driver may be end-of-life systems that preclude timely system patches.

Remediation: It is a strong practice to consider remediation when a KRI approaches the amber level and before the red level is met and the risk rises above appetite. The root cause of the increased level of the KRI should be assessed to determine how the level of risk can be brought down. If a control deficiency is identified or a control is found to be ineffective, it is a strong practice to open an issue and action plan.

Aggregation of KRIs: The KRIs should be developed so that they are consistent across businesses and functions and can be aggregated up to the enterprise level.

Number of KRIs: More is not better when it comes to monitoring and reporting on KRIs, and it is not an effective practice to overwhelm management with pages and pages of metrics. Ideally, a KRI dashboard that is reported to risk committee or the board should be no longer than one page. This requires a thorough review of the library of KRIs, and a determination of what the impactful KRIs are in terms of the enterprise's most materials risks. Some organizations only report amber and red KRIs to the committees, with an explanation of the drivers and remediations.

Monitoring: KRIs are monitored for changes in risk levels with the goal of proactively remediating issues and control deficiencies ahead of actual events, incidents, or near-misses occurring. This includes notification to senior management if there is a material issue that requires senior-level support and attention. It allows for senior management to understand the level of risk inherent in certain businesses and processes when they are engaged in strategic decision-making.

Reporting: KRIs should be reported to the risk committee and the board at least quarterly, using a dashboard that highlights where attention is necessary. Some organizations only bring the amber and red KRIs to the board. It is important to include in the dashboard, as mentioned, the underlying factors for the rising risk levels and how the risk is going to be brought down to acceptable levels.

Continuous improvement: KRIs and their thresholds should be reviewed at least annually and when there is a loss event, incident, or near-miss that was not captured by existing KRIs. In that case, a review should be conducted on the KRI thresholds and if they are adequately reflecting the appropriate risk levels, if the KRI should be modified, or a new one developed.

KRI Dashboard

Table 5.1 lists sample key risk indicators with thresholds and sample reportable values. Each organization will need to determine thresholds based on past events, industry peer events and losses. KRIs can be applied at the business unit or enterprise level, although not all metrics will apply to each. The thresholds are simply examples of what they could look like and, ideally, are linked to risk appetite. Table 5.1 can form the basis of a reporting dashboard.

Table 5.1 Sample KRI Dashboard

Category	Metric	Green	Amber	Red	Current Quarter	Past Quarter	Comments
OpRisk Losses	Operational Risk Losses Quarterly (% of revenue)	<0.5%	0.5–1%	>1%	<0.5%	<0.5%	Losses within Appetite
OpRisk Losses	Operational Risk Losses 12 months rolling (% of revenue)	<1%	1–2%	>2%	<0.5%	<0.5%	Losses within Appetite
Self-Identified Issues	Self-Identified Issues (% of all issues)	>60%	40–60%	<40%	35%	30%	Self-Identified Issues have not reached benchmark; will conduct additional communication on importance of self-identification
Regulatory	Formal Regulatory Findings (# outstanding MRA/MRIA, consent orders)	0–2	3–5	>5	0	1	Outstanding regulatory issues within appetite; no new findings
Financial Reporting	Financial Statement Errors (% requiring revision/unreconciled entries)	<1%	1–3%	>3%	0%	<0%	Errors within appetite
SOX	SOX control testing results with exceptions	<3%	3–7%	>7%	2%	3%	SOX exceptions within appetite
People	Turnover (total/regretted)	<10%	10–15%	>15%	9%	8%	Turnover within appetite
People	Turnover (regretted leavers)	<5%	5–10%	>10%	7%	4%	Regretted leavers trending high; will review exit interviews to understand driver
People	Training overdue (%)	<5%	5–10%	>10%	3%	6%	Overdue % brought down within appetite due to targeted communication plan

Technology	Network Downtime (per year)	<4 hours	4–12hours	>12 hours	3 hours	2 hours	Network downtime within appetite
Technology	% Software Patches Timeliness	>90%	70–90%	<70% timely	60%	70%	Software patching continues to be challenged by end-of-life systems; prioritization plan for replacing legacy systems is in process of being drafted for management approval
Technology	% Security Breaches blocked	>95%	90–95%	<90%	100%	98%	Security breaches within appetite
Technology	System Capacity Utilization	<70%	70–90%	>90%	60%	65%	System capacity within appetite
Business Continuity	% BCP Plans up-to-date	100%	90–99%	<90%	98%	99%	Following plans that are not up to date; targeted reach-outs to businesses that are overdue are in process
Business Continuity	% BCP Testing Exceptions	<5%	5–10%	>10%	3%	4%	BCP testing results with appetite
Transaction Processing	Trading Errors (% of transactions)	<1%	1–2%	>2%	2%	3%	Business with OpRisk are reviewing root cause for trading errors and working on opening an issue and action plan to address the development of additional controls
Transaction Processing	Wire Transfer Errors (% of total)	<0.2%	0.2–0.5%	>0.5%	0.01%	0.01%	Wire transfer errors within appetite

Bibliography

Basel Committee on Banking Supervision. *Principles for the Sound Management of Operational Risk*. Basel, Switzerland: Bank for International Settlements, June 2011. https://www.bis.org/publ/bcbs195.htm.

COSO (Committee of Sponsoring Organizations of the Treadway Commission). *Enterprise Risk Management Integrating with Strategy and Performance, Executive Summary*. June 2017. https://www.coso.org/_files/ugd/3059fc_61ea5985b03c4293960642fdce408eaa.pdf.

Financial Stability Board. *Principles for an Effective risk appetite Framework*. November 18, 2013. https://www.fsb.org/uploads/r_131118.pdf.

Office of the Comptroller of the Currency. *Corporate and Risk Governance*. July 2019. https://www.occ.treas.gov/publications-and-resources/publications/comptrollers-handbook/files/corporate-risk-governance/pub-ch-corporate-risk.pdf?utm_source=chatgpt.com.

Chapter 6

Developing and Deploying Risk Assessments

Risk and Control Self-Assessment Overview

A risk and control self-assessment (RCSA) is foundational to managing operational risk and has become the standard platform for the plethora of other stand-alone risk assessments that reside in a large financial institution. There have been efforts over the years to bring all risk assessments onto a standard platform. This is prudent as it does an organization a disservice to present different views of risk to senior management and the board and to manage and mitigate them in silos. It also does a disservice to the first line who are increasingly called upon to participate in risk assessment workshops across multiple disciplines. I have witnessed risk assessment reports going to the board by two different risk groups that showed different risk ratings for the same risk. Their explanation was that they were rating risk from "different lenses," but that just created confusion and a mandate by the board to go back and work together on one view of risk.

At its essence, assessing risks and controls in an organization is a collaborative exercise, and implementing an RCSA program requires close partnership among the first and second lines. (See the interview with Aarona Chou in Chapter 3.) Larger banks have all implemented RCSA, with one large institution calling it *control self-assessment* (CSA). I would argue that the "R" is critical to the discipline, and an effective RCSA requires a focus on risk prioritization, which requires an assessment of risk. I have heard some argue that it's a pointless exercise because all operational risks at the highest level of a taxonomy are essentially high. That is not necessarily the case, however, for each risk assessment unit (essentially, the unit of measure for the risk assessment). No institution, unless it has endless pockets, can afford both in terms of time and resources to assess controls for every risk that exists and for every risk assessment unit every year. For this reason, it is important to assess risks and create a rating and ranking of those risks that assists with prioritizing the control work.

RCSA has come under a great deal of criticism, but I would argue that it's a result of the second line making it too complicated and difficult to implement and being disconnected from the strategy of the firm and the first line not giving it enough attention and taking the time to integrate it into decision-making. There is no denying that it has become a behemoth of an activity with a lot of time and attention given to holding workshops, debating risk ratings, testing controls, challenging residual risk outcomes, and socializing and reporting on the results. In the past this has been an entire year of work during an annual cycle, and the results could be viewed as dated by the time they reached senior management committees and the board.

The industry has moved to a trigger-based approach and off the standard one-year cycle of identifying and assessing. Once the baseline is built during the first few cycles for all the risk assessment units, the assessment of risks and controls are updated when certain triggers, or predefined metrics and events, occur. This is a more efficient and real-time approach. The other efficiency that can be gained is pulling in all the other risk assessments that exist in an organization into the RCSA platform. This includes the compliance, money laundering, sanctions, anti-bribery and corruption, fair lending, community reinvestment act, fraud, cyber, technology, data, and third-party risk assessments. The idea is to "assess once" and "report many." As described, this is not only efficient but leads to better risk management. Many years ago in my career, I managed both RCSA and compliance risk assessments for a large global bank. We were not yet at a state of maturity to combine risk assessments as most were still being built. The regulators alerted me that they would line the risk and control ratings up across the various assessments. This put a fire in me to work on bringing them all together under a single platform.

The other efficiency that is being gained is the rapid embrace of the power of artificial intelligence, which is improving as a tool as quickly as I can write this chapter. I have mostly experienced manual crunching of operational risk and control data, issues, testing results, and audit and regulatory findings to determine risk and control ratings. The process of pulling together and aggregating these fact packs can be laborious and tedious. AI can analyze these documents; identify control gaps, events, and process breakdowns; and model likelihood and impact. Can you imagine a day (it's now) when AI can create risk and control ratings for each risk assessment unit and update the ratings as certain triggers occur? Management will need to validate and review and challenge the results, as there needs to be subject-matter experts (i.e., humans) at the center of the process. But no organization of any size needs to continue spending its precious resources on manually aggregating data.

As mentioned previously, no framework element exists in a silo. The results of the RCSA should be linked to the issue management program and identified control gaps and residual risks above appetite (or approaching appetite) and should result in the opening of issues and action plans. The results of the RCSA are critical inputs for capital modeling and scenario analysis work. They should be tracked against risk appetite and used as a means for monitoring its levels. Most importantly, RCSA results should inform decision-making related to investment in new controls, processes, and new business initiatives where the cost of controls is an important input.

Getting Started with Designing an RCSA

The following are the critical elements of an RCSA program:

- **Governance:** Defined roles and responsibilities, stakeholders, and subject-matter experts.
- **Communication plan:** Management should demonstrate support for the RCSA through frequent communications.
- **Leveling up:** The level that the risk assessment will be performed in the organization and the construct of the risk assessment units (legal entity, business unit, process) and level of the taxonomy.
- **The perspective:** Top down and bottom up.
- **Technology enablement:** AI, GRC systems, SharePoint.
- **Methodology:** Inherent risk, control assessment and residual risk determination.
- **Process mapping:** Integration of process maps.
- **Trigger-based approach:** Determination of cyclical or trigger-based approach.
- **Remediation:** Remediating identified control gaps and high residual risks.
- **Reporting:** Reporting on the results to senior management and the board.

Governance: Defined Roles and Responsibilities

It is always prudent to kick off any newly developed risk program with clearly defined roles and responsibilities. The key to understanding how an RCSA will be executed is the word *self* in risk and control **self**-assessment. RCSA programs are designed to be implemented by the first line and ideally with direct input from the business lines that are closest to the processes under review. The second line plays an important role in developing the methodology, policy, governance structure, defining the roles and responsibilities, and, in some instances (but not all), owning the tools. The third line (internal audit) essentially is on point to make sure the second line is providing proper oversight of the first line and has developed a fit-for-purpose framework, and the first line is implementing the RCSA program properly.

It never ends well if there is confusion among roles and responsibilities, and a key input into an RCSA policy is a well-defined matrix that includes who is responsible for executing key elements of an RCSA program.

This chart summarizes RCSA roles and responsibilities across the first and second lines:

Role	First-Line Responsibilities	Second-Line Responsibilities
Framework and Methodology	Provide business feedback on program governance and methodology, attend governance committees, assist with communication	Develop RCSA policy, taxonomy, ratings methodology, governance routines, engage stakeholders
Control Assessment	Conduct control assessments, through testing or data review	Provide review and challenge of control assessment ratings
Risk Assessment Execution	Conduct RCSA workshops, rate risks and controls	Participate in workshops in challenger role
Issue & Action Plans	Open issues and action plans for identified control gaps or residual risks above appetite	Validate that action plans are designed to mitigate the risks and close control gaps
Training	Provide training on implementation	Provide training on methodology and framework
Review & Challenge	In-business control functions provide first-level review and challenge	Review and challenge risk and control ratings and final rating conclusions
Quality Control/ Assurance	In-business control functions perform first-level quality control reviews	Perform quality assurance reviews for consistency
Reporting & Aggregation	Provide reporting of results to business leaders and risk and control committees	Aggregate results and report to risk committee, the board and senior management
Continuous Improvement	Provide feedback based on implementation lessons learned	Update methodology and benchmark practices base

The second line is responsible for establishing the policy, framework, methodology, and governance structure. It is a requirement of any policy owner to ensure it is implemented correctly. This requires second-line oversight and validation of how the program is implemented by the first line, as well as a review of required first-line procedures, to confirm that they are aligned with policy requirements.

The following are the key elements of a policy:

- **Purpose statement and scope:** The general purpose of the policy, such as establishing requirements for the RCSA program, and scope, which is usually the entire organization, including all entities, functions, and business units.
- **Definitions:** Definitions of key terms, such as inherent risk, residual risk, control, control design, control effectiveness, control type (preventative, detective, key, nonkey).

- **Roles and responsibilities:** Includes roles and responsibilities for first line, second line, third line, and governance committees.
- **RCSA program overview:** Inherent risk assessment, control assessment, cadence for performing RCSA, trigger approach, first- and second-line validation, issue and action plans when required, link to risk appetite.
- **System:** Include a statement on the system of record for recording the results of the RCSA.
- **Risk scoring:** Inherent risk, control and residual risk rating requirements.
- **Oversight and review and challenge:** First-line quality control review, second-line quality assurance, and oversight responsibilities.
- **Reporting and documentation:** First-line documentation and reporting to business-level risk and control committees, second-line aggregate reporting to risk committees and the board.
- **Training requirements:** First-line implementation training, second-line methodology and framework training.
- **Policy governance:** Policy owner, policy review cycle, policy exceptions, requirement for first-line procedures.

Many second-line functions draft standards, which provide more details on the requirements established in the policy. While a policy describes the high-level requirements for expectations and is usually a short, high-level document, a standard provides more detail on the expectations for executing the program. The first-line, however, is responsible for drafting detailed procedures that describe step-by-step how the program will be implemented.

The second line is responsible for drafting the RCSA methodology, which can be a stand-alone document or part of the standard. The methodology documentation should provide detail on how to assess risks, controls, processes, and how to arrive at a final residual risk rating. It should include the risk assessment unit schema (unit of measure), rating tables, how to determine impact and likelihood, and how to identify control gaps and open issues. There should also be a section on risk acceptance if the residual risk comes in above the risk appetite and a reference to risk appetite statements and metrics. There should be a section on required tools, templates, use of the system of record, reporting, and quality assurance. There should also be a section on requirements for reviewing and updating the methodology annually, based on feedback from stakeholders. This is a critical requirement, as the methodology should be regularly challenged and assessed for relevancy and applicability.

The results of the RCSA, including a view on whether it is within appetite, should be aggregated by the second line across processes, business lines, and entities, and reviewed through an organization's governance structure, including the operational risk and enterprise risk committees and the board. The report should include themes and trends, emerging issues, significant control gaps, and, at the board level, the 5–10 observations that are most material to the enterprise. The role of the committees is to review and challenge the results, ask questions, and determine if additional actions and remediations are required to close identified gaps or manage emerging risks.

Communication Plan

As previously mentioned, RCSA comes under a great deal of criticism for not providing value when the level of effort is accounted for. There is also a deep-seated self-interest that can be unconscious that prevents a business from doing the hard work and identifying control issues, when they have so much on their plate. (See the interview with Craig Spielman at the end of this chapter.) They also believe that they know their issues through their daily activities and do not need a formal process for identifying them. The talk-track can be "I did all this work, and you are telling me what I already know."

In addition, there can be a bias against opening issues and action plans, when an organization has created a process for penalizing businesses that have open issues through conduct score cards. Although most organizations provide credit for self-identifying issues, those responsible can see their conduct scores impacted if they miss remediation deadlines.

This is the backdrop that many operational risk and control professionals must contend with when they are working on establishing, managing, and implementing an RCSA program. If an RCSA program does not have the sponsorship of senior management, it is relegated to being a check-the-box exercise and nothing more. For this reason, the development of a robust communication plan is important to ensure the organization up and down and sideways understands the importance of implementing RCSA.

I have always kicked off RCSA programs with emails from the CEO indicating the importance of executing the program. I have asked the CEO to send supporting emails throughout the course of implementing the program to bolster acceptance of the program, rather than grudging compliance. I have also incorporated an introduction to the program by the CEO in online training modules.

I have worked in two organizations that rolled out operational excellence programs that had the identification of risks and controls at the center of their messaging. These programs highlighted the businesses and functions that identified control gaps and remediated them with quality through firmwide communications and in one organization a dinner and award ceremony at the Rainbow Room in New York. The year I was given an Operational Excellence award by the organization's CEO at the Rainbow Room was one of the highlights of my career and really drove home the importance of identifying risks and fixing control issues.

At the same time, it is important to work with compliance organizations that create conduct scorecards to ensure that they are not providing negative incentives for identifying risks and controls. Managing an RCSA program or being an ambassador in its execution is not easy work and takes a lot of patience and fortitude. You may have the symbolic equivalent of eggs thrown at you on a regular basis, but it is worth working your communication plan. When you step back and view the big picture, you are assisting the organization with enhancing its risk and control environment, assessment by assessment.

Leveling Up: Determining Risk Assessment Units

The first question I ask when I am a designing an RCSA program is "What is the unit of measure?" The unit of measure is the risk assessment unit, and it is important to have this clearly delineated ahead of implementation. If what is being assessed is unclear and undefined, the relevant question is "What are we measuring after all?" The risk assessment unit schema should reflect how the organization is structured for it to be effective. This can follow the firm's organizational hierarchy or general ledger structure.

The next question is "Are we conducting the RCSA by process, entity, business, or function?" Many large organizations have organized themselves around processes and have taken a process approach in executing RCSAs. The advantage to taking this approach is that it allows for end-to-end assessment of risks and controls in processes that cut across businesses and reflects the most material activities in an organization. A good example may be a payment process that impacts multiple businesses in an institution.

The downside to taking a process approach is that many organizations are not organized in this way, and it can be challenging to name an owner when a process crosses businesses and functions. For instance, if RCSA finds a control gap in a process that crosses several businesses, who is the accountable executive for an issue to remediate it? I have seen this issue spin for weeks on end, when no one business wanted to step in and own the issue. This can be resolved if a strong issue management policy or standard defines this up front, including who the arbitrator is when there is a disagreement.

Some organizations are very entity-based and have organized RCSA schemas by entity structure. The advantage to this approach is that regulatory and financial reporting is often by entity, and it allows for an alignment with how the organization is structured at the top level. The disadvantage is that it creates a challenge to assess processes that cut across entities and can result in duplicate assessments of the same or similar processes. I once was able to substantially reduce the number of RCSAs performed when I moved an organization from entity to a process approach, by reducing duplicate assessment units. It can also result in very high-level RCSAs which may miss risks and controls at more granular levels where processes are executed.

An additional approach with some drawbacks is a business unit or function approach that allows for more granularity in what is being assessed, as it is done at a lower level than the entity approach.

I have also executed RCSA by organizing by business (first-line revenue generating) and function (enterprise support functions, such as technology, cyber, compliance) and process within each business. I have executed this approach for organizations that did not have mature process orientations in place. This involved identifying where in the business units and functions there were material processes that required digging into based on known issues, materiality to the business, or senior management concern for lack of transparency into how they are performed (as expressed in RCSA workshops). The challenge with this approach, as discussed, is getting the view into end-to-end processes, which can cut across businesses. I have accomplished this by holding workshops with the pertinent people from impacted businesses and mapping out the end-to-end process. When taking this approach, it is critical to understand where hand-offs occur, because omissions can occur when process activities cross boundaries from one business to another.

A critical requirement is to have accountable executives assigned to each risk assessment unit. As I mentioned, that can be a challenge if a process approach is taken in an organization that is not organized by process, but it can be done by designating process owners. The accountable executive is responsible for ensuring the risk and control assessment work is completed by the respective teams, challenging the results, providing a forum for communicating the results within the business or function, ensuring issues and action plans are opened when control gaps are identified or residual risk is above risk appetite, and signing off on the final risk assessment result.

An additional critical consideration when executing an RCSA program is the operational risk Taxonomy. A process approach will require either an integrated process, risk, control (PRC) taxonomy, which allows for assessing risks and controls by process, or separate stand-alone process, risk and control taxonomies that can be cross referenced (using old-fashioned Boolean logic). Every organization I have worked with has had at minimum a risk taxonomy (see Chapter 1), derived from the seven operational risk types with operational subrisks added (such as fraud, cyber, data, technology, third party), and some but not all have had control taxonomies. A standard library of controls allows for managing the abundance of controls that exist in an organization (and they tend to grow exponentially).

A PRC taxonomy aligns the material processes in an organization with the associated risks and controls. It can be an elegant process once it is developed but can also be limiting when new combinations of risks and controls emerge. I have seen assessors try hard to fit not quite accurate results into predefined PRCs. For this reason, I have always preferred the flexibility of well-developed but stand-alone PRC taxonomies that can be mixed and matched as you work through assessments. The downside to this approach is that it is less "out of the box" than the linked PRC taxonomy, which provides a turnkey approach to assessing processes (i.e., the assessor does not have to consider among the options of what risks and controls are aligned with a process).

The following is a sample from a PRC taxonomy for third-party risk. A PRC will have the listed risks and controls for all material processes.

Sample PRC Table

Process: Third Party Onboarding

Sub-Process	Risk	Control
Vendor Due Diligence & Risk Assessment	Vendor compliance, financial, and reputational risk	Vendor risk assessment completed using standardized due diligence checklist
Vendor Due Diligence & Risk Assessment	Data Leakage	Legal review and signed contract including data protection clauses
Vendor Due Diligence & Risk Assessment	Cyber Risk	Review SOC 2 Report

The Perspective: Top Down and Bottom Up

There are two approaches to managing an RCSA program that are equally important: a top-down view with input from senior management and a bottom-up view that incorporates control testing, process mapping, and the view from the people who execute processes. The two views inform each other, and it is important to create a strategy for linking them. I have done this by kicking off the RCSA process with workshops with senior leaders of the firm and then using their articulated views to prioritize the intensive bottom-up work. I have also used their views to challenge the results, as there can be a disconnect between what senior management sees as material risk and control issues and the view from the "factory floor."

I developed the top-down approach when I was hired by a major bank to "fix" the RCSA program. The bank had recently experienced a public risk event that created significant financial losses and reputational damage. I pulled the RCSA for the business unit that was at the center of the loss to see what it said. I was surprised and only partially relieved to discover that it had identified many of the issues that later contributed to the loss. But it was evident that the RCSA was executed by a junior person, and it ended there. There was a lack of senior management involvement in the process, and the identified issues were not escalated to the level of business decision-makers.

That experience led me to put in place what I called at the time *top-down workshops*. The idea was to get the senior leadership team together for each business and to simply discuss "what keeps them up at night." I did not want to talk "taxonomy talk" or "operational risk talk" but to have them simply discuss their concerns. While I mapped their concerns later to the organization's taxonomy, I did not want them to get side-tracked by trying to pinpoint the exact risk language. (It is worth mentioning that I have worked in an institution where everyone from the CEO on down was able to organize their thoughts by the risk taxonomy, but that is not the case with every organization.)

The top-down workshop is simply a discussion with senior management. I have been asked for scripts and questionnaires, but my preference is to go with the spirit of facilitating a deep and impactful discussion about risks and controls. I had a lot of resistance the first time I kicked off this exercise, and painfully, attendance during the first session was sparse. This led me to go back to my communication plan and ask senior management to provide more messaging around the importance of the exercise. I have kicked the process off with an email from the CEO of explaining why the workshops are important and stressing that participation is mandatory. I have found that once people show up (and yes, some are heads down on their laptops or phones until they hear something that perks them up), they generally become engaged in the process. The best stuff usually happens in the last few minutes of the workshop. Someone as the workshop nears the end may throw out, "What about XYZ?" And XYZ is a big and hairy topic, and although I wonder why it was not discussed earlier in the session, it is important that it was raised.

The top-down workshops establish clear ownership of the RCSA process and allow senior management to establish priorities for the year through their discussion of what keeps them up at night, which might be emerging risks, control issues, or processes they have no insight into. This allows for prioritization of control testing, process mapping, and the business risk rating of risks and controls. I facilitated a top-down workshop for the technology function of a large foreign bank. The chief technology officer said that one of his largest concerns was the recruiting of technology talent. He ranked this as very high on his list of risks. When I ran a more granular workshop with his team who were risk rating the top risks, they said that the level of people risk is very low, because "developers are easy to recruit and replace." There was a clear disconnect between the two perspectives, but I was able to ensure the two views were aligned (and convince the team to rate people risk much higher).

Top-down workshops with senior management require a fair amount of prep work. I like to interview a few "friendly" people on each team ahead of the workshop and construct a starter list of risk and control concerns to help get the discussion started. This also includes reviewing the open issues, regulatory findings, scenarios, risk events, and near-misses. Having a starter list of risk and control issues helps get over the silence that might ensure when you first inquire about what they are most concerned about. I also bring in external peer events and pose the question, "Can this happen here and if so, what would it look like?" In some cases, the business launches directly into their concerns, but in others, it is helpful to have something for them to respond to. Having a starter list and scenarios drafted also helps with making sure that any critical issues are not missed.

Although I am not an advocate of going into a workshop with a script, and in addition to having a starter list of concerns drafted, here are some sample questions to consider starting things off with:

- What risks and controls associated with your function keep you up at night?
- What key processes or activities within your function are you most concerned with?
- Are there emerging risks, themes, or trends that you believe should be monitored in your business?
- Are there places where there is a lack of transparency associated with operations that concern you?
- What areas do you believe this RCSA process should focus on and where can we best utilize the RCSA aligned resources?
- Are there known risk or control issues that have been highlighted by regulators, auditors or your business that we should focus on?
- Are there events that have happened to your peers that you believe you may also be exposed to? (Be prepared with a list of examples.)
- What have we not discussed that you believe is material?

Although I originally facilitated top-down workshops in my second-line operational risk role, that is no longer the standard within most institutions. The first line, following the edict that the first line owns implementation of the RCSA program, should facilitate the workshops. This is often facilitated by someone in a control officer, business unit risk manager, in-business risk manager, or chief operating officer role. I have most recently attended these workshops in a review and challenge and observer role rather than a facilitator one. But smaller organizations or nonbank organizations without the first-line control structure may still rely on a second-line risk person to facilitate the workshops.

It should be mentioned that organizations that have moved to continuous RCSA programs through a trigger-based approach should still hold the top-down senior management workshops annually to refresh the top-down view.

The next step is to translate senior management's feedback into risk and control language and to link to the taxonomy. This should then inform the bottom-up work and drive the prioritized plan for assessing processes, risks, and controls. This work includes testing or assessing through a review of data controls associated with the prioritized risks and mapping out the material processes. The risk and control work can be executed through the process mapping exercises. The top-down view should inform the roadmap for subsequent work. As previously stated, prioritization is important, as it is not prudent, efficient, or effective to assess every control within an organization.

The following lists the key attributes of the top-down and bottom-up approaches. They work together to establish the roadmap for executing the RCSA program.

Top-Down Approach

- **Strategic alignment:**
  Senior management demonstrates accountability of the process and articulates prioritization for the bottom-up work by aligning with the organization's overall risk appetite and strategic objectives.
- **Focused risk identification:**
  By concentrating on the key risks identified at the executive level, critical issues are highlighted that can impact the business that require assessment.
- **Efficient resource use:**
  Prioritizing risk and control issues articulated by senior management allows the RCSA process to focus on "what matters most" and to use limited resources most efficiently in conducting the bottom-up work.

Bottom-Up Approach

- **Detailed operational perspective:**
  Employees who work directly with processes are closest to day-to-day potential breaks and issues and round out the process by providing their "on-the-ground" perspective.
- **Identification of emerging risks:**
  Employees who are closest to the process can be the first to identify emerging issues that may not have yet been escalated to senior management.
- **Process and control view:**
  A bottom-up approach that assesses risks and controls at the process and control level, is best equipped to inform the design and implementation of remediation measures.

Technology Enablement

RCSA can result in a complicated execution process, and an organization of any size will need more sophisticated tools than SharePoint. These have come to be known as governance, risk, and compliance (GRC) systems, and most have multiple modules for different components of an operational risk program, such as RCSA, loss data, and issue management. It is ideal to contract with one vendor that can provide support for the primary components of an operational risk program, which allow for connecting the dots among them. For instance, a GRC system that has modules for RCSA, loss data, and issue management will allow for the seamless opening of issues when there is a loss event or RCSA residual risk above appetite. I have also witnessed organizations that have different systems for several components of their program due to the required functionality. It is worth mentioning that a small organization or one that is just getting started may find SharePoint effective if they have in-house resources that can assist with setting up templates and reports.

I started my career in the early days of the discipline working for several operational risk start-ups, including Operationalrisk.com and Netrisk. These two companies were early pioneers in developing operational risk solutions at a time when the discipline was still being defined. They both ended up in the Risk Solutions division of Fitch Ratings, which also acquired the risk firm Algorithmics and folded them into a single entity under the Algorithmics branding. I learned a lot of lessons in the early days of developing the FIRST external loss database and participating in the first industry implementations of operational risk solutions, including RCSA.

One of the most important lessons I learned that I carried with me when I moved into bank risk practitioner roles is the importance of good collaboration with a vendor. I witnessed organizations that have had combative relationships with their vendors, which often do not end well. It is also important to understand a vendor's capabilities and track record and to ensure that they have the capacity and experience to implement an operational risk solution for your organization. Every few years a new GRC vendor emerges who the industry falls in love with. I have seen these newly emerged vendors struggle to deliver if they grow too quickly and take on too many clients at once.

The other lesson I learned is that RCSA is among one of the most complicated installations because it must be aligned with how a firm is organized. It is difficult to implement an RCSA solution straight out of the box. This requires customized approaches, including bespoke solution upgrades. Technology advancements have made it easier to implement these upgrades, but it is important to map out the RCSA lifecycle that is specific to your institution and ensure that the vendor can align it with their solution.

The following is a list of functionalities to consider when reviewing RCSA solutions that are offered by GRC vendors:

- **Lifecycle:** An RCSA solution should support the entire lifecycle, including risk and control assessment, process mapping, workshops, data aggregation, and reporting.
- **Workflow:** RCSA workflow should include alerts when risks and controls are required to be rated and validated, when triggers occur that require updating, accountable

executive and second-line validations, review and challenges, and notification for when each cycle is required to be kicked off.

- **Taxonomy:** The solution should allow for multiple taxonomies and approaches, included integrated PRC taxonomies, or stand-alone risk, control, and process taxonomies that can be combined. It should also allow for "drag and drop" functionality when changes occur.
- **Data integration:** The solution should allow for the integration of risk and control data, including issues, action plans, KRIs, scenarios, and loss data.
- **Integrated modules:** The modules should be integrated so that if you need to open an issue as the result of the RCSA findings, you can easily do so without a lot of extra steps.
- **AI integration:** The more forward solutions have AI capabilities built into the modules, which assist with data integration and initial ratings.
- **Unit of measure:** The solution should be able to cope with ease when functions or businesses or processes are reorganized through "drag and drop" functionality.
- **Process mapping:** There should be the ability to ingest process maps and link the risks and controls to process-based risk assessment units. This includes identifying hand-offs and linking the risks and controls on the map to the assessment templates.
- **Reporting:** The solution should have reporting capability built in or linkages to tools such as Tableau or Business Objects. There should be real-time dashboards that can be easily manipulated for identifying themes and trends and top risk ratings.
- **User experience:** The solution overall should provide the ability to easily configure its modules and be accessible to various levels of users.

AI is a game changer and promises that the days of manually aggregating data and consolidating "fact packs" are behind us. RCSA leverages a lot of data from losses, peer events, issues and action plans, scenarios, risk appetite metrics, KRIs, and other assessments. AI can make the process much more efficient through its ability to aggregate data and derive a first pass of risk and control ratings. It also can automate the control testing process and identify where there are duplicate controls that require reconciliation.

The approach for getting started with integrating AI into the RCSA process is to work with your GRC vendor. Several vendors can assist with this as the mainstream GRC systems have integrated AI capability (or are in the process of doing so). If your GRC system does not have AI capabilities or you do not have a GRC system, you will want to work with someone in your organization who can help you get started with structuring prompts and setting up "tasks" within ChatGPT.

It is effective to bring together a small group of RCSA stakeholders and inquire where the pain points are. They will likely say in the data aggregation process that has traditionally been manual, but they may have other areas as well. For instance, they may complain about too many workshops. AI can streamline this process by assisting with preliminary ratings, which would turn the workshops into more efficient validation sessions. This should lead to the creation of AI use cases and a plan for implementing a pilot with a risk assessment unit that is representative of the organization.

AI hallucinations are notorious, but AI is becoming more accurate by the day. The important part of the process is the "human in the middle." The ratings will require validation through workshops and feedback from the stakeholders, and you may want to check a few of the results manually. The governance around the process is critical. A good rule of thumb is to never accept a rating (of any kind) from a machine or from an aggregation methodology or model without validating it. It is necessary to always apply the lens of the people who understand the process, risks, and controls in finalizing the rating.

The following are standard data points that should be incorporated into the RCSA process, which AI can assist with integrating and aggregating:

Sample RCSA Fact Set

Category	Description
Process Maps	Process maps with risks, controls, and hand-offs
Loss Events	Internal and external loss events and near-misses
Metrics	KRIs, KCIs, risk appetite metrics
Issues and Action Plans	Outstanding issues, including those identified across three lines of defense and by regulators
Scenario Analysis	Operational risk scenarios by taxonomy
Control Testing Results	Including testing from compliance, fraud, data governance and other functions
Risk Assessments	Results from compliance, AML, fraud, third-party, and other risk assessments
Workshop results	Results from top-down and bottom-up workshops

Methodology: Rating Risks and Controls

Assessing Risks

The place to start when determining a risk rating once the initial work has been completed through the top-down workshops is with the risk taxonomy. The taxonomy along with the risk assessment units provide the structure for assessing risk. I earlier mentioned that you do not want to bring the taxonomy into the top-down workshops, but you will want to map everything to the taxonomy afterwards. You will also want to decide at what level in the taxonomy to risk rate each assessment unit. Most taxonomies have two or three levels.

A risk assessment conducted at level 1 of a taxonomy may be too broad and provide difficulties with identifying specific risk types. To conduct the risk assessment at level 3 may lead to too many individual assessments and unmanageable incremental work. A good middle ground is to conduct the assessment at level 2, but with a callout to the individual level 3 risk types. Some organizations will organize around level 2 but will conduct deep dives at level 3 in areas where there are major concerns.

The following is an example of a node from a taxonomy for fraud risk. A taxonomy will be built out at multiple levels for each risk category.

Sample Taxonomy Node with 3 Levels

Level 1: Risk Category	Level 2: Risk Subcategory	Level 3: Specific Risk Types/Examples
Fraud Risk	Internal Fraud	Employee theft; unauthorized trading; falsification of records
Fraud Risk	Internal Fraud	Misuse of confidential information
Fraud Risk	External Fraud	Check fraud; card fraud; cyber-enabled fraud
Fraud Risk	External Fraud	Account takeover fraud; ATM skimming

Inherent risk has customarily been assessed for both Impact (how big can the risk be) and Likelihood (how often can it happen). Some organizations have moved away from Likelihood, as it is much harder to determine how often a risk can manifest than to imagine how big in terms of impact it can be. (See Craig Spielman's perspective on Likelihood in the interview at the end of this chapter.) I personally have moved away from imposing Likelihood on the risk-rating process, but there are many people in the industry who believe it is an important risk dimension.

The development of an impact table is important for consistency in ratings. It is a strong practice to have one impact table for all the operational risk program elements, including RCSA, loss data, and issue management. This allows for a consistent approach in determining high, medium, and low ratings. High is the same high across the organization if all program elements are determining impact from the same table.

Table 6.1 is a high-level example of an impact table. The more specific the table is, with detailed guidance for considering the impact categories, the more consistency an organization will experience in how risks are rated. The categories should be customized for each organization, including the potential loss amounts (based on the company's loss experience and revenue), reputational impact, operational impact, and regulatory impact. For operational impact, a strong practice is to align with the company's business continuity policy and risk categories concerning business disruptions.

Likelihood, if incorporated into inherent risk, should be considered on a time horizon. For instance, the following is an example of how to consider likelihood. In this case it is on a 10-year time horizon. Traditionally the industry has considered the "rare" category on a 100-year time horizon, but catastrophic events have been occurring much more frequently than that, and the 100-year time frame is very difficult for most people to imagine.

- **Rare:** Risk manifests in less than 10 years.
- **Unlikely:** Risk manifests at least one time in 5–10 years.
- **Possible:** Risk manifests at least one time in two to four years.
- **Likely:** Risk manifests at least one time in one year.

Table 6.2 provides an example of how to plot the Impact and Likelihood to arrive at the final Inherent Risk Rating. It is a strong practice to build into the GRC

Table 6.1 Sample Impact Table

Severity Level	Financial Impact	Regulatory/Legal Impact	Operational Impact	Reputational Impact
Low	$0–$100K impact on financial statement	Informal regulatory feedback; no fine; No compliance testing issues, or low rated issue	A service disruption of business activities for less than five hours. RTO of a business activities is a Tier 4 Rating.	Minor local media coverage; no brand or client relationship damage
Moderate	$100K–$1M impact on financial statement	Regulatory written observations or small fine; minor violation of law; compliance testing issues rated Moderate	A service disruption of business activities for less than one day. RTO of a service disruption is a Tier 3 Rating.	Regional or industry press coverage; moderate brand or client relationship damage
Mod High	$1M–$10M impact on financial statement	Regulatory formal finding or moderate fine; moderate violation of law; compliance testing issues rated Moderate High	A service disruption of business activities for one to two days. RTO of a service disruption is a Tier 2 Rating.	National press coverage; significant brand or client relationship damage
High	>$10M impact on financial statement	Regulatory censure – Cease and Desist Order, Consent Order; License suspension; major monetary fine; significant violation of law; regulatory intervention; compliance testing issues rated high	A service disruption of business activities for three days or more. The RTO of a service disruption of business Tier 1 Rating.	Sustained national press coverage; major reputation damage; long term irreparable brand or client relationship damage

Table 6.2 Sample Impact and Likelihood Risk Rating Chart

	Likelihood			
Impact	**Rare**	**Unlikely**	**Possible**	**Likely**
Low	Low	Low	Low	Moderate
Moderate	Low	Moderate	Moderate	High
Mod High	Moderate	Moderate	High	High
High	Moderate	High	High	High

tool a formula that translates the table into a formula and automatically calculates the final ratings.

Another consideration is the rating scale itself, and I have been involved in many heated discussions about this. Smaller organizations have done fine with a three-point rating scale—High, Medium, and Low. The downside to this approach is that there is a large gulf between Low-Medium scores and High-Medium scores, and there is a tendency for ratings to all land in the middle of the scale.

I prefer a four-point rating scale that creates room for a wider range of ratings with greater sensitivity and allows for tracking the upper range of medium which is an important indicator for increasing risk. For this reason, I prefer a rating scale along these lines: Low, Medium, Medium-High, and High. I would be remiss in mentioning that I have been involved in long debates on three-, four-, or five-point rating scales and risk professionals are passionate about their preference!

Assessing Controls

Assessing controls, along with process mapping, comprises a great deal of the bottom-up work. Controls should be tagged to risks (and risks tagged to processes if you take that approach) and prioritized for assessment according to the level of risk they are designed to mitigate. Controls are assessed based on design effectiveness and implementation effectiveness.

The two questions you want to ask when assessing a control are the following:

- Is the control designed to mitigate the intended risk?
- Is the control implemented as designed?

The first question should be a gating item, and if the control is not designed to mitigate the risk, the control overall is not effective. It makes no sense to test a control for effectiveness that is not designed in the first order to mitigate the risk. The determination of design effectiveness can be determined by a walk-through with subject-matter experts, depending on the type of control, who can opine of its design effectiveness. For instance, if the control is designed to prevent data leakage in the human resources department, the subject-matter experts who review the control design should include those from Human Resource and Data Governance functions, along with operational risk, who should opine ahead of its effectiveness.

A design review will want to consider the following questions to derive a control rating:

- Is the control effectively designed to mitigate the specific risk in alignment with the business' articulated risk appetite and industry standards?
- Does the control support compliance with rules and regulations?
- Is the control designed to be preventative (preferred) or detective?
- Is this a key control (the primary control to mitigate a risk), a nonkey control (a secondary control to support the primary control), or a compensating control (a temporary, tactical control while the strategic control is under development)?
- Does this control mitigate the risk on its own or is reliant on other controls? Is this control designed to be part of a suite of controls?
- What is the expected output or result of the control?
- Are rules and responsibilities articulated in relation to design, execution and oversight of the control?
- Is the frequency of the control aligned with the risk that it is designed to mitigate?
- Is the control designed to be manual, automated, or semi-automated?

Controls are classified as preventative (they prevent the risk event from occurring), detective (they detect a potential risk event either concurrent to execution of a process or after its occurrence), directive (they direct behavior), or corrective (they fix a problem that has occurred). It is preferable for a control to be preventative. When control design is considered, it should be determined if a control gap that is being mitigated by a detective control would be better addressed by a preventative one (if possible). Controls can also be key or nonkey.

The following is the lexicon of controls:

- **Preventative:** Controls are implemented ahead of execution of the process or activity associated with the risk they are designed to prevent. Example: Know-your-client (KYC) controls are preventative as they identify high-risk clients ahead of bringing then onto the bank's accounts.
- **Detective:** controls are implemented either concurrent of execution of the process or activity associated with the risk they are designed to prevent or post-execution. Example: Transaction monitoring is designed to detect high-risk activities of clients currently on the bank's accounts.
- **Directive:** Controls designed to achieve desired behavioral outcomes. Example: Policies, standards, directives, procedures.
- **Corrective:** Controls designed to remediate, rectify, or recover from a control deficiency or operational risk event.
- **Compensating:** A tactical control put in place in the absence of a primary or strategic control. Example: A manual reconciliation implemented on an interim basis while an automated solution is under development
- **Key:** Primary controls that are designed to be the primary mitigants of a risk. Example: KYC is a key control for identifying high-risk clients who apply for accounts with a financial institution.

- **Nonkey:** Controls that supplement key controls but do not mitigate the risk by themselves. They often are part of a suite of controls. Example: Governance committees or forums that review risk materials but are not the primary mitigants.
- **Manual Control:** A control activity performed by a person and, as such, is more susceptible to errors and breakdowns.
- **Automated Control:** Control activity that is embedded in a system and occurs without human interaction.

Control effectiveness can be determined through testing, data reviews, or the design of a survey that assesses the quality of its execution. In many cases, testing may be available in pockets of the firm, and control implementation effectiveness will need to supplement testing results with data reviews and surveys. The first step in determining control effectiveness is to identify where testing occurs in the firm and ingest the results into the RCSA control assessment. For instance, compliance often has robust testing programs aligned with rules and regulations; fraud, data governance, model risk management, cyber risk, and technology functions may also conduct testing which can be leveraged for the RCSA.

If control testing is not available, then the next route is to consider control data, such as issues, loss events, near-misses, regulatory, and audit findings. These can be supplemented by consideration of the following:

- Has the control been consistently and comprehensively executed as designed?
- Is the control performed at the required frequency as required by the design?
- Is the control performed by personnel with the right level of experience and authority?
- Is the control properly documented through procedures?
- Did the control fail to operate completely or partially over the time frame being assessed?
- Is the continued operation of the control sustainable, as demonstrated by the knowledge and expertise of the control operators, sufficient in-house capacity, adequate budget, and management support?
- Are their open issues, regulatory, or audit findings related to the control's effectiveness?

Determining Residual Risk

Residual risk is determined through the consideration of inherent risk and controls. A rule of thumb is that regardless of the effectiveness of controls, residual risk can never be higher than inherent risk. For this reason, even low inherent risks with ineffective controls can only result in a low residual risk.

The formula for determining residual risk, which is widely circulated, is quite simple:

$$\textit{Inherent Risk} - \textit{Control Effectiveness} = \textit{Residual Risk}.$$

Residual risk is the amount of risk remaining after controls are applied to inherent risk. It is a strong practice to evaluate residual risk against risk appetite. For instance, if risk appetite for fraud in a financial institution is Medium and the RCSA, after assessing fraud as High and controls as Partially Effective, determines that residual risk for fraud is Moderate High, it is out of appetite. This would necessitate the opening of an issue to enhance the controls to bring down the residual risk and align with the articulated appetite.

The following charts demonstrate two approaches to determining residual risk. As mentioned with determining inherent risk, it is a strong practice to build into the GRC tool a formula that translates the residual risk table into a formula that automatically calculates the final rating.

Depending on the institution, you may want to consider an extremely conservative approach when designing the residual risk methodology, which will impact the overall risk rating landscape for the final RCSA results. Table 6.3 is the approach I recently took with a design of an RCSA residual risk methodology, which allowed for the lowering of just one notch when the controls were rated to be effective and no benefit for partially effective or ineffective controls. I took this approach based on the maturity of the organization, including the maturity of its control assessment processes, which were very nascent.

Table 6.4 is a more typical residual risk methodology that provides two notches of benefit for controls that are effective, one notch for partially effective and no benefit for ineffective. More mature organizations with robust testing programs and confidence in the accuracy of their control assessments typically allow inherent risk to drop by two notches when the controls are effective and one notch for partially effective controls. On the other hand, I have heard some professionals argue that controls are either effective

Table 6.3 Sample Conservative Residual Risk Chart (with One Level of Benefit for Effective Controls)

	Controls		
Inherent Risk	**Effective**	**Partially Effective**	**Ineffective**
Low	Low	Low	Low
Moderate	Low	Moderate	Moderate
Mod High	Moderate	Mod High	Mod High
High	Mod High	High	High

Table 6.4 Alternative Sample Residual Risk Chart (with Two Levels of Benefit for Effective Controls)

	Controls		
Inherent Risk	**Effective**	**Partially Effective**	**Ineffective**
Low	Low	Low	Low
Moderate	Low	Low	Moderate
Mod High	Low	Moderate	Mod High
High	Moderate	Mod High	High

or not, and a partially effective control should provide no benefit. The final design will depend on the institution and will benefit from lessons learned from a back-testing exercise to see what the best methodology is.

Once the residual risk results are obtained, it is a strong practice to hold calibration sessions with the representatives from each risk assessment unit to check for reasonableness of the ratings and to ensure that there is consistency in how they were applied. For instance, something would need be adjusted if a unit known to carry a lot of risk and control issues is rated lower than one that is lower risk with effective controls. This is also an opportunity to use AI to review the risks across the enterprise and provide a summary of the ratings.

Process Mapping

There is nothing more illuminating than mapping out a process to understand where things can go wrong. Regardless of whether an organizational assesses risks and controls through a process, entity, or business approach, a process map can add a lot of value to the exercise. I have built process maps and process inventories from scratch for major organizations by taking a top-down approach by first identifying the critical processes in an organization, gathering key people in a room, and mapping from end-to-the end the process through two or three levels, depending on the complexity of the underlying activities.

I once took a lot of heat when I worked in a big bank and was asked to assess their mortgage processes, which were under regulatory scrutiny. I pulled representatives from the mortgage businesses for a full-day workshop to map out the processes front to back, from originations to collections, and heard some harsh words for taking so many people out of their day jobs. In the end, we got a good result, and it is one of the risk assessments I am most proud of due to the depth of analysis and review of key processes. It was helpful to have people from various stages in the mortgage lifecycle in the same room to discuss hand-offs.

Today, most GRC systems include process mapping modules, which allow for integration with RCSA assessments. There are also tools that allow for visualization when producing process maps. One concern when creating a library of process maps is that they become stale over time. The care and maintenance of them requires at least annual reviews and interim updates when certain predefined triggers, such as reorganizations, occur. Process maps, like control testing, often exist in various parts of the organization and can be incorporated into the RCSA work when they exist. Most likely, operations functions have created them for their most material processes. They should be located and integrated into the RCSA process.

The benefits of making a commitment to creating and maintaining a library of process maps are that they allow for the visualization of how a process is executed from end to end. They are less useful but still workable, if they represent only a partial process due to organizational structures and an assessor needs to piece together documents to get a full view. Process maps should be prioritized like everything else in an RCSA program and focus on the highest risks and most process-intensive activities, such as payments and wire transfers. Less process-intensive activities, such as those that are based on building client relationships, may not require the creation of process maps but still may benefit from process walk-throughs.

It should be noted that an RCSA process walkthrough, or the design of a process map, is not a process re-engineering activity and does not require the commensurate level of detail. They should be detailed enough to incorporate risks and controls at the right level but not so detailed that it is hard to align them with RCSA assessment units. Their overall benefit is to visualize where the control activities occur in the activities on the map and if they are aligned with where the risks occur. An additional advantage is to understand on the process map where there are hand-offs. It is often when hand-offs occur between two functions that errors and omissions happen. If the process is divided by two or more maps due to organizational structure, it is difficult (but not impossible) to get a view into these potential control hand-offs and breakpoints.

The following are the important components to include on a process map; see chapter eleven for a sample process mapping exercise:

- **Process owner:** Name of process owner and function
- **Risk points:** Where in the process risks are manifested, with risk name and identifiable numbers if available (example: R1, R2, R3)
- **Control points:** Where in the process controls are executed, with control name and identifiable numbers if available (example: C1, C2, C3)
- **Hand-offs and hand-ins:** Where processes cross boundaries, swim-lanes, business units, or entities
- **Regulatory requirements:** Applicable regulatory and compliance requirements that impact the process
- **Control breakpoints:** Identified areas that experienced control breaks or gaps in the past

The Trigger-Based Approach

The industry has mostly moved away from updating RCSAs on a regular annual schedule. Even when a cyclical approach is taken and only the higher risk assessment units are updated annually, the RCSA has been a resource-intensive exercise. As soon as one cycle is completed, it is often time to start the next one. The ratings may be as old as six months by the time the results are published and presented to risk committees and the board.

Once the initial RCSA baseline is developed and all risk assessment units have been risk rated, a trigger-based approach can allow for more timely assessments and updates, according to a set of predefined qualitative and quantitative measures. When the predefined criteria are triggered, the risk and controls will necessitate a review and a ratings revision if required. This solves the problem of the lag time between assessment and reporting and allows for a closer to real-time approach. It is more dynamic than assessing risks and controls on a standard cycle and creates an opportunity for both better risk management and operational efficiency. The approach should be aligned with risk appetite and allows for more timely monitoring of thresholds. A strong industry practice is to incorporate risk appetite metrics into the trigger factors.

What always concerned me when I introduced the approach was the front line's reluctance to identify triggers and update risks and controls accordingly. For instance, I always included external peer events as a trigger. If a peer institution has a significant event, an assessment should be undertaken of a firm's own controls and vulnerabilities and the risk and control assessments updated accordingly for the impacted business or function. The front line may tend to reject the relevancy of such an event if has not occurred to an organization or business that is organized exactly like them, rather than considering the relevancy of the control breakdowns. Ensuring the RCSAs are updated when triggers are breached has kept me up at night when I moved to this approach. It takes active monitoring by the second line and partnership across the lines of defense.

The automation of metrics and incorporation into a GRC workflow assists with acting on the triggers when they are breached. One option is to do a parallel run and continue implementing the cyclical approach while the triggers are being introduced to allow time for training and socialization, and to get some assurance that the first line understand the process and update their RCSAs as triggers are breached. I have followed this option before moving entirely to the trigger-based approach. Some firms have implemented a hybrid approach that addresses the challenge of ensuring RCSAs are updated if triggers are not properly dispositioned and incorporates updates. But it does not allow for the efficiencies that are built into the trigger-based approach and may result in first-line complaints of extra strains on their resources.

It is important to define RCSA quantitative and qualitative triggers that are actionable and well understood by the organization. It is a strong practice to align them with risk appetite metrics. I have suggested a few in the following sections. The thresholds and actual metrics will need to be specific for each organization.

Sample RCSA Trigger Metrics

Loss Events and Incidents

- Operational risk losses over the past quarter and year aligned with risk appetite. Example: 1% of revenue for the most recent quarter, or 2% of revenue on a rolling 12-month basis.
- Material near-miss events that would meet the thresholds of high-risk operational risk losses or issues (according to the firm's Impact Tables), if they had occurred.
- Repeat near-miss events or incidents that emanate from the same root cause. Example: Failure to execute trades timely due to repeated communication breakdowns.
- Peer events that are relevant to a business, a function, or the organization. Consider the relevancy of the control breakdowns and what the event would look like if it occurred internally and the potential risk rating.
- Third-party breaches of SLAs that impact critical services or processes.
- Tier 1 system outages.
- Increase in cyber alerts above average for the firm.

Staffing

- Staff turnover rate in key risk, control, compliance, or executive functions that are above the firm's average. An industry standard is 15%.
- Number of open key risk, control, compliance, or executive roles that are above the firm's average.
- Greater than firm's average time to fill key risk, control, compliance, or executive roles. Consider greater than 90 days as an industry standard.

Audit & Regulatory Findings

- New regulatory MRA, MRIAs, consent orders, or enforcement actions.
- Repeat audit or regulatory findings that impact the same business, function, or enterprise.

Operating Environment Metrics

- Increase in volatility in the markets (monitor the VIX) that could lead to increased operational errors in trading and markets businesses.
- Increase in volume of transactions exceeding historical averages.
- Number of new products, services, or system implementations (2–3 on a business level, 5–10 on an enterprise level).
- Rapid business growth (% increase in AUM, revenue, or clients based on historical averages).
- Customer complaints (consider increase of 10–20%).

Remediation

What are we going to do about it? This is the question that should be asked when an RCSA uncovers material control deficiencies or results in residual risk above appetite. The answer is to open an issue and action plan.

As discussed in Chapter 4, issues are an important input into the RCSA process and especially control assessments. This is where it is a strong practice if you have a GRC system, to have interconnectivity between RCSA and Issue Management modules. Ideally, if a control gap is identified during the assessment process, there should be ease of use in opening an issue and action plan and linking it to the RCSA. This is why it is also important to have a single impact table for risk rating issues and RCSA inherent risk.

In most instances, the issue is assigned to the Accountable Executive who is responsible for the risk assessment unit. The action plans are assigned to whomever is best equipped to work on the remediation; they may not be in the same business unit as the accountable executive. I have witnessed this as a pain point, as there is a hesitancy to fix an issue that is not under someone's direct remit. This can be a particular challenge when a process approach is taken for the RCSA, and a control gap is identified for a process that crosses over several businesses and functions. I have witnessed extensive back and forth when no one wanted to step up and take ownership of an issue or action plan when more than one business or function is impacted. In several instances, ownership ended up with second-line operational risk, which was not the right answer. This led me to write into the issue management policy in one organization where I owned the process the escalation path for when there was a disagreement regarding issue ownership. In that instance, if there was a disagreement that could not be resolved within two weeks, the issue would be escalated to the chief risk officer, who would make the final determination.

It is a strong industry practice to assign closure requirements when the issue and action plans are designed, and sustainability criteria, to demonstrate that the fix has longevity. Sustainability criteria should include demonstration through testing or post-implementation reviews that the issue has appropriately resolved the root cause of the control gap for design and implementation. The testing or review should occur after the action plans have been completed and later integrated into the firm's control testing program if it exists, or if not, retested or reviewed 6–12 months later. Sustainability criteria should also include demonstration that the business or function responsible for the remediation has the appropriate capacity and skills to manage the new or remediated control moving forward. If new processes are involved, training should be documented.

The following is the process for identifying an issue and designing an action plan:

- The issue is identified through the RCSA process where a control gap has been identified, or the residual risk is above appetite.
- The accountable owner for the RCSA risk assessment unit is assigned ownership of the issue and in turn assigns ownership of linked action plans to the appropriate people who are best positioned to lead the remediation.
- Closure requirements and sustainability criteria are identified as part of the planning process for the issue and action plan design.
- The issue remains open until all linked action plans are remediated.
- A root-cause analysis is conducted to determine the driver of the control gap or the heightened risk level, and the action plan is designed to close the gap, bring down residual risk to an acceptable level, and address causation.
- The issue is risk-rated according to an impact table and aligned with the rating of the RCSA risk assessment unit that it is associated with.
- Issues are aligned with the RCSA taxonomy and ideally, with references to each other in the GRC system.
- Issues and action plans are designed and executed by the first line. The second line should validate the design of the action plans to ensure they address root cause. If the issue is owned by the second line, because it is linked to a process that the second line directly owns, they should identify an independent party to validate their action plan. An audit may also provide validation for very highly rated issues (or issues they assign).
- Progress associated with implementation of the action plan should be monitored through governance committees; it is a strong practice to monitor the progress of high rated issues through the operational risk and ERM committees and the board, while all issues are monitored by each business or function in their respective risk and control committees.

- Closure of the action plan should go through a formal validation process that ensures it has addressed root cause for control gaps and brought down residual risk where it was out of appetite.

Reporting on the Results

The final residual risk results of the RCSA should be thoroughly validated ahead of formal reporting. This should occur at the end of the cycle for organizations that are still following the cyclical approach and on an as-needed basis when there are significant changes through the trigger-based approach. The accountable executive and control executive for a business or function in organizations that have in-business control or risk teams should provide the first level of validation of the ratings. This may also include validation through business or function risk and control committees and sessions with the respective management team. The second line will be on point for review and challenge of the results. Any disagreement among the first and second lines should be resolved ahead of reporting. If escalation is necessary, the appropriate senior-level executive should make the final determination. For example, if the disagreement is over the final residual risk rating for cybersecurity (I have been there!), the chief information security officer (CISO) of the firm or impacted business should make the final determination.

Reporting on the results of RCSA should be focused, impactful, and designed for specific audiences. Ideally, a GRC system will provide real-time reporting functionality, which allows the first and second lines to review program progress and risk and control ratings at any point in time. Systems that do not have strong reporting functionality should include linkages to reporting packages, or at the very least offer downloading functionality that is not too onerous.

The level of detail should be aligned with the audience for the report. A business and function department will want to produce detailed reports by risk type for their respective areas and risk and control committees. The second-line operational risk function is responsible for creating aggregated reports across the enterprise that highlight the highest level of risks, themes, and trends for the enterprise risk committee and the board. The reporting at the business, function, and enterprise levels should focus on top risks, emerging trends, changes in risk ratings from previous cycles, control weaknesses, root-cause themes, and any opened issues and action plans.

When the reporting is for the risk committee and most importantly the board, the question "so what" should be addressed. I have done a lot of reporting in my past roles, including board reporting, and have always challenged myself and my team with the "so what." There is a tendency to become enamored with reporting capabilities in GRC reporting modules that can create reports, but they need to be scrutinized to tease out the themes and trends and a dump of ratings from the system does not meet this bar.

Visualization always helps. Heatmaps are maligned in the industry because they tend to just show traffic light colors that represent low, medium, and high. They can be useful because they can provide a quick view of the ratings across the enterprise, but *they* must include details on the drivers for the high ratings, the remediations, and any themes and trends. I have seen risk radars work well, with ratings plotted against a risk continuum which provides a quick view into what requires prioritization. There are a lot of creative solutions for visualization that should be explored.

The following are key considerations when designing reports:

- Know your audience, and tailor the messaging and amount of detail to the respective governance committees (more is less at the most senior levels).
- Provide the detail behind the ratings, including top risks, emerging risks, trends, themes, drivers, and root causes for the ratings.
- Include remediations and issues and actions plans and identify the accountable executive.
- Align the results with risk appetite.
- Provide a visualization that maps out the ratings across the enterprise (at the top level) or for a specific business or function (at a more granular level).
- Be consistent with the use of the risk taxonomy, risk assessment units, ratings, and control types.
- Include changes from prior periods, with identified driver for the change.

Interview with Industry Veteran on RCSA: Craig Spielman

Craig is truly an operational risk pioneer. He started an emerging technologies Audit group at JPMorgan followed by leading and creating JPM's information technology risk team in the days before it was top of the agenda for large banks. He developed and commercialized the Horizon RCSA application when he was at JPMorgan, which became the prototype for the governance, risk, and compliance (GRC) applications that are in use today. He held additional roles at Citigroup where he managed technology risk, Royal Bank of Scotland (RBS) where he was head of operational risk for the Americas, and global head of operational risk systems and analytics. Later in his career, he worked at First Data where he was global head of ERM strategy and today is the "Risk Intelligence Leader" with CNM LLP Consulting Group.

1. Question

How did the concept of RCSA first emerge in the operational risk landscape, and what motivated its development?

Answer

I first had exposure to the RCSA process in 1996 when I was at JPMorgan. The Sumitomo trading event (see "About the Sumitomo Trading Event") caused us to roll out RCSA throughout the entire firm. I was mandated to roll it out for all of technology within one year. This involved training a large global organization and facilitating risk sessions to identify risk and potential issues. We created 220 RCSAs in that first year. After it was over, the CIO and I were not satisfied with the results versus the effort and decided to change the approach and created the first risk and control templates that laid out the risks and expected controls. We asked people to opine on the strength of their controls and, if there were weaknesses, either to create an action plan or risk acceptance. We used prepopulated spreadsheets to make the process efficient. We then created the technology solution Horizon and rolled it out throughout JPM. This took the RCSA process to a new level as we had workflow, weightings, risk templates, and graphical reporting. Horizon was the first major GRC system and later was licensed by a major US regulator to manager their operational risks and global financial institutions. We added an Audit Module that compared the answers from the business and audit. Lastly, we implemented a loss module, which was essential to our "Triangle Approach."

2. **Question**

   What were the key challenges you faced in implementing RCSA frameworks in those early days?

   Answer

   The RCSA framework was evolving and maturing, and there were cultural challenges with implementing an RCSA for the first time in a global bank. At times, it felt like we were asking the "inmates to run the prison," as they were not necessarily used to identifying risks and controls in such a transparent manner. In time, the investment bank started using RCSA as a management tool to assess mergers and acquisitions, and this served as an impetus for the front line to understand its value. The smart people got it, and we gained some acceptance when we were able to get the process down from 85 hours to just 3 with the Horizon tool. Developing Horizon helped to make the process more efficient.

3. **Question**

   How did you engage business lines and leadership to take ownership of their risks and controls during the initial rollouts?

   Answer

   Simply, we talked their language. We linked the business' strategic goals to the RCSA methodology. I used to start my training sessions by telling people that I was there to help increase their compensation. That was unexpected and welcomed. I rarely said it was for the regulators or auditors. It helps to speak the business' language, and especially when you can tie it to compensation, people will listen. We used the RCSA results to assist the business with making strategic decisions, such as determining whether to shut down a business or where to make investments.

4. **Question**

   How does the first RCSA (via the Horizon application) framework compare with modern practices today?

   Answer

   What we did back then in the 2000s formed the foundation for what we have today. We created a standard methodology, linked risk and control templates to processes with various weightings, and most importantly attached dollar values to potential losses. We incorporated actual losses and estimated potential losses through scenarios, to arrive at a projected view of risk exposure. This is the approach that is widely adopted in today's world.

5. Question

Looking back, is there anything you would have done differently in designing or implementing early RCSA programs?

Answer

Yes! I would have gotten rid of the probability and likelihood discussion. I think as an industry we need to stop pushing these because at the end of the day we have no idea what is going to happen during any given time frame. We should be worried about what assets need to be protected at what level. Each institution should look at inherent risk and controls separately and then make an investment decision on what they want to control. And to go even further—residual risk is an archaic bad formula. It means nothing from a business sense. Instead, organizations should look at the value of their assets, what could go wrong, what they could lose, and the condition of their controls. At the end of the day, real risk management does not need a formula for residual risk. This was developed to give people "comfort," but it misrepresents actual risk. As risk managers, we should never put something in front of management that we have very little confidence in.

About the Sumitomo Trading Event

Yasuo Hamanaka was the chief copper trader with Japanese trading firm Sumitomo Corporation in 1996. He was found to have engaged at that time in unauthorized trading activities that had taken place over the course of a decade, with the apparent goal of manipulating the global copper market by cornering a significant portion of LME copper futures. The unauthorized trading, which started in 1985, came to a head in 1996. This event eventually cost the company USD $2.6 billion. JPMorgan had extended USD $400 million in credit to Hamanaka along with several other financial institutions. Hamanaka was convicted of fraud and sentenced to an eight-year prison term. Sumitomo paid USD $158 million in fines to US and UK regulators to settle charges related to market manipulation.

Bibliography

Archer Technologies. *Archer Evolv™ Platform Overview*. https://www.archerirm.com.

Craig Spielman. *Risk and Control Self Assessment—This time it's personal*. Cefpro Connect, January 27, 2025.

IBM. *IBM OpenPages with Watson*. Accessed June 8, 2025. https://www.ibm.com/products/openpages-with-watson.

MetricStream. *MetricStream Intelligence: AI in GRC*. https://www.metricstream.com.

Peter Truell. J.P. Morgan Cited for Loans to Sumitomo Trader. *The New York Times*, April 3, 1997.

Penny Cagan. *RCSA: The Changing Dynamics of Self-Policing Risk*. Cefpro Connect, January 27, 2025.

Reuters. Former Copper Trader Gets 8 Years in Prison. *The New York Times*, March 26, 1998.

Shira Ovide. Going Rogue: Rogue Traders Through History. *The Wall Street Journal*, September 15, 2011.

Chapter 7

Internal and External Loss Data

The collection, monitoring, analysis, and reporting of operational risk events are critical to the discipline. These tasks are the foundation upon which the discipline was founded to manage losses within risk appetite and to proactively address control deficiencies so that they do not occur again.

I participated in early discussions in industry forums ahead of the implementation of Basel II, and there was a great deal of debate on how to collect losses, what to collect, and how to index them. The last item led to the development of the *operational risk event taxonomy* (see Chapter 1). The focus was not just on collecting loss events internally but collecting them in a consistent way across the industry, and using the universal taxonomy, so that there could be learnings from trends and themes. When I look back on that time, I am struck with how the community came together to develop a common language of risk through the event taxonomy and shared common practices on managing operational risk.

We have come a long way since those early days when there was so much debate around what an operational risk taxonomy should look like. But there was never any debate on the importance of collecting loss events, and today it is more relevant than ever. There are many reasons today to collect operational risk loss data. If you are a regulated financial institution of any size, you are required to have an up-to-date, indexed, well-maintained operational risk loss database. The expectation is that you are collecting losses that have occurred within your institution, remediating them when control deficiencies are identified, aggregating and reporting on losses through governance committees, and tracking them to risk appetite.

Regulatory mandates are important, but they are not the only reason to collect loss data. Organizations should track their losses and near-miss events to understand where they are exposed to control deficiencies and, in the simplest terms, are leaking money.

The following are the benefits of tracking operational risk losses, incidents, and near-misses:

- Allows for tracking where events occur that are outside of risk tolerance (i.e., outside of expected losses that are often described as the cost of doing business).
- When an event occurs, a root-cause analysis conducted to understand the driver of the event allows for identification of control deficiencies where the loss occurred but also where else it can occur through a "look across" exercise.
- Allows for monitoring levels of risk appetite and risk tolerance, with defined measures for how much loss an institution is willing to take on an enterprise level and for any given business.
- Serves as critical inputs into scenario analysis and RCSA and assists with understanding risk exposure and assessing controls.
- Contributes to a culture of excellence, through root-cause analysis of process and control breakdowns and the opening of issues and action plans.
- Serves as important inputs into regulatory operational risk capital models, comprehensive capital analysis and review (CCAR), and stress testing.
- Banking regulators expect larger and midsize institutions to maintain a loss database and collect event data from across the industry on a regular basis for comparative purposes.

The Basel Committee on Banking Supervision (BIS) provided an overview of industry standards in developing an operational risk loss data program and database in its 2020 guidance titled "Revision to the Principles for the Sound Management of Operational Risk."The following is an excerpt from their guidance:

Banks often maintain a comprehensive operational risk event dataset that collects all material events experience by the bank and serves as basis for operational risk assessments. The event dataset typically includes internal loss data, near misses, and, when feasible, external operational loss event data (as external data is informative of risks that common across the industry). Event data is typically classified according to a taxonomy defined in the ORMF policies and consistently applied across the bank. Event data typically includes date of the event (occurrence date, discovery date, and accounting date) and, in the case of loss events, financial impact. When other root cause information for events is available, ideally it can also be included in the operational risk dataset. When feasible, banks are encouraged to also seek to gather external operational risk event data and use this data in their internal analysis, as external is often informative of risks that are common across the industry. source: https://www.bis.org/bcbs/publ/d508.pd

Types of Loss Data

There are four types of loss data that an organization would benefit from collecting (and larger and midsize banks are expected to collect):

Internal operational risk loss events: An internal operational risk loss event is an event that has occurred inside a firm. It is a realized event that has resulted in a direct financial loss. Most institutions define a specific threshold at which they will collect losses, as it is not an efficient practice to collect everything (although I know organizations that do this). A small or midsize institution may collect losses more than $10,000, while a large global bank may have a much higher threshold of $100,000. It is strong industry practice (and a regulatory requirement for banks) to track both the gross loss, which is the loss amount before any recoveries, and the net loss, which includes recoveries such as insurance payments for covered events. Direct losses include fines, settlements, write-downs, restitutions, legal liabilities, and the cost of damage to physical assets. Any accidental gains that are earned from an operational risk event (such as an error that results in a profit rather than a loss) are also expected to be included in the database.

Internal operational risk incidents: Incidents are realized events that do not result in a direct loss. They are material from a control deficiency perspective because they provide an opportunity to identify weaknesses, and they can result in indirect losses, such as reputational harm, regulatory censures, opportunity costs, and remediation expenses. Examples include a technology outage or a data leakage intentionally or unintentionally by an employee or third party where there are no direct losses. Indirect losses in these instances can include loss of access to systems and disruption to customers and data security remediations, such as firing the employee or third party, hiring a consultant to enhance data controls, or sending a notification to customers that their personal information has been compromised.

Internal operational risk near-misses: A near-miss event is an event that could have resulted in direct or indirect losses but was prevented, either because controls detected it before it was realized or by chance. These events should be tracked and assessed because although they may have been detected by a control it might have happened later than anticipated or they were detected by a secondary control (such as a secondary review), or the control failed, and the event was averted by luck. A good example from the banking industry is when funds are misdirected from one institution to another. The receiving institution realizes the mistake and returns to the sending institution the misdirected funds. The sending institution got lucky because the funds were returned, but it still would be a strong practice to understand why the error occurred and what controls did not operate effectively. (See the case study at the end of this chapter.)

External operational risk events: External events are events that have occurred to peer institutions. It is a strong practice to track peer events either through external database services, consortiums, or news searches to understand how your own organization might be vulnerable. External events should be assessed for relevancy to an organization's own control environment and essentially provide an early warning if internal deficiencies are identified because of the review. They provide an opportunity to close a control gap before an event occurs.

Roles and Responsibilities

As in other components of the operational risk framework, the second line and most typically the operational risk function is responsible for the policy, framework, oversight, and review and challenge of the operational risk program. The first line is responsible for identifying, researching, tracking, and reporting on losses. It should be noted that if an event occurs in the second line, they are responsible for identifying and tracking their own losses.

Table 7.1 is a high-level view of roles and responsibilities across the first and second lines of defense. Each organization will need to develop a detailed responsibility matrix, which includes the roles of first-line business owners, control or in-business risk managers, subject-matter experts, and second-line operational risk. It should be noted that the third line of defense (internal audit) is responsible for ensuring the program is fit for purpose, and the first and second lines are adequately performing their duties.

Table 7.1 Loss Data Roles and Responsibilities

First Line	Second Line
Monitors events for business unit or function	Owns policies, standards, methodology, training; oversees implementation of program
Identifies events as they occur and determines if loss event, incident or near-miss	Provides advisory support as needed; ensures events are properly identified
Investigates attributes of event; works with first line control or in-business risk (if relevant)	Provides advisory support; assists with determining if event meets criteria for loss event, incident, near-miss
Escalates high-risk events to senior management; works with first line control or in-business risk	Define escalation protocol; ensures proper escalations occur
Prepares details of event and works with second line on notifying regulators	Works with first line and regulatory affairs on notifying regulators if required (example: cyber and data leakage events)
Enters event into database if criteria are met	Reviews and challenges event details, including event type, risk rating and loss event
Conduct root-cause analysis	Reviews and challenges root-cause analysis
Creates issues and action plans and owns remediation through to issue closure	Reviews and challenges issues and action plans to ensure they address underlying root cause
Conducts look across to determine if control deficiencies exist elsewhere and opens additional issues and action plans if necessary	Assists with identifying where else control deficiencies may exist in the organization
Reports to business risk and control committees	Provides aggregated reporting to governance committees

Framework and Methodology

As with every operational risk program element, it all begins with a framework and a methodology. It is critical to precisely define the program elements, including the thresholds for collecting events, specific date types, and inclusion of gross and net loss amounts, as well as how to account for recoveries and reserves. It's important to spend the time defining and socializing the details. Consistency matters in how events are defined and how loss amounts are calculated and thresholds determined. The methodology should be clearly articulated in a policy or standard document that sets out the requirements for the program.

The following are items that an operational risk policy or standard must include. The policy will be higher level and state the principles for collecting, monitoring, and reporting data, while the standard will include details on how to calculate recoveries and track reserves. Many firms include a few paragraphs in the operational risk policy on the importance of collecting loss events, including the thresholds and responsibilities across the lines of defense, and write a specific standard that provides the details on implementing the program (see Chapter 8).

Items to Include in an Operational Risk Loss Event Policy or Standard

- **Purpose statement and scope:** The general purpose of the document, such as establishing requirements for the operational risk event program, and scope, which is usually the entire organization, including all entities, functions, and business units.
- **Definitions:** Definitions of key terms, such as inherent risk, residual risk, control, root-cause analysis, discovery date, recovery, net and gross loss amount, loss event, incident, near-miss event, loss amount thresholds.
- **Roles and responsibilities:** Define roles and responsibilities for first line, second line, third line, and governance committees.
- **Operational risk event program lifecycle program overview:** Identification, assessment, mitigation, monitoring, and reporting.
- **Threshold for mandatory collection of events:** All losses over a certain defined threshold (e.g., \$10,000) are required to be captured and entered in the loss database.
- **Mandatory data field:** Mandatory data fields include the event start date, event end date, discovery date, financial impact, business line, event type, taxonomy category, financial impact, flags for near-miss, incident, loss event, and boundary events.
- **Calculation of gross and net amounts:** Requirement for recording gross amount (initial loss amount) and net loss amount (include recoveries, such as insurance payments or settlements).
- **Reserves:** Guidance for allocating reserves primarily associated with legal cases, including requirements to update as estimates change.
- **Inclusion of near-misses and incidents:** Clear definitions should be included on near-misses and incidents, and requirements for inclusion should address root-cause and control issues.

- **Direct and indirect loss amounts:** Include definitions and clear guidance on direct financial losses (fines, settlements, write-downs, restitutions, legal liabilities, and the cost of damage to physical assets) and indirect losses (loss of access to systems, loss of market share, opportunity costs, cost of enhancing control environment).
- **Gain:** Provide guidance for inclusion of accidental gains.
- **Grouped events:** Provide guidance for linking related events to a single root cause, such as complicated litigation with multiple settlements, which may be tracked separately, but should be aggregated into a single loss.
- **Definitions and inclusion of date:** All relevant dates should be required, including start date, end date, discovery date, and reporting date.
- **Boundary events:** Credit and market risk boundary events occur when there are operational risk drivers that lead to a credit or market loss. Basel provides guidance on excluding credit boundary losses from the capital calculations while market events should be included; they should be collected in the database and tagged as boundary events.
- **Opening of issues and action plans:** Events should be evaluated for control deficiencies and issues and action plans opened to remediate the underlying root cause.
- **System of record:** Every organization, no matter the size, should have a system of record for collecting operational risk events; in midsize and large institutions, it will be a GRC system while smaller institutions may use an application already in their institution, like JIRA or develop an in-house repository.

Internal Loss Data

The structured collection of operational risk event data is an important part of the overall framework and requires a policy, standard, methodology, and defined lifecycle for identifying, assessing, mitigating, monitoring, and reporting events.

Figure 7.1 is a generic workflow that demonstrates at a high level the process for identifying, remediating, and reporting on loss events. Each organization will need to map their own process according to their policies, procedures, and organizational structure.

Stage 1: Identify

A potential operational risk event can be identified by anyone in the organization. I have worked in organizations where we ran campaigns encouraging people to identify an event as soon as it occurs. I have also witnessed a tendency for an event to languish outside the system of record while it is being investigated and details are being researched. It is strong industry practice to require an event to be entered into the

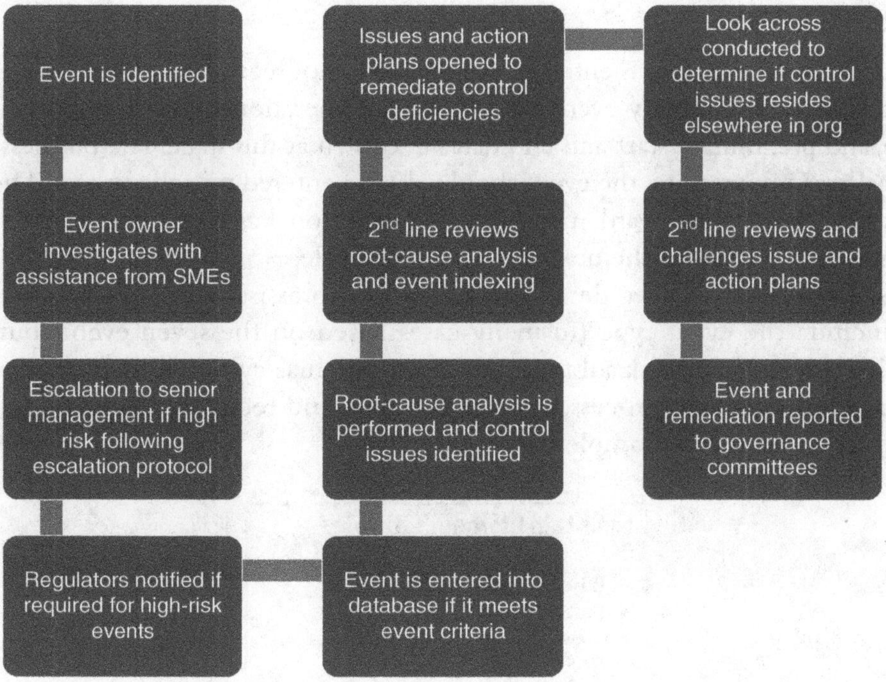

Figure 7.1 Operational risk event process flow

system of record as soon as it has been identified and escalated as necessary depending on the severity; the event details can be determined later, but within a required timeframe, such as 30 days.

There should be strong written guidance to assist with determining if an event meets the criteria of an operational risk event. If the person who has detected the event is unsure, they should have access to a list of subject-matter experts, usually in second-line operational risk, but also a first-line risk person, such as a technology specialist for a technology event, who can assist with determining the nature of the event. The second-line operational risk team is the best source to determine if it qualifies as an operational risk event and requires tracking in the system of record.

Here are some questions that the person who detected the event will want to consider in determining if the event meets the criteria of an operational risk event:

- Does the event meet the organization's operational risk definition?
- If so, does the event meet the loss amount threshold?
- If it does not meet the loss event threshold, does it qualify as a near-miss or incident?
- Does the event require immediate escalation, including large dollar events and cyber or data compromise events that require immediate reporting to regulators?
- Is the event a boundary event that has operational risk drivers for credit or market losses?

Indexing the Event

The initial information that is entered into the system of record should include an event title, description, preliminary event type (from the operational risk taxonomy), discovery date, and preliminary start and end dates if known at this stage. The business line or functional area impacted by the event should also be entered into the system. The event, unless it is very straightforward, may require an additional assessment and investigation, which will be the focus of the next step in the lifecycle.

Most organizations have detailed taxonomies to assist with indexing the event, which include the event type (in many cases based on the seven events but might also include operational risk subtype categories, such as cyber, third-party, data risk), root cause, business unit, process, control, product, and recovery type. The following figure (7.2) demonstrates sample data items.

Maintain Element Libraries

- Business Application Types
- Business Lines
- Causal Classes
- Causal Types
- Client Types
- Control Classes
- Control Types
- Cyber Incident Types
- Direct Impact Types
- Distribution Channels
- Exposure Drivers
- External Event Types
- Geographic Regions
- Indirect Impact Types
- Industry Types
- Process Natures
- Process Types
- Product Types
- Recovery Types
- Response Types
- Risk Categories
- Risk Themes
- Risk Types

Figure 7.2 Sample taxonomy. *Source*: Courtesy of www.riskbusiness.com

Figure 7.3 is an example of the details for several risk types.

As a reminder, we discussed the seven Basel event types in Chapter 1 of this book:

- Internal fraud
- External fraud
- Employment practices and workplace safety
- Clients, products and business practices
- Damage to physical assets
- Business disruption and system failure
- Execution, delivery, and process failure

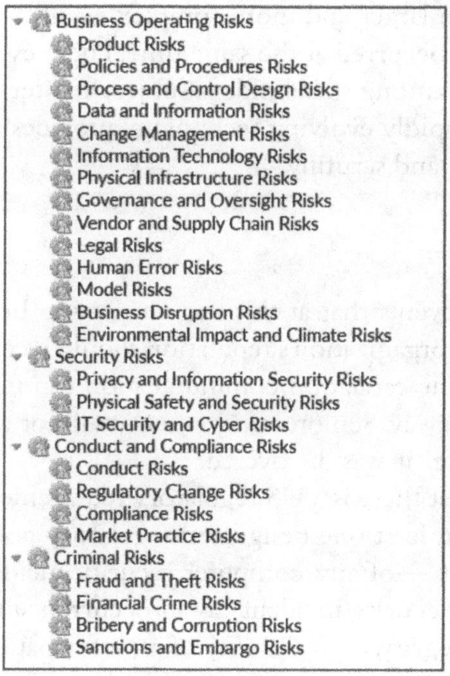

Figure 7.3 Risk themes table. *Source*: Courtesy of www.riskbusiness.com

Many institutions have developed alternative approaches to indexing operational risk events. Figure 7.4 is an alternative approach from Risk Business.

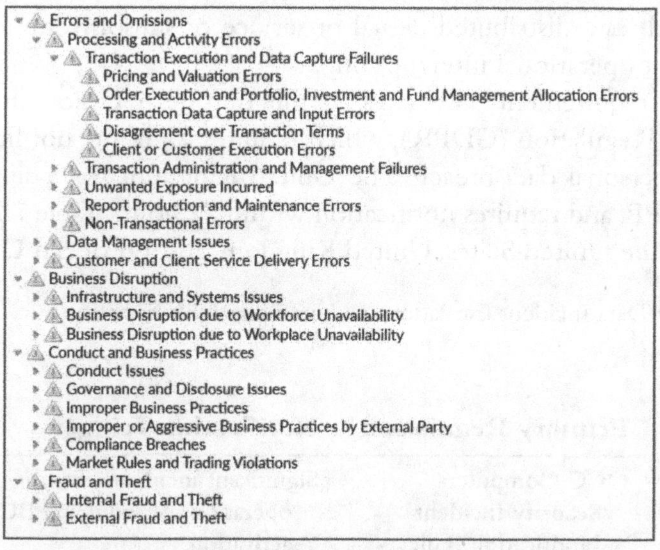

Figure 7.4 Alternative approach. *Source*: Courtesy of www.riskbusiness.com

Some organizations are starting to train their internal versions of ChatGPT to index batches of loss events. This is a promising development that allows for indexing low-level events that happen with high frequency. I have found indexing at times to be more of an art than a science with larger and more complex events where there may be a confluence of risks that have occurred at the same time. These events require a great deal of judgment and discussion among stakeholders, subject-matter experts, and the impacted business. But using this rapidly evolving technology provides a head start, and as always, the results require review and scrutiny.

Notification

It should be noted that events that at this stage appear to be material in terms of loss amount or impact on the organization's reputation should be escalated as soon as possible to senior management. The escalation communication can indicate that the assessment and investigation is underway. Senior management will not appreciate being informed of a large event weeks after it was discovered.

It should be noted that there is a US regulatory requirement for banks and their service providers to notify at least one designated regulatory point of contact—the OCC, Federal Reserve, or FDIC—of any computer security incident within 36 hours. The rule defines a computer-security incident "as an occurrence that results in actual harm to the confidentiality, integrity, or availability of an information system or the information that the system processes, stores, or transmits." A notification incident is described in the interagency guidance as "a significant computer-security incident that disrupts or degrades, or is reasonably likely to disrupt or degrade, the viability of the banking organization's operations, result in customers being unable to access their deposit and other accounts, or impact the stability of the financial sector." The rule further stipulates that a notification incident "may include a major computer-system failure; cyber-related interruption, such as a distributed denial of service or ransomware attack; or another type of significant operational interruption."

Notification requirements also exist in the European Union under the General Data Protection Regulation (GDPR), which requires 72 hours notification of becoming aware of a personal data breach. The United Kingdom has a similar requirement that mirrors GDPR and requires notification within 72 hours. Table 7.2 summarizes the requirements in the United States, United Kingdom, and European Union.

Table 7.2 Cyber/Data Incident Escalation Requirements by Jurisdiction

Jurisdiction	Primary Regulation	Notification Trigger	Regulator Notification Deadline
United States (OCC/Federal Reserve/FDIC)	OCC Computer-Security Incident Notification Rule	Significant incident affecting operations or requiring BCP activation	36 hours
European Union (EU)	GDPR	Personal data breach or major incident	72 hours
United Kingdom (UK)	UK GDPR & Network and Information Systems Regulations	Personal data breach (or major incident	72 hours

It should be noted that although cyber and personal data breaches require formal regulatory notification, regulators should be notified of any significant event following a firm's regulatory affairs protocols. It does not bode well for a regulatory relationship if they find out about significant events or incidents from external sources. (See the interview with Tom Balogh in Chapter 9) Regulators can be notified of less critical events through regular touchpoints.

Stage 2: Assess

Organizations typically require events to be entered into the system of record as soon as they are identified, with a requirement to complete the due diligence on the event within 30 days. This process includes further refinement of the original information, including description and event type from the operational risk taxonomy. The dates should be verified and confirmed, including start and end dates, in addition to discovery date. The start and end dates of the event if known provide a view into the firm's control environment. The longer the duration of an event that was able to occur without being detected, the greater the control deficiency.

The following is an anonymized and generalized event that I helped to mediate:

- **Event title:** Legacy Credit Card Interest Payment Error
- **Event description:** Customers of a specific credit card type that was no longer offered by the bank, were overcharged interest. The error was believed to have first occurred 10 years previously and was specific to a certain pricing model. The card has not been offered to its customers for two years prior to the discovery of the issue and has been discontinued. The error was discovered when all the pricing models were moved to a new platform and a retrospective reconciliation was undertaken. There was no recovery in this instance.
- **Gross loss amount:** XXX
- **Net loss amount:** XXX
- **Recovery:** 0
- **Event type:** Execution, Delivery & Process Management
- **Business line:** Credit Cards
- **Geographic location:** United States
- **State date:** January 2012
- **End date:** March 2022
- **Discovery date:** April 2024
- **Root cause:** Legacy pricing model that did not go through model validation process. Failure to assess the pricing model for accuracy over the years that the credit card was offered to clients. The model was not included in the model inventory, was implemented by the business, and did not follow model and credit risk protocols.
- **Remediation:** Working with legal, finance, and communications, to determine approach for identifying impacted customers and reimbursing overpayment interest amounts. Working with Regulatory Affairs to notify regulators of the issue. Reviewed

model risk protocols to ensure all cards, including legacy ones, have validated models. Move any models that live in the business to a central function.

Determining Loss Impact

The assess stage of the lifecycle should involve a thorough assessment of the actual cost of the event. As previously discussed, all events above a predetermined threshold should be entered into the system of record. But it is not always so straightforward in determining the actual cost of the event or how it is allocated.

It is important to collect both gross loss amount (loss before any recoveries) and net loss amount (loss after recoveries are accounted for). BIS provided guidance on determining loss amount in its 2024 guidance "Calculation of RWA for operational risk." The following is an excerpt from the guidance on determining what qualifies as gross loss amount:

- ***Direct charges***, *including impairments and settlements, to the bank's P&L accounts and write-downs due to the operational risk event;*
- ***Costs incurred as a consequence of the event*** *including external expenses with a direct link to the operational risk event (e.g., legal expenses directly related to the event and fees paid to advisors, attorneys or suppliers) and costs of repair or replacement, incurred to restore the position that was prevailing before the operational risk event;*
- ***Provisions or reserves*** *accounted for in the P&L against the potential operational loss impact;*
- ***Losses stemming from operational risk events with a definitive financial impact***, *which are temporarily booked in transitory and/or suspense accounts and are not yet reflected in the P&L ("pending losses"). Material pending losses should be included in the loss data set within a time period commensurate with the size and age of the pending item;*
- ***Negative economic impacts*** *booked in a financial accounting period, due to operational risk events impacting the cash flows or financial statements of previous financial accounting periods ("timing losses"). Material "timing losses" should be included in the loss data set when they are due to operational risk events that span more than one financial accounting period and give rise to legal risk.*

The Basel guidance also specifies what is not included in direct losses:

- *Costs of general maintenance contracts on property, plant or equipment;*
- *Internal or external expenditures to enhance the business after the operational risk losses: upgrades, improvements, risk assessment initiatives and enhancements;*
- *Insurance premiums*
https://www.bis.org/basel_framework/chapter/OPE/25.htm

Allocating Loss Amount

Allocating a loss amount to the general ledger is straightforward when a specific business unit can be identified, as demonstrated by the previous credit card example. Tracking the business unit where the loss occurred is important for modeling purposes, attribution in the general ledger, and most importantly, for tracking where there are control vulnerabilities. If there are two or more business units involved, the loss should be divided among them, with guidance from the finance department. If the loss occurs in a function that does not own a profit and loss statement, the loss should be allocated to the frontline business that the function supports. If the function supports the enterprise, as is the case with many technology departments, the loss should be evenly distributed among the frontline businesses.

Root Cause

The process to determine root cause is critical to fixing issues so that the underlying driver of an event is understood. This will require some digging to get to the true root cause, rather than what might be evident on the surface. One process widely used in the industry involves the "Five Whys." This includes asking the question repeatedly as to what caused an event, until the true root cause is identified.

Once the root cause is identified, the next step is to open an issue and action plan to remediate a control deficiency. For small events, the control deficiency may be risk accepted through a formal process that is incorporated into many institutions' issue management policies and procedures.

The following is an example of a "Five Whys" exercise based on an anonymized event I helped to remediate:

Event: A FX trade resulted in a significant monetary loss and regulatory scrutiny when the wrong currency was entered into the trading system.

- Question 1: Why did this event happen?
  - Answer: The system defaults to the US currency, and you need to override the default manually, which is not easy to do.
- Question 2: Why did this error happen now, when the system override has always been necessary for FX trades?
  - Answer: We were under a lot of pressure to execute trades.
- Question 3: Why were you under a lot of pressure to execute trades at this point in time?
  - Answer: It was the end of the quarter, and we were understaffed.
- Question 4: Why were you understaffed?
  - Answer: Several experienced team members recently left, and we were told we still needed to meet the terms of our client SLAs with smaller and less experienced teams.
- Question 5: What type of pressure were you under to meet the SLA?
  - Answer: We have been under constant pressure from management to meet client SLAs and the pressure was so great that several team members found jobs elsewhere. Management only cared about meeting the client SLAs, and we were told we could not go home until all trades were executed.

In this example, the initial response to this event was that there was a system user interface issue and there was initial discussion on how to make changing the default currency easier with additional pop-ups and warnings to check the currency. That led to a modification of the trading system interface, but it did not identify the deep-rooted issues, which struck at the heart of this business unit's culture to meet SLA deadlines at all costs and without the required capacity and skills. This led to a review of the function's capacity, skill-set and culture by human resources and additional management training for its director.

Stage 3: Mitigate

Once the root cause has been identified, an issue and action plan should be opened to address the potential control deficiency. A well-designed GRC system will have linkages between the operational event and issue management modules. In the previous example, the remediation included modifying the user interface of the trading system to make it easier to change currencies and to include alerts to check for accuracy, but also an assessment of the skills and capacity of the current team. The matter was escalated to HR who worked with management on addressing cultural issues.

It is a strong practice to conduct a "look across" and determine if there are similar issues elsewhere in the organization. It is not an adequate remediation if a control deficiency is addressed in one business unit, while the same issue resides in others. This will entail working across businesses and functions to determine if there are similar vulnerabilities elsewhere and opening additional issues and action plans if necessary.

Stage 4: Monitor

Monitoring includes tracking the status of remediations to close any control gaps and to escalate when there are delays. The newly designed or enhanced control should be tested when it is implemented and 6–12 months later to ensure it is designed to mitigate the risk and operating as designed.

Recoveries

An event should also be monitored for any incoming recoveries. Recoveries can take the form of insurance payouts, legal settlements, or payments from third parties. The recovery must be directly attributed to the loss amount and be accounted for in the period that it is realized. The loss database should include both the gross loss amount, the recovery amount, and the net loss amount and be updated as new recoveries come in.

Estimating Legal Reserves

Estimated legal reserves require monitoring as they can change over time. A complicated legal event will require working with legal, finance, and operational risk teams in continuous evaluation of the legal reserves. I have typically worked with legal in my past roles to revise estimated reserves on long-running litigations (in some cases going back to the financial crisis of 2008) and updating the loss model and database. This involves estimating the probability that the case will settle for some amount which is usually less than the litigants are requesting.

Let's look at an example of how estimating reserves can work in a financial institution.

Say a financial institution is sued for allegedly misrepresenting certain bonds as low risk to its retail clients between 2020 and 2022. The courts allow the litigation to move forward as a class action suit. The class is requesting a settlement of $100 million in damages.

Legal conducts an assessment and identifies the following three scenarios:

- **Best Case:** 20% chance of the best case occurring with the case dismissed resulting in a $0 payout
- **Moderate Case:** 60% chance that a moderate settlement out of court would occur resulting in a $25 million settlement.
- **Worst Case:** 20% chance that a court judgment would occur resulting in a $75 million payout

Legal is in the best position to determine which of the three scenarios are most appropriate for the organization. One strategy is to take the average of the three scenarios, which would result in a reserve of $33 million. Another strategy is to assume the moderate approach and take a reserve of $25 million. The reserve amount should be reassessed on a regular basis (often quarterly) and adjusted as new information comes available from discovery, court rulings, discussions with the class action lawyers and general sentiment in the courts. The legal assumptions should be carefully documented and reviewed and challenged by senior management and risk management.

Stage 5: Report

The details of a high-risk loss event (according to a firm's impact table—see an example in Chapter 5) should be included in management, risk committee, and board reports. All losses should be included in the lower-level committee reports, including operational risk committee and business and risk committees. The low-risk events may be aggregated and reported through trends and themes, which should be included in all committee reports. The basic details, including loss amount, recoveries, business unit impact, taxonomy terms, should be included along with the root cause and any issues and action plans that were opened resulting from the analysis. If a look across is performed that has detected similar control deficiencies or vulnerabilities elsewhere in the firm, this should also be included in the reporting.

In addition, regulators routinely ask for loss data, which I provided on a quarterly basis. As discussed previously, they should be notified of any material events. A report should include tending and comparison to a prior period.

External Data

FIRST Database of Case Studies

I began my operational risk journey with the development of an external loss database. The year was 2000, and Basel II was coming. The Basel II requirements for assessing operational risk included four elements: internal loss data, external loss data, scenario analysis, and business environment and internal control factors. These elements were mandatory for modeling operational risk capital under the Advanced Measurement Approach but were also essential for managing operational risk. I participated in many debates at the time that divided the community between qualitative and quantitative approaches.

Very few banks had data of any kind ahead of Basel II. Bankers Trust, which was acquired by Deutsche Bank in June 1999, had loss data. Douglas Hoffman, who became a mentor to me and gave me the "operational risk bug," had headed the Operational Risk and Insurance Management Department at Bankers Trust from 1989 through 1999. Bankers Trust had one of the industry's first internal and external loss databases of operational risk events and losses.

I was hired by a Deutsche Bank venture in 2000 called Operationalrisk.com, which was led by Doug. He gave me a spreadsheet with the external losses that he had collected during his tenure at Bankers Trust, and I worked with a technology company owned by Dr. Hans-Peter Guellich, in the development of an external operational risk loss database. Hans-Peter was an early innovator in the risk management application of fuzzy logic.

I spent some time reviewing the spreadsheet that Doug had given me and knew there had to be more than collecting loss data points. As a trained writer with a master's degree in creative writing, I got to work and started drafting case studies. The case studies included the basic details of each event but also focused on root cause and contributing factors. They were structured to assist firms with conducting health checks of their own control environment by analyzing the control breakdowns of peer events. The case studies were also designed to provide content for scenario programs and to be inputs into RCSA.

I named the database FIRST, which stood for Financial Institutions Risk Scenario Trends. It was also the first of its kind! It moved past just collecting information concerning financial institutions, and the team and I wrote up large corporate events, with the understanding that they also provided content for understanding control, conduct, and compliance issues. Within a few years, I had most major banks signed on as customers, because the appetite for operational risk data in those early days was huge.

The database was sold to Fitch Ratings, which folded it into its Algorithmics subsidiary. Fitch later sold Algorithmics to IBM, which integrated the database into their Open Pages platform, where it lives today. Although Algorithmics was later spun off by IBM, the First Database remains on the Open Pages Platform. The database is called IBM FIRST Risk Case Studies and includes 17,000 case studies. More information about the subscription service can be found here: https://www.ibm.com/products/first-risk-case-studies.

Consortium Data

The IBM FIRST database is a subscription service, where organizations pay a fee to access its data, case studies and taxonomies. The other model for acquiring loss data is consortiums, which function on a give-to-get approach. You need to give data to receive operational risk loss reports. The data is anonymized and consists of basic information that allows for comparative purposes. Unlike a subscription database, the information is vetted internally by each contributing institution.

Table 7.3 compares the FIRST database with three well-known consortiums.

The following are the three operational risk data consortiums that are well-known (although there are other specialized ones), with descriptions from their websites:

- ORX (Operational Risk data eXchange Association)
  - *ORX is the largest operational risk management association in the financial services sector. Established in 2002 by financial firms looking to share loss data, ORX is committed to improving the management and measurement of operational risk. Owned and driven by our member institutions, we bring together hundreds of operational risk professionals to share their knowledge, expertise and experience in the financial services industry. We are a not-for-profit industry association incorporated in Geneva, Switzerland.* www.orx.org
- ORIC International (Operational Risk Insurance Consortium)
  - *Founded in 2005, we are run by our members, for our members, ensuring our services are finely tuned to the specific needs of the financial industry. We empower financial services firms*

Table 7.3 FIRST vs. Others

Feature	Commercial Databases (IBM Algo, SAS OpRisk Global)	Consortium Databases (ORX, ORIC, GOLD)
Data Source	Public disclosures (news, legal, regulatory filings)	Member-contributed internal operational loss data
Event Detail	Includes case studies; deep indexing of events	Anonymized data does not include detailed event descriptions by design; case studies available for large events; include deep indexing of events
Access	Subscription-based	Membership-based; requires data contribution
Update Frequency	Real-time or monthly	Quarterly or semi-annual
Industry Breadth	Cross-industry (banks, corporates, insurers)	Primarily financial services
Pros	Broad coverage, timely updates, no data contribution needed; detailed case studies; consistent indexing approach	Detailed, validated data; strong for modeling and benchmarking
Cons	Public-only, subscription cost	Requires ongoing contribution; slower data availability

Source: Courtesy of Risk Business, www.riskbusiness.com

to proactively address operational risk, enhance resiliency, and secure a competitive edge. Our member-driven organisation offers unparalleled access to comprehensive data, cutting-edge analytics, and peer benchmarks. www.oricinternational.com

- GOLD (Global Operational Loss Database)
  - *Established by the British Bankers Association (BBA) in 2000, GOLD represents the first organised non-financial or operational risk data sharing initiative amongst banks. Facilitated by RiskBusiness since 2010, management of GOLD transferred to UK Finance when the BBA merged with several other trade associations in 2017, before being completely outsourced to RiskBusiness at the beginning of 2022.* https://riskbusiness.com/gold/

Monitoring Loss Events in the Press

Collecting external events is one of the most proactive forward-looking activities that an operational risk team can undertake. You do not need a subscription to the FIRST database or a consortium membership to track external operational risk events. I have routinely conducted lessons learned on large events that appear in the business press and have set up alerts from the major regulatory agencies that disclose public consent orders and censures. I have also set up automated searches in ChatGPT that are partially helpful. The searches suffer from hallucinations as ChatGPT has a habit of citing sources that do not exist, but it's a start. As in all uses of ChatGPT, a high level of review and scrutiny is required. Risk Business provides helpful news flashes on its website that I track on a regular basis: https://riskbusiness.com/newsflashes/.

Citibank Revlon Bond Case Study

It is not atypical for banks to misdirect funds to each other. These are classic near-miss events, because the funds are customarily returned to the sending institution that made the error. The Citibank Revlon incident sent a chill through the financial community because it was a reminder of what can happen when the funds are not returned. These errors occur frequently in large institutions, and there was always the expectation that misdirected funds would be returned, until one day they were not.

Citibank was the loan agent for a Revlon loan that included a consortium of 10 lenders. In this capacity, Citi was responsible for administering interest payments to the lenders. In August 2020, Revlon mistakenly paid out the principle on the loan, rather than the interest payment. They should have wired $7.8 million in interest payments but instead wired the full principal amount of $894 million. This error occurred even though Citi had a "six-eyes" review process in place that required reviews ahead of payment by three individuals. The cause was attributed to a human error in the payment release process. When Citi discovered the error, it attempted to recall the payments, but the funds were not forthcoming when the lenders indicated that they would not accommodate the recall request.

The dispute over the funds went to the courts and was initially ruled in the lender's favor in February 2021. An appeals court overturned that decision in September

2022. Citi reached a final settlement in December 2022 that allowed it to recoup approximately $500 million of the funds in dispute. From an operational risk database perspective, this would represent a partial recovery that should be factored into the net loss amount.

Citi experienced another fat finger event in April 2024. The event was widely reported by the business press in February 2025. A Citi banker had intended to credit a client account $280 but instead entered $81 trillion. The near-miss was attributed to an input error resulting from a "cumbersome user interface" that came prepopulated with 15 zeros, which required deletion by the person inputting the transaction. The error was missed by two employees but caught by a third within 90 minutes of posting. It was reversed, and there was no monetary loss to the bank.

Bibliography

Basel Committee on Banking Supervision. *OPE. Calculation of RWA for* Operational Risk. OPE *25. Standardized Approach.* July 5, 2024. https://www.bis.org/basel_framework/chapter/OPE/25.htm.

Basel Committee on Banking Supervision. *Revisions to the Principles for the Sound Management of Operational Risk.* March 31, 2021. https://www.bis.org/bcbs/publ/d515.htm.

Basel Committee on Banking Supervision. *Sound Practices for the Management and Supervision of Operational Risk.* Basel: Bank for International Settlements, February 2003. https://www.bis.org/publ/bcbs96.htm.

Basel Committee on Banking Supervision. *Operational Risk – Supervisory Guidelines for the Advanced Measurement Approaches.* Basel: Bank for International Settlements, June 2011. https://www.bis.org/publ/bcbs196.htm.

IBM FIRST Risk Case Studies. https://www.ibm.com/products/first-risk-case-studies.

Jon Hill. *2nd Circ. Give Citi Win in $500M Revlon Wire Transfer Fight.* Law 360, September 8, 2022.

Office of the Comptroller of the Currency. OCC Bulletin 2021–55: *Computer-Security Incident Notification Requirements Final Rule.* November 2023. https://www.occ.gov/news-issuances/bulletins/2021/bulletin-2021-55.html.

Office of the Comptroller of the Currency (OCC). OCC Assesses $400 Million Civil Money Penalty Against Citibank. *OCC Press Release,* October 7, 2020.

ORX (*Operational Riskdata eXchange* Association). The ORX Reference Taxonomy for operational and non-financial risk, by ORX and Oliver Wyman, 2020, https://orx.org/resource/event-type-operational-risk-reference-taxonomy.

ORX Annual Banking Loss Report: an analysis of the operational risk loss data in the ORX global banking database from 2019–2024. June 2025. https://orx.org/resource/annual-banking-operational-risk-loss-data-report.

Philippa Girling. *Operational Risk Management: A Complete Guide for Banking and Fintech,* Chapter 7. Hoboken, NJ: Wiley, 2022.

Regulation (EU) 2016/679 (General Data Protection Regulation). *Notification of a Personal Data Breach to the Supervisory Authority.* https://gdpr-info.eu/art-33-gdpr/.

Reuters. *Citi, Revlon Lenders Reach Deal Over $500 mln Accidental Payment.* Reuters, December 16.

Stacy Cowley. Citi loses its bid to reclaim cash from a $900 million mistake. *New York Times,* February 16, 2021.

Stephen Gandel and Joshua Franklin. Citi erroneously credited client account with $81tn Near Miss. *Financial Times,* February 28, 2025.

Tarpley Hitt. Citibank Accidentally Paid out $900 Million. Then It Had to Get It Back. *The New Yorker*, February 24, 2021. https://www.newyorker.com/news/our-columnists/citibank-accidentally-paid-out-900-million-then-it-had-to-get-it-back.

United Kingdom. *UK General Data Protection Regulation*, as amended by the Data Protection, Privacy and Electronic Communications (Amendments etc) (EU Exit) Regulations 2019, SI 2019/419. London: The National Archives, 2019.

Chapter 8

Setting Up the Guardrails: Operational Risk Governance

I consider governance the heartbeat of any risk management program. Governance is also a broad concept that can mean everything or nothing. I like to think of it in its essence as "doing the right thing."

In a risk management context, doing the right thing means behaving with ethical standards and being willing to speak up when you see something wrong. It is what Mike Silva in his interview for this book (see Chapter 2) referred to when he said that risk management will likely at some point in your career call for courage.

Here is how I think about doing the right thing in a risk management context:

- Acting with integrity in everything one does
- Treating customers fairly
- Respecting the interests of shareholders
- Being transparent with regulators
- Being compliant with laws, rules, and regulations
- Following the firm's policies and procedures
- Raising one's hand when they see something wrong
- Tackling issues as they arise
- Challenging the status quo when it is no longer an effective risk management strategy
- Holding oneself accountable for managing risk
- Supporting team members
- Making prudent risk decisions and managing risk within appetite

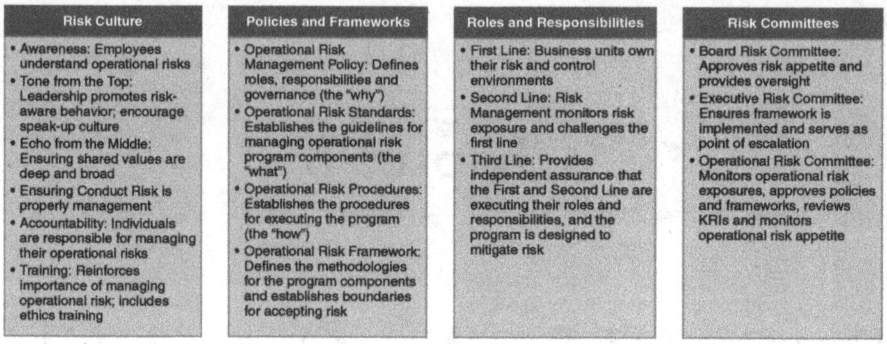

Figure 8.1 Four key governance themes

I have distilled this big meaty topic of risk governance into the four key themes shown in Figure 8.1.

Risk Culture

I had to go back to a 2014 paper by the Financial Stability Board to find a decent definition of risk culture, which quoted a 2009 International Institute of Finance report titled "Reform in the Financial Services Industry: Strengthening Practices for a More Stable System."

The IIF defines risk culture as "the norms of behaviour for individuals and groups within an organisation that determine the collective ability to identify and understand, openly discuss and act on the organisations current and future risk."

Note the emphasis on behavior, collective ability, open discussion, and acting on current and future risk. Risk culture depends on the collective consciousness of a firm to do the right thing, and it starts with tone from the top and resonates through echo from the middle. No one individual with the best of intentions and all the bravery in the world can be successful in an organization that has bad values and is anathema to doing the right thing. Bad culture that reflects poor values can ripple through an organization to the extent that "doing the wrong thing" is expected and normalized behavior.

The Financial Conduct Authority (FCA) in its 2018 paper titled "Transforming Culture in Financial Services" defines culture as "a key root cause of the major conduct failings that have occurred within the industry in recent history, causing harm to both consumers and markets." The regulator targets four main drivers for a firm's culture: purpose, leadership, approach to rewarding and managing people, and governance.

The FCA adds to the IIF's definition of culture by focusing on purpose, leadership, incentives, people management, and governance. Leadership and tone from the top are universally accepted as important drivers for a strong culture. But there can be a disconnect between what management says and the incentives that drive behavior throughout the organization. All the emails that come from senior management with the theme of "doing the right thing" fall on flat ears when they are not carried through with how employees are incentivized and assessed.

The Wells Fargo fake account event that came to light in 2016 is an example of a high-pressure sales culture that had misaligned incentives. Bankers were pressured to sell up to eight distinct consumer products to their clients. When you consider how many consumer products a client needs—perhaps a deposit and savings account, mortgage, and credit card—it is difficult to envision how this could have made sense in the context of treating customers fairly and doing the right thing. Not only were employees incentivized to meet this eight-product target through a compensation scheme, but they were also penalized or terminated if they fell behind the goal. (See the ORX Wells Fargo case study at the end of this chapter.)

The inclusion of "purpose" in the FCA's definition identifies an important driver of culture. A sense of purpose that addresses the question "What are we doing here?" fosters an environment where doing the right thing is embedded in a firm's DNA. I previously worked for a "purpose-led" organization that made a significant investment in sending its senior employees to "purpose training." This was a valuable three days out of the office where not only did the group in attendance walk-through the organization's purpose but we drafted our own purpose statements that allowed everyone to understand their unique contribution. Ultimately, it is about being able to articulate the "why"—why does this organization exist and why do I show up every day?

The European Central Bank in its "Guidelines on Internal Governance" highlights the following factors that contribute to a strong risk culture, which are aligned with the FCA:

Tone from the top: *the management body should be responsible for setting and communicating the institution's core values and expectations. The behaviour of its members should reflect the values. Institutions' management, including key function holders, should contribute to the internal communication of core values and expectations to staff. Staff should act in accordance with all applicable laws and regulations and promptly escalate observed non-compliance within or outside the institution (e.g., to the competent authority through a whistleblowing process). The management body should on an ongoing basis promote, monitor and assess the risk culture of the institution; consider the impact of the risk culture on the financial stability, risk profile and robust governance of the institution; and make changes where necessary.*

Accountability: *relevant staff at all levels should know and understand the core values of the institution and, to the extent necessary for their role, its risk appetite and risk capacity. They should be capable of performing their roles and be aware that they will be held accountable for their actions in relation to the institution's risk-taking behaviour.*

Effective communication and challenge: *a sound risk culture should promote an environment of open communication and effective challenge in which decision- making processes encourage a broad range of views, allow for testing of current practices, stimulate a constructive critical attitude among staff, and promote an environment of open and constructive engagement throughout the entire organisation.*

Incentives: *appropriate incentives should play a key role in aligning risk-taking behaviour with the institution's risk profile and its long-term interest.*

Source: https://www.eba.europa.eu/sites/default/files/document_library/Publications/Guidelines/2021/1016721/Final%20report%20on%20Guidelines%20on%20internal%20governance%20under%20CRD.pdf

Each culture is different, but the ECB distills the essence of fostering a strong risk culture in all types of organizations. The tone from the top is critical, but it needs to be authentic and reflect senior management's true beliefs. Employees will see right through communication that is inauthentic or divergent from senior management's actions, and I am sure many of us heard in some form gripes when these communications come out and are contrary to observed practices.

Accountability is equally important, and there is no room in any organization for protecting bad actors out of some sort of reverence for the revenue they procure. This is not only bad risk management, it is bad management in general, because recent history has shown that bad behavior associated with profit-taking at all costs without regard for "doing the right thing" can result in significant losses, as was the case with Wells Fargo that suffered significant losses and a brutal regulatory mandated asset cap that was only recently removed as a result of their sales practices related regulatory issues.

Open and transparent communication and the ability to challenge practices and behaviors are critical for the health of an organization's risk culture. This is very much aligned with an organization's values, which often state that they value a "speak up" culture. However, this is another example where the statement may not reflect reality in an organization. I have heard far too many people say, "It's wrong but I am not going to say anything because no one will listen," or "I am not going to say anything because I don't want to antagonize management" or "I am not going to say anything because it will go nowhere." To get this right, senior management should be willing to reach down into the organization and go on a listening tour and put plans in place to respond to what they have heard. They need to create a safe space for people to speak up, challenge, and offer their perspective.

Incentives drive behavior, especially in financial institutions and sales-oriented organizations where people are clearly motivated by incentive compensation. Incentive schemes can have unintended consequences if they are not examined closely, and it's a strong practice to have risk management and compliance review and opine on them. They should be aligned with the firm's risk appetite and impacted when a particular business or function exceeds risk appetite. It is a strong practice in banks to have risk management and compliance review designated "material risk takers" each year and to provide feedback.

It should also be mentioned that some organizations have created compliance matrixes for their senior employees and risk takers that if not carefully thought out can have unintended consequences. For instance, many organizations with mature issue management programs provide benefit to businesses and functions that self-identify issues. But they get negative points on their compliance matrix if the action plans associated with their self-identified issues go overdue. As a result, they can be reluctant to self-identify issues, because at the end of the day, it means additional work. In addition, I have witnessed the business pushing back on accepting second-line-identified issues and suspected that the underlying reason was that it would impact their compliance matrix and, in turn, the team's incentive compensation. This is an example of how this type of matrix may not drive the right behavior even though on the surface they are designed to do so.

Training

Training helps to instill the right risk culture in a firm and reinforce the value of "doing the right thing." Operational risk training serves this function through the following:

- **Risk awareness:** Educates employees on the importance of identifying, managing, mitigating, and escalating operational risks
- **Accountability:** Reinforces the concept of the three lines of defense and educates the first line on its responsibility for managing operational risk and executing the components of the operational risk framework
- **Risk taking:** Educates the firm on the concept of risk appetite, and assists with embedding risk taking into decision-making and strategic planning
- **Value-based:** Reinforces the concept of "doing the right thing" and expected behaviors
- **Escalations:** Reinforces the concept of "if you see something say something" and encourages rapid escalation of issues
- **Speak-up:** Reinforces the value of engaging in a "speak-up culture" and reinforces that the organization does not retaliate against people who raise their hands when they uncover issues
- **Risk framework:** Offers practical training in implementing components of the operational risk framework, including RCSA, operational risk event reporting, risk appetite, and scenario analysis

Most organizations offer asynchronous training that is assigned to relevant stakeholders through online training systems. There are off-the-shelf operational risk training modules that can be purchased and customized for firms that do not have large training departments or the capability to design their own content. It is an effective strategy to offer continuous opportunities for in-person training through sessions devoted to emerging risk topics, such as managing AI risks. The worse modality for training is a pre-recorded session by someone on the operational risk team that is not designed to be interactive. Sometimes this is the only option for offering training, but it is not a good user experience to listen to these pre-recorded sessions, which can be quite flat.

Conduct Risk

In many ways, conduct risk can be considered the manifestation of corporate culture. It has become an important focus of managing risk within an organization. The regulators in the United States focused on sales practices (a form of conduct risk) following the Wells Fargo cross-selling event, while the United Kingdom established an entire regulatory regime focused on conduct (the Financial Conduct Authority).

The United Kingdom has made the most progress in establishing the key components of what a conduct risk program should look like, which include the following core principles:

1	Integrity	A firm must conduct its business with integrity.
2	Skill, care, and diligence	A firm must conduct its business with due skill, care, and diligence.
3	Management and control	A firm must take reasonable care to organize and control its affairs responsibly and effectively, with adequate risk management systems.
4	Financial prudence	A firm must maintain adequate financial resources.
5	Market conduct	A firm must observe proper standards of market conduct.
6	Customers' interests	A firm must pay due regard to the interests of its customers and treat them fairly.
7	Communications with clients	A firm must pay due regard to the information needs of its clients and communicate information to them in a way which is clear, fair, and not misleading.
8	Conflicts of interest	A firm must manage conflicts of interest fairly, both between itself and its customers and between a customer and another client.
9	Customers: relationships of trust	A firm must take reasonable care to ensure the suitability of its advice and discretionary decisions for any customer who is entitled to rely upon its judgment.
10	Clients' assets	A firm must arrange adequate protection for clients' assets when it is responsible for them.
11	Relations with regulators	A firm must deal with its regulators in an open and cooperative way, and must disclose to the FCA appropriately anything relating to the firm of which that regulator would reasonably expect notice.
12	Consumer Duty	A firm must act to deliver good outcomes for retail customers.

Source: FINANCIAL CONDUCT AUTHORITY / https://www.handbook.fca.org.uk/handbook/PRIN/2/1.html / Last accessed by Nov 07, 2025

Managing conduct risk and in turn bolstering an organization's risk culture should draw on all the elements of the operational risk framework as outlined in Chapter 4 of this book. This includes incorporating conduct issues into risk appetite, key risk indicators, RCSA, scenario analysis, issue management, and monitoring and reporting.

The following are examples of conduct issues:

Personal dealing: Most financial institutions have policies in place that regulate personal dealing. Controls are established to prevent employees from trading on insider information on behalf of their personal accounts that they may glean from their day-to-day business activities. Standard controls include watch lists of stocks that are not allowed to be traded for a period of time (for instance, ahead of a securities offering that the bank is managing) and monitoring of personal trading accounts through pre-approved broker-dealers.

Unauthorized trading: Unauthorized trading is a classic operational risk (see Chapter 1 for background on the Barings event) that has bad conduct at its core. Large unauthorized trading events have led regulators to examine the firm's risk culture and controls (including front office supervision, training, handling of misconducts) and have led to sizable regulatory fines (in addition to the actual trading losses).

Information barriers: Financial institutions are expected to protect private and confidential information and create barriers among certain trading groups, or departments within the bank (research, trading, investment banking) so that the firm cannot manipulate the markets based on insider information. Creating barriers among these groups used to involve ensuring that they were on different floors and behind locked doors. However, with the advent of technological advances, organizations are increasingly deploying advance monitoring techniques, including the monitoring of chat rooms, email, telephone conversations, and company texting services.

Conflicts: Conflicts arise when an organization is able to realize a gain at the expense of a client or places the interest of one client (perhaps a large institution) over another (perhaps a smaller institution or individual), has an interest in the execution of a client's transaction that is not aligned with the interest of the client, or accepts a reward (financial or nonfinancial) from an entity other than the client to execute a transaction on the client's behalf. Conflicts became a hot topic in the wake of the 2008 financial crisis, when it became apparent that some banking firms were "betting against their clients" through proprietary trading positions. The passage of the Volcker Rule prohibits banks from engaging in trading of certain investment activities on their own accounts. In addition to limiting speculative trading, the rule has limited the ability of banks to essentially "trade against their clients."

Third-party risks: Operational risk functions manage risks associated with the actions of third parties through policies, frameworks, oversight, and monitoring. Third parties are expected to be fully compliant with applicable rules and regulations. Third-party risk is often incorporated into risk assessments that assess risk from a variety of perspectives, including third-party compliance with SLAs in force and compliance with regulations. They should be assessed as well for any potential conduct issues that can blow back on the firm they are providing services for. For instance, in the 2013–2015 timeframe, several large US banks received consent orders as the result of improper add-on products offered by third parties to their client base. This included adding on identity protection and credit monitoring to credit card benefits. Customers paid for these benefits but did not receive the service.

Market conduct: In November 2014, global regulators around the world (including the FCA, OCC, FINMA) levied fines on global banks, including Citigroup, UBS, JPMorgan Chase, Barclays, and HSBC, for colluding to manipulate global FX benchmark rates. This led the banking industry to establish global codes of conduct that prohibit traders from sharing transactional information that can create unfair market advantage for the largest institutions. At the essence of managing market conduct is ensuring that the markets behave fairly and without bias for all parties involved (including large institutions and individuals) and are free from manipulation, price fixing, bid rigging, and collusion. The overriding value is the expectation that markets will operate freely and competitively and without manipulation by any participating party, regardless of size or influence.

Reputational risk: Noncompliance with any of the risks a financial organization faces—money laundering, sanctions, fraud, consumer protection, anti-bribery, market manipulation—can lead to bad press, a loss of faith in the institution on the part of shareholders, customers, employees and regulators, and ultimately a hit to the firm's reputation that may not be recoverable in the near term. Several large industry events over the past decade resulted in reputational hits to some of the world's largest and most respected financial institutions. In addition to regulatory fines, new business barriers, and increased scrutiny over all their operations (and not just the ones at the center of the event), loss of customers, and market share, these institutions had a long path to regaining faith in how they manage their operations, including compliance risk.

The Boeing Example

Conduct risk is not specific to financial institutions. I have been following the Boeing event that involved the blowout of a plugged door panel since the event occurred in early January 2024 because it provides a lesson on the criticality of strong quality control programs and also because the possibility of sitting next to a hole in a fuselage on an in-flight aircraft is simply terrifying.

Former Boeing and FAA employees and experts testified before Congress in 2024 that when employees raised their hands and reported quality issues, they faced barriers to action or retaliation. A Boeing engineer who worked on the 787 and 777 programs testified that he was threatened when he came forward with concerns and was told by one supervisor that "I would have killed someone who said what you said." The engineer indicated that he was transferred to work on the 777 program as a form of retaliation. He found problems in that program as well, including employees who forced parts together by jumping on top of them. In addition to putting added stress on the parts by applying such aggressive pressure, this is presumed to not meet FAA quality standards.

Sen. Richard Blumenthal, the chair of the investigation committee into Boeing's quality issues, commented following the hearings that Boeing appeared to have "a broken safety culture." He added that the "whistleblowers have come forward at great personal risk."The *Washington Post* in its coverage of the event reported that Boeing did not respond directly to these allegations but released a statement indicating that "retaliation is strictly prohibited at Boeing."

It is likely that Boeing's top executives believe that they have communicated from the top that retaliation is prohibited in the firm. But the fact that its employees felt threatened regardless of what senior management communicated suggests a cultural problem and an issue with its tone from the middle. Often, it's the managers, like the one who commented that he would "kill someone," who impact the tone for the firm.

One of the previous findings from the review of Boeing's quality culture is that there was a disconnect between senior management and the factory floor. A firm should absolutely get tone from the top right when it communicates its values, but the echo from the middle is equally important. What happens in the middle is often driven by pressures that are put upon it from above and compensation policies. And it is in the middle where tone from the top meets action.

One of the primary lessons learned from the Boeing event is that is pays to get quality right. The consequences can be dire if the company is found liable for loss of life. In addition, issues do not age well, and the most critical quality issues should be prioritized and remediated. Top-down initiatives should incorporate bottom-up process reviews (see Chapter 6 on RCSA). And most importantly, a firm's culture should empower employees to speak up. (See Chapter 11 for the Boeing case study.)

Policies and Frameworks

If conduct risk is the manifestation of an organization's culture, the policy framework serves as the mechanism to ensure conduct risk is managed in its broadest sense through the organization's frameworks. It is what an individual in an organization turns to in order to understand what they need to do to stay within compliance of an organization's expectations. A policy framework is designed to provide the why, what, and how.

Most organizations have a policy governance policy that sets out the consistent standards for managing a policy framework. This policy defines how all the policies within an organization are organized and establishes requirements for creating, approving, maintaining, communicating, and retiring a policy. It is often owned by an Enterprise Risk Management function within Risk Management but can be owned by Operational Risk or Compliance. It is a strong practice to have a template that risk functions use so that all policies across risk stripes have a consistent look and feel.

There are three universal components of a policy framework: the policy, standard, and procedures. Some organizations have directives or handbooks instead of standards, and supplement the framework with guidance documents, which are recommendations for implementing the requirements, or desktop aids, which serve as reference documents. Every regulated financial institution will have some form of the three primary components.

The policy framework will establish governance standards for reviewing and updating a policy, which is typically annually, and requirements for approvals. The framework will also establish what is expected of a policy owner, including initiating the annual process for updating a policy.

It is important that a policy owner engage a large cohort of stakeholders when the policy is being drafted and, annually, when it is reviewed for changes. I can attest that this can be a protracted process and a challenge with bringing all the various perspectives from stakeholders into a single coherent document. It is critical, however, because a failed policy is a policy that is thrown over the wall at stakeholders with the expectation that it is adhered to. If the stakeholders feel that they were not consulted (and how many times have you heard people complain that they don't think a policy makes sense, but no one consulted them?), they will grudgingly comply at best.

A policy owner is not done when the policy is finally finalized and published. It is a strong practice for the policy owner to provide oversight of the policy and to ensure

Table 8.1 Policy Hierarchy

Element	Purpose	Example
Policy (owned by the second line)	Outlines why something must be done; establishes strategic direction and expected behaviors	Cyber policy establishes the requirement that all employees must use strong passwords to access applications and systems; requires protection of passwords
Standard (owned by specialized function in the first or second line)	Outlines the specific requirements and criteria that must be met; defines enforceable requirements	Cyber standard sets out requirements for password complexity, such as required upper and lower case, letters, numbers and characters
Procedure (owned by first line—owned by second line if it refers to a process they own)	Outlines the day-to-day instructions for meeting requirements of policy and standards	Cyber procedures outline step-by-step process for creating and updating passwords

it is being implemented by the stakeholders. This may be through testing or an RCSA. I have worked in organizations that conducted annual risk governance assessments that were focused on assessing compliance with policy requirements. The policy owner is also responsible for monitoring the operating environment and making changes between the annual review and update cycle if there are immediate requirements to do so, such as a change in regulations.

Table 8.1 is an overview of the differences between the three components of the policy framework.

Operational risk policies are owned by the Operational Risk function in the second line of defense. The operational risk policy establishes in clear and concise language the high-level requirements for following an operational risk framework. The policy will typically include a few paragraphs on each framework element, but it will not go into detail on each. For example, an operational risk policy may have a few paragraphs stating the importance of collecting operational risk events, will establish the threshold for collecting losses, and have a statement that the system of record is the required repository. But it will not go into the level of detail that the standard would, which provides guidance on each lifecycle element of an operational risk event program.

A policy also serves as a mechanism for incorporating regulatory requirements into business requirements for the firm. It is a strong practice to map regulatory requirements to policies to ensure there are no gaps. This can be a resource-intensive process, and there are new solutions in the market that use AI to conduct rules mapping to business processes and policies. As a former policy owner, I conducted regular reviews of outstanding and new regulatory requirements to determine if the policies I was responsible for required updating. I would receive on a regular basis a list of new or revised regulations that I would review for any required policy updates or changes in risk management practices.

I mentioned earlier that the policy owner is ultimately responsible for ensuring adherence. The first thing a regulator or auditor requests when they prepare for an examination is for all relevant policies. They will proceed to check that the policy has been adhered to by all stakeholders, including second line in its role as owner and first line in its role as implementor. It is not good to have a missing policy for a critical risk function, but it is even worse to have a policy in place that is not followed. Regulatory consent orders often target a firm's policies either for being missing or more frequently deficient and require that the policies be implemented or enhanced as part of the required remediation.

The following is an example of what an operational risk policy would include:

- **Purpose statement and scope:** The general purpose of the policy, establishing requirements for the operational risk program, and scope, which is usually the entire organization, including all entities, functions and business units.
- **Definitions:** Definitions of key terms, such policy, standard, procedure.
- **Roles and responsibilities:** Includes roles and responsibilities for first line, second line, third line, governance committees.
- **Operational risk framework overview:** Requirements to conduct an RCSA, track and monitor operational risk events, threshold for tracking operational risk losses, risk appetite, issue management, scenario analysis, key risk indicators, reporting, monitoring and oversight, review and challenge, reporting, governance committees (operational risk committee); include a referral for each to the relevant standard.
- **System:** Include a statement on the system of record for RCSA, operational risk events, issue management.
- **Operational risk subtypes:** Include statements concerning the management of data, model, third party, technology, cyber, fraud, transaction processing, and business continuity risks; include a referral for each to the relevant standard.
- **Reporting and documentation:** Include sections on governance, senior management, committee, and regulatory reporting.
- **Training requirements:** Include requirements for conducting operational risk training.
- **Policy governance:** Indicated policy owner, policy review cycle, policy exceptions, requirement for first-line procedures, required approvals.

A standard provides details on the "what" that is defined in the policy. For instance, a policy may have a high-level overview of each of the operational risk framework elements, while in many organizations there is a standard stacked against each of those elements that explain in detail the requirements of the specific program. A standard will have a roles and responsibilities matrix that delineates the roles across the first and second lines in much more detail than the high-level three lines of defense matrix that would be found in a policy. The standard is owned by the function that owns the program that it addresses, which is typically, but not always second-line operational risk. The second line will likely own the standards for the operational risk framework components, but a first-line function may own the documents for risk disciplines under their domain, such as a cyber-risk management standard.

As an example, an RCSA standard will describe how to determine inherent and residual risk, include impact tables, and describe the requirements for holding risk

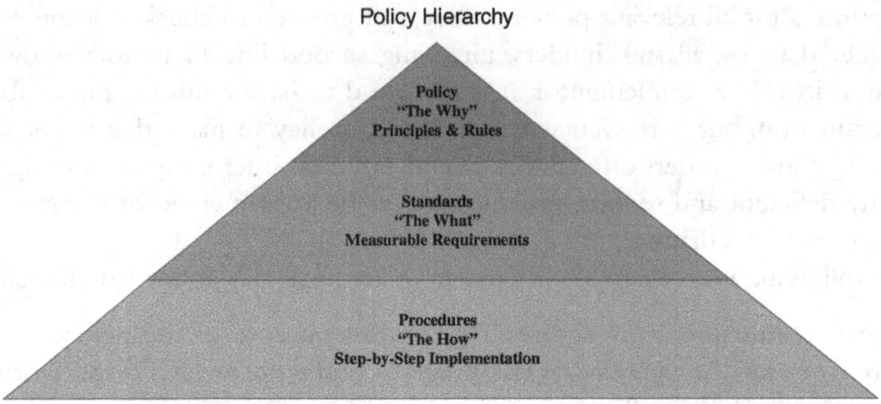

Figure 8.2 Policy hierarchy

workshops, assessing controls and when issues and action plans are required. An operational risk event standard would include the requirements for identifying, accessing, and reporting on events, including the requirement to conduct root-cause analysis, event classification, and escalation. An issue management standard would include the requirements for opening issues and action plans, assigning owners, reporting and monitoring.

Procedures provide granular documentation on how to implement a program, such as RCSA. While the policy will state that all businesses and functions are responsible for executing an RCSA according to a schedule and the standard will include the detail on each component of the RCSA lifecycle, the procedure will detail step-by-step how to execute an RCSA. This will include details on who to invite to workshops, how to structure the session, how to test controls and integrate into the control assessment, how to determine the control ratings, and how to communicate and report on the final results.

Figure 8.2 shows the standard policy hierarchy that exists in most regulated institutions.

Operational risk policies, standards, and procedures provide the structure for implementing the operational risk framework across the lines of defense. See Chapter 4 for a discussion of the importance of the operational risk framework and its standard elements.

Governance

Roles and Responsibilities

Governance provides the guardrails for managing risk across the three lines of defense. It is critical to get the lines of demarcation correct and to clearly define the roles and responsibilities for managing and implementing the operational risk framework across the first, second, and third lines. Role confusion will result in challenges in implementing the operational risk framework and management scrutiny on why duplicate resources are assigned to similar tasks. It's a strong practice to review the lines of demarcation for key elements of the framework on a regular basis to ensure roles and responsibilities are clearly defined and understood.

Key roles in the first line of defense usually flow from the chief operating officer (although organizational constructs vary), while key roles, including the chief operational risk officer, flow from the chief risk officer in the second line of defense. The third line is governed by the chief audit officer.

In large institutions, the requirement on the first line to implement the operational risk framework is significant. As an example, the RCSA process requires teams that are knowledgeable about their business and its risks and controls. This is not an exercise that can be relegated to a junior analyst without proper oversight and management engagement. The process requires an understanding of the data that goes into the assessment of the level of risk and expert qualitative judgment in making the final determination. This includes the ability to properly assess the effectiveness of the controls both individually and from the perspective of the overall control environment and establish remediation plans where they are not operating effectively.

The board and chief risk officer also play critical roles in the governance of the operational risk program. The US Federal Reserve's Enhanced Prudential Standards (EPS, Regulation YY) stipulates that the board of directors are responsible for approving a written risk management framework, which includes risk appetite for all risk stripes. EPS holds the chief risk officer responsible for the oversight of all financial and non-financial risks in their organization. This includes ensuring that risk appetite is reviewed and approved by the board.

Senior management, often with significant input from the chief risk officer, plays a critical role in ensuring that an organization has an operational risk framework in place that is appropriate to its size and complexity. They are responsible for providing the resources and support for an adequate operational risk function. The Basel Committee in its Revisions to the Principles for the Sound Management of Operational Risk (2021) includes the requirements for senior management to translate the board-approved operational risk management framework into policies and procedures:

> *Senior management should translate the ORMF approved by the board of directors into specific policies and procedures that can be implemented and verified within the different business units. Senior management should clearly assign authority, responsibility and reporting relationships to encourage and maintain accountability, and to ensure the necessary resources are available to manage operational risk in line with the bank's risk appetite and tolerance statement. Moreover, senior management should ensure that the management oversight process is appropriate for the risks inherent in a business unit's activity.*
>
> *Source:* https://www.bis.org/bcbs/publ/d515.pdf

See Chapter 3 for a discussion of the three lines of defense.

Risk Committees

Strong governance starts at the top of the house with the board of directors, which is responsible for overseeing all risks, including operational risk. They are responsible for setting the risk appetite at the top of the house for each risk stripe and for monitoring the levels of risk within the thresholds established by the risk appetite framework.

Many larger organizations have established risk committees of the board, while others manage risk through the audit committee. Smaller organizations may manage the risk disciplines through the full board committee.

The Basel Committee in its "Revisions to the Principles for the Sound Management of Operational Risk" (2021) provides guidance for establishing a risk committee structure:

> *A bank's governance structure should be commensurate with the nature, size, complexity and risk profile of its activities. When designing the operational risk governance structure, a bank should take the following into consideration:*
>
> **a)** ***Committee structure***—*Sound industry practice is for larger and more complex organisations with a central group function and separate business units to utilise a board-created enterprise-level risk committee for overseeing all risks, to which a management level operational risk committee reports. Depending on the nature, size and complexity of the bank, the enterprise-level risk committee may receive input from operational risk committees by country, business or functional area. Smaller and less complex organisations may utilise a flatter organisational structure that oversees operational risk directly within the board's risk management committee.*
>
> **b)** ***Committee composition***—*Sound industry practice is for operational risk committees (or the risk committee in smaller banks) to include members with a variety of expertise, which should cover expertise in business activities, financial activities, legal, technological and regulatory matters, and independent risk management.*
>
> **c)** ***Committee operation***—*Committee meetings should be held at appropriate frequencies with adequate time and resources to permit productive discussion and decision-making. Records of committee operations should be adequate to permit review and evaluation of committee effectiveness.*
>
> *Source:* https://www.bis.org/bcbs/publ/d515.pdf

In organizations that I worked in, I was responsible for reporting on the operational risk profile to the risk committee of the board on a regular basis. Reporting, including board reporting, is among the most important responsibilities of an operational risk function, because it is how they communicate with the top echelon of the organization, and the messaging must be finely crafted to be effective. I always asked myself and my team when we worked on board reporting the board the following questions:

- What does the board need to know?
- What action do I want the board to take?
- Why am I reporting on these specific topics?
- What is the "so what?"

In my operational risk role, I was responsible for consolidating the view of operational risk across the enterprise, including the current level of risk appetite, the top risks as identified through RCSA and thematic reviews, emerging risks, critical control breakdowns, regulatory and audit findings, and the status of critical remediations. My teams would pull this information from across all businesses and functions, and the art would come into play when working on distilling the messaging. For instance, many of the functions, such as technology and cyber, would submit very technical updates that required translating into language that would resonate and be understandable to the board.

Most boards understand risk appetite and are responsible for approving its thresholds and levels on at least an annual basis and more frequently if significant changes are required. In my reporting function, I would bring the current risk appetite assessment for operational risk as a whole and by subtype to the board. If there was a breach of some sort, I would frame it within the context of risk appetite, because that is the language that resonates with the board. It is worth noting that I was often limited to just a few pages in the overall risk report for the board and had to decide what were the most important items to highlight. From my experience, no board wants to read through hundreds or even dozens of pages for any one risk stripe. There is always the option to include background materials in the board report appendix, but this needs to be monitored because it can get out of hand.

I always encouraged my teams to not fall into the trap of simply counting—counting number of open issues, loss events, near-miss events, RCSAs performed, vendor risk assessments, number of vendors, number of fraud events. It is satisfying to put these numbers on paper, but simple counts do not tell the board or senior management what they need to respond to. As an example, when presenting issue management data, it is important to do the analysis and determine what the underlying root cause trends and themes are. If the count of high rated issues has increased on a material basis, what are the underlying drivers for the increase? What can be done to remediate the identified trends related to control deficiencies? And why is this being reported to the board? What do they need to know and react to?

The following are the items I would typically include in a board report:

- **Executive summary:** Key messages, significant OpRisk events, emerging risks, overall risk profile
- **Risk appetite metrics:** Metrics for overall operational risk and subtypes (cyber, third party, data, continuity, model, fraud)
- **Events and losses:** Large operational risk losses, including root cause and trends, and any relevant peer events with a statement on internal exposure to similar risks and control issues
- **RCSA results:** High-rated residual risks outside of appetite, or approaching lower band of thresholds, with statements for drivers and remediations to bring level down; high-level inherent, control and residual risk ratings by business unit or entity
- **Issues and remediation:** New high-rated issues and issues coming due; drivers for high rated actions that are overdue; root-cause trends and themes
- **Regulatory and audit:** Results from regulatory exams, with remediations if necessary

Key components of the governance framework include committee hierarchies, with the structure flowing downward from the board. Sitting underneath the board or the risk committee of the board or the audit committee is the enterprise risk committee in many larger organizations. In the organizations where I worked, my monthly operational risk report would first be presented to the operational risk committee, followed by the enterprise risk committee, and finally, the risk committee of the board. It would be heavily vetted by the chief risk officer to ensure the messaging was concise and consistent.

The operational risk committee in many organizations reports into the enterprise risk committee, along with the other risk stripes, such as credit, market and liquidity risk. The hierarchy is important because the escalation path flows upwards. If an issue cannot be resolved in the operational risk committee, an escalation can be brought to the enterprise risk committee. The enterprise risk committee in turn can escalate issues to the risk committee of the board, or the board if the governance structure is flat.

The members of the operational risk committee should include a cross section of representatives from the three lines of defense. I would typically include from the second line the leads for each of the operational risk subtype programs (transaction processing, fraud, third party, continuity, model, data), the framework programs (RCSA, loss data, scenario analysis, reporting), and the head of enterprise risk and compliance representatives. I would include from the first line the business risk and control leads for each of the businesses and representatives from the firm's functions, such as technology and cyber, fraud, and third-party. I would also include the lead auditor for operational risk from the third line. There is no right number for operational risk committee membership, but it can become unwieldly with more than 20 or 25 members. I have worked in an organization that limited committee membership to just 10–12 people, and I found this challenging to get the right cross section. It is ultimately a balancing act when the membership roster is created.

It should be noted that sitting beneath the operational risk committee are subcommittees or forums, dedicated to topics specific to the subtypes, such as cyber, fraud, and third-party. Committees are formal structures with requirements for charters and minutes and are often monitored by regulators. I was routinely asked for monthly operational risk committee reports by my regulators. Forums are less structured and do not require the formality of a committee, including the taking of formal minutes or structured reports. Committees should exist as decision-making bodies, while forums can exist for sharing of information. For instance, the operational risk committee should be the first step in approving risk appetite statements and metrics, ahead of approval by the enterprise risk committee and the risk committee of the board. A forum can be the place where you can bring a presentation on a new tool to manage cyber risk.

Figure 8.3 shows a sample committee structure hierarchy that I have experienced in large financial institutions.

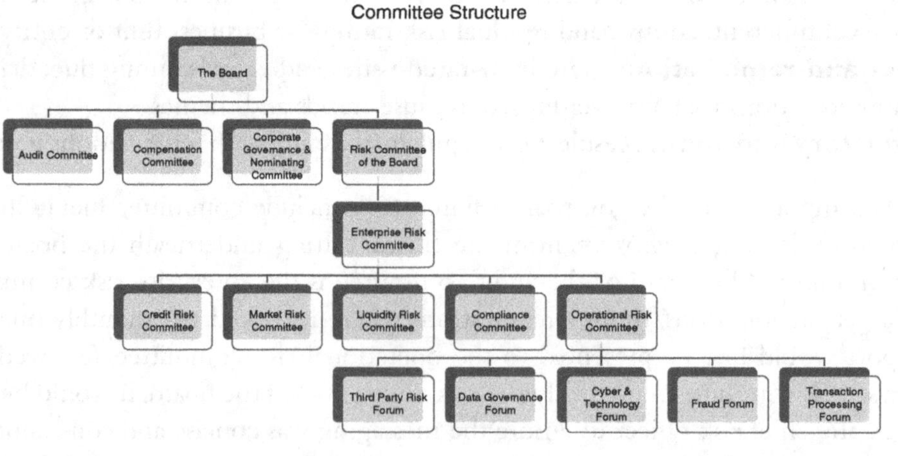

Figure 8.3 Sample committee structure

Interview with Industry Veteran: Maureen Day

Maureen is a retired senior Ernst & Young partner, who has worked on complicated regulatory and compliance challenges for some of the most complex financial organizations. She started her career as an audit professional and most recently led EY's Financial Services compliance consulting practice. She is a respected industry expert on conduct issues and brings deep knowledge and practical experience to the topic.

1. **Question**

   What in your view distinguishes a mature conduct risk framework from a developing one?

   Answer

   Because of its broad and pervasive nature, conduct risk is often challenging to identify, measure, monitor, and control, and we see conduct risk frameworks at different levels of maturity. More mature conduct risk frameworks focus not only on specific conduct risk programs (such as a conduct risk assessment, conduct risk monitoring and metrics, etc.) but also on the firm's culture and norms as well as messaging by management, including outright messaging and leadership by example. Conduct risk cannot be effectively managed without both.

2. **Question**

   How would you define conduct risk, and why is it often misunderstood by financial institutions?

   Answer

   Conduct risk is generally defined in a broad context and most often includes the risk of detrimental customer outcomes or negative impacts to the markets in which the firm operates. In some cases, conduct risk definitions extend to risk of adverse impact to other stakeholders or to market competition. These risks manifest through actions of the firm itself and of its employees and often involve reputational and legal risk. Thoughtfully defining conduct risk is one of the gating activities that a firm should undertake as it further develops its conduct risk management framework.

   Oftentimes misconduct is thought of stemming only from the actions of a lone, bad actor or solely motivated by money or activity present at only one firm. The challenge in establishing effective conduct risk frameworks is providing enough flexibility to be able to identify both singular and pervasive events that can lead to conduct risk.

3. **Question**

   What are some red flags or early warning indicators you have witnessed that suggest potential conduct risk?

   Answer

   The transactional nature of consumer financial products and potentially huge associated transaction volumes provides a wide range of analysis that can help in identifying red flags. Since firms are seeking to identify inappropriate customer outcomes, customer complaints provide a wealth of information that can be mined to identify potential conduct issues. The challenge is differentiating conduct issues from other causal factors such as need for employee training, IT performance issues, and other operational matters. Analysis of complaint data in and of itself is a necessary practice, but to be most effective at identifying conduct risk issues, the output of that analysis should be connected with other data including data related to compensation programs, employee exit interviews, whistleblower information, and customer account activity such as early account or product closure, all of which taken together could be indicative of mis-selling and sales practices issues, for example.

With respect to the wholesale businesses—commercial banking, corporate banking, and investment banking—analysis of profit and loss statements (P&L) and particularly analysis of new deal, new product, and new business P&L are great methods to detect potential conduct risk issues. These analyses are performed routinely by financial institutions, and the key is to also look at the data through a conduct risk lens.

4. **Question**

   How should boards and senior management be effectively engaged in overseeing conduct risk?

   Answer

   As with other risks present in the organization, boards and senior management must challenge the frameworks and approaches being utilized, including the approach to conduct risk monitoring and also challenge and probe the results, conclusions, and actions taken. Of equal importance is ensuring an appropriate and balanced tone at the top, which includes reactions and consequences for conduct breaches throughout the organization. It is important to react appropriately and in some cases strongly and visibly to actions that are not in line with the firm's culture.

5. **Question**

   In your experience, how can firms balance strong sales performance with appropriate conduct oversight?

   Answer

   We see a number of ways to promote an appropriate sales culture and a culture of compliance. Appropriate employee conduct related to the selling process, for example, is so closely tied to the customer experience, that managing and monitoring sales, P&L, and customer experience can serve both purposes. Additionally, messaging around customer satisfaction, focusing on the long-term client health and relationship also serve to promote an appropriately focused sales culture as well as manage conduct risk.

6. **Question**

   How do emerging technologies (like AI and machine learning) change the landscape for managing conduct risks?

   Answer

   Emerging technology provides great promise in management of conduct risk and also poses risk that must be mitigated and managed. For example, use of AI and large language models has been successfully deployed in the analysis of potentially anomalous behavior in large sets of unstructured data such as customer complaints. While such emerging technology can promote effective risk management, its use in certain applications pose risk. For example, financial institutions are generally proceeding with caution with respect to the use of AI in customer-facing applications. AI-based analysis and decisioning may introduce unintended results that cannot be fully explained or may introduce unintended bias, all of which could lead to increased legal and compliance risk. See Table 8.2.

Wells Fargo Pays USD $7.57 Billion in Penalties and Redress Over Retail Customer Violations

As of May 16, 2023, Wells Fargo has agreed to pay and provision at least USD $7.57 billion (EUR 6.72 billion) over improper trade practices. The violations included employees setting up accounts in the names of customers without their knowledge or consent in order to meet sales targets.

On May 14, 2019, 20 current and former officers and directors, including former Wells Fargo CEO John Stumpf, agreed to pay USD $240 million to Wells Fargo over their role in the bogus accounts scandal, Law360 reports. Payments would be made by the bank's directors and officers liability insurers. As this settlement was an indirect recovery, ORX News has not subtracted it from the total loss amount.

The following is a breakdown of the total loss amount in USD, ordered according to settlement date:

September 6, 2016: 35 million, fine, Officer of the Comptroller of the Currency
September 8, 2016: 100 million, fine, Consumer Financial Protection Bureau
September 8, 2016: 5 million, restitution, Consumer Financial Protection Bureau
September 8, 2016: 50 million, fine, Los Angeles City Attorney
April 21, 2017: 142 million, class action settlement, accountholders
August 2017: 2.8 million, reimbursement, following PwC audit
September 2017: 910,000, reimbursement, following PwC audit
May 4, 2018: 480 million, class action settlement, shareholders
October 18, 2018: 65 million, fine, New York Attorney General
December 28, 2018: 575 million, settlement, 50 states and District of Columbia
August 22, 2019: 6.5 million, settlement, Navajo Nation
October 15, 2019: 1.6 billion, provision, legal expenses
February 21, 2020: 3 billion, settlement, DoJ and SEC deferred prosecution agreement
December 20, 2022: 506 million, restitution, Consumer Financial Protection Bureau
May 15, 2023: 1 billion, class action settlement, shareholders
Total: USD 7.57 billion

On September 8, 2016, it was announced that Wells Fargo had been fined USD $100 million and ordered to set aside USD $5 million for customer restitution by the US Consumer Financial Protection Bureau (CFPB), ordered to pay a USD $35 million penalty to the US Office of the Comptroller of the Currency (OCC), and ordered to pay USD $50 million to the City and County of Los Angeles. The CFPB also ordered the bank to hire an independent consultant to conduct a review of its sales practices.

Between May 2002 and July 2015, Wells Fargo retail branch employees signed up existing customers for deposit accounts, credit cards, debit cards, and online banking services for which they did not apply. As part of this, employees made payments from customers' legitimate accounts into the unauthorized accounts without their knowledge, used customer information to submit applications for credit cards, faked email addresses to create accounts, and created personal identification numbers (PINs) for debit cards that the customers were unaware of.

According to the CFPB, a combination of high sales targets and pecuniary incentive programs drove the employees' misconduct. According to the *Guardian*, employees were expected to cross-sell a minimum of 20 products per day in 2013. This figure dropped to 15 in 2014. Employees risked losing their jobs if they did not meet these targets.

The CFPB found that since January 1, 2011, the employees opened more than 2.1 million unauthorized deposit and credit card accounts. This included more than 1.5 million deposit accounts, around 85,000 of which incurred fees of approximately USD $2 million, which as of September 8, 2016, the bank was refunding. These fees included overdraft fees on linked accounts and monthly service fees for failing to maintain minimum account balances. The employees opened 565,443 unauthorized credit card accounts, of which 14,000 incurred fees totaling USD $403,145, which as of September 8, 2016, the bank was refunding. These fees included annual fees and overdraft protection fees, in addition to interest charges and other late fees. In 2017, PricewaterhouseCoopers (PwC) found that the actual number of unauthorized accounts totaled around 3.5 million.

The CFPB also found that around 5,300 Wells Fargo employees had lost their jobs as a result of their misconduct since January 1, 2011.

The OCC found that Wells Fargo's employee incentive plan was not adequately aligned with local branch traffic, staff turnover, or customer demand, and that it encouraged unsafe and unsound banking practices. In addition, the OCC said that the bank had failed to implement an enterprise-wide sales practice oversight program to prevent the illicit sales and lacked comprehensive customer complaint monitoring procedures and sufficient audit coverage.

The *New York Times* reported on September 8, 2016, that the majority of the fraudulent accounts were not discovered because employees would close the accounts soon after opening them.

Wells Fargo stated that customers who had improperly paid fees and charges on unauthorized accounts had been refunded around USD $2.6 million following an internal review. The average amount refunded was USD $25. ORX News has attributed this to the USD $5 million in restitution ordered by the CFPB.

In April 2017, Wells Fargo's independent directors concluded an investigation that revealed that former CEO John Stumpf had been aware of problems since 2002 and that employees had been terminated for misconduct since at least then.

On April 21, 2017, it was reported that Wells Fargo had agreed to pay an additional USD $142 million to settle a class action lawsuit brought by account holders who suffered damages, such as fees, after Wells Fargo employees had opened unauthorized accounts in their names. This comprises an initial USD $110 million settlement announced on March 28, 2017, to which USD $32 million was added.

The class originally consisted of any Wells Fargo customers who had accounts opened in their name, were enrolled in products, or had applications for products submitted in their name without consent from January 1, 2009, until the date the settlement was to be finalized. This was later extended to include customer accounts dating back to May 2002.

The settlement was granted preliminary approval on May 18, 2017, subject to certain conditions, including that the parties drew up provisions to deal with customers whose credit was damaged by the fraudulent accounts. Upon approval, the bank said that it expected the settlement to also resolve claims in 11 other related pending class actions.

In April 2017, the bank ordered Stumpf and former head of retail banking Carrie Tolstedt to return a total of USD $75 million in compensation for their ineffective oversight of sales conduct. Wells Fargo said it would "claw back" USD $28 million from Stumpf and seize USD $47 million in stock options from Tolstedt. This was in addition to USD $60 million that the pair had already agreed to give up.

On August 31, 2017, an external audit conducted by PwC revealed the total number of fictitious accounts to be around 3.5 million. The expanded third-party review examined more than 165 million retail banking accounts opened from January 2009 to September 2016.

A statement from Wells Fargo on this matter read: "The account review analyzed consumer and small business checking, savings, and unsecured credit card and line of credit account data to identify potentially unauthorized accounts." The firm further stated that due to the data-driven analysis that monitored account usage patterns, some authorized accounts opened with a customer's consent can exhibit similar account usage patterns. Therefore, some authorized accounts might have been identified as unauthorized.

In this instance, Wells Fargo agreed to reimburse an additional USD $2.8 million to its customers.

The PwC audit further conducted a review of online bill payment services, as required by the consent order of September 8, 2016. This part of the review revealed that approximately 528,000 customers were enrolled in potentially unauthorized online bill payment services in which they made an unauthorized introductory payment for an online service never used. However, Wells Fargo stated that it might be possible that the affected customers did in fact sign up for the online bill payment service and later decided not to use it. According to Wells Fargo, the customers who experienced the enrolment would be reimbursed USD $910,000.

On February 2, 2018, the US Federal Reserve (Fed) announced an enforcement action against Wells Fargo in response to "widespread consumer abuses and compliance breakdowns." The enforcement action restricted Wells Fargo from expanding beyond its total asset size at the end of 2017 and required the bank to replace four board members before the end of 2018. The action was to be terminated when the Fed judged Wells Fargo to have adequately strengthened its governance and risk management processes, including oversight by its board of directors.

On May 4, 2018, Wells Fargo announced that it had reached an agreement in principle to pay USD $480 million to settle a securities fraud class action lawsuit brought by shareholders who claimed that the bank had failed to disclose or had misstated the details of its sales practices in its financial statements. Asset manager Union Investment, lead plaintiff in the lawsuit, claimed that the inadequate disclosure had caused Wells Fargo's share price to be artificially inflated. Wells Fargo denied the claims, the *Financial Times* reports.

On October 18, 2018, Wells Fargo agreed to pay a USD $65 million penalty to the New York Attorney General for failing to disclose to investors that the success of its cross-sell efforts was built on systematic sales practice misconduct.

On December 28, 2018, the Iowa Attorney General announced a USD $575 million settlement between Wells Fargo and 50 states and the District of Columbia over the bank's violation of state consumer protection laws through its sales practices between October 15, 2005, and July 19, 2018. The sales practices in question included: creating unauthorized bank accounts; submitting insurance policy applications to Wells Fargo's partners without customers' consent, for which Wells Fargo would remediate over USD $1.1 million to customers; force-placing collateral protection insurance with vehicle finance customers, for which Wells Fargo anticipated paying remediation of more than USD $385 million; failing to provide refunds to which some customers were entitled on guaranteed asset/auto protection (GAP) products, for which remediation was expected to exceed USD $37 million; and charging unwarranted rate lock extension fees to residential mortgage borrowers, for which refunds of USD $100 million would be made.

ORX has not included the previous remediation and refunds in the overall loss amount as it is not clear whether these amounts are already included in the class action settlements and reimbursements listed above.

On February 27, 2019, Wells Fargo announced in an annual regulatory filing that it had entered into preliminary settlement discussions with the US Department of Justice (DoJ) and the US Securities and Exchange Commission (SEC) over its improper sales practices. Wells Fargo also confirmed that it had reached an agreement in principle to resolve a lawsuit alleging that current and former directors and officers of the bank had breached their fiduciary duty in failing to detect and prevent sales practices issues. Pursuant to the agreement, insurance carriers would pay Wells Fargo USD $240 million to cover the bank's damages, and the bank would pay the plaintiffs' attorneys' fees. As of February 27, 2019, it was not known how much the bank would contribute to the settlement of the case.

Wells Fargo also disclosed that several cases against it were ongoing. These included numerous shareholder derivative lawsuits alleging breach of fiduciary duty for failure to detect and prevent sales practices issues, multiple employment litigations, including an Employee Retirement Income Security (ERISA) class action, a class action of employees alleging they protested the misconduct and/or were terminated for failing to meet sales goals, various wage and hour class actions alleging that sales pressure resulted in uncompensated overtime, and multiple Sarbanes-Oxley Act complaints and state law whistleblower actions alleging adverse employment actions for raising sales practice misconduct issues.

On August 22, 2019, the Navajo Nation announced that Wells Fargo had agreed to pay USD $6.5 million over its "long campaign of predatory and unlawful practices that targeted and harmed the Navajo people." Reuters reports that the Navajo Nation sued Wells Fargo in federal and tribal courts in 2017, alleging that the bank opened unauthorized accounts for vulnerable tribe members.

On October 15, 2019, Wells Fargo announced in its Q3 earnings report that it had taken a USD $1.6 billion litigation charge. According to InvestmentNews, the charge related to sales malpractice lawsuits.

Wells Fargo has therefore paid and provisioned at least USD 3,062,210,000 for failures related to the opening of potentially unauthorized customer accounts, the potentially unauthorized set-up of online bill payment services, making unauthorized insurance policy applications, force-placing insurance policies, failing to provide refunds on GAP products and charging unwarranted mortgage fees as of October 15, 2019.

On January 23, 2020, the OCC announced that it had fined three former Wells Fargo executives a total of USD $21 million and issued notice charges against five others seeking USD $37.5 million.

The OCC found that the executives had failed to adequately perform their duties and responsibilities, which contributed to the creation of millions of unauthorized customer accounts. According to an OCC consent order, Stumpf failed to react to several warning signs, such as team complaints regarding pervasive sales pressure, fear of dismissal for not meeting unreasonable sales goals, and illegal and unethical sales activity across the bank.

The OCC fined Stumpf USD $17,500,000; Hope Hardison, the bank's former chief administrative officer and human resources director, USD $2,250,000; and Michael Loughlin, the bank's former chief risk officer, USD $1,250,000.

Additionally, as of January 23, 2020, the OCC was seeking:

USD 25,000,000 from Tolstedt
USD 5,000,000 from group risk officer Claudia Russ Anderson
USD 5,000,000 from general counsel James Strother
USD 2,000,000 from chief auditor David Julian
USD 500,000 from executive audit director Paul McLinko

On February 21, 2020, the DoJ and the SEC announced that Wells Fargo had agreed to pay a total of USD $3 billion as part of a deferred prosecution agreement. This agreement settles civil and criminal investigations brought by the DoJ and SEC into the pressuring of employees to meet unrealistic sales targets, resulting in millions of accounts or products being fraudulently opened on behalf of customers. Of the USD $3 billion, USD $500 million was paid to the SEC to remunerate investors.

The DoJ's allegations centered around the criminal liability Wells Fargo faced for falsifying bank records and identity theft. In the deferred prosecution agreement, Wells Fargo admitted that:

- Employees had created false records and forged customers' signatures on account opening documents to open accounts that were not authorized by customers.
- Employees had falsely created a PIN to activate unauthorized debit cards as the unrealistic sales targets rewarded employees for opening online banking profiles, which required a debit PIN to be set up.

- Employees had transferred funds to these unauthorized accounts to meet the bank's funding requirements. Employees either moved customer funds into these accounts or used their own funds or other methods to meet the requirements.
- Employees had submitted falsified consumer and business credit card applications using customers' names and personal identification.
- Employees had opened bill pay products without customer authorization.
- Employees had altered customers' contact information on the account opening documents so that the customers would not find out about the unauthorized accounts or to prevent Wells Fargo contacting the customers as part of a customer satisfaction survey.

Wells Fargo also admitted that executives had been aware of these practices since at least 2002 when a group of employees were fired from a branch in Colorado for these acts. Further, the bank admitted that senior executives knew that sales targets were too high and that employees were struggling to meet them, which resulted in employees' fraudulent activities. Despite knowing this, executives continued to set unrealistic sales targets every year until 2013 and employees continued to miss sales targets even though Wells Fargo had begun retroactively lowering sales targets after 2012.

The SEC's investigation centered around Wells Fargo and its misleading of investors. According to the SEC, Wells Fargo misled investors regarding the success of the core business strategy. Wells Fargo reportedly claimed that its strategy was needs-based. However, the SEC found that between 2012 and 2016, Wells Fargo had failed to disclose to investors that its sales model was instead volume-based and was causing widespread unlawful and unethical sales practices. The SEC ordered Wells Fargo to cease-and-desist from committing or causing any violation of Section 10(b) of the Exchange Act and ordered the bank to pay USD $500 million to investors.

In entering into the deferred prosecution agreement, the DoJ and SEC said that it had considered several factors, including Wells Fargo's cooperation with the authorities, and its admission of wrongdoing. The deferred prosecution agreement also meant that Wells Fargo would not be prosecuted for identity theft and creating false banking records, nor breaching the Financial Institutions Reform, Recovery and Enforcement Act of 1989 (FIRREA) or for breaching Section 10(b) and Rule 10b-5 of the Exchange Act. Prosecution on these matters was deferred for three years provided that Wells Fargo abides by certain agreements, including continued cooperation with the government's investigations.

On September 21, 2020, the OCC announced its settlements with three former Wells Fargo executives for their roles in the bank's systemic sales practices misconduct. The settlements included:

- A prohibition order and a USD $925,000 civil money penalty (CMP) to former Community Bank Group Finance Officer Matthew Raphaelson;
- A personal cease and desist order (PC&D) and a USD $400,000 CMP to former Head of Community Bank Deposit Products Group Kenneth Zimmerman; and a PC&D and a USD $350,000 CMP to former Head of Community Bank Human Resources Tracy Kidd.

The settlements are in addition to the actions the OCC announced on January 23, 2020, which included the issuance of a notice of charges against five other former senior bank executives and settlements with three others.

On November 13, 2020, the SEC announced that it had charged Stumpf and Tolstedt for their roles in allegedly misleading investors about the success of the Community Bank, Wells Fargo's core business. Stumpf agreed to pay a USD $2.5 million penalty and the SEC opened a litigated action for fraud against Tolstedt.

According to the SEC order against Stumpf, in 2015 and 2016 he signed and certified statements regarding Wells Fargo's cross-sell strategy and its reported metric, which he should have known were misleading.

The SEC complaint against Tolstedt alleged that from mid-2014 through mid-2016, Tolstedt publicly described and endorsed Wells Fargo's "cross-sell metric" as a means of measuring Wells Fargo's financial success despite the fact that this metric was inflated by accounts and services that were unused, unneeded, or unauthorized. Tolstedt was further accused of signing misleading subcertifications as to the accuracy of Wells Fargo's public disclosures when she knew or was reckless in not knowing that these disclosures were materially false and misleading.

On January 15, 2021, the OCC announced that it had fined Wells Fargo's former executive from the General Counsel, James Strother, USD $3.5 million for his role in the bank's systemic sales practices misconduct. The penalty also included a personal cease and desist order. The settlement is in addition to the settlements with six other former senior bank executives announced on January 23, 2020, and September 21, 2020.

On December 20, 2022, the CFPB ordered Wells Fargo to pay USD $3.89 billion in penalties and remediation over repeated violations across many of the bank's largest product lines and widespread management failures in relation to automobile loans, mortgage loans and deposit accounts. ORX News has allocated remediation amounts as updates to individual stories and covered the USD $1.7 billion penalty separately in digest 11172. Of the total USD $2.19 billion worth of redress ordered by the regulator, Wells Fargo would refund USD $506 million over issues covered in this digest concerning the servicing of consumer deposit accounts, including wrongful account freezes and the application of authorized-positive overdraft fees.

On March 15, 2023, the OCC announced it had issued a penalty of USD $17 million and a prohibition order against former executive Carrie Tolstedt for her responsibility in perpetuating the systemic sales practices misconduct at Wells Fargo. Tolstedt also pleaded guilty to obstructing an examination of the bank and was facing 16 months in prison.

On May 16, 2023, shareholder representatives announced a USD $1 billion settlement with Wells Fargo in a class action lawsuit alleging that the bank had misled investors. After the Fed, the OCC and the CFPB issued orders in 2018 against Wells Fargo over its misconduct, the bank assured investors that it was complying with the orders. In fact, regulators had rejected Wells Fargo's compliance plans, which were "missing key elements" and "so inadequate as to raise concerns about the company's leadership." Then-CEO Timothy Sloan falsely testified to the US Congress that the bank was complying with regulatory requirements. When the bank's misrepresentations were uncovered publicly, its stock price fell sharply. Shareholders claimed a loss of USD $54 billion in market capitalization due to false statements by bank executives and their inability to comply with the 2018 orders, further compounded by the extension of the asset cap imposed by the Fed.

On January 14, 2025, the OCC announced further settlements with three former Wells Fargo executives for their roles in the bank's systemic sales practices misconduct. The settlements included a prohibition order and a USD $10 million CMP to former group risk officer Claudia Russ Anderson; a PC&D and a USD $7 million CMP to former chief auditor David Julian; and a PC&D and a USD $1.5 million CMP to former executive audit director Paul McLinko.

The settlements were in addition to those the OCC reached with multiple other former senior bank executives in January 2020, September 2020, January 2021, and March 2023. Later, on April 25, 2025, the OCC announced that the CMPs issued to Julian and McLinko had been reduced to USD $100,000 and USD $50,000 respectively, following appeals.

On June 3, 2025, the Fed announced that it had removed the growth restrictions it imposed on Wells Fargo in February 2018. The regulator said that the bank had made substantial progress addressing its deficiencies in its governance and risk management program. The FT estimated that the asset cap caused Wells Fargo to lose out on an extra USD $9 billion each year in earnings and cost it nearly USD $120 billion in market capitalization. Reuters reported that the bank was to give a USD $2,000 award to each full-time employee to commemorate the accomplishment.

Courtesy of O.R.X. (www.orx.org)

Table 8.2 Wells Fargo Cross-Selling Case Study (From ORX)

Wells Fargo & Company	USD 7,568,210,000.00 | US Dollar
USD 7,568,210,000.00 | US Dollar	EUR 6,720,309,376.76 | Euro
BL0301—Retail Banking	EL0401—Suitability, Disclosure & Fiduciary
US—United States	North America
Loss Event	Published in media September 08, 2016

Bibliography

Basel Committee on Banking Supervision. *Principles for the Sound Management of Operational Risk.* Basel, Switzerland: Bank for International Settlements, June 2011. https://www.bis.org/publ/bcbs195.htm.

Basel Committee on Banking Supervision. *Corporate Governance Principles for Banks.* Basel, Switzerland: Bank for International Settlements, July 2015. https://www.bis.org/publ/bcbs294.htm.

Basel Committee on Banking Supervision. *Revision to the Principles for the Sound Management of Operational Risk.* March 2021. https://www.bis.org/bcbs/publ/d515.pdf.

Board of Governors of the Federal Reserve System. *Enhanced Prudential Standards for Bank Holding Companies and Foreign Banking Organizations (Regulation YY).* Washington, DC: Federal Reserve, February 2014. https://www.govinfo.gov/content/pkg/FR-2014-03-27/pdf/2014-05699.pdf.

European Banking Authority. *Final Report on Guidelines for Internal Governance* - EBA/GL/2021/05). London: European Banking Authority, June 2021. https://www.eba.europa.eu/publications-and-media/press-releases/eba-publishes-its-final-guidelines-internal-governance.

European Banking Authority. *Supervision Newsletter: Strong Risk Culture - Sound Banks*. February 15, 2023. https://www.bankingsupervision.europa.eu/press/supervisory-newsletters/newsletter/2023/html/ssm.nl230215_3.en.html.

Federal Aviation Administration (FAA). *Expert Panel Review*. February 2024. https://www.faa.gov/newsroom/Sec103_ExpertPanelReview_Report_Final.pdf

Financial Conduct Authority. *Transforming Culture in Financial Services. Discussion Paper DP 18/2*. March 2018. https://www.fca.org.uk/publication/discussion/dp18-02.pdf.

Financial Conduct Authority. *FCA Handbook. Conduct Rules*. https://www.handbook.fca.org.uk/handbook/COCON/2/?view=chapter.

Financial Stability Board. *Guidance on Supervisory Interaction with Financial Institutions on Risk Culture: A Framework for Assessing Risk Culture*. April 7, 2014. https://www.fsb.org/uploads/140407.pdf.

KPMG. *Translating Risk Culture into Action*. New York: KPMG International, April 4, 2025. https://kpmg.com/be/en/home/insights/2025/04/rr-translating-risk-culture-into-action.html.

Office of the Comptroller of the Currency. *Heightened Standards for Large Banks: Guidelines Establishing Minimum Standards for Risk Governance*. Washington, DC: OCC, September 2014. https://www.occ.gov/newsissuances/federalregister/2014/79fr54518.pd f.

Washington Post. *Boeing Engineer Set to Testify on 787 Dreamliner Quality Issues*. April 17, 2024. https://www.washingtonpost.com/transportation/2024/04/17/boeing-whistleblower-787-dreamliner/.

Chapter 9

The Fourth Line: Managing Regulatory Risks

The Regulatory Climate

There is a lot of uncertainty concerning the regulatory environment in the United States at the time that I am drafting this book. The Consumer Financial Protection Bureau (CFPB), which was created on the heels of the Great Credit Crisis with the sole focus on consumer protection, has been defunded. The SEC has withdrawn the climate disclosure rule, and both the OCC and Federal Reserve have removed reputation risk from their supervisory frameworks. Basel III Endgame (see Chapter 1) has been stalled in the United States, and some think it is essentially dead. The overall tone in the United States is one focused on deregulation and growth.

The United Kingdom has been ahead of the United States in its focus on a pro-growth agenda with the introduction of the Edinburgh Reforms in December 2022. The exit from the European Union provided the United Kingdom with the opportunity to review its regulations and determine how to pose itself for growth without the obligations of the European Union's regulatory regime. The Edinburgh Reforms consist of 31 measures that were designed to revise and update the United Kingdom's financial regime post-Brexit. The overall focus is on a more agile regulatory regime that promotes growth in the country, with a focus on proportionality of regulation. The country's regulatory regime continues to have pillars in place to protect consumers and remains committed to climate reform and net zero goals.

The European Union is still full steam ahead in terms of its regulatory regime and has introduced several "weighty" regulations related to AI and data protection. (See the interview with an industry veteran and former regulator at the end of this chapter.) Together these acts promise to enhance risk management and set standards not just in the European Union but for global firms operating in the region, as well as influence worldwide risk management. Even if your organization does not operate in the European Union, it would be a strong practice to map to the key provisions of its acts, to determine where you may want to enhance your risk management programs.

The following sections are an overview of two recent critical EU regulations that are focused on managing emerging risks.

Digital Operational Resilience Act (DORA)

Dora was designed to encompass management of operational resilience broadly, with a focus on information and communication technology (ICT). The act went into force in January 2025 and requires financial institutions to safeguard their institutions against ICT-related events. The act includes requirements for notifying regulators of incidents (see Chapter 6). The act, however, is designed to put in place a framework for proactively preventing such incidents from occurring. The pillars of DORA include the following:

- **ICT risk management:** Establishes the framework for managing ICT risks. Stipulates that financial institutions shall have a "sound, comprehensive and well-documented ICT risk management framework," which includes strategies, policies, procedures, ICT protocols, and tools to protect the information and ICT assets of the firm. Risk management provisions also include the importance of establishing and maintaining an internal governance framework to manage ICT risk, including oversight and support by senior management.
- **ICT-related incidents:** Establishes a framework for defining, establishing and implementing an incident management process focused on detection, management, and notification of ICT-related incidents. Includes requirement to establish procedures for consistent identification, classification, and monitoring of events; determining criticality and severity; and ensuring root causes are identified. Requires informing senior management and eternal stakeholders of significant events, including the "relevant competent authority."
- **Digital and operational resilience testing:** Provides guidance on risk-based testing, including "vulnerability assessments and scans, open-source analyses, network security assessments, gap analyses, physical security reviews, questionnaires and scanning software solutions, source code reviews where feasible, scenario-based tests, compatibility testing, performance testing, end-to-end testing and penetration testing." Stipulates that the testing should be undertaken by internal or external independent parties.

- **ICT third-party risk management:** Establishes requirements for monitoring and contracting with third parties following a risk-based approach that accounts for the "nature, scale, complexity and importance of ICT-related dependencies." This includes the potential impact on the availability of the contracted services and concentration risks incurred when contracting with third parties and any sub-outsourcing relationships that they may have. Also stipulates that contracts with third-party providers should include requirements for transparency and allow for "access, inspection and audit rights."
- **ICT information sharing:** Provides guidance for sharing intelligence on cyber threats among financial institutions, including "indicators of compromise, tactics, techniques, and procedures, cyber security alerts and configuration tools." The purpose is to enhance overall systemic resilience and to raise awareness in the industry of current and emerging threats.

Source: https://eur-lex.europa.eu/legal-content/EN/TXT/?uri=uriserv%3AOJ.L_.2022.333.01.0001.01.ENG&toc=OJ%3AL%3A2022%3A333%3AFULL

EU Artificial Intelligence Act

The European Union published the text of the first of its kind Artificial Intelligence Act in July 2024 in the Official Journal of the European Union. The act serves as a strong framework for global financial institutions as they work on framing standards for managing the operational risks associated with AI. Existing frameworks may not be nimble and robust enough to account for rapidly changing risks associated with the use of a technology that is by its very nature generative. The act is being rolled out in stages, with most of its provisions expected to be in place by August 2026.

The act includes the following key points:

- **Risk-based:** The AI Act classifies AI according to its level of risk, and high-risk activities are deemed unacceptable. Prohibited activities include those designed to distort behavior or impair decision-making, causing significant harm; exploiting vulnerabilities related to age, disability, or socio-economic circumstances; biometric systems designed to infer sensitive attributes such as race, political opinions, religious affiliation, sex orientation; social scoring; assessing the risk of an individual committing criminal offenses; compiling facial recognition databases from the Internet or CCTV footage; inferring emotions in workplaces; real-time biometric identification by law enforcement except in certain law enforcement related circumstances.
- **Risk management:** The act stipulates that a risk management system should be in place to manage high-risk AI throughout its lifecycle. This includes implementing data governance protocols; drafting technical documentation; recording events relevant for identifying national level risks; providing instructions for use to downstream deployers; designing the high-risk AI system to allow for human oversight and for achieving appropriate level of accuracy, robustness and cybersecurity; and establishing a quality management system to ensure compliance.

- **Responsible developers:** The majority of obligations fall on developers of high-risk AI systems. This includes developers based in the European Union or a third country where the AI system's output is used in the European Union.
- **Responsible users:** Users that deploy AI systems in a professional capacity (not affected end users) have some obligations, although this is less than the developers. This applies to users in the European Union and those in a third country where AI system's output is used in the European Union.
- **General-purpose AI:** All providers of general-purpose models must provide the requisite technical documentation associated with use and development of the model, including training content. If the models present systemic risk, model evaluations and adversarial testing should be conducted and serious incidents tracked and reported.

Source: https://artificialintelligenceact.eu

The regulatory pendulum swings in cycles, from a tightly wound regulatory regime as was experienced in the aftermath of the Great Credit Crisis to one that is less restrictive and more focused on allowing for growth. This is a result of political pressure from the current administration in power and industry lobbying. The swings can happen quite rapidly, as during just two years there has been a major shift in the United States in the wake of the failure of Silicon Valley Bank and the call for more regulation of smaller entities to the current climate of deregulation.

What the current US regime has in common with the United Kingdom and the European Union is the concept of proportionality. The Edinburgh Reforms were drafted with consideration of size and complexity of regulated entities, while there are provisions in DORA for smaller institutions. The concept of proportionality ensures that regulations are tailored to the size, complexity, risk profile, and systemic importance of an institution, with the most stringent requirements reserved for the largest banks. Its main goal is to avoid overburdening smaller or less complex firms, while ensuring that larger or riskier firms are subject to stricter regulatory requirements.

Proportionality has been central to the US Federal Reserve's tier system, with the highest requirements related to stress testing, single counter-party credit limits, and liquidity reserved for the Global Systemically Important Banks (GSIBs). These include the big four banks in the United States (JPMorgan Chase, Bank of America, Wells Fargo, Citibank) plus four additional institutions (State Street, Morgan Stanley, Bank of New York Mellon, and Goldman Sachs). These are essentially the US-based organizations that are deemed "too big to fail" and require the most stringent regulatory oversight.

The Prudential Regulatory Authority in the United Kingdom introduced the concept of a "strong and simple" framework for nonsystemic banks and building societies that is designed to simplify the prudential requirements for these smaller institutions. This applies to financial institutions that have total assets on average over the past three years that are no more than £20 billion; operate domestically; have limited trading activity; do not use Internal-Ratings Based (IRB) models; do not provide clearing, transaction settlement, custody, or correspondent banking services; and do not have a foreign parent.

The following is a summary table of the primary regulatory regimes we have discussed in the United States, United Kingdom, and European Union:

Region	Regulator	Approach	Primary Responsibility
US	Federal Reserve (Fed)	Risk-based, safety, and soundness	Monetary policy, supervision of bank holding companies and systemic risk; primary regulator for foreign banks operating in the United States (FBOs)
US	Office of the Comptroller of the Currency (OCC)	Rules-based, safety, and soundness	Supervision of nationally chartered banks; primary regulator for US-domiciled banks
US	Federal Deposit Insurance Corporation (FDIC)	Deposit insurance, resolution-focused	Insures deposits and resolves failed banks; primary regulator for smaller banks (with assets under $10 billion)
UK	Prudential Regulation Authority (PRA)	Prudential, safety and soundness	Supervision of banks, insurers, and major investment firms
UK	Financial Conduct Authority (FCA)	Conduct and consumer protection	Market conduct, consumer protection, and competition
EU	European Central Bank (ECB)	Direct supervision of eurozone banks via SSM	Supervises significant euro area banks under Single Supervisory Mechanism (SSM)
EU	European Banking Authority (EBA)	Harmonized rule-making and supervisory convergence	Develops banking rules and conducts EU-wide stress testing

Managing Regulatory Relationships

Regulators are important stakeholders. The regulators can be considered the fourth line of defense (see the following discussion on the fourth line of defense) in the management of operational risk. Although they are independent of the in-house business, risk, and audit teams, they are critical partners. They observe practices in a variety of organizations and can provide a unique perspective on the industry. Developing a strong and mutually respectful relationship with one's home regulators (and host regulators in global institutions) is one of the most important responsibilities of any risk management team. The regulators ultimately have the same mission as the internal risk teams to protect an organization's safety and soundness through strong risk management.

Building a mutually respectful relationship with regulators starts with proactive and transparent communication. This includes formal regular briefings on current and emerging risks. I would meet with my prudential regulators at least quarterly and walk through the operational risk reports that I had prepared for the operational risk and enterprise risk committees and the risk committee of the board. The regulators had access to these materials, but my regular meetings were an opportunity to provide a picture of the overall operational risk landscape.

It is imperative to respond to regulatory requests in a timely manner, which is usually within two or three days. The response should be complete and address the request directly and without obfuscation. If an event occurs where the regulator is required to be informed, such as a data breach (see Chapter 7 for notification requirements), it is important to respect the required notification timelines. However, this type of notification should not be done unilaterally and should be with involvement of the regulatory affairs department (if there is one), the executive in charge of regulatory affairs, compliance, or legal.

Preparing for regulatory exams can be a very intense experience, especially when there are multiple regulatory exams happening at the same time. As mentioned in Chapter 8, one of the first requests associated with an exam will likely be for policies, standards, and procedures. The regulators will check if the policy framework is adequate to manage the organization's risk, but also if it is being implemented. From my experience, the regulators will look to the policy owners for their insight into how it is being implemented and where potential gaps may reside.

Many organizations have centralized regulatory functions, which help manage the exams and function as the first level of communication with examiners when they have specific requests. I have witnessed a variety of practices, with regulators reaching out directly to the risk teams or the business or going through the regulatory affairs office. Regulatory affairs functions are staffed with dedicated regulatory subject-matter experts and often lawyers, who can provide a great deal of support and insight when interacting with a regulatory team. They assist with managing complicated exams and track the status of the myriad requests for documents that inevitably come through.

The tenor of a regulatory relationship is especially important in jurisdictions like the United States, where many of the regulations are open to interpretation. This is especially true for operational risk. For instance, there is no specific regulation that says a risk and control self-assessment (RCSA) must be performed. The OCC's Heightened Standards and the Federal Reserve's Enhanced Prudential Standards (Regulation YY) require banks to identify their risks. But when I was asked by a senior executive to name the specific US regulation that requires an institution to perform an RCSA, my response was very nuanced.

The US prudential regulators primarily supervise operational risk through handbooks and published guidance. This includes the Interagency Guidance on Third Party Risk (2023), which documents the third-party risk management lifecycle that many organizations have adopted, the OCC's Large Bank Supervision Handbook, the OCC's New, Modified or Expanded Bank Products and Services Bulletin, and the Federal Reserve's Supervisory Guidance on Model Risk (SR Letter 11-7).

These bulletins and handbooks do not comprise precise regulation. They provide strong guidance for establishing risk management frameworks, but how they are implemented can be interpreted differently. This makes it especially important to communicate with the supervisory team on the ground concerning their expectations and to have established a mutually respectful relationship.

The quality of regulatory communication is critical when responding to formal regulatory findings. When drafting the remediation plan, you should clarify the regulator's expectations for how you can close their identified issues. Many regulatory teams will not opine directly on your remediation approach, but it is important to understand what their concerns are and how you can address the root cause. It is also important to walk them through your remediation plan, even if they are not going to give you specific feedback (although some regulators will). If there are any ambiguities in the language of the formal findings, and sometimes the language is not precise, it is important to seek clarity ahead of designing action plans.

It is a strong practice to share remediation progress with the regulators on a regular basis. Again, it comes down to constant and consistent communication. The worse outcome is to complete a remediation and to discover that there was a disconnect with what the regulators had expected. This also holds true when there is a change with a regulatory team. If this happens midway through a remediation, it is important to walk through the plan with the new team and ensure they are comfortable with the approach.

Audit teams can provide significant support when working on regulatory remediations, because they are often the first level of validation ahead of turning in a closure package of materials to the regulators. They can provide insight into the interpretation of regulatory expectations, and they should be comfortable with the remediation plan that they will validate. It is equally painful to complete a remediation plan and to discover that it was not what an audit envisioned and will fail their validation.

The response to a regulatory finding should be comprehensive. In the long run, it does not protect the organization and is not a strong risk management practice to respond to the finding in the narrowest manner possible. Of course, you also do not want to respond broadly and sweep in more than is required or can be responded to within the required timeframe. It is important to respond in a way that addresses the root cause of the issue and closes any control gaps.

I have heard some risk teams complain that they received regulatory findings that they do not agree with or were the result of a misunderstanding on the part of the regulator. Communication is important in these circumstances, but sometimes there is not much to be done except to address the required remediation. It is hoped that this can be avoided if the channels of communication are open all along the way (see the discussion on the fourth line of defense that emphasizes strong communication).

Many organizations track regulatory remediations through their existing issue management programs, although many have heightened approval requirements for regulatory issues. This will include the development of action plans, which will require audit and second-line approval before the remediation begins. Some organizations will require approval by the chief risk officer and chief compliance officer for action plans that are designed to address high-risk regulatory findings. Progress on the action plans should be tracked by the impacted business management, regulatory affairs, and operational risk, and any delays or challenges should be escalated through the committee structure (see Chapter 8).

Consent order and formal censures require an additional level of scrutiny. They are often monitored through risk and regulatory committees and forums. If they are serious enough, as in the case of a consent order that addresses multiple risk management failings, a special executive committee will be formed to monitor progress. The board will also want to be kept abreast of progress addressing consent orders and censures. Regulators routinely meet with the board of directors to provide their overall view of risk management within the organization and their assessment on progress of material findings. The board should be fully informed of any challenges or missed remediation deadlines before this happens.

It is important to work across the lines of defense in managing a regulatory engagement program. The regulators will often want to meet with the first line during exams or regular meetings to gain an understanding of how they are implementing the operational risk framework and if they have a good grasp of the risk and control environment. They often require that these meetings occur without the presence of the second line. It is helpful to make sure ahead of these meetings that there is consistent messaging and documentation. The regulators will pick up on inconsistent messages. Of course, each line of defense will have its own perspective, but they should have a consistent view on their most material risks and the efficacy of their controls.

This is also where regulatory affairs can play a strong role in managing regulatory exams and bringing the key parties together through pre-exam exercises, where the messaging is assessed for consistency. It is a strong practice to maintain a regulatory playbook that covers the exam process, including preparing for exams and response procedures.

Tracking Regulatory Changes

A critical responsibility for an operational risk function is the tracking of regulatory changes. Financial institutions are expected to maintain regulatory inventories that track obligations and include mappings to the relevant businesses and functions. This process is often owned by compliance. I have received in my operational risk roles quarterly lists of new regulations that I was required to review and determine if they have operational risk impact. Any changes that impacted operational risk required an assessment of current policies, standards, and procedures to determine if updates were required.

Operational risk can also play a role in assisting compliance with mapping regulations to RCSA processes so that they can be assessed for their control effectiveness. Most compliance functions have programs in place that test for compliance with regulations. By linking this effort to RCSA processes, it is possible to assess the compliance controls directly. It leads to a more efficient process for determining the effectiveness of compliance controls and allows for aligned risk identification. It is not a good outcome, when the RCSA and compliance testing programs have different views of certain risks. For instance, I have witnessed RCSA and compliance risk assessments that went to the board with different views of compliance risks. In this instance, the board asked for everyone to go back and agree on one view of risk.

There is a lot of interesting work going on in the industry in the regulation mapping space. Several firms have come to market with AI-driven solutions that make what was once a painful, manual process more efficient.

Regulatory Expectations

The Basel Committee on Banking Supervision originally introduced its "Principles for the Sound Management of Operational Risk" in 2003. A notable update was released in 2011 that incorporated the lessons from the great financial crisis. The 2011 version was my "bible" for a long time when I was establishing and implementing operational risk programs. The Basel Committee updated the principles in 2021 with the recognition that ICT had not been previously covered. As is the case with many of the Basel guidance documents, they are relevant across disciplines and provide strong industry guidelines for all types of enterprises that have operational risk at their core (which is all of them!).

The following 12 principles are from the 2021 guidance that provide a roadmap for assessing an organization's operational risk program against regulatory expectations:

Principle 1: *The board of directors should take the lead in establishing a strong risk management, culture, implemented by senior management. 11 The board of directors and senior management should establish a corporate culture guided by strong risk management, set standards and incentives for professional and responsible behaviour, and ensure that staff receives appropriate risk management and ethics training.*

Principle 2: *Banks should develop, implement and maintain an operational risk management framework that is fully integrated into the bank's overall risk management processes. The ORMF adopted by an individual bank will depend on a range of factors, including the bank's nature, size, complexity and risk profile.*

Principle 3: *The board of directors should approve and periodically review the operational risk management framework, and ensure that senior management implements the policies, processes and systems of the operational risk management framework effectively at all decision levels.*

Principle 4: *The board of directors should approve and periodically review a risk appetite and tolerance statement for operational risk that articulates the nature, types and levels of operational risk the bank is willing to assume.*

Principle 5: *Senior management should develop for approval by the board of directors a clear, effective and robust governance structure with well-defined, transparent and consistent lines of responsibility. Senior management is responsible for consistently implementing and maintaining throughout the organisation policies, processes and systems for managing operational risk in all of the bank's material products, activities, processes and systems consistent with the bank's risk appetite and tolerance statement.*

Principle 6: *Senior management should ensure the comprehensive identification and assessment of the operational risk inherent in all material products, activities, processes and systems to make sure the inherent risks and incentives are well understood.*

Principle 7: *Senior management should ensure that the bank's change management process is comprehensive, appropriately resourced and adequately articulated between the relevant lines of defence.*

Principle 8: *Senior management should implement a process to regularly monitor operational risk profiles and material operational exposures. Appropriate reporting mechanisms should be in* *place at the board of directors, senior management, and business unit levels to support proactive management of operational risk.*

Principle 9: *Banks should have a strong control environment that utilises policies, processes and systems; appropriate internal controls; and appropriate risk mitigation and/or transfer strategies.*

Principle 10: *Banks should implement a robust ICT (Information and Communication Technology) risk management programme in alignment with their operational risk management framework.*

Principle 11: *Banks should have business continuity plans in place to ensure their ability to operate on an ongoing basis and limit losses in the event of a severe business disruption. Business continuity plans should be linked to the bank's operational risk management framework.*

Principle 12: *A bank's public disclosures should allow stakeholders to assess its approach to operational risk management and its operational risk exposure.*

Source: Revision to the Principles for the Sound Management of Operational Risk (March 2021) https://www.bis.org/bcbs/publ/d515.htm

The Four Lines of Defense Model

The Bank of International Settlements Financial Stability Institute (FSI) published a paper in 2015 that introduced the concept of a four lines of defense model, which incorporated regulators and external auditors into the overall control framework. The FSB argued that the three lines of defense model (see Chapters 3 and 8) could be improved. Specifically, the FSI report identified the following weaknesses in a three lines of defense model:

- Misaligned incentives for risk-takers in the first line of defense
- Lack of organizational independence of functions in the second line of defense
- Lack of skills and expertise in second-line functions
- Inadequate and subjective risk assessment performed by internal audits

The FSI proposed its alternative model to address the "deficiencies" that it perceived in the three lines of defense model by assigning specific roles to regulators and external auditors. Instead of ignoring the role these external parties play, they incorporated them into the internal control system, while acknowledging that they remain external to an organization. This model was specifically developed for highly regulated bank entities but would apply to any regulated industry.

The advantage with this model, according to the FSI's "Four Lines of Defense Report," is more streamlined communication between the internal and external parties and an extra level of assurance by external auditors that the regulatory supervisors could leverage for their assessments. The report indicates that an additional advantage is "an improvement to the tools and methods that could be used by supervisors in order to intensify their oversight of financial institutions, aiming at delivering preemptive, rather than reactive and outcome-based supervision." The report further states that with "improved communication channels with internal audit, supervisors might be provided with useful and reliable information to support their judgments and enable them to be more forward-looking in their assessments of risk."

Enhanced communication and more aligned information gathering among the three lines of defense and external parties, and especially the third line, external auditors, and external regulators, would be a good outcome, as a disconnect with a supervisory team, especially in the context of responding to regulatory findings, can be painful if the feedback comes late in the remediation process. There is an opportunity today, with the shift toward lighter regulations and a focus on growth for the relationships between the three lines and regulators to consider a more collaborative approach. This is a line, of course, regulators would have to walk in terms of maintaining their independence, and the internal functions would have to trust that establishing a more collaborative relationship with their supervisors will not have unintended consequences.

The four lines of defense in essence exist today, although in a less prescribed model than what the FSI has proposed. It is worth mentioning that regulators often rely as their "first line of defense" on validation by a financial institution's internal audit department before they evaluate a regulatory deliverable. A remediation package will not be turned into a regulator in many institutions if it has failed audit validation. Regulators also have access on an ongoing basis to committee materials, risk assessment results, issues, and audit reports.

Seeking Help

It is possible that an organization that has received a regulatory finding, consent order, or censure will require additional resources in terms of both subject-matter expertise and capacity. This may require the hiring of a consulting firm or an individual consultant for assistance. Organizations deal differently with regulatory communication when they hire consultants, with some highlighting the addition of experts with industry perspective who will assist with remediating findings according to industry standards. Other organizations prefer to focus on their internal capabilities. The hiring of consultants, however, like all matters regarding regulatory findings, should be disclosed. It is how they are positioned to regulators that may vary according to circumstances and organizational preference.

When hiring either a consulting firm or an independent consultant through industry contacts or companies that specialize in outsourcing, the following factors should be considered:

- Do the consultants assigned to the project, or the independent consultant, have the required knowledge and background to provide the requisite industry perspective?
- Have they worked on similar projects? Have they assisted with closing enforcement actions?
- What type of safeguards will the consultant put in place to protect firm and customer (if relevant) data?
- How familiar are the consultants with the relevant regulations and the specific regulators that issued the findings?

- Will they provide proper training and transfer of knowledge when the project concludes?
- Do they have any conflicts related to working with multiple clients?
- Will the pricing model be a fixed fee or an hourly rate?

The closure package should include a list of sustainability factors to demonstrate that the remediation solution will "stick." (See Chapter 6 for issue management closure packages and sustainability factors.) An organization that has hired outside consultants for assistance with closing a regulatory finding will want to demonstrate that the "fix" is sustainable and they have the appropriate internal resources, subject-matter expertise, and budget to sustain the effort. One of the worse outcomes is to receive a repeat regulatory finding a few years after the initial one was closed, due to a drift in focus or pullback from dedicated resources to support the enhanced controls. Repeat regulatory findings can end up in consent orders, and repeat consent orders can result in fines and penalties and sustained reputational consequences.

Confidential Supervisory Information

All employees who interact with US regulators, engage in remediating regulatory findings, and have access to regulatory information in regulated US financial organizations must understand the requirements related to the handling of Confidential Supervisory Information (CSI). The United Kingdom has similar restrictions, as outlined in the Financial Services and Markets Act.

The US regulators, including the Federal Reserve, OCC and FDIC, have defined CSI accordingly:

> *Confidential supervisory information means nonpublic information that is exempt from disclosure pursuant to 5 U.S.C. 552(b)(8) and includes information that is or was created or obtained in furtherance of the Board's supervisory, investigatory, or enforcement activities, including activities conducted by a Federal Reserve Bank (Reserve Bank) under delegated authority, relating to any supervised financial institution, and any information derived from or related to such information. Examples of confidential supervisory information include, without limitation, reports of examination, inspection, and visitation; confidential operating and condition reports; supervisory assessments; investigative requests for documents or other information; and supervisory correspondence or other supervisory communications. Additionally, any portion of a document in the possession of any person, entity, agency or authority, including a supervised financial institution, that contains or would reveal confidential supervisory information is confidential supervisory information.*
>
> *Source:* https://www.law.cornell.edu/cfr/text/12/261.2

Regulatory approval is required ahead of sharing CSI with external parties. The following is the OCC's guidance on the sharing of confidential information:

> *OCC regulations provide that nonpublic OCC information is the property of the OCC (see 12 CFR 4.32(b)(2)). This information may not be disclosed without the prior written permission of the OCC, except in very limited circumstances (see 12 CFR 4.36(d) and 4.37(b)). The circumstances for release of nonpublic OCC information may include disclosure to a parent holding company, director, officer, attorney, auditor, or other specified third party, to the extent consistent with the OCC's regulations (see 12 CFR 4.37(b)(2)).*

Any person who discloses or uses nonpublic information except as expressly permitted by the OCC or as provided by the OCC's regulations may be subject to the criminal penalties provided in 18 USC 641. This legal prohibition on the release of nonpublic OCC information applies to all financial institutions supervised by the OCC.

Source: https://www.occ.gov/news-issuances/bulletins/2019/bulletin-2019-15.html

Violating CSI regulations can lead to fines and penalties and reputational damage. The Federal Reserve issued an enforcement action against the Industrial and Commercial Bank of China Ltd and its New York branch in January 2024 for the unauthorized use and disclosure of CSI. The Federal Reserve fined the bank $2.4 million, and the New York Department of Financial Services issued an additional $30 million penalty. The Federal Reserve enforcement action accused the bank of "unauthorized use and disclosure of confidential supervisory information." The Federal Reserve action also stated that the bank's New York branch "lacked any formal policies, procedures, training, or other internal controls designed to instruct employees regarding how to properly handle CSI or how to prevent the unauthorized dissemination and use of CSI; whereas, after receiving confirmation from Board and Reserve Bank staff that proposed communications with a third party included CSI and would therefore require a waiver from the Board prior to disclosure, the Bank and Branch nonetheless caused the unauthorized, and therefore impermissible, disclosure of CSI to occur."

Source: https://www.federalreserve.gov/newsevents/pressreleases/files/enf20240119a1.pdf

Abiding by CSI requirements when working in the US branch of a foreign banking organization can require special finesse and understanding of how global regulators interact. The censure of the Industrial and Commercial Bank of China was the result of the bank sharing information with a foreign regulator without securing permission from the Federal Reserve and New York Department of Financial Services. This is an important nuance to be cognizant of when sharing reports with foreign regulators, which may require scrubbing of any mention of US regulatory findings.

Goldman Sachs also found itself the recipient of a Federal Reserve censure in August 2016 resulting from its "unauthorized use and disclosure of confidential supervisory information." The Federal Reserve fined Goldman $36.3 million over the issue. The Fed also instituted enforcement proceedings against a former Managing Director with the bank for improper usage of CSI in presentations to current and prospective clients to win business. The regulator found that the bank lacked "sufficient policies, procedures, or adequate employee training" to ensure compliance with CSI regulations.

Every regulated organization should have a program in place to manage CSI, which includes the following:

- **Governance:** Policy or directive and procedures that include the responsibilities for managing CSI. These documents can be owned by regulatory affairs (if the function exists), compliance, or enterprise or operational risk management.
- **Training:** Regular training on CSI for all employees to reinforce the importance of adhering to the requirements and consequences associated with violations. It is a

strong practice to offer the training annually. The training can be offered by regulatory affairs, compliance, or enterprise or operational risk management.

- **Assessment of CSI risks and controls:** CSI risks and controls should be assessed through RCSA, compliance testing, and, if managed separately, compliance risk assessment.
- **Segregation of information:** CSI should be segregated from other data and handled with enhanced controls. All reports that contain CSI should be labeled clearly.
- **Compliance and risk reports:** Progress on regulatory findings that are included in compliance, risk and board reports, and any mention of CSI should be excised before the reports are shared with foreign regulators. There should be a process in place to scrub these reports ahead of submission.
- **Regulatory permission:** A process should be in place to receive regulatory permission ahead of sharing CSI with external parties, including external consultants, advisors, and regulators.
- **Consult:** Legal, compliance, and/or regulatory affairs should be consulted if in doubt about sharing CSI with any external party.

Interview with Industry Veteran on Managing Regulatory Risk: Tom Balogh

Tom Balogh is an experienced risk professional who spent 10 years working as a UK regulatory in telecommunications and financial services and 13 years as a consultant. He recently started a new position as the chief risk officer with a UK real estate firm.

1. **Question**
   From your time as a regulator, what were the most common weaknesses you observed in how financial institutions managed regulatory risk? Were there recurring themes that you observed?
   Answer
   I believe the most critical weakness is the lack of open and transparent engagement. This can lead to skepticism by regulators and ultimately, more intrusiveness, which has creates additional regulatory burdens and costs. This also means there can be a financial incentive for being open and engaging with regulators. If they trust you, they are more likely to give you space to remediate without ongoing supervision (such as consent orders or monitors) which means financial impacts can be less onerous and require fewer remediation resources.

   One of the recurring themes that I have noticed over the years is the lack of a clear home and ownership for regulatory relations. Often, responding to regulatory inquiries or even findings do not land with the people who understand the risk the best and where formal regulatory affairs functions do exist, they often act as a "post office" which delayed responses. Timing counts, and it's important to have the right person available on a timely basis who knows the business and the risk.

2. **Question**
What does "effective regulatory engagement" look like from a regulator's perspective?
Answer
When there is a material event, timing in terms of regulatory notification and speed of engagement is critical. It's important to get ahead of the papers. This goes back to what I originally said about openness and trust. Building a trusted relationship with a regulatory is critical. When a regulator reads something in the papers, before they have been told by the firm, can really damage that trust and it takes a long time to build it back up.

3. **Question**
How should firms balance proactive regulatory engagement with the need to manage reputational and legal exposure?
Answer
I just mentioned openness, speed of engagement, and transparency, which are all important toward developing a trusted relationship with a regulator. But of course, as in all things, there is a balance. You will want to engage senior management and legal when notifications are required. But some lawyers are very conservative in what should be shared with a regulator. I have always reminded them that the rules tend to favor the regulator, and they must be notified of any issues within a reasonable timeframe.

The balancing needs to be determined on a case-by-case basis, and it is also important to not set hares running, but timeliness is key when critical issues arise.

4. **Question**
How do you see the use of technology and data analytics transforming regulatory compliance and risk management? Are there emerging expectations from regulators regarding the use of RegTech or AI in compliance programs?
Answer
This is an exciting time, and I am looking forward to seeing how it unfolds. It may be a scary for someone just entering financial services, like a junior compliance person to see what AI can do.

But I am hopeful that what they will lose are the tedious tasks that no one really wants to do. This should lead to more interesting roles in the long term as human judgment and intervention becomes ever more important. For example, KYC and Transaction Monitoring seem ripe for AI because they can translate weaker signals into strong ones and provide direction on where to look for anomalies. AI can also help with sorting through the relevant rules, turn them into obligations and scan a policy against relevant regulations. These are all examples of where jobs that used to take large numbers of inexperienced people could be reduced to a few intelligent people undertaking quality checking.

As for regulatory expectations, I think there is both an expectation that technology is used (intelligently) and concern related to its risk. There is certainly the expectation that it is used in the market abuse and surveillance space. There is also a huge focus on using technology appropriately to manage cyber risk. But at the end of the day, many regulators are focused on outcomes rather than how firms achieve them, so it is up to firms to decide.

5. **Question**
   What advice would you give to operational risk professionals on navigating today's evolving global regulatory landscape?
   Answer
   Regardless of which direction the regulatory pendulum swings, understanding that managing operational risk is not at its core about managing to regulations, but rather good risk management which provides an organization with a business advantage. This is an important concept at a time when you can't rely on a regulator to force a firm to give you budget. We are currently on a deregulatory swing, but the past 20 years have taught us that deregulation can lead to conduct issues which can be costly in terms of fines, penalties, losses and reputational harm.

   So, currently we see some pullback in the United Kingdom on regulations. It might be less ideologically motivated than in the United States, but the focus is currently on allowing for growth. At the same time, the post-Brexit United Kingdom is still mostly aligned with the European Union, which limits the potential for change and the focus is not on getting rid of compliance requirements but trying (perhaps not very successfully) to reduce some of the red tape.

   For foreign organizations doing business in the European Union, there are some weighty EU regulations that they must abide by which are setting the standards globally. This includes AI and crypto regulations, which are big and weighty. I suppose this might make specializing in EU regulation a good career advantage.

6. **Question**
   Are there specific cross-border regulatory risks or geopolitical factors they should prioritize?
   Answer
   These are critical times for geopolitical risks, including what is happening in the Middle East. But putting the Middle East aside, I think global firms need to consider their alignment with the world powers. Determining if you align with China or the United States is critical because it is becoming difficult to do business with both. It is challenging to have both an east and west strategy in the same way you could have 10 years ago. In the short term, most big firms that have seen the United States as a major market are potentially experiencing it as less welcoming, and China is there as a business partner. And there are still many EU/UK Brexit business issues to work out, the need for professional services to be able to work across that border is a major issue that needs to be fixed, to my mind.

7. **Question**
   When you look back on your career, what lessons learned would you like to share with the profession?
   Answer
   It is important to be flexible and willing to look at the next project and work out how your skill set fits into it. Realistically, knowing how to work with emerging technology is important. But, while we don't know what our jobs will look like in

10 years for now, I am certain people will be needed, and the successful ones will be those who embrace change, have strong communication skills, good judgment, and, the rarest of all skills, common sense and the ability to be pragmatic.

The other lesson I would highlight is how important it is to have a good relationship as risk professionals with your business partners, and to be able to explain the importance of strong risk management. This has to be more than telling them "because a regulator says so," it means really being committed to risk as a business-improving discipline and one that has a long-term benefit to the bottom line.

Bibliography

Bank of England. Prudential Regulation. *"Strong and Simple."* January 2025. https://www.bankofengland.co.uk/prudential-regulation/strong-and-simple.

Basel Committee on Banking Supervision. *Compliance and the Compliance Function in Banks.* Basel, Switzerland: Bank for International Settlements, April 2005. https://www.bis.org/publ/bcbs113.htm.

Basel Committee on Banking Supervision. *Revision to the Principles for the Sound Management of Operational Risk.* March 2021. https://www.bis.org/bcbs/publ/d515.pdf.

Basel Committee on Banking Supervision. *Corporate Governance Principles for Banks.* Basel, Switzerland: Bank for International Settlements, July 2015. https://www.bis.org/bcbs/publ/d328.pdf.

Board of Governors of the Federal Reserve System. *Supervisory Guidance on Model Risk Management (SR 11-7).* Washington, DC: Federal Reserve, April 2011. https://www.federalreserve.gov.

Board of Governors of the Federal Reserve System. *Federal Reserve Board Issues Enforcement Action and Fines the Industrial and Commercial Bank of China Ltd. and its New York Branch Approximately $2.4 Million for Their Unauthorized Use and Disclosure of Confidential Supervisory Information.* January 19, 2024. https://www.federalreserve.gov/newsevents/pressreleases/enforcement20240119a.htm?utm_source=chatgpt.com.

Board of Governors of the Federal Reserve System. *Federal Reserve Board Orders Goldman Sachs Group to pay $36.3 Million Civil Money Penalty and Announces it is Instituting Enforcement Proceedings Against Former Goldman Sachs Managing Director.* August 3, 2016. https://www.federalreserve.gov/newsevents/pressreleases/enforcement20160803a.htm#:~:text=The%20Federal%20Reserve%20Board%20on,solicit%20business%20for%20the%20firm.

Digital Operational Resilience Act. *Dora, Updates, Compliance.* https://www.digital-operational-resilience-act.com.

European Banking Authority. *Guidelines on Internal Governance (EBA/GL/2021/05).* London: European Banking Authority, June 2021. https://www.eba.europa.eu.

Federal Reserve. *Requirements for Domestic and Foreign Banking Organizations.* Adapted from https://www.federalreserve.gov/aboutthefed/boardmeetings/files/tailoring-rule-visual-20191010.pdf.

Financial Stability Institute 2015 / Bank for International Settlements. *The Four Lines of Defense Model for Financial Institutions.* Basel, Switzerland: Bank of International Settlements, December 2015.

Gov.Uk. Financial Services: *The Edinburgh Reforms.* December 2022. https://www.gov.uk/government/collections/financial-services-the-edinburgh-reforms.

Interagency Advisory on the Confidentiality of the Supervisory Rating and Other Nonpublic Supervisory Information. https://www.federalreserve.gov/boarddocs/srletters/2005/SR0504a1.pdf.

Lathan & Watkins. *The Edinburgh Reforms – Two Years on.* December 2024. https://www.globalfinregblog.com/2024/12/the-edinburgh-reforms-two-years-on/.

LII Legal Institute. *12 CFR Part 261 - RULES REGARDING AVAILABILITY OF INFORMATION.* Cornell Law School. https://www.law.cornell.edu/cfr/text/12/part-261.

Legislation.gov.uk. *Financial Services and Markets Act 2000.* Part XXIII. Disclosure of Information, Section 348. https://www.legislation.gov.uk/ukpga/2000/8/section/348.

Office of the Comptroller of the Currency. *Heightened Standards for Large Banks: Guidelines Establishing Minimum Standards for Risk Governance.* Washington, DC: OCC, September 2014. https://www.occ.gov.

Official Journal of the European Union. *Regulation (EU) 2022/2554 of the European Parliament and of the Council on Digital Operational Resilience for the Financial Sector and Amending Regulations (EC) No 1060/2009, (EU) No 648/2012, (EU) No 600/2014, (EU) No 909/2014 and (EU) 2016/1011.* December 14, 2022. https://eur-lex.europa.eu/legal-content/EN/TXT/?uri=uriserv%3AOJ.L_.2022.333.01.0001.01.ENG&toc=OJ%3AL%3A2022%3A333%3AFULL.

Office of the Comptroller of the Currency. OCC Bulletin 2019-15. *Supervisory Ratings and Other Nonpublic OCC Information: Statement on Confidentiality.* https://www.occ.gov/news-issuances/bulletins/2019/bulletin-2019-15.html.

PWC. *Government Announces Sweeping Edinburgh Reforms.* December 2022. https://www.pwc.co.uk/financial-services/assets/pdf/government-announces-sweeping-edinburgh-reforms.pdf.

PWC. *Digital Operational Resilience Act.* https://www.pwc.com/mt/en/services/pwc-digital-services/cyber-security-and-privacy/cyber-security-services/dora.html.

Sidley. *Federal and State Regulators Fine Foreign Bank for Unauthorized Disclosure of Confidential Supervisory Information.* January 24, 2024. https://www.sidley.com/en/insights/newsupdates/2024/01/federal-and-state-regulators-fine-foreign-bank.

U.S. Department of the Treasury, Financial Crimes Enforcement Network (FinCEN). *Anti-Money Laundering and Countering the Financing of Terrorism National Priorities.* Washington, DC: FinCEN, June 2021. https://www.fincen.gov.

World Economic Forum. *The Global Risks Report 2024.* Geneva: World Economic Forum, January 2024. https://www.weforum.org.

Chapter 10

It Could Happen Here: On Developing Scenarios

I have been a fan of scenarios since the inception of the FIRST external operational risk event database that I brought to market (see Chapter 7). I blew out the basic risk event descriptions with a focus on control failings so that they could serve as the genesis for an organization's operational risk scenario program. I continue to believe today that external loss events provide a strong foundation for developing scenarios. The basic concept in designing scenarios is that they must be severe but plausible. Large external events meet this standard because they meet both the severe (they are severe enough to be in the public domain) and plausible (they have occurred) benchmarks. They can be stressed to determine their potential severity under certain conditions specific to one's own organization.

The Basel Committee defines scenario analysis as "a method to identify, analyse and measure a range of scenarios, including low probability and high severity events, some of which could result in severe operational risk losses" (https://www.bis.org/bcbs/publ/d515.pdf). Scenarios have been a foundational element of an operational risk program from the first publication of the Basel Operational Risk Basel II guidance, which included external data, internal data, business environment and internal control factor assessments, and scenario analysis (see Chapter 1) as the pillars of an operational risk framework.

Scenarios remain a critical component of current operational risk frameworks, but I would argue that they have not been used to their full potential. They are heavily used in the operational risk Comprehensive Capital Analysis and Review (CCAR) process and are important inputs to operational risk capital models. Basel II was focused on the use of scenarios as primarily a data input into advanced measurement approach (AMA) models. With the movement away from AMA, they are primarily used today from a quantitative perspective in CCAR and Internal Capital Adequacy Assessment Process (ICAAP) stress models. (See the interview with the industry expert at the end of this chapter.)

But that is not where the story ends. Scenarios also are the ingredient for cracking the struggle in the industry to identify emerging risks. A critical request from management is often to "tell me what I do not already know." When considering how to cross the current versus emerging risk timeline, scenarios are a good place to start. In our current operating environment, they should account for the most critical risks, including cyber, geopolitical, pandemics, and climate change. Scenarios can be used to create or update resiliency playbooks, assess, and plan for emerging risks, as well as create risk awareness among senior management and the board.

I have managed the operational risk scenario program in several of my past positions and would update them annually. Shortly before the COVID pandemic came to a head and sent us all home, I worked with my team on updating our organization's scenario library. We reviewed the pandemic scenario that had been in our library since the bird flu became prevalent; it had been collecting dust, and we decided that it was no longer relevant. As soon as we decided to retire it, we were all sent home when COVID was declared a pandemic.

I confess that it was a lack of imagination that led me to the conclusion that since the bird flu was relatively contained in our geographic location, we would not be subject to a severe pandemic.

At the heart of building a scenario library is imagining what could happen, based on what has happened in the industry and what risks could emerge in a stressed environment. The example I often use in workshops is that imagining an invasion on Earth by extraterrestrial beings is not plausible, while a pandemic that is more severe than what we experienced during COVID is plausible and credible for inclusion in a scenario library.

The Basel Committee has broadened its perspective on the use of scenarios with the publication of its "Revisions to the Principles for the Sound Management of Operational Risk." The document provides a good summary of the purpose, implementation, and use of scenarios and data inputs:

> *Scenario analysis is a method to identify, analyse and measure a range of scenarios, including low probability and high severity events, some of which could result in severe operational risk losses. Scenario analysis typically involves workshop meetings of subject-matter experts including senior management, business management and senior operational risk staff and other functional areas such as compliance, human resources and IT risk management, to develop and analyse the drivers and range of consequences of potential events. Inputs to the scenario analysis would typically include relevant internal and external loss data, information from self-assessments, the control monitoring and assurance framework, forward-looking metrics, root-cause analyses and the process framework, where used. The scenario analysis process could be used to develop a range of consequences of potential events, including impact*

assessments for risk management purposes, supplementing other tools based on historical data or current risk assessments. It could also be integrated with disaster recovery and business continuity plans, for use within testing of operational resilience. Given the subjectivity of the scenario process, a robust governance framework and independent review are important to ensure the integrity and consistency of the process.

Source: https://www.bis.org/bcbs/publ/d508.pdf#:~:text=Operational%20risk%20is%20defined%20in%20the%20capital,people%20and%20systems%20or%20from%20external%20events.&text=f)%20Scenario%20Analysis%20%2D%20Scenario%20analysis%20is,could%20result%20in%20severe%20operational%20risk%20losses

Note the emphasis on qualitative uses of scenarios, including impact assessments for risk management purposes, and integration with disaster recovery and business continuity plans and testing of operational risk resilience. The Basel passage also emphasizes the subjectivity of the scenario process, which relies on consensus derived in primarily workshop settings and requires acknowledgment of biases and a tendency to anchor on what the most critical risk is at any given moment.

Scenarios were designed in the early days of Basel II implementation to support quantification of operational risk capital. They are used heavily today in stress testing programs to determine an institution's ability to withstand severe disruptions. I participated in scenario building in one organization that stressed RCSA results to determine how the organization's controls would withstand highly stressed conditions.

Some organizations have multiple scenario programs residing within their walls. This approach should be aligned with RCSA assessments, where the controls are stressed to determine their ratings, in a fully integrated approach.

The following are how scenarios are used today in operational risk programs:

Use	Description
Risk Identification and Assessment	Identify emerging risks and potential vulnerabilities that are not represented in historical data. Allow for assessment of confluence and concentration of risks.
Emerging Risks	Explore "what if" scenarios associated with new technologies, external operating environment, geopolitical risks, emerging threats.
Capital Allocation	Support quantification of potential losses used in calculating operational risk capital under regulatory frameworks.
Stress Testing and Resilience Planning	Provides content for stressing the institution's ability to withstand severe operational disruptions.
Risk Appetite	Assist with validating risk appetite thresholds.
RCSA	Incorporate known but stressed risks into RCSA and identify potential control gaps under stressed conditions. Assist with identifying forward looking risks, themes and trends.
Resilience	Provide input into the organization's business continuity plans and assist with planning and assessing a firm's resilience.
Training and Awareness	Promote risk culture by engaging First Line in thinking about their risks and controls and allows for a top-down strategic view from senior management participants.

The Scenario Program

Establishing a scenario program requires defined governance and a framework that allows for a documented and repeatable process. The Basel Committee's "Operational Risk Supervisory Guidelines for the Advanced Measurement Approaches" (June 2011) establishes guidelines for a scenario program regardless of whether the focus is on models or qualitative risk management:

- *A clearly defined and repeatable process;*
- *Good quality background preparation of the participants in the scenario generation process;*
- *Qualified and experienced facilitators with consistency in the facilitation process;*
- *The appropriate representatives of the business, subject-matter experts and the corporate operational risk management function as participants involved in the process;*
- *A structured process for the selection of data used in developing scenario estimates;*
- *High quality documentation which provides clear reasoning and evidence supporting the scenario output;*
- *A robust independent challenge process and oversight by the corporate operational risk management function to ensure the appropriateness of scenario estimates;*
- *A process that is responsive to changes in both the internal and external environment; and*
- *Mechanisms for mitigating biases inherent in scenario processes. Such biases include anchoring, availability and motivational biases.*

Source: https://www.bis.org/publ/bcbs196.pdf

The Scenario Framework

Figure 10.1 shows a high-level overview of a scenario framework, which is based on the Basel Guidance.

Governance and Framework

As with any framework element, establishing an articulated governance structure that allows for consistency is the first step in creating and implementing an operational risk scenario program. The program should be supported by the requirement in the operational risk policy to maintain operational risk scenarios, a standard that describes the

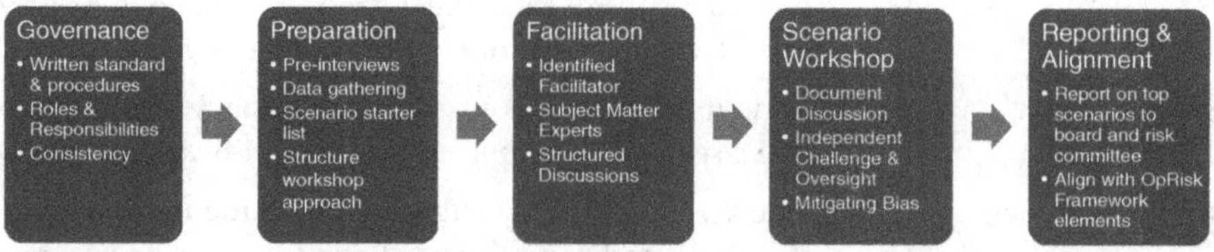

Figure 10.1 Scenario framework

program requirements, and a procedure that breaks down the implementation steps. (See Chapter 8 for the discussion of the types of governing documents.) The methodology for selecting and determining severity of scenarios should be included in the standard document or published as a separate methodology document.

The second-line operational risk function is typically responsible for developing the framework and methodology for operational risk scenarios, although some organizations have ownership of this function in a second-line enterprise risk department (and in smaller organizations they can be a single function). There is some logic to this approach as the scenarios are an input into the material risk ID effort, which is typically owned by enterprise risk. However, in the later example, the operational risk department works with their risk colleagues in designing and structuring the program.

The first line of defense is usually responsible for gathering the relevant risk data, attending workshops, and providing their perspective on the identification of operational risk scenarios. Subject-matter experts should be identified in the first and second lines that can provide insight into their specific risk domains depending on the scenario under development. For instance, representatives from HR departments should be available for assisting with scenarios associated with people issues, cyber experts should be available for cyber scenarios, and payments experts for scenarios that touch their business areas.

I have experienced significant involvement of senior management in scenario workshops when the scenarios are inputs into the CCAR and capital planning process, as they are very aware of the impact of the results on operational risk capital. This was an opportunity to engage the most senior executives of the organization in discussing potential severe operational risks and their related controls; the workshops served as an opportunity to raise awareness and garner support at the highest level of the firm.

The development of the methodology and framework for determining scenarios should include the following considerations that are incorporated into the standard or methodology document:

Questionnaire, interview, or workshops: Scenarios can be determined through a questionnaire, interviews with key stakeholders, or workshops. I prefer the workshop approach, because there is something powerful in the "room where it happens" and the discussions that occur among a cross section of workshop participants. Questionnaires and interviews can be used to prepare for a workshop, but something is lost if the discussions are bypassed. However, smaller organizations may consider alternative approaches to scenario workshops, and it is possible to alternate years between a questionnaire or a workshop approach.

Single or multiple scenarios: It should be determined how many scenarios will be brought into the workshop for discussion. Ultimately, one scenario will be selected for inclusion in the stress and capital models for each risk type. Multiple scenarios can be considered during the workshop, each with different root causes, business impacts, and severity, but ultimately, a single scenario should be agreed upon for inclusion in stress and capital models. It is a strong practice to combine the elements of the multiple scenarios into one, considering the confluence of potential underlying drivers and impacts.

Scenario selection: Scenarios should be selected according to alignment with the operational risk taxonomy and at a predetermined level (level 1 or 2). I have customarily constructed scenarios at level 1 in the taxonomy to consider the broad underlying factors driving potential extreme events and to allow for consideration of combined scenarios that incorporate more than one event type. The loss data history and external peer events should be considered in constructing scenarios. (See the "Preparation" section).

Scenario development: A narrative should be drafted for each scenario that includes the underlying root causes, impacted businesses and functions, loss estimates and impact, duration of event, and relevant assumptions for selection and impact determination.

Impact assessment: Determining the ultimate impact of a scenario will be critical for incorporation into stress and capital models. Some firms determine low, medium, and high impacts and adjust the levels according to the control environment associated with the scenario. I have experienced scenarios that are estimated at the high level the first year when there were known control issues and then brought down to the medium level in subsequent years as remediations were completed and validated. The determination of impact should include all inputs, including direct loss amount, revenue impact, fines and penalties, and remediation costs. The determination of inherent and residual risk should follow RCSA or other risk assessment standards that already exist in the firm. If the concept of "confidence level" is introduced, it should be stipulated in the methodology.

Inherent versus residual risk: I have worked in organizations that have considered the inputs into scenarios, and particularly the risk levels determined from RCSA, on an inherent basis and other organizations that considered residual risk. If the later approach is taken, it is a strong practice to consider the controls in the RCSA under stressed conditions, with an assumption of the impact on scenario severity if the controls were operating at partially effective or ineffective levels under stress.

Macro-economic versus idiosyncratic scenarios: Macro-economic scenarios incorporate external events and contain systemic risks with widespread impact, such as a market shock or global geopolitical issue. Idiosyncratic scenarios are internal and specific to an institution, with more localized impact, such as a system integration failure. The Federal Reserve requires the incorporation of both types of scenarios into its CCAR models. (See the interview with the industry veteran at the end of this chapter for more background on the two types of scenarios.)

Data inputs: The required data inputs should be specified and documented for determining which scenarios are selected and their severity. (See the following discussion on what the Fact Pack should contain.)

Validation and documentation: The second-line review and challenge process should be defined in the documentation along with a process for validating the scenarios. It is a strong practice to back test the scenarios both on an individual scenario and portfolio level. At the portfolio level, the loss data should be analyzed for how often events over a certain severe threshold occur in the industry and within the historical experience of the institution. The loss estimate ranges should correspond with the high, medium, and low loss estimates for the portfolio of scenarios and for each individual scenario. As an example, if the totality of scenarios selected add up to $1 billion at the high level, how many events in the last 10 years has the organization suffered in total, and how many events on average has a group of industry peers suffered? Do the number of events correspond with the frequency assumptions that helped to determine the loss ranges for the scenarios? This approach will depend on the use of likelihood in determining estimated loss amounts and access to consortium data (see Chapter 7) to determine the industry average. The same approach can be taken on an individual scenario basis.

Here is how the validation process can work:

- Aggregate high, medium, and low estimated losses at the portfolio level for all scenarios.
- Count the number of historical internal loss events over the selected threshold for a predetermined timeframe depending on available data for each loss bucket. (example: 10 years).
- Use consortium data (ORX, Gold), to assess average frequency of high-severity events for each loss bucket among a set of pre-determined industry peers.
- Check whether the loss frequencies from the scenarios align with internal and external loss data.
- Document findings and adjust scenario loss estimates or likelihoods if needed.
- Apply same approach at the individual scenario level using the internal and external data.
- Document, document, document.

Documentation: All assumptions going into the determination of the selection of scenarios and their severity should be carefully documented, along with the minutes of the scenario workshops. This includes the assumptions regarding loss amount, stressed controls, inputs from the Fact Pack, back testing results, independent validation, and review and challenge.

Preparation

I start the scenario analysis preparation process by identifying the current state of the scenario library. My goal is to have a scenario for each of the level 1 operational risk types in the taxonomy. This can take a few cycles to build a comprehensive library, as the first few cycles should focus on the highest and most immediate risks that would be critical for the stress testing models. It is also critical to consider the confluence and concentration of risks, as risks do not tend to occur in distinct categories. For instance, market volatility and extreme market events can result in large transaction processing events, frauds, and business disruptions. With the concentration of third-party service providers in certain domains, such as the cloud, a severe business disruption might have systemic impact that will increase the severity of an event across the industry. The CrowdStrike business interruption event that occurred in July 2024 and is characterized as the largest documented IT outage provides a good example of how a vendor so concentrated in offering cyber protection services can cause so much systemic havoc when a system upgrade goes wrong.

Once the library is reviewed, the next step is to create a workshop plan that includes the primary operational risks, as reflected in the top level of the taxonomy but also considers the intersection of risks, such as cyber, third-party, resiliency, and data protection. This has the benefit of allowing for combined workshops by operational risk type and cross-functional discussions of risks.

The planning process should include identification of key stakeholders for each scheduled workshop, which will be a cross section of representatives from the first line and functions. For instance, a workshop that is dedicated to cyber, third-party, and resilience will want a representative from each impacted business and the subject-matter experts for each of the functional domains. This would include someone from first- and second-line cyber, third-party, and resiliency risk management. I also like to interview a few subject-matter experts (SMEs) ahead of the scenario workshops so that I can present an initial view during the session.

The scenarios should rely on data and risk assessments. Fact Packs should be created ahead of each workshop and disseminated to the participants that include the following:

- Internal loss data history
- Relevant peer events
- Open issues
- Audit findings
- Regulatory findings
- Recent news stories that impact risk domain
- RCSA results
- Risk appetite and/or key risk indicator metrics
- Compliance testing results
- Scenario starter list (past scenarios and suggested ones by SMEs during planning process)

Facilitation

A facilitator should be identified who has the gravitas to move the discussion forward and break through any impasses. The facilitator is most often a member of the operational risk team. It is important to be able to move the discussion forward and provide challenge to the ongoing discussion so that a result can be reached concerning the content of the scenario and estimated severity.

Developing a template for use in a workshop along with the Fact Pack helps structure the discussion. It is also a strong practice to take notes during the workshop, as regulators and auditors may ask for this down the line. This is especially true if the scenarios are inputs into stress models, as the regulators will want to understand the underlying assumptions.

The template may include the following information:

- Workshop title and date
- Facilitator
- Attendees (includes business, function, risk, and subject matter representatives)
- Scenario narrative
- Underlying driver and root cause for scenario
- Operational risk event type (from taxonomy)
- Scenario assumptions
- Underlying root cause
- Total loss amount (some firms create high, medium, and low estimates)
  - Direct loss amount following loss event guidance (see description in Chapter 6)
  - Estimated revenue loss amount
  - Estimated remediation costs
  - Estimated regulatory fines
  - Estimated legal fees
- Total loss amount (some firms create high, medium, and low estimates)
- Downtime duration (if business interruption scenario)
- Impacted controls
  - Control deficiencies identified
  - Control enhancements required
  - Required remediations
- Review and challenge statement by operational risk

Once the materials are pulled together, a calendar should be created with the scheduled workshops and required attendees. This is no small chore and requires strong project management to get the right cross section of people together for the scenario sessions. In my experience, workshops are often initially held in one-hour slots due to scheduling challenges, but they are rarely concluded in just one hour and require additional sessions. The session's agenda should include sufficient time to provide background, review prior relevant scenarios to level-set the discussion (if they exist), to draft the scenario narrative, and to walk through the high, medium, and low estimates. There will inevitably be a follow-up session to complete and validate the analysis and a session ultimately at the end of the process with senior management for final validation. The process can be significantly aided if some pre-work occurs on the part of the facilitators and subject-matter experts in constructing straw-person scenarios ahead of the workshops.

The invitees should be at an appropriate senior level to provide insight into the construction of scenarios, their business, or function risk exposures and potential loss estimates. If they are unavailable at the slotted time, they should send appropriate delegates. The process is not effective if the delegates do not have enough knowledge and seniority to fully participate in the workshops.

The invitation should be sent out with the Fact Packs, and the attendees should have sufficient time to review the data ahead of the workshop.

Scenario Workshop

Once all the pieces are in place—the methodology is determined and published, the attendees are identified, the invites are sent out with the Fact Pack, the working template is ready to go, predetermined initial scenarios are drafted—it is time to hold the workshop. I have found these risk discussions to be among the most profound of my career. This is because of the nature of the workshops and the participation of senior level people (this is a must!) who come together from a cross section of businesses and functions to discussion risks. And the discussion is not just about what has happened in the past but what *could* happen. This is where emerging risks are often identified that can provide inputs into other framework elements (see Chapter 4).

There has been a lot written about workshop bias, and it is certainly a concern. I always worry that because scenarios are inputs into stress and capital models, there would be some gamesmanship associated with trying to keep the loss estimate numbers as low as possible. This for the most part has not been the case, but it can be managed by anchoring on the data available in the Fact Pack and through a strong independent challenge during the workshop sessions.

Here is the list of potential biased responses that should be acknowledged up front and managed through strong workshop facilitation and challenge:

- **Availability bias:** Gives more weight to events that have recently occurred, such as the most recent transaction processing error that the participants may be actively involved with remediating.
- **Anchoring bias:** Over-reliance on initial estimate for losses. Everyone in the workshop will anchor around this number, which may be an over or under the estimate.
- **Motivational bias:** This occurs when the participants are influenced by personal or company interest, as in the example provided where there might be a bias toward keeping the loss estimates that impact stress and capital models.
- **Overconfidence bias:** Participants are overly confident in their estimates, without reviewing the underlying data.
- **Status quo bias:** Assuming the loss estimates of past scenarios will be the same in the new cycle and failure to consider emerging risks.

As mentioned, the workshops focus for each event type on the representative scenario or scenarios. Although there may be more than one scenario developed for management purposes, there should be one designated for incorporation into the stress and capital models. I have been restricted in my past organizations to submitting three to four scenarios for modeling purposes. This involves a prioritization exercise and consideration of what handful of scenarios best represent the organization's risks. This would often involve additional workshops once the scenarios were drafted or refreshed for the current cycle to determine the final selection. It was also an opportunity to consider combining the underlying drivers of multiple scenarios, to capture the interconnectivity among risks.

The workshop requires imagination, as the purpose is to envision what can happen, while keeping the discussion within the boundary of the probable. The group of stakeholders that have come together brainstorm for each risk category the severe yet probable outcome. This requires considering both internal and external threats and vulnerabilities, including cyberattacks, natural disasters, severe economic downturns, IT incidents, financial crimes, AI-driven frauds, suitability issues, and transaction processing failures.

Reporting and Alignment

The final set of scenarios should be added to the library of scenarios. A few may be selected for incorporation into the models, but the library itself should be used as inputs into the other operational risk framework components. The scenarios represent forward-looking risks, which can supplement the tendency in RCSAs to look at current state. The RCSAs should be updated once the scenarios are drafted to incorporate this perspective. It would also be a proactive response to open an issue and action plan if it is determined that certain controls require strengthening through the assessment of how they would perform in stressed conditions.

The scenarios related to technology and cyber events, manmade and natural disasters, and resiliency should be aligned with the business continuity program. Principle 3 of the Basel Committee's Principles of Operational Resilience specifically call this out: "Banks should have business continuity plans in place and conduct business continuity exercises under a range of severe but plausible scenarios in order to test their ability to deliver critical operations through disruption." The scenarios can assist in developing business continuity recovery plans based on the assessment of how the organization would respond to a disruption scenario.

A report should be prepared for the board each year when the scenario exercises are complete that summarize the selection of the key scenarios, with a high-level description and justification for inclusion (if relevant) in the stress models.

The following is a high-level view of what a report summary might look like:

Basel Event Category	Scenario Description	Frequency*	Low Estimate ($)	Medium Estimate ($)	High Estimate ($)	Scenario Selected	Inclusion in Stress Model
Internal Fraud	Wealth management employee embezzles wealthy elderly customer's funds over several years.	Medium	50,000,000	100,000,000	250,000,000	Medium estimate due to history of related issues that have been in the moderate range and industry events	No
External Fraud	Sophisticated deep fake event results in transactions to fraudster's accounts and financial losses.	High	30,000,000	75,000,000	100,000,000	High estimate due to industry events and recent fraud attempts and open issues	Yes
Employment Practices and Workplace Safety	Major discrimination lawsuit leads to a high-profile class action settlement.	Low	5,000,000	10,000,000	15,000,000	Low estimate due to lack of recent history of significant settlements, including class action lawsuits	No
Clients, Products, and Business Practices	Widespread mis-selling of structured products leads to regulatory sanctions and customer class action.	Medium	150,000,000	300,000,000	500,000,000	High estimate due to outstanding class action lawsuit and open issues	Yes

Basel Event Category	Scenario Description	Frequency*	Low Estimate ($)	Medium Estimate ($)	High Estimate ($)	Scenario Selected	Inclusion in Stress Model
Damage to Physical Assets	Category 5 hurricane destroys regional data center.	Medium	95,000,000	250,000,000	500,000,000	Medium estimate due to recent peer events	No
Business Disruption and System Failures	Critical trading systems go offline for three days due to system upgrade failure.	High	110,000,000	300,000,000	600,000,000	High estimate due to two recent business disruption events and recent peer events and open issues	Yes
Execution, Delivery, and Process Management	Series of trading errors on client accounts results in regulatory action and customer remediation.	High	85,000,000	225,000,000	350,000,000	Medium estimate due to history of manual processing errors and open issues	Yes

***Note*: Assume the following frequency ranges:

High: At least once a year; medium: at least once every two to five years; low: less than once every five years

Scenario Examples

The following are example scenarios that could be considered for workshops by Basel Category based on real-life events. These events serve as a basis for constructing scenarios for your own organization, with consideration of how the event would unfold, what controls could fail, and what the ultimate high, medium, and low impacts would be. It takes some imagination to apply them to your own organization and asking the questions: Could it happen here? And if so, what would it look like?

Internal Fraud

- **Insider Trading:** A trader executes trades based on insider knowledge of a pharmaceutical company's drug trials that resulted in $276 million profit. (See S.A.C Capital Advisors event; https://www.justice.gov/usao-sdny/pr/sac-capital-portfolio-manager-mathew-martoma-sentenced-manhattan-federal-court-nine.)
- **Employee Embezzlement:** CFO of a nonprofit embezzles $40 million over 12 years. (See Detroit Riverfront Conservancy event; https://www.justice.gov/usao-edmi/pr/former-detroit-riverfront-conservancy-chief-financial-officer-sentenced-embezzling.)
- **Data Theft:** Insider bribery leads to exposure of sensitive personal information of approximately 70,000 customers' confidential data. (See Coinbase insider data leak; https://www.exterro.com/resources/data-privacy-alerts/insider-bribery-leads-to-major-coinbase-data-breach.)

External Fraud

- **Cyberattack:** Hackers infiltrate a healthcare company's systems, stealing confidential information, including health information. (See United Healthcare cyber event; https://www.unitedhealthgroup.com/ns/health-data-breach.html.)
- **Deep Fake Fraud:** A finance employee at a multinational firm is tricked into paying out $25 million to fraudsters using deepfake technology to pose as the company's chief financial officer in a video conference call. (See deepfake event involving Hong Kong company; https://www.cnn.com/2024/02/04/asia/deepfake-cfo-scam-hong-kong-intl-hnk.)
- **ATM Skimming:** A criminal gang installs skimming devices on ATMs to steal card information in banks located in multiple states. (See event involving criminal gang; https://www.justice.gov/usao-ri/pr/second-defendant-admits-his-role-atm-skimming-bank-fraud-conspiracy.)

Business Disruption and System Failures

- **System Outage:** A major outage at critical third-party service provider left banking customers without access to online banking services. (See event involving Fiserv; https://thecollegeinvestor.com/57421/banking-outage-leaves-customers-without-account-access/?srsltid=AfmBOooMu8JlSJrKaq0H_eNej-qFb0IJKOtXJK2cGgXYca0ESWVm77Dh.)

- **Cloud Service Failure:** Human error resulting from mistyping a command leads to cloud service provider outage, impacting multiple organizations and resulting in significant financial losses. (See AWS; https://www.datacenterknowledge.com/outages/aws-outage-that-broke-the-internet-caused-by-mistyped-command.)
- **Third Party Failure:** A third party that offers cyber protection services suffered an outage resulting from a botched software update, that resulted in significant outages across multiple industries. (See Crowdstrike; https://edition.cnn.com/2024/07/24/tech/crowdstrike-outage-cost-cause.)

Execution, Delivery, and Process Management

- **Trade Settlement Errors:** A trader accidentally executes an order for $1.4 billion rather than $58 million of equities, which results in a significant drop in a major market index. (See Citi trading error; https://www.marketwatch.com/story/a-citi-trader-intending-to-sell-58-million-of-shares-ended-up-selling-1-4-billion-now-the-bank-has-been-fined-c3e631eb?utm_source=chatgpt.com.)
- **Fat Finger Payment Event:** A bank in its capacity as loan agent for a bond, sent investors payments for the entire principle amount on the bonds, rather than interest payments. (See Citi Revlon event; https://prmia.org/common/Uploaded%20files/ORM%20Designation/PRMIA_Citibank-Revlon_021122.pdf.)
- **Risk Management Failings Related to Payment Processing:** A payment processor is fined by a prudential regulator for failing to remediate risk management and governance weaknesses that were previously identified. (See Vocalink; https://www.bankofengland.co.uk/news/2025/july/boe-fines-vocalink-limited.)

Employment Practices and Workplace Safety

- **Age Discrimination:** A class action is opened against a firm that offers talent acquisition software, alleging age discrimination is built into the algorithms. (See Workday; https://www.lawandtheworkplace.com/2025/06/ai-bias-lawsuit-against-workday-reaches-next-stage-as-court-grants-conditional-certification-of-adea-claim/.)
- **Gender Discrimination:** A $200 million settlement was reached at a major financial firm alleging gender bias and a hostile workplace. (See Goldman Sachs; https://www.nytimes.com/2023/05/09/business/dealbook/goldman-sachs-discrimination-lawsuit.html.)
- **Health & Safety Violations:** OSHA brought forward ergonomic injury complaints related to 10 warehouse facilities, citing high rates of musculoskeletal injuries due to repetitive motions and heavy lifting. (See Amazon; https://www.osha.gov/news/newsreleases/national/02012023.)

Damage to Physical Assets

- **Building Collapse:** A massive explosion occurred at the base of a multi-story building that contained a bank branch. The explosion resulted in collapse of the building façade, the death of a bank employee and injury to several others (See JPMorgan Chase; https://www.nytimes.com/2024/05/28/us/gas-explosion-youngstown-ohio.html.)

- **Terrorist Attack:** A foreign national was arrested after attempting to detonate a bomb outside the New York Federal Reserve Building. The suspect aimed to strike at the heart of the financial system. (see DOJ sentencing of suspect; https://www.justice.gov/usao-edny/pr/al-qaeda-inspired-operative-sentenced-30-years-prison-attempting-bomb-federal-reserve.)
- **Vandalism:** A bank branch is burned down during protests. (See Union Bank; https://timesofsandiego.com/business/2022/12/09/la-mesa-marks-reopening-of-union-bank-branch-burned-during-2020-riot/.)

Clients, Products, and Business Practices

- **Sanctions Violations:** A bank is fined by a prudential regulator and its growth is restricted due to deficiencies in its anti-money laundering compliance program. (See TD; https://www.occ.treas.gov/news-issuances/news-releases/2024/nr-occ-2024-116.html#:~:text=The%20OCC%20found%20that%20the,directed%20to%20the%20U.S.%20Treasury.)
- **Mis-selling of Financial Products:** A bank makes good will payments to investors who suffered significant losses related to the sale of derivatives, who may not have understood or been informed of the risks. (See UBS; https://www.ft.com/content/c8816f71-112c-40f2-a11f-aacd3229c1aa?utm_source=chatgpt.com)

Interview with Industry Veteran on the Use of Scenarios: Evan Sekeris

Evan is one of the industry's most knowledgeable risk management subject-matter experts, with deep knowledge in operational risk, model risk, and quantification methods, including scenarios. Evan has previously led model risk functions at PNC and Capital One and was America's head of nonfinancial risk at MUFG. His previous positions include a partner role in the risk management practice at Oliver Wyman and time with two Federal Reserve Banks.

1. **Question**
   Can you provide a background on the evolution of scenarios? What is their origin as an important component of the operational risk framework?
   Answer
   The short history is that Basel II's Advanced Measurement Approaches (AMA) listed scenarios next to internal and external loss data as inputs to capital quantification. This original characterization of scenarios as a data element influenced how the industry has perceived and treated scenarios ever since. Many practitioners treated scenarios were just another "data element"—an object to be stored, aggregated, and resampled. In reality, scenarios are an estimation technique, the equivalent of

qualitative models, synthesizing expert judgment, process knowledge, and relevant evidence into a forward-looking forecast.

Scenarios were useful in the context of the AMA, particularly in the early days when data was scarce. AMA aimed at the 99.9% one-year loss quantile. That is the extreme tail of the distribution, where data are scarce, model assumptions dominate, and minor specification choices lead to large swings. It is no surprise the estimates were sometimes unstable and sensitive. Scenarios flourished because they allowed institutions to reason from process—how things actually break—rather than to stretch thin data to fit an extreme-tail distribution.

Then CCAR came along, and the industry faced the same problems that we faced when working within the AMA framework. The operational risk data was not always representative of the risks that the organization was exposed to. I should mention one important technical point: AMA models were tasked with achieving a 99.9% loss distribution, which meant that a bank would not exceed its estimated losses in 1 out of 1,000 years. Stress testing models had a different mandate. They were estimating losses in much different levels of probability and mostly in 1 in 50 or 100 years. Models developed for stress testing purposes were different from the LDA type models used for capital purposes, trying to link operational losses, particularly their frequency, to macroeconomic variables and other firm specific variables. However, the use of scenarios remained limited at first.

This changed in 2015, when the Federal Reserve issued guidance on capital planning through SR15-19. This is when they started asking banks to use scenarios in stress testing to complement their models. This essentially led to the recycling of AMA scenarios, but without clear guidance on the distribution approach. It was never clear if banks should consider not exceeding losses in a 1 in 50-, 100-, or 1,000-year time horizon. What was also unclear was whether scenarios should still be considered a data element or if they were seen as an alternative forecasting methodology complementing quantitative models. In this push for an increased use of scenarios, the Federal Reserve started pushing for two types of scenarios: top-of-the-house enterprise scenarios that are tied to macro assumptions, and idiosyncratic scenarios that are nonsystemic and tied to internal factors such as control weaknesses, business process breakdowns, and technology failures.

The introduction of stress testing for operational risk brought a new challenge: operational risk failures have large idiosyncratic drivers and tend not to be as dependent on the macro-economic environment. Unfortunately, the AMA practices and, more importantly, the resulting large capital numbers anchored expectations for stress testing. Models tying operational risk losses to the macroeconomy show some cyclicality of losses, but even a tripling or quadrupling of the expected losses pales in comparison to the tail events driving capital numbers. Furthermore, large operational risk losses can happen at any time during the economic cycle in addition to any movement driven by the cycle. As a result, the Fed turned to requiring the use of idiosyncratic models to get the estimates they would have expected for operational risk and had previously seen through capital modeling exercises. This is how we got to where we are today with the combination of models and scenarios driving stress testing.

The industry today is using a dual approach of macro and idiosyncratic scenarios, which is appropriate, because idiosyncratic events can happen during times of macro-economic stress. They may be unrelated, but the impact of this happening should be considered. A good example is the Fukushima earthquake that struck Japan in 2011 when the world was still recovering from the impact of the 2008–2009 financial crisis. This is a reminder of the importance of considering the interconnectedness of risks when designing scenarios because unexpected things happen.

Another aspect of operational risk that is not sufficiently discussed is the importance of resilience and how it is probably even more critical to the survival of a firm than any amount of capital it might be holding. A firm's ability to withstand an operational risk event depends on the strength of its controls under stress, not just its capital. Even if it is adequately capitalized and is in a position to absorb the losses resulting from the event, it will remain a going concern only if it has the ability to continue operating under duress.

2. **Question**

What are the primary uses of scenarios outside of capital and stress testing? How do they integrate into the broader operational risk framework?

Answer

It is important to integrate scenarios into broader operational risk frameworks. There is a lack of integration even among scenario programs, such as AMA versus stress testing and overlapping workshops. Scenarios can be used for much more than estimation; they can be used to look at practical outcomes to better manage operational risks. Scenarios provide insights into the risks that cannot be obtained with traditional modeling techniques which for the most part ignore the drivers of the risk. The industry is working today to improve this situation and to use scenarios for multiple purposes. An important use is to identify process areas where there are weaknesses that could assist risk management with fixing identified issues.

We are making progress as an industry but still have far to go. Many organizations still design scenario workshops with a specific purpose, such as CCAR or capital, as opposed to designing workshops that would look at broader scenarios from process and control failures and be used for multiple purposes. Developing broader scenarios is certainly more time consuming in the front end as scenarios are designed to more completely understand potential weaknesses, but in the long run it lead to a stronger risk management process that is more efficient if the scenarios have multiple uses.

There is a significant opportunity to integrate scenarios into the RCSA process. Scenarios could be constructed through the implementation of RCSAs, which is a logical way of identifying potential control weaknesses. It would also bring a forward looking perspective to the RCSA process, allow for better identification of emerging risks, and a deeper understanding of control vulnerabilities.

Ideally, firms would run a single enterprise scenario program with shared standards and a common library. Then wire that program into multiple uses:

- *Capital and stress testing*—Configure probability and horizon explicitly. Make clear whether scenarios are primary or challenger and how overrides sunset.

- *RCSA*—Start from process maps and control breakpoints. Use scenarios to test how controls degrade under stress—or fail together.
- *Operational resilience*—Use scenarios to quantify impact tolerances, map recovery time objectives, and stress playbooks.
- *Risk appetite and control investment*—Translate scenario ranges into decision metrics: overlays, investment prioritization, and pre-committed actions.

A reusable scenario library with owners, refresh cadences, and traceable links to processes, KRIs, incidents, and control testing is the backbone. Scenarios should be easily adapted to the various needs without having to completely being redesigned or re-run.

3. Question

How do you determine which operational risk scenarios are most material to an institution?

Answer

First, I want to mention that we have a chicken and egg challenge that is inherent in the question. How do you define materiality for a class of risks? You need to understand how bad things can get. How do you know if a risk is material before you have quantified it? There are a lot of biased assumptions in determining materiality, and especially when using it as factor in determining what scenarios you need to develop.

For this reason, I advocate for a two-layer quantification approach. The first past would be a quantification of all risks through a process that is not too onerous and would lead to establishing a rank order of risks. This could then inform a second deeper dive into quantifying the risks. This second level of quantification can be integrated into the RCSA process, and as mentioned, linked to scenarios.

4. Question

In your experience, has senior management been properly engaged in the scenario process? How can engagement be improved?

Answer

There is a wide range of practices in the industry but it is common for scenarios to be developed without full engagement from senior management. I have seen the development of scenarios to be a perfunctory exercise at some organizations but similarly, I have seen firms where the process is taken very seriously. Lack of adequate senior engagement is more common at firms suffering for the proliferation and duplication of scenarios we discussed earlier. At these banks, executives have grown tired of participating in repetitive scenario workshops that are run to satisfy the duplicative scenario processes. Even when senior executives are more involved in the scenario process, they often only get involved at the end of the process as a validation point. It would be helpful to have their participation much earlier and in the drafting of narratives, as they can bring expert opinion based on their top-down strategic view. The drafting of narratives is conducted in workshops with more junior people who may not see the big picture and focus on narrower problems, not the ones that can cause a cross departmental problem. It is important to have their on-the-ground perspective, but it should be balanced with the top-down view as well. I know this would require a lot of effort and commitment on the part of senior executives.

I have seen more robust and impactful scenarios designed when senior executives get involved earlier in the process.

5. **Question**

What challenges have you encountered in managing scenario programs?

Answer

One challenge is the absence of a clear objective in constructing scenarios. It is difficult to end up with effective scenarios if objectives are ill-defined. I also think it is wrong to solely focus on outcome—meaning the loss estimation numbers—rather than the ability of an organization to be resilient under a particular scenario. It is important to be able to articulate the ways processes and controls can fail. operational risk materializes through process and control breakdowns, which is where you should start in constructing a scenario and walk forward from there, rather than walking backwards from a loss estimation.These focus on the outcome, on the loss, is directly driven by the fact that scenarios were originally developed to support capital numbers or stress testing projections.The key objective of these exercises is to put a dollar amount on the potential losses, not to get a full understanding of the mechanisms that led to them. Unfortunately, this view of scenarios has influenced how the workshops are run. Some institutions have invested in so-called structured scenarios which focus first and foremost on the processes and mechanisms that cause the losses. These firms have found these scenarios to be significantly more valuable from a risk management perspective, but, very interestingly, also much more accurate from a loss forecasting point of view! This is because by breaking down the loss mechanism in its different steps, they can collect data on the steps and build up a data driven view of how the loss occurs and of how severe it can be. Investing in such scenarios represents, of course, a significant commitment and a certain vision by the bank's operational risk management, which is why it is not as common yet of an approach as I would like it to be.

I mentioned that many institutions are not using scenarios more broadly. It's not efficient or good risk management to construct scenarios for narrow purposes, as opposed to understanding the risk. There should be one scenario program in an institution, and the scenarios should be used for various purposes. It is possible to create a single scenario process that serves all needs, including as discussed, resiliency and RCSA.

Bibliography

Basel Committee on Banking Supervision. *Revisions to the Principles for the Sound Management of Operational Risk.* March 31, 2021. https://www.bis.org/bcbs/publ/d515.htm.

Basel Committee on Banking Supervision. *Principles for the Sound Management of Operational Risk.* Basel, Switzerland: Bank for International Settlements, June 2011. https://www.bis.org/publ/bcbs196.pdf.

Basel Committee on Banking Supervision. *Operational Risk—Supervisory Guidelines for the Advanced Measurement Approaches.* June 2011. https://www.bis.org/publ/bcbs196.pdf.

Basel Committee on Banking Supervision. *Principles for Operational Resilience.* March 2021. https://www.bis.org/bcbs/publ/d516.pdf.

Michael Grimade. *Ten Laws of Operational Risk*, Chapter 8. Hoboken, NJ: Wiley, 2022.

Operational Risk Exchange (O.R.X.). *Scenario Analysis in Operational Risk at a Turning point.* https://orx.org/blog/scenario-analysis-operational-risk-turning-point.

Operational Risk Exchange (O.R.X.). *ORX Scenarios White Paper: State of the Industry*, October 2024.

Philippa Girling. Operational Risk Management: *A Complete Guide for Banking and Fintech*, Chapter 11. Hoboken, NJ: Wiley, 2022.

Chapter 11

Know Your Process: Managing Execution Risks

Regardless of what type of institution you work in, execution risk is where you will spend a great deal of your time if you are in a risk function or, for that matter, in almost any other function. Execution risk encompasses the day-to-day errors, mistakes, and, simply, things that go wrong on a frequent basis. Being an operational risk manager entails dealing with the daily "they did what and why" category of events. In the past, management would first look to operational risk to explain what went wrong and how the issue can be remediated. I have experienced a change in the response to errors over time with more awareness of business ownership, with the first line in the "hot seat" for explaining what went wrong and remediating the issue.

The Basel Committee defines the Execution, Delivery, and Process Management (EDPM) category as "Losses from failed transaction processing or process management, from relations with trade counterparties and vendors."The category is the second largest in terms of frequency in the ORX data from 2019 to 2024 (fraud is the top loss category) and severity (Clients, Products, and Business Practices is the top loss category). (See Chapter 7 for more about ORX loss data.) The Basel taxonomy (see Chapter 1 for the complete Basel operational risk taxonomy) includes transaction capture, execution and maintenance, monitoring and reporting, customer intake and documentation, and customer/client account management in the EDPM category.

The following is the EDPM branch of the Basel operational risk taxonomy:

Execution, delivery, and process management	Losses from failed transaction processing or process management, from relations with trade counterparties and vendors	Transaction capture, execution, and maintenance	Miscommunication Data entry, maintenance, or loading error Missed deadline or responsibility Model/system misoperation Accounting error/entity attribution error Other task misperformance Delivery failure Collateral management failure Reference data maintenance
		Monitoring and reporting	Failed mandatory reporting obligation Inaccurate external report (loss incurred)
		Customer intake and documentation	Client permissions/disclaimers missing Legal documents missing/incomplete
		Customer/client account management	Unapproved access given to accounts Incorrect client records (loss incurred) Negligent loss or damage of client assets

Source: Adapted from https://www.bis.org/basel_framework/chapter/OPE/25.htm

Operational risks live in organizational processes, and it's critical that a firm maintains a list of its processes, with a determination of criticality based on a documented methodology. It is difficult to get a true handle on execution risks if there is a lack of understanding of how the processes truly work and where potential breaks can potentially reside. Most financial services organizations have business resilience programs in place that have identified the most material processes, which can be leveraged for process risk assessments. However, there is work to do in the industry to identify end-to-end processes more broadly, as this continues to be a challenge in complex organizations where processes do not line up neatly with business responsibilities.

It is especially critical that "handoffs" that exist in a firm's processes are mapped. I have experienced operational risk events that occur where these handoffs exist, because an activity was not completed at the other end of the process. The handoff can occur between two people who are associated with different functions or between automated and manual processes. A point of failure can occur where an automated process passes an activity to a manual one (such as an email confirmation) that is missed. The key to managing these handoffs is to have them mapped and assessed for control coverage. A strong practice is to create "handshake" controls where these handoffs occur so that there is confirmation that what is passed over is properly picked up on the other side.

Innovative firms are organizing their functions around customer journeys, which are essentially processes that have the customer at their center. This creates an opportunity for an operational risk function, whether in the first or second line, to re-envision how it assesses risks and controls. Aligning risk and control self-assessments (RCSAs), compliance assessments, and other risk activities with the customer journey is a strong practice.

Many financial institutions continue to operate in environments that are heavily reliant on manual processes and controls. This results from years of underinvestment in automating the control environment. An example of a manual control is a four-eyes control, where an activity requires separation between a "maker" and a "checker." However, several notable operational risk events have had the failure of these controls at their center. A lack of investment in controls can in the long run cost an institution a great deal in terms of actual and reputational losses. (See the Boeing case study at end of this chapter.)

The following are examples of execution risks from the financial services industry. Data errors are central to many of these risks and apply across all industries.

Sample Execution Risks

Execution Risk Type	Description
Human Errors	Fat finger errors, manual processing errors, miscommunication, untrained staff
Systemic Errors	Data feeds not working properly; incorrect data embedded in systems or model, system processing errors
Reporting Errors	Failure to meet regulatory or corporate reporting requirements, errors in data or narratives, data or reporting errors require resubmission
Data Errors	Incorrect, incomplete or untimely data
Transaction Booking Errors	Incorrect trade entry, wrong account booking, wrong market rates, duplicate entries, omissions
Trade Execution Failures	Timing delays, failure to meet requirements, mismatched trades
Settlement and Confirmation Failures	Late or failed settlements, confirmation mismatches, missing documentation
Valuation and Pricing Errors	Pricing model errors, wrong inputs, pricing discrepancies, incorrect product pricing
Reconciliation Failures	Breaks in trade or cash positions, failure to reconcile with general ledger
Technology and Systems Failures	System failures during upgrades or deployments, system downtime, broken system links, failure to back-up or mirror system activity
Process and Control Failures	Processes are not adequately executed, process handoff errors, controls fail to perform as designed
Regulatory and Compliance Breaches	Failure to meet regulatory or compliance requirements resulting from failed or inadequate processes

Managing Through the Operational Risk Framework

All operational risk subtypes (including execution, third-party, fraud, resilience, data risks) should be managed through the standard operational risk framework as a starting point so that there is ultimately one methodology for assessing risks and controls and one view of risk. As previously mentioned, I have worked in organizations where there were multiple risk assessments covering the operational risk subtypes that resulted in bringing conflicting risk reports to the board and senior management.

Figure 11.1 shows the components of the operational risk framework. (See Chapter 4 for a discussion on the operational risk framework.)

Some risks may require a "double-click" or deep dive when designing the risk and control assessments according to specific industry frameworks (such as the Cyber NIST framework discussed in Chapter 13), but these should be ultimately aligned with the operational risk framework. I discussed in Chapter 1 how a taxonomy is the "risk language" of the firm. The operational risk framework in essence provides the guiding principle for managing risks across all nonfinancial risk disciplines and serves as the "control language" of the firm.

Figure 11.1 Components of the operational risk framework

The following are applications of the framework to the management of execution risks.

Governance

It is critical that the roles and responsibilities are adequately defined for the management of execution risks. The first line is closest to the "factory floor" and will have the best perspective on where the processes are most vulnerable. Boeing's management implemented control enhancements after catastrophic plane crashes and loss of life and established senior-level control committees, but there was a disconnect with what was really happening on the faculty floor. (See the Boeing case study at the end of this chapter.) There needs to be strong communication among the three lines of defense in managing execution risks and also between the people on the ground managing the processes, their management, and the firm's executive management and the board.

Policies and Procedures

Managing execution risks should follow the requirements for managing operational risk in the operational risk policy. However, it is a strong practice to complement the operational risk policy with a standard that includes the specific requirements (in essence, the "double-click") for managing execution risks. Some firms create an execution risk policy, given the criticality of the risk type. The first line would be expected to create a procedure that describes the step-by-step requirements for implementing the policy or standard.

The policy or standard should include the following:

- **Purpose statement and scope:** The general purpose of the policy or standard, establishing requirements for the management of execution risk, and scope, which should be the entire organization, including all entities, functions, and business units, as execution risks reside in almost every process.
- **Definitions:** Definitions of key terms, such as execution risk, escalation, issue, action plan, process mapping, material process, RCSA, key risk indicators, key performance indicators, and risk appetite.
- **Roles and responsibilities:** Roles and responsibilities for first-line, second-line, third-line, and governance committees that are responsible for monitoring execution risks.
- **Operational risk framework and policy:** Linkage to operational risk framework and policy requirements, including requirements to conduct RCSA, track and monitor execution related risk events, threshold for tracking losses, risk appetite, issue management, scenario analysis, key risk indicators, reporting, monitoring and oversight, review and challenge, reporting, governance committees.
- **Types of execution risk:** Description of the types of execution risks, including manual process errors, human errors, financial reporting errors, transaction booking and execution errors, settlement and confirmation errors, valuation and pricing errors,

reconciliation errors, technology and system errors, process and control failures, regulatory and compliance breaches, third party errors.

- **Escalations:** Section on requirements to escalate execution related incidents, including thresholds and regulatory notification requirements (see Chapter 8).
- **System:** A statement on the system of record for tracking execution incidents.
- **Reporting and documentation:** Section senior management, committee and regulatory reporting related to execution risks, including any specific committees of forums
- **Training requirements:** Requirements for conducting training on managing execution risks, escalations and reporting.
- **Policy governance:** Indicated policy or directive owner, review cycle, exceptions, requirement for first-line procedures, required approvals.

Risk Appetite and Key Risk Indicators

It is impossible to reduce errors and execution-related risks to zero while remaining in business. As with all risks, it is necessary to define the level of execution risk an organization or business is willing to accept and where the thresholds reside for crossing over the line into unacceptable risk. The risk appetite for execution risks should be anchored to the overall risk appetite for the firm, with specific thresholds called out for the types of errors that can occur related to specific execution types, such as transaction processing, manual processing, and system errors. I am a huge advocate of having one set of risk metrics that flow from the risk appetite statements, which also serve as key risk indicators.

The following are five categories of execution risks with sample risk appetite statements and suggested metrics. The metrics include low, medium, and high thresholds. It is a strong practice to put an action plan in place proactively when a metric hits a yellow threshold or to determine if a risk acceptance is appropriate. Developing a set of metrics and monitoring them against risk appetite is essential to understanding the current level of exposure to execution errors and whether the firm is within its stated appetite.

Human Error Risk Appetite Statement

The firm maintains a low appetite for human error that results in material financial loss, regulatory breaches, and client or reputational harm. All errors above the risk appetite lower threshold must be promptly escalated and remediated (i.e., in the medium and high threshold). The organization is committed to maintaining strong controls and systems to reduce manual errors. See Table 11.1.

Table 11.1 Examples of Human Error Risk Appetite Metrics

Metric	Low	Medium	High
Error Rate per 1,000 Transactions	<=1	1.01–3	>3
% of Manual Workarounds	<=5%	5.01–10%	>10%
% Staff Completing Execution Training	>=98%	90–97.99%	<90%

Reporting Risk Appetite Statement

The firm has no appetite for reporting errors that lead to regulatory noncompliance, market misinformation, or misinformed executive decisions. Reports must be accurate, timely, and appropriately reviewed prior to distribution. The firm supports data quality programs and robust controls to ensure reporting integrity. See Table 11.2.

Table 11.2 Examples of Reporting Risk Appetite Metrics

Metric	Low	Medium	High
% of Reports Delivered on Time	>=99%	95–98.99%	<95%
Number of Regulatory Reporting Errors	0	1–2	>=3
Re-submission Rate for Regulatory Filings	<=1%	1.01–3%	>3%

Data Risk Management Risk Appetite Statement

The firm maintains a low appetite for data integrity failures that impact business decisions, client outcomes, regulatory compliance, or cybersecurity. Data must be accurate, complete, timely, and governed through robust data management practices. The organization invests in data governance and controls to mitigate data risk. See Table 11.3.

Table 11.3 Examples of Data Risk Management Risk Appetite Metrics

Metric	Low	Medium	High
% of Critical Data with Defined Owners	100%	90–99.99%	<90%
Data Quality Score (Accuracy)	>=98%	95–97.99%	<95%
Unauthorized Data Access Events (monthly)	0	1	>=2

System Risk Appetite Statement

The firm maintains a low appetite for system outages or failures in critical business applications. Systems supporting client transactions, financial reporting, and regulatory compliance must maintain high availability, performance, and resilience. Planned downtime must be minimal and well-communicated, and unplanned outages must be investigated promptly. See Table 11.4.

Table 11.4 Examples of System Risk Appetite Metrics

Metric	Low	Medium	High
System Uptime for Critical Platforms	>=99.9%	99.0–99.89%	<99.0%
Number of High-Severity Incidents	<=1	2	>=3
Mean Time to Recover (MTTR)	<=1 hour	1.01–3 hours	>3 hours

Trade Execution Risk Appetite Statement

The firm maintains a low appetite for trade execution errors that result in client harm, financial loss, or regulatory breaches. All trades must be executed promptly, accurately, and in accordance with internal policies and external regulatory requirements. While minor and recoverable execution errors may occur in high-volume environments, such events must be infrequent, promptly detected, and addressed through effective controls, monitoring, and remediation. See Table 11.5.

Table 11.5 Examples of Trade Execution Risk Appetite Metrics

Metric	Low	Medium	High
Booking Error Rate (per 1,000 trades)	<=1	1.01–3	>3
Trade Confirmation Timeliness (%)	>=99%	95–98.99%	<95%
Settlement Failures (%)	<=0.5%	0.51–1%	>1%
Mean Time to Detect Execution Errors	<=30 minutes	31–120 minutes	>120 minutes

Loss Data, Incidents, Escalations, and Issue Management

Execution-related risks contribute significantly to an organization's operational risk loss events but also to its incidents and near-misses. (See Chapter 7 for definitions of operational risk loss events.) The actual documented loss events do not always tell the complete story when tracking execution errors as many do not rise to the level of a defined event. Still, the execution events that are below the reported thresholds are important to track to understand if they in aggregate suggest a pattern of process and control failings and if in aggregate they add up to something that is noteworthy and could impact the firm's risk appetite. These events do not necessarily need to be tracked at the same level of detail as loss events that are above the reporting threshold, but they should be monitored through a "portfolio approach" that is not too onerous given the level of risk each individual event poses.

An important component of managing execution risks is to have a clear understanding of when events require escalation, to whom, and within what timeframe. Some institutions have escalation policies, directives, or procedures, while others incorporate "escalation ladders" into their loss event governance documents. It is helpful to create a distribution list with the firm's senior executives for when a high or critical event occurs and some institutions have the communication list built into the workflow of their GRC systems.

Opening issues and action plans should follow the identification of an event or incident that meets the criteria outlined in the issue management policy, which is usually an identified control deficiency that requires remediation. The identified control deficiency will be remediated through an action plan designed to address the root cause of the missing or ineffective control and the risk it is designed to mitigate. If the incident is deemed to be rated low risk, it may not meet the issue management threshold for required remediation. However, if there is a pattern of similar incidents that are tracked through the portfolio review approach, it is prudent to open an issue proactively to address the pattern of control issues that have emerged.

The second-line operational risk department may want to conduct a thematic review of a firm's processes, including assessing the effectiveness of controls and walking through process maps, when a large execution risk event occurs. It is a strong practice to look across the organization through the review to determine if similar control vulnerabilities exist elsewhere. The risk function may want to also conduct a thematic review if a pattern of smaller events occur to determine where controls can be enhanced proactively. Conducting a narrow thematic review and examining only one small area where an incident occurred will produce narrow results that does not fully protect the organization.

It is critical (see Chapter 3) for there to be a strong partnership between the first and second lines of defense. This is ever more critical when it comes to managing execution risk, because it is not effective for the second line to be disconnected from the on-the-ground processes. When an event, incident, or near-miss occurs, the first and second lines will need to work together to remediate the issue, stop the bleeding, conduct a root-cause analysis and a look-across to determine if there are similar issues elsewhere. This can be effective only if the basis for a strong collaborative relationship has been formed and both sides trust each other and assume positive intent. I have witnessed operations people who move from the first line to a second-line function be successful in their oversight and review and challenge role, as they understand the processes profoundly. They are well positioned to know where to look for control issues.

Risk and Control Assessment

Risk and control self-assessments are critical for all operational risk types, including execution risk. At the heart of execution risks are processes, and when processes and their associated controls go wrong, you are likely to have an event of varied magnitude. It is not possible to manage this risk without understanding the processes from end to end. Process mapping is an essential component of an RCSA program, as it allows for the assessment of where in the process risks reside and control activities occur. It is important to ensure, for instance, that the controls are occurring in the correct stage of the process, as a timing mismatch can result in a control breakdown. The risks and controls identified in the process mapping exercises can be pulled directly into the RCSA assessment.

The benefits of making a commitment to creating and maintaining a library of process maps are that they allow for the visualization of how a process is executed from end to end. It is important to decide at what level the process mapping exercise will be conducted and how detailed the maps will be. I have always preferred conducting process mapping exercises as either "level 2" or "level 3" depending how a certain process is structured. A too high-level process map is essentially boxes on a page, while a too detailed one creates challenges with "seeing the forest through the trees" as it is difficult to identify the overriding risks and controls. A process map created for RCSA purposes is not a process reengineering exercise, but rather a risk and control exercise. I start with a level 2 or 3 processing mapping exercise and then dig deeper if I need to get a more detailed view into where controls may be breaking down.

It is possible to leverage process maps that have been created for other purposes, as they often reside in operations functions. They may need to be rolled up if they are too detailed, but often these efforts include both the high-level view of an end-to-end process and the more detailed views. The challenge ultimately in complex organizations is getting the end-to-end view of risks and controls. This is especially challenging for processes that cross business units and functions, because there may be multiple people involved in managing the various streams inherent in the process. An RCSA that is organized by process as the first principle, with risks connected to processes and controls connected to risks, or the PRC approach, allows for easier view into end-to-end processes (see Chapter 6).

It is a strong practice to name process owners who are responsible for the end-to-end management of a process, including assessing risks and controls, regardless of how they stack up in business units or functions. Many organizations are adopting process-driven organizational structures that allow for closer alignment with the firm's process inventory and process-based approach to risk and control. A firm that is not organized in this way can still create end-to-end process views and process ownership, if someone is willing to accept ownership of processes that may not be entirely within their business remit. This level of end-to-end ownership of a process is critical, as breakdowns often happen where there are handoffs among businesses and functions. I have worked in organizations that spend a long time debating on who will own an issue when this happens, because no one wanted to own a remediation that was not entirely within their remit.

Here is how I work with stakeholders on the creation of a process map:

- Schedule workshop with SMEs and representatives from the businesses and functions that are impacted by the process. Ensure that the right cross section of people is present. As an example, for regulatory reporting, I would include regulatory reporting (see sample regulatory reporting process map below) and data governance risk people, along with the first-line business—in many cases a finance function—that are responsible for submission of certain required regulatory reports.
- The workshop will start with a review of existing process maps if they exist or the creation of a high-level end-to-end view, which can be built out.
- The workshop participants walk through the high-level diagram of the process and confirm that the end-to-end view is complete.
- Each stream (i.e., each box under the high-level view) would be built out and mapped across distinct swim lanes. For the sample process map below, the processes are mapped out for the data analyst, data owner, and report owner activities.

- I always start with a whiteboard or a paper and easel for the initial creation of the process flow. Once the whiteboard view is agreed on by the participants, the flow can be transferred to an application.
- The activities are mapped by their swim lanes into a process mapping application, such as Microsoft Visio or IBM Blueworks. Excel also works, which is what I used to create the example process map shown in the next section.
- Activities that cross over swim lanes (and functions) are identified as potential areas of "handoff" risks.
- Risks and controls are added to the maps, based on workshop discussions. It is a strong practice to add any rules or regulations to the map that apply to the process.
- It is a strong practice to add handshake controls where there are handoffs. A handshake control can be a documented acknowledgment through an email or workflow tool that the process activity has been handed off and "caught" by the business or function on the other side.
- The process works the same for a map that requires updating, with the walkthroughs validating the process and identifying any changes that are incorporated into the process map.
- Once the process map is created, the workshop participants validate the view and provide additional feedback.
- The risks and controls are incorporated into the RCSA; the risks are rated for inherent risk, and the controls are rated for effectiveness.
- The process maps are updated following a risk-based approach. The highest rated processes should be reviewed and updated annually, the moderate ones every two years and the lowest rated ones every three years.
- It is a strong practice to update the process maps when there is a change in the process, a reorganization, or a process breakdown that requires remediation. (Learn about the RCSA trigger-based approach in Chapter 5.)

Example Process Map for Regulatory Reporting with Risks and Controls

Figure 11.2 shows a high-level view of a process map that contains risks and controls for the regulatory reporting process. It is an example of a process map at level 2. A real process map would have additional steps related to data validation.

The following are the risks and controls:

Risks	**Controls**
R1: Inaccurate data	C1: Validate of system rules
R2: Data corruption	C2: Access controls
R3: Template errors	C3: Reconciliation against regulatory thresholds
R4: Late or inaccurate submission	C4: Reconciliation to GL and financial statements
	C5: Senior manager attestation
	C6: Independent validation (four-eyes review)

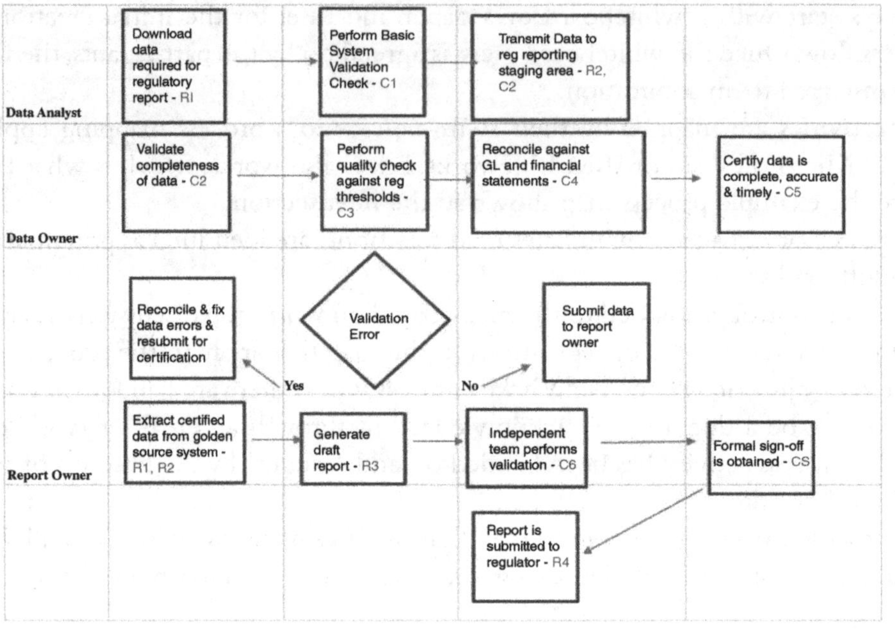

Figure 11.2 A high-level view of a process map

Scenario Analysis

Dissecting and analyzing a process from end to end provides rich content for the construction of scenarios, and this is especially true for execution risk, where the exposure resides primarily where processes break. Process maps can assist with the development of severe but plausible scenarios. As discussed, breakdowns often occur where there are handoffs that can be identified through the process maps and stressed to develop execution risk scenarios. Areas to highlight in the construction of scenarios, in addition to handoffs, are where there are manual processes, third-party dependencies, and process intensive activities.

When constructing the execution risk scenario, the focus should be on where the process breakdown can occur, what the upstream and downstream impacts are, and what the impact would be if the controls failed under stress. As discussed in Chapter 9, determining loss impact through the assessment of past internal and external events, issues, audit and regulatory findings is a good way of anchoring the loss estimation. If controls are found to be deficient under stress, it is a strong and proactive practice to open an issue and action plan to enhance the control environment.

The following are suggested execution-related scenarios:

Scenario Title	Description	Root Cause	Severity	Likelihood	Low Loss ($)	Medium Loss ($)	High Loss ($)	Impact
Fat-Finger Payment Error	The loan operations department entered an interest payment of $500M instead of $50M in the payment processing system.	Failure to properly catch error during four-eye review.	High	Medium	$1,000,000	$10,000,000	$100,000,000	Payment loss, regulatory fines related to payment controls, reputational damage
Derivatives System Outage	Third-party provider of derivatives trading execution support goes down due to ransomware attack. Bank shuts off connection to vendor and manually executes trades.	Third party vendor had vulnerability in trading platform and insufficient cyber security controls.	High	High	$2,000,000	$15,000,000	$150,000,000	Missed trades, data exposure, regulatory inquiry into third party controls, customer harm
Misrouting of Large Wire Transfer	$75M settlement payment sent to wrong counterpart; mistaken funds are not returned upon receipt.	Manual input error; lack of dual authorization and four eyes review.	High	Medium	$5,000,000	$25,000,000	$100,000,000	Losses, costly litigation, reputational harm
Losses, Failed Collateral Substitution on a Cleared Repo	Required collateral substitution not executed, creating margin shortfall.	Poor coordination; unclear ownership.	High	Low	$3,000,000	$20,000,000	$75,000,000	Regulatory breach, penalties, strained counterparty relationships
Settlement Failure in Sovereign Bond Trade	$1B sovereign bond trade fails to settle due to incorrect account instructions.	Static data error; reconciliation breakdown.	High	Medium	$10,000,000	50,000,000	200,000,000	Counterparty claims, interest penalties, capital impact

Monitoring and Reporting

Reporting on execution risks should occur at several levels within the firm. Each impacted business, such as payments and operations, should report on recent events, incidents, and near-misses through forums and committees for their respective business and function areas. Second-line operational risk should incorporate reporting of execution-related events, incidents, near-misses, and risk appetite metrics that are above or approaching the appetite, RCSA results, issues and regulatory and audit findings into its regular risk committee and board reporting.

Culture and Awareness

Human errors are at the heart of many execution risk events, incidents, and near-misses, and there are few organizations that exist today that can attest to not relying on manual (being human) processes. Organizations are highly dependent on humans doing their jobs correctly, which when it comes to processes, such as payments, reporting, trade execution, collateral management, and wire transfers, require attention to detail and the proper execution of controls. It should be noted that AI will reduce many of these manual processes and associated errors over time.

I have worked at several firms that had operational excellence initiatives in place that were designed to remind employees of the importance of doing their jobs with care, intention, and attention. I worked at one firm that gave out awards each year as part of their excellence initiative. As someone who received an award, I was invited to a special session with the chief executive officer and a dinner at the Rainbow Room in New York in celebration of that year's awardees.

It is an effective strategy to acknowledge the people who go above and beyond, execute their duties with extreme care, and raise their hands when they identify problems.

Here are the core components of how an operational excellence program works:

- **CEO communication:** The CEO communicates regularly on the importance of executing with care, continuous improvement, identifying issues, raising one's hand when there is a problem and taking pride in one's work. These communications are specific so that they resonate and are distributed on a regular basis. It is a strong practice to reinforce the message through taped videos or even better, in-person townhalls.
- **Echo from the middle:** The CEO's message is reinforced by line managers for each area where they are responsible. This should include discussions during team meetings and all-hands sessions and positive reinforcement when issues are self-identified.
- **Self-identified issues:** A strong practice is to set targets for the self-identification of issues (versus identification by second-line regulators or auditors). I have seen the target at several organizations for self-identified issues be in the 50–60% range. I worked at one organization that set it at 80%, which drove some bad behavior with issues that did not meet the issue management criteria or duplicate issues being entered into the system to meet the self-identified benchmark.

- **Training:** Training sessions are conducted on the importance of executing one's responsibilities with care. Teams are so inundated with online assigned compliance training that an in-person or Zoom or Teams session may have more impact than something that is prerecorded, where the session can be interactive and a safe place to discuss execution challenges.
- **Culture carriers:** Individuals who consistently do the right thing, execute with care, step up and identify areas for process improvement, complete major initiatives on time and budget, and exude all the strong cultural qualities of an organization's mission should be recognized each year, through a nomination process. One organization posts the recipients of its annual excellence awards on LinkedIn. I mentioned the organization where the recipients were treated to a special evening event.
- **Performance management:** Goals can be added to the performance management system that assesses an individual's ability to perform their duties with quality, including delivering projects on time with minimal errors, remediating outstanding issues, effectively implementing controls, self-identifying issues, and continuously improve processes under their remit.

Payments

Execution risks associated with retail and wholesale payments are significant. On the retail side, in addition to traditional check and credit card payments, there are emerging technologies that pose new risks that require integration into an operational risk management program, including digital wallets, real-time payments, blockchain, and the use of payment applications as primary bank accounts. Execution risks associated with wholesale payments include faster transactions, real-time processing, and digitization. Both retail and wholesale payments are highly dependent on technology and exposed to risks associated with fraud, operational failures, data privacy, system reliability, and third-party vendors. This is a heavily regulated sector that carries significant compliance risk. It is a risk type that results in significant financial losses. Stripe, in its paper on risk management, estimated in 2024 that more than 60% of operational failures in payment systems result in at least $1 million in total losses.

Stripe outlines the following operational risks associated with payment systems: fraud (characterized as the main risk in retail payments), chargebacks (losses associated with retail client disputes), technical issues (technical issues and system failures), regulatory compliance (complying with payment system standards), emerging threats (includes synthetic identify fraud and deep fakes), and third-party risks (third-party payment processes and service providers).

The risk management solutions for managing payments risk are relying heavily on technology and are evolving as I write this, with AI allowing for more efficient and accurate monitoring. Advanced fraud detection systems that are AI driven are important tools in tracking fraudulent transactions and are reducing the multitude of false positives that have occurred with more rules-based traditional systems. AI is also being used in behavioral analytics that are being used to detect anomalies through user profiling.

Biometric verification is increasingly being used to detect credential compromises and unauthorized transactions.

Payment risk management should leverage all the components of the operational risk framework including scenario analysis, risk appetite and RCSA. Process mapping these systemic processes is critical, with a deep dive into where the systems handoff processes to humans, as this is where errors, omissions, and oversights can occur. There are still quite a lot of organizations that rely on human processing for some portion of the payments process.

The Automated Clearing House (ACH) Network is extremely critical to the US banking industry. It is the infrastructure for movement of money and serves as the primary rails for direct deposits (our paychecks!) and bill payments. If there was a disruption in the ACH Network, our paychecks might be delayed, and there could be severe disruption in our payment systems, including liquidity issues. National Automated Clearing House Association (NACHA) is the governing body responsible for managing the development, administration, and governance of the ACH Network in the United States. NACHA provides extensive guidance on managing ACH related frauds, along with typical scenarios in its risk management framework (https://www.nacha.org/RiskFramework).

The European Union released a Payment Services Directive that became applicable in 2018. It established standards across the European Union, including multifactor authentication, consumer protection, fraud prevention, customer rights, and transparency requirements related to fee disclosures. In addition to introducing new compliance and risk management guidelines, it was designed to open its payment infrastructure to digitization and create seamless passage for European payments (see https://www.ecb.europa.eu/press/intro/mip-online/2018/html/1803_revisedpsd.en.html).

Boeing Case Study

Execution risks occur in all industries. The challenges experienced by Boeing provides a good example of how overlooking execution risks and underinvesting in quality controls can lead to serious ramifications down the line, including fines, penalties, shareholder lawsuits, business interruption and reputational consequences.

The event involving the blowout midflight of a plugged door panel on an Alaska Airlines Boeing 737 Max 9s Jet in January 2024 is a reminder that operational risk resides everywhere and in every industry. It is frightening to consider how much worse this incident could have been, and I can only imagine the terror passengers onboard the flight must have felt. This follows a history of issues with the Boeing 737 Max. This family of aircraft has been under scrutiny since the global fleet was grounded in March 2019 following two fatal incidents that resulted in the death of 346 people.

There are a lot of lessons learned associated with the blown-out door incident, which thankfully did not result in a loss of life. It includes the importance of testing, testing, testing, following a rigorous quality control program, oversight of third-party providers, understanding the impact of cost-cutting, and paying close attention to the quality of process execution. One lesson is that issues do not age well. Several reports, including an assessment by the National Safety Transportation Board and the Federal Aviation Administration, along with investigations by the *Financial Times*, the *Wall Street Journal,* and PBS Frontline, all pointed to long-standing quality issues that were never remediated at their root cause.

The remediations that management put in place over the years did not seem to fix Boeing's underlying quality issues. There were several top-level initiatives that the CEO put in place when he took over in 2020. He established a board-level safety board and reorganized reporting lines so that top-level engineers reported directly to the company's chief engineer, rather than the business executives they previously reported to. He created a product and services safety group that reported to the chief engineer and a chief safety officer was appointed. The *Financial Times* reported, however, that there was a "disconnect between top-level initiatives and the reality on the shop floor."

It was also reported that Boeing relied on a process called *traveled work* that stressed its ability to manage quality. If a quality issue was found on the assembly line, instead of stopping work, the plane was passed on with the problem until it was fixed down the line. The challenge is that leaving a plane with a quality issue in place instead of advancing it to the next station during assembly holds up the process at a time when Boeing was under pressure to meet increasing demand. But repairing the issue down the line increases exposure to additional execution risks, including a failure to properly repair the issue or missing it entirely.

This has emerged as one of the root causes of the problem with the Alaska Air plugged door. Workers spotted faulty rivets after the fuselage arrived at the factory but did not make the fix right away. The fuselage then spent three weeks moving through the assembly line without the needed fix. Boeing workers opened the plane to complete the repair several weeks later but failed to replace the critical bolts on the plug door. They also failed to properly document the fix. This ultimately led to the January 2024 incident where the door fell off an inflight aircraft.

The National Transportation Safety Board (NTSB) in its investigation of the incident issued findings indicating the evidence pointed to missing bolts that prevented the movement of the door plug. The report points to the absence of "contact damage or deformation" around the impacted holes as evidence that the bolts were simply missing. It turns out that the issue was not loose bolts, but rather no bolts on the plugged door.

The NTSB evidence included a photo that was attached to a text message that was sent by a Boeing team member on September 19, 2023, that displays the missing bolts. Boeing opened the panel at that time to repair damaged rivets on the plane's fuselage, and it appears never replaced all the bolts after they removed them. The NTSB indicated that the photo showed three of the four bolts missing in the September photo. The fate of the fourth bolt was unclear, because the photo that was examined showed the location of the fourth bolt obstructed by insulation. The plane was delivered to Alaska Airlines the following month.

The Federal Aviation Administration (FAA) released an expert panel review of the incident. The structure of the panel's investigation was based upon a principle that is intrinsic to its Safely Management System (SMS) framework: organizations must manage safety with the same level of priority that they give to other business processes. The FAA required Boeing to review its 53 findings and develop a remediation action plan.

The FAA panel identified a disconnect between senior management and other members of the organization on safety issues. There were concerns about the ability of its safety reporting systems to function with open communication channels. The panel found that the safety cultural initiative that was implemented with five components was confusing and inadequate. It also found that safety training, implementation of the FAA's SMS framework and safety metrics were equally confusing. The report did mention that training became more effective as Boeing moved to a more scenario-based approach.

The FAA also found that Boeing's safety procedures lacked transparency when updates were made, with one document simply indicating "major updates" without explaining the changes. The panel found that roles and responsibilities in the procedures for managing implementing the SMS framework were high level and mostly implied. The report found that there was a decline in employee knowledge and expertise of safety measures as more experienced staff left or took retirement during the pandemic.

The fuselage for Boeings 737 was supplied by Spirit Aerosystems and over time became heavily dependent on suppliers. A Boeing engineer published a paper in 2001 warning of the company's subcontracting strategy and observed that the quality of the overall manufacturing process is only as good as the "least proficient of the suppliers." In fact, Boeing put a lot of cost pressure on Spirit, which may have contributed to some of the quality issues that were resident in the delivered fuselages.

Here are some of the lessons learned from this event:

- **Outcomes matter:** Risk management should be outcome based. A program to improve quality falls flat if it cannot be substantiated by evidence of actual improvement.
- **Connect the dots:** From a lesson learned perspective, it's important to connect top-down initiatives with bottom-up ones. Boeing's Senior management appear to not have had enough insight into the quality of the company's manufacturing processes on the factory floor.
- **Processes matter:** There should be strategies in place to inventory all processes to pinpoint where they can fail and to monitor and report on vulnerabilities. The people who manage day-to-day operations should have a means for raising red flags when necessary.
- **Problems don't age well:** Boeing was dealing with quality problems associated with Spirit AeroSystems' components for some time. They appear to have never gotten to the root cause of all the issues that were emerging and conducted a comprehensive look across.
- **Experienced workers are critical:** The industry in general suffered from a loss of experienced workers due to layoffs and retirement.

Citigroup Fat Finger Case Study Courtesy of IBM

IBM **FIRST**
RISK CASE STUDIES

FIRST Report for Loss Event 18732

Short Description

Citigroup confirmed it had mistakenly transferred USD $900 million to creditors of cosmetics company Revlon on August 11, 2020. As the administrator of a $1.8 billion term loan for Revlon, Citigroup should have transferred only the interest due on the loan to the creditors. Instead it transferred amounts nearly 100 times greater, paying off the full amount -- principal and interest -- from its own funds, as a result of a manual error. When Citigroup asked creditors to return the funds some did so, returning approximately $400 million of the funds received in error. Ten creditors, including Brigade Capital Management, HPS Investment Partners and Symphony Asset Management, refused to do so, leaving the bank with a loss amount of $501 million. Because the loan had been underperforming, these creditors were unlikely to recoup their investment and they said they viewed the transfers as repayment of their loans. Citigroup then sued the remaining creditors for the return of its funds. On February 16, 2021, a judge in the US District Court in the Southern District of New York ruled that Citigroup wasn't entitled to get the funds back from what he described as "one of the biggest blunders in banking history." Citigroup said it strongly disagreed with the court's decision and appealed. On September 8, 2022, the 2nd US Circuit Court of Appeals in Manhattan ruled 3-0 in favor of Citigroup, ordering lenders to Revlon Inc to return about $500 million of Citigroup's own money. Citigroup announced on December 20, 2022 that it had finally resolved the matter a reached a settlement with the last remaining counterparties, and that all "all ten" creditors having signed agreements with the bank, litigation in the case would end.

Organizations

Name	Firm	Country
Citigroup Inc.	Citigroup Inc. - No Firm Available	North America\United States\New York

Details

Loss Amount:	
Currency:	USD
Loss Amount Current:	
Currency Original:	USD-United States Dollars
Original Currency Amount:	
Status:	CLOSED
Geography:	North America\United States\New York
Created Date:	Aug 20, 2020
Revision Date:	Dec 20, 2022

Dates

Start Occurrence: Aug 11, 2020	End Occurrence: Aug 11, 2020	Settlement Date: Sep 12, 2022

Long Description

Event Summary

Citigroup confirmed it had mistakenly transferred USD $900 million to creditors of cosmetics company Revlon on August 11, 2020. As the administrator of a $1.8 billion term loan for Revlon, Citigroup should have transferred only the interest due on the loan to the creditors. Instead it transferred amounts nearly 100 times greater, paying off the full amount -- principal and interest -- from its own funds, as a result of a manual error. When Citigroup asked creditors to return the funds some did so, returning approximately $400 million of the funds received in error. Ten creditors, including Brigade Capital Management, HPS Investment Partners and Symphony Asset Management, refused to do so, leaving the bank with a loss amount of $501 million. Because the loan had been underperforming, these creditors were unlikely to recoup their investment and they said they viewed the transfers as repayment of their loans. Citigroup then sued the remaining creditors for the return of its funds. On February 16, 2021, a judge in the US District Court in the Southern District of New York ruled that Citigroup wasn't entitled to get the funds back from what he described as "one of the biggest blunders in banking history." Citigroup said it strongly disagreed with the court's decision and appealed. On September 8, 2022, the 2nd US Circuit Court of Appeals in Manhattan ruled 3-0 in favor of Citigroup, ordering lenders to Revlon Inc to return about $500 million of Citigroup's own money. Citigroup announced on December 20, 2022 that it had finally resolved the matter a reached a settlement with the last remaining counterparties, and that all "all ten" creditors having signed agreements with the bank, litigation in the case would end.

Event Details

Cosmetics company Revlon was struggling with a large debt load during the Covid-19 pandemic, when retail markets collapsed. This included a 2016 $1.8 billion term loan from creditors including Brigade Capital Management, HPS Investment Partners and Symphony Asset Management. Citigroup was the administrative agent on the loan and made interest payments on Revlon's behalf.

On August 10, 2020, the creditor group sued Revlon over its debt-restructuring practices after the cosmetics giant transferred intellectual property assets, including those for American Crew and Elizabeth Arden, to subsidiaries. The group alleged that Revlon then pledged these assets as collateral for other creditors as the company tried to raise more funds, when they were the collateral backing for their $1.8 billion loan. Revlon was "stealing away the 2016 term lenders' collateral" the creditors alleged. The loan was trading for less than 30 cents on the dollar, compared with 77 cents at the start of the year, which indicated that the creditors were unlikely to recoup all of their investment.

The next day, the creditor group was surprised to discover that the exact amount of the loan, both principal and interest, had been repaid in full. Citigroup, the loan administrator, said a mistake had been made and that it had accidentally transferred amounts 100 times greater than were due to the creditors. Brigade Capital was supposed to receive $1.5 million in interest on a loan principal of $174.7 million. Instead, Citigroup transferred $176.2 million. The bank also wrongly transferred $127.3 million to HPS Investment Partners and $109.7 million to Symphony Asset Management. The total amount sent in error to multiple creditors was $900 million.

Revlon confirmed it had not made the repayments and Citigroup said the payment was made from its own funds. Citigroup said the overpayment was discovered within hours, during its daily cash reconciliation process, and the bank asked the recipients to return the money. However, some of the creditors refused, saying the funds should be regarded as repayment for the loan.

Citigroup sued Brigade Capital in federal court to return the $175 million it had been sent in error. The bank said Brigade should have known that a surprise repayment of principal could not be made under the governing credit agreement. The case was Citibank NA v Brigade Capital Management, 20-cv-6539, US District Court, Southern District of New York (Manhattan).

The following day Citigroup also sued HPS Investment Partners and Symphony Asset Management for the return of their funds. The case was Citibank NA v. HPS Investment Partners LLC and Symphony Asset Management LLC, 20-cv-6617, U.S. District Court, Southern District of New York.

Control Failings and Contributory Factors

Human Errors; Failure to Test for Data Accuracy: In order to ensure that only the interest amount was paid to the creditors, the person processing the transaction had to select three fields from the Flexcube system used by Citigroup. However, the processor and two other people involved in approving the payments all believed, incorrectly, that they only needed to enter data into the 'principle' field on the database. This meant that Citigroup paid the exact amount of principal and interest owed. Brigade Capital, HPS and Symphony disagreed there had been a mistake and said that Citi could not have transferred such a large sum in error.

Lack of Dual Control: Citigroup's manual 'six-eye' approval procedure, which requires three people to review and approve a transaction before it is executed, failed.

Inadequate Technology Planning: Citigroup was criticized for trying to process a complex payment, to pay only a certain number of multiple creditors who had recently agreed to a new payment schedule, using old technology. The bank confirmed that Flexcube, the IT system used to make the payment, dated back to the 1990's and was being replaced with the industry standard, Loan IQ. The rollout was ongoing when the incident took place, but it was not clear if any specific system contributed to the incident.

Corrective Actions and Management Response

In August 2020 a federal judge temporarily froze $175 million received by Brigade Capital Management, $238.3 million received by HPS Investment Partners and $109.7 million received in error by Symphony Asset Management. Some creditors chose to return approximately $400 million of the funds received in error but ten creditors refused, saying they did not know how Citigroup could expect them to know a payment was a mistake when the bank itself couldn't explain what had gone wrong. This left a loss amount of $501 million for Citigroup.

Citigroup said it was investigating how the mistake occurred. The bank said it was phasing out the system that allowed the accidental payment and upgrading it with a new loan-operations platform.

In October 2020, Citigroup was fined $400 million by the OCC and Federal Reserve Board for inadequate risk management practices, data governance and internal controls (see #18799).

Citigroup sued the ten creditors for return of the $501 million. The bank said the repayment was a human error and that the creditors knew or should have known that the transfers were a mistake and that Revlon could not afford such a large payment.

At a bench trial in December 2020 in the US District Court for the Southern District of New York (SDNY), Judge Jesse Furman ruled that under New York law, Citigroup wasn't entitled to get the funds back from what he described as "one of the biggest blunders in banking history." Judge Furman said the recipients could keep the money they received in error because the funds we "discharge-for-value" of a valid debt, the recipients had made no misrepresentations to induce the payment, and the recipients did not have notice of the mistake. They had reasonable grounds to believe the payments were intentional. "To believe that Citibank, one of the most sophisticated financial institutions in the world, had made a mistake that had never happened before, to the tune of nearly $1 billion, would have been borderline irrational." the judge said.

Citigroup said it strongly disagreed with the decision and intended to appeal.

Citigroup's appeal was successful and on September 8, 2022, a panel of the 2nd US Circuit Court of Appeals in Manhattan ruled 3-0 in favor of Citigroup Inc. The court ordered lenders to Revlon Inc to return about $500 million of its own money that was accidentally sent to them by wire transfer. Judge Pierre Level wrote in the 131-page ruling "Here, the debt on which Citibank mistakenly made a payment was not due for another three years. Defendants may not invoke the discharge-for-value rule as a shield against Citibank's claims for restitution."

Citigroup said in a statement on September 8: "Today's ruling reaffirms our long-held belief that these mistakenly transferred funds should be returned as a matter of law, as well as ethics. While Citi has taken steps to reduce the likelihood of such an error in the future, today's decision provides welcome stability and upholds the concept of cooperation needed for a well-functioning syndicated lending market."

Citigroup disclosed on December 20, 2022 that it had recently asked the Southern District of New York to dismiss litigation in the case after it reached a settlement with Revlon's creditors. The bank said it had settled over a USD500m portion of a payment that was made by the bank in error in August 2020. Citi also said it had already received repayment on about three quarters of the erroneous payment. In a court order dated December 19, the judge in the case gave the parties 60 days to reopen the action "if the settlement is not consummated."

Lessons Learned

From an operational risk perspective, the Citigroup Revlon miskeying event can be considered a "near miss" -- Citi won a favorable ruling in the Second Circuit Court of Appeals when the judges on the panel found unanimously that the payment was clearly made in error. However, the bank lost access to hundreds of millions of dollars for period of one to two years, and likely incurred significant unspecified legal expenses.

Keywords Indexing	
Entity Type	FINANCIAL SERVICES\BANKING\COMMERCIAL/FULL SERVICE BANK
Business Unit Type	COMMERCIAL BANKING (BIS)\LENDING/LOANS SERVICES -- COMMERCIAL
Service/Product Offering Type	LENDING PRODUCTS & FINANCING SERVICES\COMMERCIAL LOANS & FINANCING SERVICES\FINANCING SERVICES\FINANCING (MISC.)
Contributory/Control Factors	EMPLOYEE ACTION/INACTION\HUMAN ERRORS

	LACK OF CONTROL\FAILURE TO TEST FOR DATA ACCURACY LACK OF CONTROL\LACK OF DUAL CONTROL STRATEGY FLAW\INADEQUATE TECHNOLOGY PLANNING
Loss Type:	Known
Loss Impact	DIRECT LOSS\WRITE-DOWN (BIS)\GENERAL MONETARY LOSS
Loss Detection Sources	PERIODIC INTERNAL REVIEWS\BACK OFFICE REVIEWS
Market Focus	INSTITUTIONAL SERVICES
Event Trigger	PROCESS RISK CLASS\ERRORS AND OMISSIONS\EMPLOYEE ERRORS\MISKEYING
Basel Levels I & II	Execution Delivery and Process Management\Transaction Capture, Execution & Maintenance\Data entry, maintenance or loading error
Basel Business Line	Commercial Banking\Commercial Banking
Industry Event	

Rules and Regulations Indexing

Ratings

Ratings Action	Ratings Code	Effective Date	Ratings Watch/Outlook
Affirmed	A	Apr 22, 2020	Rating Outlook Negative
Review - No Action	A	Jun 9, 2020	Rating Outlook Negative
Affirmed	A	Dec 26, 2020	Rating Outlook Stable
Review - No Action	A	Dec 27, 2020	Rating Outlook Stable
4 Ratings found			

Source

2022-September-8: 2nd U.S. Circuit Court of Appeals "Citibank August 11, 2020 Wire Transfers" No. 21-487.

2022-December-20: Bloomberg News / Yahoo Finance "Citigroup's $900 Million Revlon Blunder Ends With a Dismissal After Bank's Victory"

2022-December-20: Mint / Bloomberg News "Citigroup's $900 million Revlon blunder ends with a dismissal"

2022-September-12: Computer Weekly "Mistakenly transferred $504m to be returned to Citigroup"

2022-September-9: Wall Street Journal "Citi Wins Appeal of Errant Payoff"

2022-September-8: Reuters "Citigroup wins appeal over mistaken Revlon wire transfer"

2021-February-16: US District Court Southern District of New York, "Citibank August 11, 2020 Wire Transfers, findings of fact and conclusions of law."

2021-February-23: FCPA Compliance &Ethics, "Too complex to succeed: Citibank incorrectly wires out $900 million."

2020-August-26: Bloomberg News, "Citi's $900 million misfire happened during software switch," by Jennifer Surane.

2020-August-20: National Post, "Citigroup gets part of Revlon funds frozen; nearly half of $900m paid in error locked," by Katherine Doherty.

2020-August-19: The Wall Street Journal, "Citi widens hunt for Revlon loan payments as lenders question mistake," by Becky Yerak.

2020-August-17: The Wall Street Journal, "Citi Sues Revlon Lender Brigade for Return of Payment It Says Was a Mistake," by Alexander Gladstone.

2020-August-17: Reuters News, "Citi sues Revlon lender Brigade for not returning part of $900 mln transferred mistakenly."

2020-August-13: The Wall Street Journal, "Citigroup pays Revlon lenders nearly $900 million by mistake," by Becky Yerak.

Claimant

Claimant Name:	US District Court for the Southern District of New York
Claimant Type:	REGULATORY

Scaling Data

Scaling Date	Employees	Total Assets(USD $M)	Total Equity(USD $M)	Total Deposits(USD $M)	Net Income(USD $M)
Dec 31, 2022	240,000	2,416,676.00	182,843.00	1,615,494.00	14,934.00
		Tier I Capital (USD $M)	**Tier I Capital Ratio (%)**		
		169,145.00	13.85		

Supporting Material

Loss Amount: Given that Citigroup's appeal was ultimately successful, we have removed the Loss Amount. However it should be noted that Citi has had legal expenses, as well as the lost opportunity to use more than $500 million for two years.

Revision Comments

12/20/2022: Citigroup announces a settlement with remaining counterparties, asks court to dismiss its lawsuit. Left Loss Amount blank
09/12/2022: Removed Loss Amount and added comment from Citigroup.
09/09/2022: Second Circuit Court of Appeals overturns SDNY verdict, ordering lenders to return $501 million to Citigroup; updated case, let Loss Amount stand.
02/22/2021: Updated event with details of US District Court Southern District of New York ruling that 10 creditors were not required to return $501 million they received in error. Changed loss amount to $501 million to reflect the fact that some creditors returned $400 million of funds received in error to Citigroup. Changed Settlement

Date to February 16, 2021.

09/01/2020: Updated event with more details from Citigroup about the manual error. Added Control Failings, Lack of Dual Control, Inadequate Technology Planning.

Copyright Information

IBM.

Source: Reprint Courtesy of IBM Corporation © 2025

Bibliography

Claire Bushey and Sylvia Pfeifer. Grounded Boeing Planes Won't Return to Service Until They Are Safe. *Financial Times*, January 10, 2024.

Claire Bushey and Sylvia Pfeifer. It Ain't Working: Boeing's Quality Pledges in Question after Max 9 Incident. *Financial Times*, January 15, 2024.

European Central Bank, Eurosystem. *The Revised Payment Services Directive (PSD2) and the Transition to Stronger Payments Security*. March 2018. https://www.ecb.europa.eu/press/intro/mip-online/2018/html/1803_revisedpsd.en.html.

Federal Financial Institutions Examination Council. *Retail Payment Systems IT Examination Handbook*. Washington, DC: FFIEC, April 2016. https://ithandbook.ffiec.gov/it-booklets/retail-payment-systems.aspx.

Federal Financial Institutions Examination Council. *Wholesale Payment Systems IT Examination Handbook*. Washington, DC: FFIEC, July 2004. https://ithandbook.ffiec.gov/it-booklets/wholesale-payment-systems.

Federal Aviation Administration. *Expert Panel Review Report*. https://www.faa.gov/newsroom/Sec103_ExpertPanelReview_Report_Final.pdf.

International Organization for Standardization (ISO). *ISO 20022: Financial Services—Universal Financial Industry Message Scheme*. Geneva: ISO, 2013. https://www.iso20022.org.

NACHA. *A New Risk Management Framework for the Era of Credit Push Fraud*. September 2022. https://www.nacha.org/RiskFramework.

National Transportation Safety Board. *In-Flight Separation of Left Mid Exit Door Plug, Alaska Airlines Flight 1281, Boeing 737-9, N704AL*. https://www.ntsb.gov/investigations/Pages/DCA24MA063.aspx.

Niraj Chokshi, Sydney Ember, and Santul Nerkar. Shortcuts Everywhere: How Boeing Favored Speed Over Quality. *The New York Times*, March 28, 2024. https://www.nytimes.com/2024/03/28/business/boeing-quality-problems-speed.html.

Office of the Comptroller of the Currency. *OCC Bulletin* 2012-16: *Mobile Payments Risk Management*. Washington, DC: OCC, April 2012. https://www.occ.gov/news-issuances/bulletins/2012/bulletin-2012-16.html.

Office of the Comptroller of the Currency. *OCC Bulletin* 2021-29: *Third-Party Relationships—Risk Management Guidance*. Washington, DC: OCC, June 2021. https://www.occ.gov/news-issuances/bulletins/2021/bulletin-2021-29.html.

Object Management Group (OMG). *Business Process Model and Notation (BPMN) Version 2.0*. Needham, MA: OMG, 2013. https://www.omg.org/spec/BPMN/2.0.

PBS Frontline. *Boeing's Fatal Flaw*. March 12, 2024. https://www.pbs.org/wgbh/frontline/documentary/boeings-fatal-flaw/?utm_source=Iterable&utm_medium=email&utm_campaign=ICYMI&utm_content=031624#video-1.

Sharon Terlep. Behind the Alaska Blowout: A Manufacturing Habit Boeing Can't Break. *The Wall Street Journal*, March 11, 2024. https://www.wsj.com/business/airlines/behind-the-alaska-blowout-a-manufacturing-habit-boeing-cant-break-c05a2ba5?mod=hp_lead_pos2.

Stripe. *Payments Risk Management: Key Components and Best Practices*, August 12, 2024. https://stripe.com/nz/resources/more/payments-risk-management-101-key-components-and-best-practices.

Chapter 12

Managing Change, and Product and Service Risk

Change Management

There are many forms of change in an organization. There is change associated with changes in laws and regulations (which has been significant lately), such as the new Basel III Capital Regulations or the introduction of DORA in the European Union. There is change related to operations, such as centralizing or decentralizing certain functions, outsourcing processes, or bringing them back in-house. There is change associated with products and services, such as the introduction of new or modified products or services. There is technology change, such as the introduction of a new banking deposit or finance system or moving data and systems to the cloud. There is organization change, such as changes to organizational structures, including downsizing the workforce or shifting responsibilities from one group to another. Finally, there is strategic change, such as shifting a firm's priorities on what markets it wants to operate in or what products it wants to offer.

There are many reasons why change is difficult. This can include failure of executive management to properly communicate the value proposition of why the change initiative is being undertaken, the lack of stakeholder buy-in and engagement, lack of planning and identifying risks, poor project management and governance, inadequate resources to execute the change initiative, failure to properly test (especially related to systems changes), and the deep-rooted human tendency to resist change. After all, who would expect a team to openly embrace moving their resources offshore or cost cutting initiatives?

Change brings increased risk, and it is critical to approach change initiatives with rigor and a structured risk management process, that includes assessing and mitigating identified risks, communicating the benefits of the initiative to all impacted stakeholders (you cannot overcommunicate), and testing, testing, testing ahead of any implementation. Operational risk functions in both the first and second line play important roles in assessing the initiative risks and providing oversight.

The following are some risks to consider when assessing a change initiative:

- **People:** Many people are inherently resistant to change, and the level of resistance should be assessed through interviews, committee briefing sessions, and reach-outs to the key stakeholders. It is good to know ahead of implementing an initiative where people's pain points might be and if there is at best less than enthusiastic support for the change initiative. It is also important from a communication perspective to work all bases and make sure the message from executive and middle management is positive. A bad outcome will likely result from a middle manager telling their team "I don't know why they are doing this, but we have to go along with it." Communication at all levels is critical to gain stakeholder support, and training sessions focused on "what is coming our way" are very helpful. It is a strong practice to map out a communication plan, which includes briefing sessions at committees and forums and information sessions that are aimed at a large cohort of stakeholders.
- **Project management:** Developing an implementation plan, regardless of whether the approach is Agile or Waterfall is important for keeping the project on track. Poor planning and poor project management often result in failed projects. It is also important to assess the project risks up front and identify the controls that will help mitigate them. If the controls do not exist, they should be developed ahead of implementation. Poor planning and project management, and failure to adequately assess project risk, can lead to a failed or challenging implementation.
- **Technology:** It is important to understand the risks and downstream and upstream impacts of technology change initiatives and business initiatives with significant system impact. There are very few change initiatives that do not involve some type of system change. Failure to properly integrate systems, and to test for all impacts, including impacts on an organization's existing infrastructure and compatibility issues, is critical to a successful implementation. It is also important to understand third-party exposure related to the initiative and to have a realistic budget for system builds or upgrades. This should be estimated up front. It is not a great strategy to assume the budgeting will be worked out later.
- **External factors:** Regulatory considerations must be considered when planning for a change initiative and compliance must be involved in the assessment process to understand the impact to any significant changes to a firm's products and services. In addition, scenarios should be created for various market and economic conditions to understand the impact of various changes to the operating environment on the change initiatives.

- **Agile vs. waterfall:** The change initiative should be assessed to determine if an Agile, Waterfall, or hybrid approach is appropriate. Many organizations have moved to an Agile approach, which is iterative and runs project phases concurrently, but it might not be the best methodology for every change initiative.

The following are key components of an effective change risk management program:

- **Framework and lifecycle:** The operational risk framework should be applied to the change risk management program. Change management should be assessed through an RCSA, a risk appetite statement should be drafted along with monitoring metrics, progress on the change portfolio should be monitored and reported through committee meetings, and control gaps identified through the change assessment process should result in the opening of issues and action plans. In addition, it is a strong practice to articulate the change risk management lifecycle that supplements the operational risk framework. The lifecycle must provide a structure for requesting, reviewing, approving, and documenting changes, including roles and responsibilities associated with approvals, communication, testing, oversight, and deployments.
- **Risk assessment:** Ahead of implementing an individual change initiative, an impact assessment must be conducted, the risks rated, a review undertaken of the effectiveness of current controls, and action plans completed ahead of deployment where required to close any material deficiencies.
- **Release management:** Rigor associated with version control should be in place for technology change initiatives to manage any code changes and track and approve revisions. Release schedules should include timelines, resources, and communication plans. Pre-production environments should be created and tested ahead of any releases. This is critical as there is continued challenge in all industries with business interruption events occurring that are associated with system upgrades.
- **Access administration:** For technology change initiatives, only authorized people should have access to the deployment environment. This always should be monitored, but especially ahead of a major change.
- **Testing and monitoring:** For process and technology change initiatives, multiple layers of testing should occur, including post-performance, user acceptance, and stress testing to ensure performance under different scenarios. Continuous monitoring should be in place to identify any issues that may require a rapid response and potential rollback.
- **New business initiatives (NBIs):** NBIs are a critical component of a change management program. They should be assessed ahead of implementation for impact to the organization's risk profile and ability for the current operating environment to incorporate the additional activity. All critical risks should be assessed, and the initiative should be monitored post-implementation to determine whether it is delivering on expectations. In addition, many regulators have established guidelines for introducing, developing, and distributing products and services, with a global standard of due care.

Figure 12.1 Change initiative lifecycle

Lifecycle

Change initiatives have distinct lifecycles, as demonstrated in Figure 12.1, which allow for proper rigor and risk management protocols.

Identification and Assessment

Articulating and documenting the business case is the first step in planning for a new business initiative. The initiative must be aligned with the firm's strategy, which is usually outlined in a three- or five-year strategic plan. I have experienced working with a business that had a lot of creative ideas for new initiatives, but there were too many to properly implement with attention and care, and many were not aligned with the firm's strategic plan. I was able to help the business more carefully align its change initiatives with the firm's overall strategy. I did not consider this challenge as "anti-innovation," but rather I assisted the organization with focusing on its priorities to be successful where it mattered most (i.e., in their core businesses). I have also experienced businesses that have put change initiatives forward without securing funding for automation, people, or controls, under the assumption that if the "business takes off" they will ask for proper funding. This is a suboptimal approach with the potential for losses if the business does not invest in the proper infrastructure, including controls. It can also be a red flag that the initiative is not aligned with the firm's strategy or lacks deep management support.

Every change initiative should be assessed for the risks associated with people, processes, systems, market conditions, the operating environment, and regulations. As mentioned, even nontechnology initiatives often have system components that require a careful assessment. The risk assessment should identify all potential issues that could arise during deployment and post-implementation, with a thorough analysis of the impact on all stakeholders, including clients, and processes and systems. Subject-matter experts across the board should review and challenge the risks, and any necessary control uplifts that the business sponsor has identified.

Review and Approval

Board approval is often required for complex initiatives that are assessed as high risk, which can result in significant change to critical business processes or result in transformation of an organization's systems. All initiatives except for ones in the low-rated business-as-usual category will require review and approval by subject-matter experts for their coverage area.

Before the approval process is kicked off, the business sponsor will provide their approval for the initiative. This is the stage where the go-no-go decision is made. Second-line operational risk will review and challenge the initiative, and higher-risk initiatives will be reviewed by the enterprise risk committee. However, the ultimate approval must be from the business. The second line can raise concerns and request the development of additional controls, but the business owns the risk and their business strategy.

Technology development initiatives will often be reviewed and approved by technology-focused committees, which include a cross section of technology, cyber, and business management. The more complex enterprise technology initiatives should also be reviewed by the risk committee and the board for transparency into their business and risk implications.

Communication

Communication is a component in the change initiative lifecycle that is often overlooked but is critical for success of an initiative. The business plan should incorporate a risk-based communication plan that covers all stakeholder bases within the organization. This should start with the business owner's initial outreach to executive management and the board for a complex, high-rated initiative after the first iteration of the business case is drafted. This is an opportunity to incorporate senior management input into the business case, along with input from SMEs and risk management.

As a former risk reviewer of change initiatives, I appreciated the opportunity to provide feedback early in the process so that any control concerns could be integrated into the business plan. I have seen initiatives get far along in the planning process that were never going to be viable because of risk and compliance concerns without significant investment in controls, which should have been an early consideration in the planning process.

Communication should continue through the planning, review and approval, design and implementation phases of the lifecycle, presentations at relevant committees and forums, and regular outreach sessions with stakeholders. Communicating widely with impacted stakeholders is an important consideration in building awareness and acceptance.

Design

The first consideration in determining the design of an initiative is how it will be implemented and if a Waterfall or Agile approach will be taken. Regardless of the approach, a well-designed implementation plan and timeline should be drafted and reviewed by the business owner, risk management, the assigned SMEs, and, for high-risk and complex enterprise initiatives, the board. The plan should incorporate the necessary resources (which presumably were already identified and approved by management) to implement the initiative. The plan should include pre-implementation testing in a controlled nonproduction environment ahead of deployment. The plan should also include success criteria so that the initiative can be monitored during and after implementation.

Implementation

Careful monitoring against success criteria should continue throughout implementation. Testing should continue and action plans opened as issues are identified. Systems implementations are customarily scheduled for weekend overnights so that there is the least amount of disruption to business operations.

Systems upgrades or new implementations carry a great deal of risk, and comprehensive testing is critical to a successful implementation. Contingencies should be made for exception processes that occur during the implementation or afterward, including a playbook for when emergency system updates are required and a defined path for emergency approvals.

Post-Implementation Review

Once the implementation is completed, a post-implementation review should occur 6–12 months later to ensure that it has met its objectives. This includes testing against financial and nonfinancial success criteria. The success criteria should be monitored and tracked through a dashboard in the interest of transparency and lessons learned.

In my experience, the initial revenue projections for an initiative are rarely met within the timeframe proposed. The success criteria should include financial and nonfinancial measures, and the monitoring results against the defined criteria should be reported through management committees and the board for the complex and high-risk enterprise initiatives in the spirit of "how are we doing."

Once the initial post-implementation review is complete, the initiative should be monitored through the components of the operational risk framework on a BAU basis, including RCSA.

Change Management Examples by Risk Rating

As previously mentioned, managing a change initiative should be risk-based, with the most oversight and senior-level reporting and monitoring for the highest rated complex initiatives. The following provide some examples on how to segment change initiatives by risk rating.

High-risk initiatives have a high level of complexity, include a critical process change, and impact the enterprise.

Examples include:

- Outsourcing a critical service, process or system to a new vendor, or adding a new critical service agreement to an existing vendor's contract and SLA
- Introduction of an NBI that is in a new target market or incorporates a new client segment or launch of an entirely new business
- Mergers and acquisitions that impact the enterprise
- Reorganization of a bank's business and functions across the enterprise
- Upgrade of a major service platform, such as a wealth management client platform

- Introduction of a new system that impacts core business activities or customers, such as a new finance system
- A new initiative to migrate data or an application to the cloud, the selection of a new cloud provider, or expanding an existing provider's remit
- Construction of a new headquarters building
- Moving the organization to a new headquarters location

Medium-risk initiatives have a moderate level of complexity, include a significant process change, and impact two or more businesses or functions.

Examples include:

- Modification or expansion of an existing business initiative with a known client segment and target market
- Acquisition or divestiture of a business unit, service, product, or portfolio
- Consolidation of two or more business units or functions
- Upgrade of the interface on an existing system that has customer impact
- Replacement of a system that serves a single business or functional purpose
- Automation of a process, such as financial or regulatory reporting
- New branding or marketing campaign
- Renovation of headquarters building
- Update to marketing and customer disclosure materials or development of new materials
- New GRC system
- Moving several businesses or functions to a new office location

Low-risk initiatives have a low level of complexity and no upstream or downstream impact on businesses or function within the enterprise.

Examples include:

- Singe business of function reorganization
- New functionality of an existing system that has no customer impact
- Upgrade or update of certain features of an NBI
- Renovation of a floor in an office building
- Update to social media or marketing campaign
- Update of intranet site
- Introduction of new internal reporting package
- Upgrade of existing GRC system
- Moving a business or function to a new office location

Change Initiative Risk Assessment

The business case should include a thorough analysis supporting the introduction of the change initiative, including the estimated budget and people resources necessary for sustaining the effort. A comprehensive risk and control assessment, including the development of new controls when necessary, should be included in the business case. Subject-matter experts should be assigned to review and assess the impact to their risk coverage areas. Second-line operational risk usually reviews the final due diligence package, including the risk assessment, for completeness, reasonability, and impact to risk appetite and the control environment.

The following are considerations for executing the risk assessment:

- **Strategic risk:** The first consideration in constructing the business plan and assessing strategic risk is the alignment with the firm's strategy, which is often articulated in a three- or five-year plan. The strategic risk assessment should include an analysis of the impact of not doing the initiative on the firm's competitive and market position.
- **Financial risk:** An assessment should be conducted on the source of revenue that is anticipated from the change initiative if applicable, including the impact on the revenue mix for the firm.
- **Liquidity, interest rate risk, and credit risk:** The impact on the liquidity risk of the firm is an important consideration and a requirement by the Federal Reserve when assessing NBIs. A clear understanding of the impact to the firm's credit risk, including collateral management where relevant, should be documented. Interest rate sensitivities, including the impact of pricing on products, should be assessed.
- **Nonfinancial risk:** The impact of the change initiative on all the operational risk types, including cyber, technology, data, third-party, model, resiliency, execution, and fraud risk, should be assessed, including the impact on nonfinancial risk appetite, and the potential for an increase in risk events. An important consideration is the convergence among these risk types and how they can impact the risk profile when considered together.
- **Customer impact:** The overall impact of the initiative on the firm's client base should be assessed, including if there will be exposure to new high-risk clients or markets. An important consideration is the value and benefits the change initiative will bring to a customer. If the value is to the organization at the expense of the customer's best interest, it should be reevaluated.
- **Regulatory and compliance risk:** A thorough assessment of the exposure to new regulations or increased exposure to existing ones should be undertaken, including the impact on policies, procedures, marketing materials, and client disclosures.
- **Systems and cyber risk:** Risks associated with any system development work should be assessed, including if the change initiative will increase the firm's exposure to cyber risk.
- **Control environment:** A review of existing issues and action plans and identified control deficiencies should be considered when assessing the control environment. Recommendations for the development of new controls should be included in the assessment.
- **Operating environment:** The assessment should include a review of existing manual processes in the operating environment and the history of human errors. An assessment should be conducted of the overall impact on risk appetite if the change initiative adds additional manual processes into an operating environment that is already manually intensive.

- **Volume and capacity:** The assessment should include a review of the anticipated volume and capacity and the impact on the firm's existing system and processing infrastructure.
- **Resources:** The assessment should include if the appropriate resources are in place to support the change initiative, including capacity and skill set, or if additional resources are necessary, including outside support.

Roles and Responsibilities

It takes a village to implement highly complex change initiatives. The involvement of senior-level committees, such as the enterprise risk committee or the board of directors, is usually contingent on the complexity and risk profile of an initiative. Low-risk initiatives or initiatives that are isolated to a single business or function will not require review and challenge by the enterprise risk committee or the board. They may be reviewed through a business risk and control committee or forum or a function-specific committee or forum, such as a third-party committee if the initiative involves the introduction of a new vendor. For a high-profile vendor selection, such as a new cloud provider, the initiative will be reviewed through the subject-matter-specific committee, in addition to the higher-level ones. Technology functions often have their own focused committees that review technology and information security initiatives. The higher-profile technology initiatives, however, should also be reviewed by the risk and board committees.

Waterfall vs. Agile

Many organizations moved heavily into Agile as a discipline for managing change risk a few years ago. The linear, sequential method of managing projects, known as Waterfall, fell out of favor at that time in some organizations. The firms I worked in at the time seemed to be "Agile crazy," with application of the discipline to all products, services, and processes. Teams were reorganized in small cross-functional pods that allowed them to move quickly and with a great deal of "agility," and there were plans to organize enterprises completely around the Agile approach. Many have for the most part pulled away from their "Agile dreams" and applied the approach in more targeted ways to their change initiatives.

The difference between Agile and Waterfall resides in their approach to managing and implementing change. Waterfall is a methodical approach that organizes projects in sequential phases, including drafting project requirements, working on the design, developing the approach, and testing ahead of deployment. The advantage of this approach is that it includes a great deal of project planning and robust documentation. The website project-management.com suggests that Waterfall is the appropriate methodology for projects that are reliant on one phase being completed before the next one is started, such as those in the construction and manufacturing sector or highly regulated industries like healthcare and pharmaceuticals. As an example, each stage of a drug trial requires thorough documentation and is dependent on the results of the previous stage in order to move forward. The downside to implementing a Waterfall approach is that it is difficult and can be costly to change course once the project has been rolled out.

Agile relies on an iterative approach to implementing change. There is an emphasis on continuous feedback and adapting changes in the plan as feedback is obtained. The process includes daily short sprints, where cross-functional teams pull up and identify challenges that may require iterative changes to the plan. It is a flexible approach that allows for more flexibility in the implementation process than the Waterfall approach. It also incorporates strong controls, such as frequent testing that allows for issues to be identified ahead of implementation.

Agile grew out of the technology industry in the early 2000s when there was a need to be able to innovate and implement more quickly. It is well suited to technology and product development where the landscape is constantly evolving. It is also suited to teams that are flexible and fluid in their responsibilities, while Waterfall is more appropriate for teams that are highly specialized and wedded to defined roles. Some organizations utilize a hybrid approach where they adopt the rigor of Waterfall for the planning stage of a large change initiative, while following an Agile approach during the implementation stage.

I have experienced the positive impact of an agile approach in one of the organizations I previously worked in, where I was the manager of the operational risk system, which was overdue for an upgrade. I had struggled to get funding up front for all the features that I would have liked to see in the upgrade, but substantial progress was made over time through an Agile approach, and I eventually got the system to where it needed to be. On the other hand, there are many misperceptions about Agile. I once heard a senior-level executive comment that with Agile, you do not need to know where the train will eventually end up. I would argue that you always need to know the end goal of a change initiative, regardless of whether it follows an Agile or Waterfall approach. Controls and strong planning always apply regardless of the approach.

Success Criteria

As mentioned, it is important to ultimately know where the train will end up. The development of success criteria allows for monitoring of the progress of the change initiative and its overall performance post-implementation. It is the equivalent of an "on-time" metric for a train line. Success criteria should be tracked by the initiative owner and submitted for review to the relevant business committees and forums. Success criteria for complex and high-risk initiatives should be incorporated into risk committee and board materials.

Here are the suggested success criteria for consideration:

- **Strategy:** Alignment with enterprise three- or five-year strategic plan; business case approved by executive management and the board for complex enterprise initiatives
- **Project management:** Initiative delivered on time and within budget

- **Technology:** System integration and development work deployed without business interruptions or necessary version rollbacks
- **Financial:** Actual revenue versus projections; return on investment targets met or exceeded; financial risks identified and mitigated
- **Client base:** Actual onboarding of new clients versus projections
- **Market share:** Actual market share versus projections
- **Compliance:** Compliance with rules and regulations, and new exposure incorporated into policies and procedures
- **Governance:** Initiative owner provides ongoing oversight; progress and monitoring results are reported to relevant committees; roles and responsibilities for implementing and managing initiative are clearly defined
- **Risk and control:** New controls successfully implemented or existing ones updated where necessary; all control deficiencies remediated through issue management process; initiative risks and controls incorporated into RCSA, compliance and financial crime risk assessments; control testing results yield a low rate of defects, which are remediated and retested
- **Stakeholder engagement:** Communication plan executed; feedback loop incorporates stakeholder feedback; training and awareness sessions conducted
- **Capacity:** Internal resources, including capacity and skill set, are adequate to support initiative post-implementation
- **Post-implementation review:** Post implementation review conducted according to timeline; lessons learned are documented and incorporated into initiative through a feedback loop

Products and Services Change Initiatives

New business initiatives or new product and service initiatives are managed by many organizations through the change risk management program. The introduction of what I will refer to as NBI in this chapter is critical to an organization's innovation, ability to continue meeting market and customer demand, and over the long run its viability. It's a strong industry practice to manage this critical program through a single change management framework and lifecycle.

At the core of all organizations and their NBI programs, no matter the sector, is a customer offering. This is the heart of why organizations exist, which sometimes can be forgotten by operational risk functions that reside in the corporate sector and are removed from the front line. We all exist in our present organizations—or we should—to do the right thing by our customers and stakeholders, including shareholders, employees, and our communities. This emphasis on doing the right thing should be an important assessment criteria when NBIs are evaluated for their impact on customers and stakeholders.

Doing the right thing by our customers and stakeholders includes a customer-centric approach to how we think about the firm's suite of products and services. This starts with assessing each new and existing product and service for the benefits that it offers our customers, and understanding where there might be conflicts with the customer and organizational value proposition. We know from recent events involving sales practices misdeeds (see the Wells Fargo sales practices event in Chapter 8) that an offering that creates customer harm or is not in their best interest also hurts all other stakeholders of an organization, including shareholders and employees.

Operational risk personnel must be present from the start of the development of a new product and service and work together with the business development team. This includes evaluating at the Identification and Assessment lifecycle stage (see the change management lifecycle in Figure 12.1) along with the projected revenue stream and alignment with firm strategy, the customer benefits of the product, where there could be potential harm, applicable regulations, any increase in risk that would impact the level of the firm's risk appetite, building of new processes to support the NBI, and necessary investment in controls and automation. I have witnessed more than once a business getting far along with planning a new offering only to find out from a risk assessment conducted late in the assessment process that there are regulatory or risk issues that would make it too difficult to go to market without significant additional investment in controls.

Introducing a new product or service should include a risk and control assessment, along with a risk and reward one. The development and investment in new controls should be factored into the revenue estimations up front. I have experienced a business pushing back on the investment in automated controls because the projected revenue did not justify the expenditure. The reliance on manual processes in these instances should be fully understood, including how adding new manual processes will impact the operating environment, and the cost and impact of their failure. The reluctance to invest in controls should lead to a strategy discussion on whether the implementation of this product or service and the necessary investment are justified by the projected revenue.

Financial firms for the most part have programs in place to assess products and services, and as mentioned, many have incorporated them into change risk management frameworks. Risks associated with NBIs should be managed from initial implementation all the way through to offboarding when it's no longer viable for economic, regulatory, or strategic reasons. Most financial institutions have programs in place to assess the risks associated at the introduction and growth stage, but some lack formal programs to manage products and services throughout their entire lifecycle. The benefits of the product should be assessed and tracked throughout its lifecycle, including monitoring its performance from a customer, organization, and regulatory perspective over time.

A lot of the risk associated with products and services cluster in the "Clients, Products and Business Practices" category of the Basel Taxonomy, which provides a high-level view of the associated risks. The associated risks include aggressive sales practices, which was witnessed in the Wells Fargo case; fiduciary breaches; selling unsuitable products to clients; client disclosures; churning of brokerage accounts; improper business practices, such as was witnessed in the aftermath of the Credit Crisis where firms were trading against their customers interest; and the large money laundering events that impacted most global banks. An important consideration for the wealth management and brokerage business in the United States is the Securities Exchange Commission Regulation

Best Interest (Reg BI) rule that became effective on June 30, 2020, and was designed to enhance investor protections when broker-dealers make recommendations to retail customers.

The following is a snapshot from the Basel Taxonomy of the "Clients, Products and Business Practices" category:

Clients, products and business practices	Losses arising from an unintentional or negligent failure to meet a professional obligation to specific clients (including fiduciary and suitability requirements), or from the nature or design of a product.	Suitability, disclosure, and fiduciary	Fiduciary breaches/ guideline violations
			Suitability/disclosure issues (know-your-customer, etc.)
			Retail customer disclosure violations
			Breach of privacy
			Aggressive sales
			Account churning
			Misuse of confidential information
			Lender liability
		Improper business or market practices	Antitrust
			Improper trade/market practices
			Market manipulation
			Insider trading (on firm's account)
			Unlicensed activity
			Money laundering
		Product flaws	Product defects (unauthorized, etc.)
			Model errors
		Selection, sponsorship and exposure	Failure to investigate client per guidelines
			Exceeding client exposure limits
		Advisory activities	Disputes over performance of advisory activities

Source: Adapted from https://www.bis.org/basel_framework/chapter/OPE/25.htm

US Regulatory Guidance

I have kept a copy of the OCC's guidance titled "New, Modified, or Expanded Bank Products and Services: Risk Management Principles" close at hand since it was published in 2017. Its basic principles hold true today, even with its recent cross-outs of all mentions of reputation risk. The OCC was one of the first US regulators to come out with basic risk management principles for the management of NBIs, throughout their entire lifecycle. When the OCC went into institutions around the time of the publication of the guidance, they found that while many banks had NBI programs in place and were working on enhancing the upfront management of products and services, they were less focused on ongoing product management. I believe this has changed in the industry with the appointment of product managers and the incorporation of product risks into BAU processes, such as RCSA.

The OCC guidance provides the following definitions of new, modified, and expanded products and services, which incorporates the risks inherent in each:

- ***New** products and services may differ substantially from previous bank offerings and may result from relationships with third parties. New products and services include those offered for the first time, as well as offerings that the bank previously discontinued but will offer again after a substantial period of time has passed. New products and services can provide entrance into or solutions for new financial markets, add new convenience and capabilities for customers, or manage risks for customers.*
- ***Modified** products and services differ substantially from existing products and services in nature, terms, purpose, scale, or use. Modified products and services substantially alter the underlying risk qualities or characteristics of the existing products and services.*
- ***Expanded** products and services are those offered beyond a bank's current customer base, financial markets, venues, or delivery channels.*

Source: https://www.occ.treas.gov/news-issuances/bulletins/2017/bulletin-2017-43.html

The OCC guidance highlights errors, the inability to achieve business objectives, systems and control problems, violation of laws and regulation, and litigation as risks that can occur when organizations fail to assess risks and controls ahead of approving NBIs. It is important to look ahead when assessing these risks, as I have witnessed significant issues occurring when an NBI not too long after implementation has changed course and is serving a different and potentially higher-risk customer or market segment than originally intended. It is common for the NBI approval process to include conditions, such as the NBI will be restricted to a particular market or customer segment and for these conditions to fall away over time. This can lead to unmitigated risk if the NBI was approved for one environment with appropriate controls in place and then migrates to a higher risk one without the investment in additional controls.

The OCC's risk management framework contains the following elements, which are aligned for the most part with the change management framework I proposed in this chapter. Here are the basic elements of the OCC's new, modified, and expanded products and services framework:

- **Adequate due diligence and approvals before introducing a new activity:** Includes due diligence and approvals; alignment with strategic plan; impact on liquidity and capital position; consultation with relevant function areas (the SMEs); determining regulatory obligations; assessment of required expertise; ability of infrastructure to support the initiative; analysis of third-party providers; and business plan review

- **Policies and procedures to properly identify, measure, monitor, report, and control risks:** Expand or amend policies as needed to address NBI and incorporate into organization's risk management and compliance frameworks
- **Effective change management for new activities or affected processes and technologies:** Review by risk management, line managers, senior managers in business units ahead of implementation; testing; exception reporting; training
- **Ongoing performance monitoring and review systems:** Monitoring of ongoing risk exposure that board and management are willing to except; specific objectives and performance criteria; testing of controls and regulatory compliance; changes in business plan based on performance results and exit strategy

The OCC's framework includes the assessment of strategic, credit, operational, compliance, and liquidity risk, with a special call for assessing third-party relationships and financial technology. The guidance document provides a good set of criteria to assess each risk stripe, which as a strong practice should be integrated into the identification and assessment phase of the change management lifecycle. Subject-matter experts must be assigned to each risk stripe to provide feedback, review and challenge, and determine if the control environment is adequate to support the NBI. There may be recommendations to create new controls or strengthen existing ones ahead of implementation, which should be considered in the budgeting for the initiative.

Liquidity risk is an important consideration when assessing NBIs and includes requirements under the Federal Reserve's Regulation YY. The requirement is for the evaluation and approval by senior management of the NBI's impact on the firm's liquidity risk profile and if the associated liquidity risk is within established risk tolerance. The requirement includes an annual review to determine if any product or service creates "unanticipated liquidity risk" and whether it remains within established risk tolerance. It is a strong practice for all financial firms to conduct annual assessments of its suite of products and services impact on liquidity risk appetite.

The current version of the OCC's guidance has crossed out all mentions of reputational risk following a decision by the regulator to drop all references from the Comptroller's Handbook and guidance documents. The OCC has instructed its examiners that they should no longer examine for a financial institution's management of reputational risk. I have argued for years that reputational risk is an impact that flows from risk events. For instance, the Wells Fargo sales practices event included a great deal of consequences, including regulatory fines and penalties, an asset cap that prohibited growth, and most importantly a severe hit to the bank's reputation that was once considered one of the best managed banks in America. Reputational consequences should be considered when assessing all risk stripes, as a stellar reputation is an asset that is hard to retrieve once it has been tarnished.

The OCC continues to provide guidance on the management of products and services through the publication of the "Semiannual Risk Perspectives." The bulletin has highlighted product risk over the last few years as one that it is closely monitoring. The current issue highlights benefits associated with the introduction of new technologies and innovative products and services, including enhancing customer experience, but it also points out the additional risks these products pose to an organization's operating environment, which impact change management, governance, and overall risk management. The current bulletin also highlights the benefits of "responsible AI" in managing risk but points out the increased model, cybersecurity, and compliance risks that can be introduced through the adoption of any form of AI.

Every recent issue of the "Semiannual Risk Perspective" has highlighted the risks associated with maintaining legacy technology architectures. The OCC has highlighted the risk that a failure to upgrade systems will result in loss of market share and competitiveness as organizations that offer digitized services can do so with greater efficiency. The OCC targets innovations in payment systems using ledger technologies and mobile payment platforms as examples that can bypass legacy technology infrastructures and disrupt revenue streams and business models. The regulator continues to warn of the risk that "prolonged use of older or legacy systems could increase the likelihood of operational outages, introduce security vulnerabilities, create system maintenance challenges, and create other concerns that could reduce operational resilience."

The OCC along with other regulators are adapting to the recent acceptance after many years of a "wait and see approach" of crypto-asset products. The OCC announced in May 2025 that it now considered it permissible for national banks and federal savings associations to buy and sell crypto-assets held in custody at the customer's direction, including outsourcing to third parties who provide custody and execution services.

In July 2025, the OCC, Federal Reserve, and FDIC released guidance on crypto-asset risk management. The interagency documents provides guidance on assessing the following risks, which should be integrated into the change management risk assessment: "core financial risks given the strategic direction and business model; ability to understand a complex, evolving, and potentially unfamiliar asset class, including by keeping abreast of industry leading practices; ability to ensure a strong control environment; and contingency plans to address any unanticipated challenges in effectively providing services." In addition, as the sector is changing so rapidly, financial institutions should assess and manage their fiduciary risks as they take on the management of crypto-assets. The interagency guidance recommends that they "keep abreast of leading practices to meet these heightened standards."

One of the critical risks to assess when initiating a crypto NBI is the compromise of cryptographic keys. It is a common practice to transfer crypto-assets through cryptographic key pairs made up of unique alphanumeric codes. Key pairs consist of a private key that is kept confidential and a public key that can be shared during a specific transaction. The interagency guidance requires that banks follow a "standard of care" in protecting crypto-assets, which includes ensuring that no party—including the customer—has "access to information sufficient to unilaterally transfer the crypto-asset out of the control of the banking organization."

The other notable development in the United States is the passage of the Genius Act officially known as the Guiding and Establishing National Innovation for U.S. Stablecoins Act. It is landmark legislation that potentially moves a product that was held in the "wait and see" mode into the mainstream. The act, which creates clear rules for managing payment stablecoins (as opposed to investments), was signed into law on July

17, 2025. The act defines payment stablecoin as the following: "A digital asset that is, or is designed to be, used as a means of payment or settlement; and the issuer of which—is obligated to convert, redeem, or repurchase for a fixed amount of monetary value, not including a digital asset denominated in a fixed amount of monetary value; and represents that such issuer will maintain, or create the reasonable expectation that it will maintain, a stable value relative to the value of a fixed amount of monetary value." The act further stipulates that the definition does not include deposit taking using distributed ledger technology, securities or investment contracts."

The act outlines standards for the issuance of payment stablecoins. This includes maintaining identifiable reserves backing the outstanding payment stablecoins of the permitted payment stablecoin issuer on at least a one-to-one basis with guidance on what the reserves should constitute; disclosure of the issuer's redemption policy; monthly publication of the issuer's reserves; monthly certification by CEO or CFO and examination of reports by certified public accounting firm; capital, liquidity and risk management requirements including operational, compliance, and information technology, financial crime and sanctions risk management principles-based requirements and standards; and prohibition of tying (to other products and services).

The United Kingdom issued new Consumer Duty guidance that requires firms to "act to deliver good outcomes to retail customers." The Consumer principle includes three cross-cutting rules: good faith, avoid foreseeable harm, support financial objectives. Included in the guidance are four specific outcomes: product governance, price and value, consumer understanding, and consumer support. At the heart of the guidance is attention to the fairness and transparency of product designs.

The European Securities and Markets Authority (ESMA) issues guidelines on MiFID II product governance requirements, which are focused on investor protection that like the SEC's Reg BI are designed to ensure products are distributed in the best interest of clients. The key tenets of the guidance include identifying the suitable target market, ensuring suitability, and conducting periodic reviews of product performance and the target market.

The following is a brief overview of the regulatory requirements related to NBIs in the major world markets:

Regulator	Governance Requirement
OCC	Heightened standards require a new product approval process with board oversight and risk management involvement; OCC Bulletin 2017-43 requires a formal risk management process for new, modified, and expanded products and assessment of the primary risk stripes.
Federal Reserve	Regulation YY requires integration of liquidity risk management for new products under Enhanced Prudential Standards.
SEC	Reg BI establishes a "best interest" standard of conduct for broker-dealers and their associated persons when making recommendations to retail customers concerning securities transactions or investment strategies.

Regulator	Governance Requirement
FCA (UK)	Consumer Duty establishes a high standard of care for the customer, including product design, and customer support with four defined outcomes.
EU (MiFID II)	MiFID II product governance is a set of requirements focused on financial investments that are developed and distributed in the best interests of investor.

Bibliography

Basel Committee on Banking Supervision. *Prudential Treatment of Cryptoasset Exposures.* December 2022. https://www.bis.org/bcbs/publ/d545.pdf.

European Banking Authority. *The EBA Provides Further Guidance on Reporting Requirements Under the Markets in Crypto Assets Regulation.* December 18, 2024. https://www.eba.europa.eu/publications-and-media/press-releases/eba-provides-further-guidance-reporting-requirements-under-markets-crypto-assets-regulation.

European Securities and Markets Authority. *Guidelines on MiFID II Product Governance Requirements.* March 8, 2023. https://www.esma.europa.eu/sites/default/files/2023-08/ESMA35-43-3448_Guidelines_on_product_governance.pdf.

Ernst and Young. *President Trump Signs the Nation's First Federal Digital Asset Regulation into Law.* July 2025. https://www.ey.com.

Federal Reserve. *SR 10-6: Interagency Policy Statement on Funding and Liquidity Risk Management.* March 17, 2010. https://www.federalreserve.gov/boarddocs/srletters/2010/sr1006a1.pdf.

Federal Reserve. *Regulation YY (12 CFR 252): Enhanced Prudential Standards.* November 1, 2019. https://www.federalregister.gov/documents/2019/11/01/2019-23662/prudential-standards-for-large-bank-holding-companies-savings-and-loan-holding-companies-and-foreign.

Financial Conduct Authority. *PS22/9:A New Consumer Duty.* July 27, 2022. https://www.fca.org.uk/publications/policy-statements/ps22-9-new-consumer-duty.

Financial Stability Board. *FSB Global Regulatory Framework for Crypto-asset Activities.* July 17, 2023. https://www.fsb.org/2023/07/fsb-global-regulatory-framework-for-crypto-asset-activities/.

J.R. Johnivan. Project-Management.com. *Agile vs Waterfall Methodology: Differences & How to Choose.* November 25, 2024. https://project-management.com/agile-vs-waterfall.

Morgan Lewis. *Genius Act Passes in US Congress: A Breakdown of the Landmark Stablecoin Law.* July 17, 2025. https://www.morganlewis.com/pubs/2025/07/genius-act-passes-in-us-congress-a-breakdown-of-the-landmark-stablecoin-law.

Office of the Comptroller of the Currency. OCC Bulletin 2017-43. *New, Modified, or Expanded Bank Products and Services: Risk Management Principles.* October 20, 2017. https://www.occ.treas.gov/news-issuances/bulletins/2017/bulletin-2017-43.html.

Office of the Comptroller of the Currency. Interagency Guidance. *Crypto-Asset Safekeeping by Banking Organizations.* July 14, 2025. https://www.occ.gov/news-issuances/news-releases/2025/nr-ia-2025-68a.pdf.

Office of the Comptroller of the Currency. *Semiannual Risk Perspective: Spring 2025.* https://www.occ.gov/publications-and-resources/publications/semiannual-risk-perspective/files/pub-semiannual-risk-perspective-spring-2025.pdf.

One Hundred and Nineteenth Congress of the United States. *Guiding and Establishing National Innovation for U.S. Stablecoins Act or the GENIUS Act*. https://www.congress.gov/bill/119th-congress/senate-bill/1582/text?utm_source=chatgpt.com.

U.S. Securities and Exchange Commission. *Regulation Best Interest: The Broker-Dealer Standard of Conduct*. July 12, 2019. https://www.sec.gov/rules-regulations/2019/06/s7-07-18#34-86031final.

Chapter 13

Managing Data Risk, AI, and Machine Learning

An often-quoted article published by the Harvard Business Review in 2016 included IBM's stunning estimate of the cost of bad data. The estimate in 2016 was $3.1 trillion. Data has become more exponentially complex and abundant since the article was published. The article's primary thesis is that managing bad data is so costly due to the "hidden data factory" and the need to clean it up as it passes from one department to another. Thomas Redman, the author of the article, conjectured, "It is hard to imagine any sort of future in data when so much is so bad." But of course, here we are in the future. Data governance and required data controls have matured since the article was published, with the cost of checking, cleaning up erroneous data, and performing independent reviews built into data governance frameworks.

Investment in data governance frameworks is critical because data is at the heart of almost everything an organization does and, at the same time, presents enormous operational risk challenges. The task to manage such a critical asset is enormous and requires the support and attention of the entire enterprise. Many organizations continue to be burdened by "data debt," which has built up over time from a lack of investment in strong data governance programs, and automation. Such data debt requires substantial resources for remediation, while often the same resources are entrusted with managing the quality of newly created data. The issue is more critical than ever with the introduction of AI and large language models into the management of core business processes along with risk management. Institutions of all sizes continue to struggle with allocating resources to both the cleanup of historical data and oversight of the newly created data.

Data often relies on manual processes, which creates additional challenges for retrieving and using the data. But bad data can also live in automated processes, such as system feeds. I have experienced instances where bad data has been used through the execution of these feeds for years, and when the error is finally uncovered (usually through a delayed reconciliation or testing process), the remediation, including potential regulatory impact, is painful. An example is a miscalculation on mortgage rates that occurred for almost a decade and required customer remediation and regulatory notification.

One place to start in understanding the complexity of managing data is the finance department. A large publicly traded organization has the obligation under the Sarbanes-Oxley Act (SOX) for providing timely and accurate financial data. The consequences are severe for reporting inaccurate data, including a jail term for senior executives who knowingly provide false information. This necessitates the management of a control infrastructure that includes testing, usually by an independent finance team, of the financial data. Second-line operational risk must review and assess the adequacy of the control testing. When resources are allocated, SOX testing is rarely the place where there are aggressive cost-cutting initiatives, given the management consequences of misreporting. But it is also a place where AI can provide great efficiencies in the testing protocol.

Of course, critical data resides in most if not all functions within an organization. In a consumer financial setting, data can literally determine the course of a customer's life. Banks provide credit data to the credit bureaus that determine consumer credit scores and factor into decision-making including the granting of home and auto loans and the interest rate on personal loans and credit cards. If an institution provides incorrect data to a credit bureau, the consumer could be denied a home loan or pay higher interest rates. This can have dire consequences for their life, as they are denied access to home or auto ownership. It can impact where their children attend school or their ability to travel to their workplace.

Organizations are increasingly leveraging data analytics in the proprietary use of the consumer data they have access to for marketing purposes, which can present data privacy issues. Some financial institutions have sold this data to third parties. It can be used to create a "360 view" of a customer to determine if they are candidates for additional products and services. Customers do not always understand how their data is used in these commercial pursuits, which creates risks for an institution that does not want to be viewed as "predatory" in its use of consumer data.

Data also resides at the core of a strategic decision-making, and there is an assumption (ideally based on careful assessment and testing) that it is accurate, complete, and timely. The data used in strategic decision-making should be carefully curated so that it is relevant and targeted to address the task at hand and assessed and tested to make sure it can be trusted to tell us something. As AI is used increasingly in models that ingest consumer data, there is a risk of disparate impact, discrimination, and consumer harm in how credit and pricing decisions are made. With the emergence of new and not always transparent technologies, it is more critical than ever to have clean data on the front end of the data lifecycle.

Ultimately, to avoid the bad data future or rather, present, that Thomas Redman predicted all those years ago, good data quality depends on the following:

- Having the right data strategy
- Clearly articulating what the data will be used for
- Developing and implementing a well-articulated data governance framework, with a strong practice to integrate into the operational risk management framework
- A training and communication program that instills in the organization that everyone is responsible for managing data, with clear guidelines for data producers, data owners, data stewards, and data consumers
- Managing a state-of-the art data infrastructure, including a data warehouse that increasingly resides in the cloud
- Staying abreast of strong practices for managing risks associated with how data is used in AL and machine learning for decision-making and gaining insights
- Continuous monitoring of data quality and data usage, including a quality assurance testing program

Data Risk Management Framework

When I first started to get my feet wet with managing data, the source everyone pointed to was Dama International, which was founded in 1980 and originally known as the Data Administration Management Association. Dama's big blue book titled "Data Management Body of Knowledge" is my data risk management reference source. DAMA defines data governance as "the exercise of authority and control (planning, implementation, monitoring and enforcement) over the management of data assets." The other respected data industry association is EDM Council, which was founded in 2005 and publishes benchmarking results against its data maturity scale.

I have managed data risk as part of my operational risk duties, and each time the organization I was with was on a five-year journey to adopt enhanced data risk management principles. The journey for me started with the passage of what is known as "Basel 239—Principles" for effective data aggregation and risk reporting. The passage of Basel 239, or commonly known as BCBS 239, was introduced in 2014 and groundbreaking in the management of data. BCBS 239 is focused on risk reporting and ultimately influenced enterprise risk management functions in how they managed data. Basel 239 introduced 14 basic principles that established a framework for determining maturity of a data-driven risk reporting program.

As mentioned, I have seen organizations on five-year journeys for the last 12 years. The Basel Committee published a report focused on the progress of the adoption of the basic principles in 2023 almost 10 years after the publication of Basel 239. The Basel Committee assessed the progress of 31 banks and found that only two banks were fully compliant with the principles but that not a single principle had been implemented across all banks. The results 10 years later mostly support the complexity of managing data risk programs. The Basel Committee attributed the results to programs that were underfunded, limited in scope, lacked senior management and board focus, and a failure to fully understand and assess the complexity and independencies of data risk management programs. The committee also pointed to IT legacy systems and ambitious timelines. I would also argue that these programs are becoming more complex with the use of AI in models that at their core may be ingesting not so great data.

The 14 principles that are set out in Basel 239 establish clear accountability with senior management and the board for identifying, assessing, and managing data quality risks as part of its overall risk management framework. The principles focus on ensuring that data is accurate, complete, and timely. They also provide guidance for risk reports that require concise and clear communication and are distributed to relevant parties at the appropriate frequency. In addition, the principles establish the importance of designing, building, and maintaining an appropriate data infrastructure that supports risk data aggregation and reporting capabilities, which is where I have seen many organizations struggle. It is no small undertaking to upgrade a complex organization's data infrastructure, especially when they have been bolted together through a series of mergers and acquisitions.

The following are the Basel 239 principles:

Principle 1

Governance*—A bank's risk data aggregation capabilities and risk reporting practices should be subject to strong governance arrangements consistent with other principles and guidance established by the Basel Committee.*

Principle 2

Data architecture and IT infrastructure*—A bank should design, build and maintain data architecture and IT infrastructure which fully supports its risk data aggregation capabilities and risk reporting practices not only in normal times but also during times of stress or crisis, while still meeting the other Principles.*

Principle 3

Accuracy and Integrity*—A bank should be able to generate accurate and reliable risk data to meet normal and stress/crisis reporting accuracy requirements. Data should be aggregated on a largely automated basis so as to minimise the probability of errors.*

Principle 4

Completeness*—A bank should be able to capture and aggregate all material risk data across the banking group. Data should be available by business line, legal entity, asset type, industry, region and other groupings, as relevant for the risk in question, that permit identifying and reporting risk exposures, concentrations and emerging risks.*

Principle 5

Timeliness*—A bank should be able to generate aggregate and up-to-date risk data in a timely manner while also meeting the principles relating to accuracy and integrity, completeness and adaptability. The precise timing will depend upon the nature and potential volatility of the risk* *being measured as well as its criticality to the overall risk profile of the bank. The precise timing will also depend on the bank-specific frequency requirements for risk management reporting, under both normal and stress/crisis situations, set based on the characteristics and overall risk profile of the bank.*

Principle 6

Adaptability—*A bank should be able to generate aggregate risk data to meet a broad range of on-demand, ad hoc risk management reporting requests, including requests during stress/crisis situations, requests due to changing internal needs and requests to meet supervisory queries.*

Principle 7

Accuracy—*Risk management reports should accurately and precisely convey aggregated risk data and reflect risk in an exact manner. Reports should be reconciled and validated.*

Principle 8

Comprehensiveness—*Risk management reports should cover all material risk areas within the organisation. The depth and scope of these reports should be consistent with the size and complexity of the bank's operations and risk profile, as well as the requirements of the recipients.*

Principle 9

Clarity and usefulness—*Risk management reports should communicate information in a clear and concise manner. Reports should be easy to understand yet comprehensive enough to facilitate informed decision-making. Reports should include meaningful information tailored to the needs of the recipients.*

Principle 10

Frequency—*The board and senior management (or other recipients as appropriate) should set the frequency of risk management report production and distribution. Frequency requirements should reflect the needs of the recipients, the nature of the risk reported, and the speed, at which the risk can change, as well as the importance of reports in contributing to sound risk management and effective and efficient decision-making across the bank. The frequency of reports should be increased during times of stress/crisis.*

Principle 11

Distribution—*Risk management reports should be distributed to the relevant parties while ensuring confidentiality is maintained.*

Principle 12

Review—*Supervisors should periodically review and evaluate a bank's compliance with the eleven Principles above.*

Principle 13

Remedial actions and supervisory measures—*Supervisors should have and use the appropriate tools and resources to require effective and timely remedial action by a bank to address deficiencies in its risk data aggregation capabilities and risk reporting practices. Supervisors should have the ability to use a range of tools, including Pillar 2.*

Principle 14

Home/host cooperation—*Supervisors should cooperate with relevant supervisors in other jurisdictions regarding the supervision and review of the Principles, and the implementation of any remedial action if necessary.*

Source: https://www.bis.org/publ/bcbs239.pdf

Governance and Policies and Procedures

The first Basel principle establishes clear expectations for strong governance, which includes the responsibility of an institution's board and executive management to "promote the identification, assessment and management of data quality risks as part of its overall risk management framework." Additional requirements include documentation of the institution's "data aggregation capabilities, independent validation that is aligned with the institution's other independent review activities within the bank's risk management program," and integration into other initiatives, such as assessment of new products and change initiatives.

As with other risk types, the operational risk framework is suited for providing the structure for managing data risks. This includes aligning with the elements of the framework and incorporating data risks into risk appetite, risk assessments, loss data, scenario analysis, and issue management.

Roles and Responsibilities

It truly takes a village to manage data risks, as they are among the most diverse and complicated assets within a firm. Managing this risk type requires coordination and well-defined roles and responsibilities, as there is a need for strong collaboration among the first-line data governance office, second-line operational risk, technology, CISO, model governance, risk committees, and data councils.

The first line has a large role with owning and managing data and associated risks, including the integration with AI and machine learning. The first line in many organizations has established a chief data office that reports into the chief operating officer or the chief technology officer. The chief data office often owns the data governance policy, while the second line integrates the managing of data risks into the operational risk policy and may also publish a data risk management standard. Some organizations may follow the traditional model with the second line owning a data risk policy and/or standard, but that is not a construct that I have observed in the organizations where I worked.

The EDM Council conducted a benchmarking study in 2023 on the role of the chief data officer. The report found that 65% of respondents had such roles in place, which was an increase from 60% in 2020. The report also found that 86% of chief data officers reported to the "C-suite," which was up from 72% in 2020. The report found that data officers are much more experienced than they were 10 years ago, with the scope of their responsibilities increasing, to define not just their organization's data strategy but increasingly their AI and ML strategy as well. As many as 80% of respondents in all industries had data management programs in place, which reflects the universal acceptance of data as an organization's key asset and a strategic imperative.

The chief data office is responsible for pulling the "village" together through participation in the data council, which will include representatives from technology, cyber, model, operational risk, third-party risk, and compliance functions among others. These participants are responsible for reviewing and challenging data risks from the vantage point of their coverage areas.

Risk Appetite and Key Risk Indicators

Risk appetite statements and metrics should at a minimum be defined for the key components of managing data risk governance: accuracy, completeness, and timeliness. The following statements and metrics are examples of what they should look like. It is a strong practice to open issues and action plans when the metrics associated with each risk appetite statement reach the yellow threshold, and ahead of hitting the red threshold, which indicates that risk appetite has been breached.

Accuracy

Table 13.1 shows a sample risk appetite statement. We have low tolerance for inaccurate data in reports, models, or customer-facing systems that could lead to financial misstatements, regulatory noncompliance, or customer impact. The accuracy of key data elements must meet predefined control and quality standards.

Table 13.1 Sample Risk Appetite Statement

Accuracy Description	Metric	Green Threshold	Yellow Threshold	Red Threshold
Evaluates correctness of critical data fields based on defined rules	% of critical data elements passing validation rules	>99.9% accuracy	<99% triggers yellow	<97% red
Tracks incidents leading to restatements, fines, or customer complaints	# of high-impact incidents due to inaccurate data	0 tolerance	≥1 per quarter	≥1 per quarter
Manual data corrections	% of automated vs manual data corrections	<10% manual corrections	>15% manual corrections	>20% manual corrections

Completeness

Table 13.2 shows a sample risk appetite statement. We have low tolerance for data incompleteness that materially impacts decision-making, regulatory reporting, or risk modeling. The organization aims to maintain data completeness above defined thresholds for critical data elements across all core business processes.

Table 13.2 A Sample Risk Appetite Statement

Completeness Description	Metric	Green Threshold	Yellow Threshold	Red Threshold
Measures data gaps in required fields across key data reporting or risk modeling systems	% of missing required fields in critical data sets	>99.5% completeness	<98.5% triggers yellow	<96% red
Assesses alignment between authoritative sources and data reporting or risk modeling systems	% of reconciled data sets across source and target systems	>98% reconciled	<96% triggers escalation	<94% triggers escalation
Tracks missed or failed data controls where handoffs occur in reporting or risk modeling processes	# of control failures related to data handoffs	<5 per quarter	>10 per quarter	>12 per quarter

Timeliness

Table 13.3 shows a sample risk appetite statement. We have low tolerance for delays in delivery of data used in regulatory reporting, customer transactions, or risk exposure monitoring. Timeliness targets are aligned to business and regulatory needs.

Table 13.3 A Sample Risk Appetite Statement

Timeliness Description	Metric	Green Threshold	Yellow Threshold	Red Threshold
Assesses whether key reports are issued by deadline	% of critical reports delivered on time	>99% on-time delivery	<97% on-time delivery	<95% on-time delivery
Measures time lag between data generation and system availability	Data latency in critical applications (e.g., risk, finance)	<5 minutes for real-time systems	>7 minutes for real-time systems	>9 minutes for real time systems
Measures use of outdated data	% of stale data in dashboards or analytics	<2% of data >24 hours old	>4% of data >24 hours old	>6% of data >24 hours old

Loss Data

Events, incidents, and near-misses that have data issues at their core should follow operational risk Loss Data and Escalation protocols (see Chapter 6). This includes tracking events that meet the loss or near-miss threshold in the system of record, escalating issues to senior management and regulators when necessary (see data compromise requirements in Chapter 7), monitoring external events for potential relevancy, and opening issue and action plans as necessary.

The following are examples of potential data-related events:

Data accuracy failures

- **Mortgage underwriting error:** Inaccurate data inputs in automated loan processing system lead to hundreds of customers being wrongly denied mortgages. Potential regulatory fine and enforcement action and reputational harm.
- **Mutual fund mispricing net asset value (NAV):** Incorrect calculation of NAV leads to mispricing of mutual funds. Potential regulatory fines and enforcement action, required remediation, reputational harm.
- **Mispricing of credit card interest rate:** Incorrect data is fed into credit card pricing model, which results in interest rate overcharges. Potential regulatory fine and enforcement action, required remediation, reputational harm.

Data completeness failures

- **Inaccurate data transfer:** Incomplete data entered in payment system leads to the transfer of inaccurate and overpayment amount to counterparties. Potential direct loss if counterparties do not return overpayment.
- **Credit reporting:** Incomplete data submitted to credit bureau agencies results in misreporting of client credit scores. Potential regulatory fine and enforcement action and reputational harm.
- **Poor data migration:** Data migration during a finance system upgrade includes incomplete data feeds, which impact regulatory reporting. Potential regulatory fine and enforcement action and resubmission of reports.

Data timeliness failures

- **Delayed margin reporting:** Delayed data feeds from risk systems cause breaches in daily margin call reporting. Potential regulatory fine and enforcement action.
- **Transaction monitoring:** Data feed does not pick up current transaction data, which leads to incomplete monitoring of financial crime exposure. Potential miss of suspicious transactions, regulatory fine and enforcement action.
- **Payroll system:** The payroll system is not updated as required with revised salary information after annual promotion cycle and employees are underpaid. Remediation required when errors are identified.

Risk and Control Assessments and Maturity Assessment

Data risks and controls should be incorporated into the RCSA process. Many of the assessed risks will fall into the "Execution, Delivery and Process Management" category (see taxonomy in Chapter 11). Additional risk assessments that are performed by the chief data office should be integrated into the RCSA. In addition, data privacy concerns, which are often tracked and assessed by compliance and cyber functions, should be incorporated into the RCSA.

As mentioned, many data risk management programs have been on multiple cycles of five-year plans. When tracking an emerging (or emerged) risk, it is critical to understand where you on a maturity scale versus an industry standard, your destination (where the "train" is headed), and the timetable to get there. It is a strong practice to conduct a data maturity assessment so that the status of the "five-year" program can be articulated to executive management, the board, and the regulators.

The EDM Council publishes criteria that the industry uses to assess their maturity following a model known as the Data Management Assessment Model (DCAM).

This is the maturity scale that EDM uses for its maturity model:

- **Not initiated:** Ad hoc data management
- **Conceptual:** Initial planning activities
- **Development:** Engagement underway
- **Defined:** Data management capabilities established and verified by stakeholders
- **Achieved:** Data management capabilities adopted and compliance enforced
- **Enhanced:** Data management capabilities fully integrated into operation

Here is the DCAM criteria:

- Data strategy and business case
- Data management and program funding
- Business and data architecture
- Data and technology architecture
- Data quality management
- Data governance
- Data control environment

Source: https://edmcouncil.org/frameworks/dcam/

It should be noted that it is rare for firms to aim for an enhanced rating, which is the top level of maturity. The ultimate "train destination" should be consistent with a firm's size and complexity. A smaller institution might aim for a defined rating, while a large one might work toward the achieved rating. According to EDM's analysis, firms can remain in the development stage for a while as they are establishing their program.

The maturity assessment should be updated regularly. I have seen firms update the assessment quarterly or semi-annually and to share the results with the risk committee and the board on at least an annual basis (or more often if they are addressing regulatory findings). The results should be brought as they are updated to the Data Council for review and challenged by the constituents. Any issues, concerns, or control deficiencies that are identified should be integrated into the RCSA. There should be alignment with the view of data in the RCSA and the Maturity Assessment. There would be a disconnect if the RCSA residual risk rating is low and the controls are rated effective, while the maturity assessment indicates that the program is still in the development stage.

Scenario Analysis

At least one scenario involving data risks should be incorporated into the scenarios that are selected for stress and capital models. In addition, a handful of relevant and diverse scenarios should be developed and incorporated into RCSA. Any potential emerging risks or control deficiencies identified through the scenario creation process should result in the opening of issues and action plans.

The following are sample scenarios with data issues at their center:

Scenario Title	Description	Root Cause	Severity	Likelihood	Low Loss ($)	Medium Loss ($)	High Loss ($)	Impact
Delayed Regulatory Report Submission	CCAR Report is submitted past the due date due to delays in data aggregation and validation.	Inaccurate data found during QA process results in delay in creating and submitting report.	High	Medium	$100,000	$500,000	$1,050,000	Regulatory fine, enforcement action, reputational harm
Incorrect Risk Rating Due to Data Input Error	A loan is misclassified due to incorrect customer risk rating data, and loan is extended to client with a poor credit record.	Manual input error and absence of validation controls.	Medium	High	$1,000,000	$2,000,000	$5,000,000	Loan defaults resulting in credit loss
Failed Sanctions Screening from Outdated Data	A sanctions list update fails to load, and a transaction involving a sanctioned entity is processed.	Batch job failure and lack of real-time validation.	High	Low	$1,000,000	$2,000,000	$5,000,000	Regulatory fine, compliance breach, legal exposure and reputational harm
Inaccurate Customer Statements Due to Data Mapping Error	Customer statements are generated with incorrect balances due to a data mapping error after a system migration.	Insufficient testing during system changes and poor data lineage documentation.	Medium	Medium	$250,000	$500,000	$1,000,000	Customer complaints, reputational impact, remediation costs
Third-Party KYC Data Feed Delay	Customer onboarding is delayed due to a third-party KYC data provider failing to deliver files on time.	Lack of service-level monitoring and no alternate processing plan.	Low	High	$250,000	$500,000	$1,000,000	Customer complaints, operational backlog, SLA violation

Monitoring and Reporting

Reporting on data risks should be integrated into first-line reports for business line management and business risk and control committees and the second-line operational risk reports for risk committees and the board. The first-line report should include the results of the RCSA data risks and controls for the individual business and any issues and remediations. The first-line data council should include an update on the BCBS 239 work and progress on meeting the principles, data maturity assessment results and progress on moving toward the desired state, any emerging risks, regulatory findings, an update on outstanding data issues and action plans, and industry trends and themes. The second-line operational risk should incorporate reporting of data-related events, incidents, near-misses, and data-specific risk appetite metrics that are above or approaching appetite, aggregate RCSA results including data as a theme, issues, and regulatory and audit findings into their board and risk committee reports.

Cultural Awareness

Cultural awareness starts with the first principle of BCBS 239 that is centered on the board and executive management's full-hearted support of the data governance program. This includes ensuring the program has strong leadership with the appropriate stature, technology support including funding to upgrade the data infrastructure where necessary, and the budget to support a staff that is commensurate with the organization's size, complexity, and necessary work to properly mature and guide the program. I have witnessed significant delays in obtaining budget to upgrade institutions' data infrastructure. In the long run, with layers on top of layers of workarounds and manual processes, and regulatory scrutiny, managing such clunky and aged infrastructures cost more than allocating the budget up front to fix the underlying issues.

Cultural awareness of the importance of doing the right thing by properly managing the quality of data and not passing on bad data to colleagues and other functions can be incorporated into an operational excellence program (see Chapter 11) as managing data can be central to execution risk. A strong training program that includes the basics of data risk management and the roles and responsibilities of data owners, data producers, and data users should be integrated into operational risk training schedules. Acting as a strong data steward and core values around managing data with care and attention can be reinforced through inclusion in the performance management system.

AI and Machine Learning

There is "good" and "bad" AI. Good AI in a risk management context is the use of the technology to assist with the management of risk, which includes replacing heavily manual data aggregation, testing, and monitoring with machine automated routines. (See Chapter 6 and the discussion of using AI to assist with the RCSA process.)

A good place to start is with the definition of AI. The NIST Framework provides this definition:

> *The AI RMF refers to an AI system as an engineered or machine-based system that can, for a given set of objectives, generate outputs such as predictions, recommendations, or decisions influencing real or virtual environments. AI systems are designed to operate with varying levels of autonomy (Adapted from: OECD Recommendation on AI:2019; ISO/IEC 22989:2022).*
>
> *Source:* https://nvlpubs.nist.gov/nistpubs/ai/NIST.AI.100-1.pdf

As with other operational risk types, the operational risk framework should be leveraged to manage AI risks, including establishing risk appetite statements and metrics, integrating into the relevant RCSA categories such as data, fraud, cyber, technology, model risk and sales practices, and incorporating into scenarios. AI is increasingly a driver for operational risks overall and should be considered in the context of its interconnectivity to all risks in an operational risk taxonomy.

There are several frameworks that are focused on AI risks. It is a strong practice to map the specialized frameworks to the operational risk framework components. The NIST AI Framework is the one that several industry experts that I queried pointed to. The framework clearly states that "AI risk management should be integrated and incorporated into broader enterprise risk management strategies and processes. Treating AI risks along with other critical risks, such as cybersecurity and privacy, will yield a more integrated outcome and organizational efficiencies." The NIST framework further targets data privacy risks and concerns associated with the "confidentiality, integrity, and availability of the system and its training and output data."

In addition to NIST, the EU Artificial Intelligence Act was published by the European Union in July 2024 and provides guidance for financial institutions. The elements of the framework include a risk-based focus, risk management processes that including data governance protocols and event management, responsible developers and users, and guidance on general-purpose AI. (See Chapter 9 for more background.) Google has indicated that it will sign the European Union's AI Code of Practice, despite articulated concerns that it could slow Europe's development and deployment of AI. Microsoft's president indicated that it will likely sign the code.

The OECD has published a framework that provides guidance on the deployment of an AI system in specific contexts, although its framework can apply to generic AI systems. It classifies AI systems and applications along the following dimensions: People & Planet, Economic Context, Data & Input, AI Model, and Task and Output.

A research team at MIT scanned 13 key frameworks and guidance documents related to the risk management of AI that were published between 2023 and 2025. They extracted from the research 831 specific mitigations, which they defined as actions designed to mitigate the impact of AI-related risks. They organized these into a risk management taxonomy with 4 top-level categories and 23 subcategories. This research presents a view of a complicated and evolving risk management environment that can be challenging. A strong practice is to leverage as the environment evolves the operational risk framework as the guardrails and to focus on mapping one or two frameworks (such as NIST and EU) to the operational risk framework components and the operational risk taxonomy.

There is so much information breaking on managing AI. I have anchored on the following concepts:

- The risk manager must be at the center of managing AI risk. I have been recently asked about the concept of an AI compliance manager. AI has become a much-needed tool for managing risk (see Chapter 6 on the use of AI in RCSA). I like to think of AI as the junior resource who does the initial review. But there needs to be a subject-matter expert—the risk supervisor—who can make the final determination on how to apply the findings to the organization's overall risk profile.
- The business manager must be at the center of managing AI strategies, models, aggregation methodologies, and other business uses. They must be at the center of all AI-produced output to determine the best application, if it is accurate, and if any biases or unanticipated risks are present.
- Data is a critical input into all AI-driven processes, routines, and models. Data that is not accurate, complete, timely, or contains biases and is fed into an AI model will result in problematical outcomes.
- It is worth repeating that the inputs need to be managed through a strong data management program and the output needs to be heavily scrutinized and challenged by subject-matter experts. This is a difficult task as there can be a lack of transparency in how the output was derived. Humans are needed to interpret and apply the output and to manage the documentation process very carefully.

Data Is Foundational to AI and Machine Learning

There is great interconnectivity between managing data, AI, and machine learning, as the latter rely on data as their source of power. It is not possible to manage AI risks effectively without having a strong data risk management program in place. If the data is not of good quality or has inherent bias, the bad data and biases become part of the AI's knowledge base and get multiplied exponentially times over through its generative processes. This adage holds truer now than ever: "Garbage in, garbage out."

AI and machine learning pose very specific data risks as they are reliant on large data sets. If a model is trained on inaccurate or biased data, it can amplify the impact of bad data. As a result, it can lead to biased models such as those that are used for pricing or lending decisions or violate privacy laws. And there may be a lack of transparency that this is occurring. A friend of mine told me that as part of a background check on a new employee at his company, the AI-driven review returned deeply confidential information. He was horrified and deleted the results immediately. He also did not understand how this could have happened.

There is a lot of concern that AI models are opaque and lack transparency. Tracing data through its lineage and lifecycle allows for transparency into the quality of the data that is fed into a model. This work is more important than ever as companies move to the use of AI in decision-making and models. The OECD and NIST frameworks consider the impact of societal harm if the data that is used in AI and machine learning is biased and not carefully vetted.

Conducting a data lineage is a pain-staking exercise, and of course, introducing AI to the process allows for more efficiency and accuracy but also produces a risk of using AI to validate AI. This topic is being debated in the risk community: can you use AI to validate the accuracy of a model or to create a documentation trail of itself? It is an interesting discussion, but I keep coming back to one of the strongest risk mitigation strategies is to have a human with deep subject matter in the middle of the process.

AI-Specific Operational Risks

Managing AI risks must incorporate consideration of how they are drivers of other risks and assessed through an integrated approach. The following are some of the operational risks that should be assessed through RCSA and considered in the construction of scenarios:

People:

- There can be a resistance to change and fear of being replaced among the employee population, which may stymie the adoption of AI capabilities.
- There is currently a shortage of talent with the requisite skills to deploy AI and to manage its associated risks as evidenced by the war for AI talent in the technology sector.
- Talent acquisition systems that use AI can be biased, if they are based on past hiring decisions, data, or keyword matching that are inherently biased.
- Misalignment with employees and management on who benefits from AI-driven efficiencies:
  - The *Wall Street Journal* published a story on AI efficiencies that quoted a survey published by SAP. The SAP survey indicated that nearly 50% of workers felt that any efficiencies and time savings gained from the deployment of AI should belong to them. The survey also found that workers who use AI gain approximately one hour a day in efficiency. On the flip side, employers are using AI efficiencies to downsize or hold steady their current employee numbers. There is a trend for CEOs to publicize recent layoffs as a positive move to gain efficiencies, while in the past they were more circumspect about layoffs because they might have indicated slow growth.

Process:

- AI models can be biased if the underlying data is problematical and can operate as a "black box" with a lack of transparency.
- Data privacy can be compromised through feeding personal, customer, or corporate data into AI algorithms if guardrails are inadequate.
- Errors that are embedded in AI systems could go undetected if verification and validation procedures are inadequate, and it can be difficult to determine root cause.

- The lack of transparency can create challenges with documenting data lineage.
- Business continuity plans and playbooks may be out-of-date and prove to be ineffective if they have not been updated to include processes that rely on AI.
- AI is increasingly proving to be an effective tool for fraudsters, including the use of deepfakes and voice imitation software.

System:

- AI systems can be susceptible to cyber threats if the proper controls are not in place and updated regularly, with additional risk associated with the use of open-source software.
- Systems that have AI embedded within them require complex integration with existing applications.
- System capacity may be inadequate to process, store, and transform large data sets.

External:

- Any decisions, processes, or activities that utilize AI must comply with regulations, including those related to fair lending, consumer protection, employment discrimination, privacy, and cybersecurity.
  - Several wealth management firms are using AI agents to provide investment advice based on data related to a client's risk profile. This needs to be carefully vetted by the "human in the loop" to protect against suitability issues.
  - The SEC has settled with several investment advisors over "AI washing" related to how the firms document claims that their investment decisions are supported by AI.
- The AI regulatory landscape is evolving, with the recent drafting of EU rules governing its use.
- AI has played a role in the reporting of geopolitical events, with a rise in fake news and misleading social media posts.

Using AI to Manage Risk

The tide is turning (finally!) in many operational risk functions in terms of leveraging AI and technology to manage risk. A challenge that the industry has dealt with from the inception of managing operational risk as a distinct discipline is the identification of forward-looking and emerging risks. All the manual work that has gone into risk and control assessments has for the most part been at best a point-in-time view. Consider the use of internal loss events and issues as inputs into RCSA ratings that reflect known control deficiencies and risk exposures. They mostly tell you what is already known. The use of external loss events can help with proactively identifying control gaps before they manifest within one's own organization, but it takes some imagination to know how to apply them. Scenario analysis with the assistance of strong subject-matter experts is one of our most forward-looking tools, but an individual can only envision so much in this deeply challenging environment.

Now is the time to say goodbye to manual aggregation of data forever and, if you are not already doing so, to start drafting use cases for integrating AI into the components of the risk management framework. Several vendors are developing solutions that can scan the horizon for risk signals that include social media posts, news articles, regulatory filings, briefings from critical regulators, changes in rules and regulations, and financial, industry, and market reports that allow for real-time views on risk. The power of these AI systems, which are also being built in-house at some organizations, is that they can scan all of these sources and bring together trends and themes related to a broad range of topics, including fraud, loss events, cyber breaches, geopolitical developments, regulatory fines and penalties, and market events to arrive at real-time conclusions and early warning signs, which can be used for risk rating and management decision-making.

The following is an overview of where AI can be used to manage components of the operational risk framework:

- **RCSA:** RCSA leverages data, such as open issues, losses, peer events, and the results from other risk assessments. AI can add tremendous value by automating much of the data review process and determination of risk and control levels. AI would not only make the process more efficient but also more effective, as it can be used in the identification of emerging risks beyond what we know about today through a scan of the external environment.
- **Control assessment:** Control assessments are tedious, and control inventories have grown exponentially. AI can be useful in identifying duplicate controls and reconciling control inventories. It can also be used in mapping controls to policies and industry frameworks and collecting data to assess the state of controls.
- **Manual controls:** There is a reliance in many institutions on manual controls, such as the infamous four eye controls. When a manual control breaks down, often the tendency is to add an additional level of manual controls. AI can be used to monitor for mismatches in the placement of transactions where human errors often occur and errors associated with reconciliations and incomplete process implementation.
- **Data:** AI can be used to create, aggregate, identify, and monitor KRIs and metrics, which are executed through manual aggregation in many institutions.
- **Testing:** Testing is a manual process in many institutions, including SOX and control testing. AI can be used to automate much of these processes and relieve institutions of the reliance on manual testing protocols.
- **Scenario analysis:** Powerful AI agents can scan the information horizon (see the earlier discussion) for emerging themes and trends much more broadly than any individual can. They can assist with not just understanding risk themes but also the frequency of how they are evolving and the potential severity.
- **Operational risk databases:** AI can be used to manage operational risk databases, identify duplicate entries, reconcile against the general ledger, and look for anomalies and incomplete records. This is especially important as the industry implements the new standardized approach for allocating operational risk capital, which relies on loss data.
- **Risk monitoring:** AI agents can scan and process vast amounts of data that trigger risk alerts; they provide themes and trends that can be integrated into an organization's

risk profile and used to bolster, revise and develop new controls if necessary. False positives are always a challenge in traditional monitoring systems, but AI models can be trained to reduce false positives as they process data and get smarter over time.

Interview with Industry Veteran on Data and Machine Learning: Jae Kang

Jae Kang is a senior risk management executive leading financial and operational risk with emphasis in data, models, ML, and AI for leading financial institutions. Currently, he consults bank clients in credit and quantitative risk management and serves as a strategic advisor to a SPAC company. Previously, Jae was the deputy chief risk officer at Nelnet and the head of risk management at Sallie Mae, implementing and managing data management and governance, model risk management, and ML and AI risk management initiatives. Jae's experience also includes M&A where he served as the head of bank strategy and global head of M&A at notable firms, acquiring and disposing assets and companies during the financial crisis. Jae started his career as an investment banker and a strategy management consultant.

1. **Question**

   How do you view the interconnectedness between data, ML, and AI risk? What are the common elements?

   Answer

   In my experience, one of the critical elements that ties data, machine learning (ML), and artificial intelligence (AI) is a well-defined business (data) strategy, both for the business executives and risk managers. Too often, companies treat business strategy, data, ML, and AI as separate functions, each pursuing in isolation based on capabilities and emerging technologies. Without a unifying comprehensive strategy, the efforts become fragmented, misaligned, and possibly counterproductive.

   A robust business strategy is the starting point that should guide how and what data is collected and what and how ML and AI models are deployed and monitored for risk management. A key question is "What business problems are we trying to solve?" In financial services, the common business strategy clusters around improving marketing efforts, enhancing credit risk management, detecting fraud, improving compliance efforts, streamlining customer services, and improving processes for efficiencies. These strategies are dynamic and need to be anchored in strategic intent.

   From a risk manager perspective, it is particularly important for the first line and second line of defense to work together and define an optimal business strategy. The second line of defense should not simply review the strategy and implementation after the rollout but should have a seat at the table during the formation and implementation. This active involvement ensures that risk considerations are embedded into the designed and implemented correctly from the start.

2. **Question**

   How do you define effective data, ML, and AI governance, and what frameworks key components must be in place?

Answer

While the definition of good-quality data varies by industry or organization, it is generally understood as data that is accurate, complete, current, consistent, and timely. Data that is relevant for decision-making and supports unbiased outcome. Once a good quality data is established, ML and AI models should be used and designed to solve valuable business problems, operate ethically, improve consistently, incorporate human oversight, and scale effectively for maximum business benefits.

There are well-known frameworks that are utilized. For data governance, commonly used models include DAMA-DMBOK, the NIST Data Governance Framework, and DCAM, particularly in financial services. For ML and AI, the NIST AI Risk Management Framework, the AI Model Risk Management Framework from the Cloud Security Alliance, and ISO/IEC 42001:2023 are among the most recognized.

It is important to recognize that these frameworks are not enough but must be tailored to the organization's specific contexts and integrated with broader operational risk management programs, including cybersecurity, technology, third-party risk, process controls, and compliance. A governance program is most effective when it is not only structured using a framework but also practical, adaptive, and aligned with organization's strategy and risk appetite.

3. **Question**

What are strong practices for assessing and managing data-related risks (e.g., data lineage, unauthorized access, poor metadata)?

Answer

Strong data risk management begins with a clear definition of what data governance is and what it aims to achieve. As defined by DAMA-DMBOK, data governance is "the exercise of authority and control (planning, monitoring, and enforcement) over the management of data assets." For the program to be effective, it must be sustainable, embedded into daily operations, and measurable.

The critical first step is establishing an effective data governance organization with clear sponsorship and buy-in from the senior management and the board of directors. It begins by identifying the key risks to be addressed (data quality, security, privacy, model use, and compliance). It also includes data infrastructure (data warehouse, data lake etc.), metadata management, and vendor oversight. Once those factors are determined, a good governance structure includes committees, data stewards, and officers to oversee accountability and execution.

From there, the focus shifts to understanding the organization's data assets and identifying vulnerabilities across data lifecycle. Oversight can be supported through various SaaS and tools that monitor practices, including data quality, model use, storage, access controls, integration, lineage, and user training.

Building an effective data governance program is a complex journey that requires organizational change, technology know-how, and cross-functional collaboration. As stated before, however, the heart of it all is a clearly defined business strategy. With that foundation, governance can be prioritized and tailored to deliver meaningful risk management.

4. Question

What controls should be in place to manage risks associated with AI and machine learning models in production?

Answer

Managing AI and ML model risks in operation starts with understanding that these models rely on quality data to support decision-making. It is also important to recognize the strengths and limitations of different models. For example, statistical models are often preferred in credit decisions due to their transparency (e.g., credit decision for declining a borrower for a loan). ML models such as decision trees, random forest, and gradient boosting are excellent in identifying characteristic differences but may suffer from high variance. AI models such as gen AI and agentic AI are excellent in general operations but often lack the accuracy (e.g., hallucination, etc.) required for financial institution's operations.

When it comes to controls, there is no one-size-fits approach. Controls must be tailored to the specific models and risks and uses. For instance, bias is a major problem, and it can be mitigated through strong data quality check, clear data lineage, and augmentation of data using nonbiased data in real time. Lack of transparency is another risk that can be controlled using explainable AI models, the use of interpretable models where possible, and stress testing outputs to identify abnormal behaviors. Performance drifting is another common issue and requires continuous monitoring, alerting mechanisms, and periodic model validation. These are some simple examples, but there are a multitude of controls that can be deployed depending on the risks identified.

Ultimately, while the landscape of AI and ML risk is broad and evolving, there are many tools, controls, and frameworks available to support effective risk assessment and control. What matters most is that qualified professionals—both technical experts and risk managers—are actively involved throughout the lifecycle. Their engagement is essential to identifying risks early on, implementing the right controls, and ensuring that AI and ML are used responsibly and effectively.

5. Question

What challenges have you encountered in managing data, ML, and AI risks over the course of your career?

Answer

Throughout my career leading data, ML, and AI initiatives—both from a solution development and risk management oversight perspective—the most consistent challenge I have encountered is the lack of a clear business (data) strategy. In my experience, this is often the key factor that separates between a successful program versus a deficient one.

In one engagement, a client aspired to become a data-driven organization and had access to literally petabytes of data. However, teams began building a data infrastructure without fully understanding the relevance of data and the ultimate goals of using data for business outcome. Much of the data turned out to be inaccurate, incomplete, and misaligned with business needs. It lacked controls for security, privacy, bias, and other critical data lifecycle. Ultimately, this organization could not leverage the data for its ML and AI decision-making.

To address this, risk managers engaged business leadership to define a clear business strategy. Once that foundation was in place, risk managers partnered with the business to design a tailored risk management framework and worked closely with them through various stages of development lifecycle for data management and governance initiatives.

This experience reinforced a core lesson: identifying and aligning on a business (data) strategy is the essential first step in both implementation and risk management.

6. Question

What advice would you give people who are interested in pursuing a career in managing data, ML, or AI risks? What skills should they develop?

Answer

There are many paths to becoming an effective data, ML, and AL risk manager, but two qualities stand out in my experience: a strong foundation in core disciplines and a genuine sense of curiosity.

First, successful risk managers need to understand three essential components. The starting point is a solid understanding of the business, namely, strategy, objectives, processes, and capabilities. Without this context, it is difficult to design a risk management program that is both relevant and effective. Second, robust knowledge of risk management is essential. This includes, among many, developing a framework, policies, and procedures; assessing risk and controls; and engaging with relevant stakeholders. Finally, a fundamental understanding of data, ML, and AI technology can be very useful. While deep technical expertise is not necessarily required, a good risk manager should know the basic flows of how these systems work (e.g., technology and processes, etc.) and what the outcome implications are.

In my opinion, it is also important to have curiosity. The AI landscape is evolving rapidly. In 2022, we were introduced to large language models (ChatGPT), and prompting became the new discipline. By 2024, multimodel models emerged allowing texts, videos, pictures, and voices to be combined. In 2025, agentic AI emerged reshaping how organizations think about AI deployment. To stay relevant, risk management professionals must be eager to learn, adapt, and apply new technologies in real-world contexts. It is not just about understanding the theories but also engaging with the AI tool and see how they perform in real-life practice.

Bibliography

Alexander Saeri, Sophia Lloyd George, Jess Graham, and Clelia Lacarriere. *Mapping AI Risk Mitigations: Evidence Scan and Draft Mitigation Taxonomy. Massachusetts Institute of Technology (MIT)*. July 2025. https://cdn.prod.website-files.com/669550d38372f33552d2516e/6887e58496902e3bcad04a5a_Mapping%20AI%20Risk%20Mitigations.pdf.

Basel Committee on Banking Supervision. *Principles for Effective Data Aggregation and Risk Reporting*. 2014. https://www.bis.org/publ/bcbs239.pdf.

Basel Committee on Banking Supervision. *Progress in Adopting the Principles for Effective Risk Data Aggregation and Risk Reporting*. November 2023. https://www.bis.org/bcbs/publ/d559.pdf.

Callum Borchers. Your Prize for Saving Time at Work with AI: More Work. *The Wall Street Journal*, July 9, 2025.

DAMA-DMBOK. *Data Management Body of Knowledge*. Revised Edition. Basking Ridge, N.J., Technis Publications, 2024.

EDM Council. *Global Data Management Benchmark Report*. 2023. https://edmcouncil.org.

Ernst and Young. *Regulatory Reporting Technology and Architecture—Consolidated Financial and Regulatory Data Approach*. July 2023. https://www.ey.com/content/dam/ey-unified-site/ey-com/en-us/insights/banking-capital-markets/documents/ey-regulatory-reporting-technology-and-architecture-consolidated-financial-and-regulatory-data-approach.pdf.

Foo Yun Chee. *Google to Sign EU's AI Code of Practice Despite Concerns*. Reuters. July 30, 2025. https://www.reuters.com/sustainability/boards-policy-regulation/google-sign-eus-ai-code-practice-despite-concerns-2025-07-30/.

ISO. *ISO/IEC 42001: 2023: Information Technology—Artificial Intelligence—Management System*. https://www.iso.org/obp/ui/en/#iso:std:iso-iec:42001:ed-1:v1:en.

Lu Wang. *Dumb' AI Bots Collude to Rig Markets, Wharton Research Finds*. Bloomberg. July 30, 2025. https://www.bloomberg.com/news/articles/2025-07-30/wharton-experiment-finds-dumb-ai-bots-collude-to-rig-markets.

National Institute of Standards and Technology (NIST). *Artificial Intelligence Risk Management Framework*. January 2023. https://nvlpubs.nist.gov/nistpubs/ai/NIST.AI.100-1.pdf.

National Institute of Standards and Technology (NIST). *Artificial Intelligence Risk Management Framework: Generative Artificial Intelligence Profile*. July 2024. https://nvlpubs.nist.gov/nistpubs/ai/NIST.AI.600-1.pdf.

OECD. *OECD Framework for the Classification of AI Systems*, OECD Digital Economy Papers, No. 323, Paris, OECD Publishing, 2022. https://doi.org/10.1787/cb6d9eca-en.

Thomas C. Redman. Harvard Business Review. *Bad Data Costs the U.S. $3 Trillion Per Year*. September 22, 2016. https://hbr.org/2016/09/bad-data-costs-the-u-s-3-trillion-per-year.

Chapter 14

Managing Cyber Risk

Cyber risk is a material component of an operational risk management program and one of the most important risks of our day. It has a prominent place on Risk.Net's "Top 10 Risks" for the last few years (March 2025) and was cited by Federal Reserve Chairman Powell during a *60 Minutes* TV interview as the risk that keeps him up at night (https://www.cbsnews.com/news/jerome-powell-full-2021-60-minutes-interview-transcript/).

Cyber is an important operational risk and is often managed through the operational risk framework in the second line. However, this risk cannot be managed without active ownership by the first line of defense.

Key components of a cyber risk management program include mapping to components of the operational risk framework, assessing the threat landscape, and identifying vulnerabilities internally and externally in systems and processes. A robust inventory of all the applications and systems on a network must be maintained that allows for visibility into potential control issues and for comprehensive patching when vulnerabilities are identified. The implementation of firewalls, intrusion detection systems, and encryption are also critical to a robust approach to cyber risk management.

Cyber risk should be managed along with the other risks that it interacts with, including business continuity, third-party, and fraud risks. A mature and well-documented incident response program is critical to managing cyber risk, including criticality ratings associated with the day-to-day running of critical business systems. An important partner in the management of cyber and technology risks is the business resilience team, who collaborate on the development of disaster recovery plans and playbooks in the event there is a cyber breach, system malfunction, or degradation.

Another important component of managing cyber is third-party risk. There is concentration with certain critical vendors, including those that support managing data and processes in the cloud (Amazon AWS, Microsoft Azure). The "bad guys" are becoming more sophisticated in how they exploit vulnerabilities within third-party providers, who are becoming more concentrated in the sectors that they serve. A cyber incident at a third-party provider that has a concentrated market presence can have impact across an entire sector. This can result in multiple organizations being unable to serve a client segment, the breach of customer data industry wide, and, ultimately, a catastrophic systemic event. At the same time, organizations that experienced the breach will suffer reputational consequences if they do not have robust resiliency programs in place, and they will be compared with each other by how long it takes them to resume normal operations.

A Tale of Two Attacks

The United Healthcare event is the one that stopped my heart. As a customer, I received the letter that so many received detailing the extent of my compromised data. This includes highly personal and confidential data, including Social Security numbers, medical records, health diagnoses, test results, and billing and payment information. United Healthcare's Change Healthcare subsidiary was hit by a ransomware attack in February 2024. The attack was perpetrated by a criminal group called AlphV/BlackCat, which infiltrated United Healthcare's operations. The criminals caused widespread delays in the processing of electronic claims and prescriptions services, which impacted health facilities across the United States.

In response to the cyber event, United Healthcare paid a $22 million ransom in Bitcoin to the AlphV group to contain the damage and restore services. Although it is not confirmed, a second ransomware group, RansomHub, claimed to have access to the stolen data after the initial ransom was paid and demanded a second payment. It is unclear if this was in fact paid, but some have speculated that it was. In addition to my personal impact, I was deeply concerned at the time of the impact of the criminals getting access to so much personal health information. What if it became public that a CEO of a major public company had certain health issues? Could this have impacted the stock price of the firm or the company's ability to manage itself through what might become serious governance issues? (See the IBM FIRST case study at end of this chapter.)

A few months before the United Healthcare event hit the press, the British Library disclosed on October 28, 2023, that it was the victim of a significant cyberattack that brought its services to a standstill. Most services provided by the British Library were down, including their website, phone lines, and everything accessed online. Delivery of materials from the library's offsite storage facility in Yorkshire was suspended. The main catalog with more than 36 million records was only brought back some time later in a read-only format.

The attack was perpetrated by a hacking group called Rhysida, which has been described as a "ransomware-as-a-service" provider. The group operates by exploiting networks, such as virtual private networks, and conducting phishing campaigns. Once it has the information it needs to gain network access, it deploys software that encrypts data and demands a ransom.

The British Library's response was notable because unlike United Healthcare it refused to pay a ransom. Rhysida demanded 20 bitcoins, which are the approximate equivalent of £600,000, in exchange for restoring the data. It was estimated following the attack that the cost to the library for recovering its data and online access was approximately £7 million. The ransomware group eventually made most of the data it appropriated available on the dark web with the message "Data hunters, enjoy."

Both events contain lessons about the importance of investing in cybersecurity controls, network security, intrusion detection systems, and education. Training and awareness are important because at the heart of these cases, and many like them, is the ability of the bad guys to collect the information they need through network vulnerabilities. It is also a reminder that we need to protect our public institutions, which require resources and expertise to secure critical services, such as those provided by libraries, utilities, hospitals, and governments.

The contrast between the two responses is significant and highlights that planning for a cyber response must include the decision on whether a ransom will be paid. In the case of the British Library, the cost of recovering the data and the length of it service disruption may suggest that paying a ransom would have been more advantageous. When ransoms are paid to bad guys, however, there is never assurance that once the systems are back up and running the data has been returned. In the case of the United Healthcare event, there is speculation that a second ransom was demanded by another bad guy threatening to expose private data.

An organization should have a well-designed and thorough playbook ready at hand if they are the victim of a cyberattack. This includes the factors that would lead to the decision to pay a ransom. Of course, the best approach is to have strong controls in place. For instance, United Healthcare admitted that the Change entity did not have basic multifactor authentication (MFA) controls in place, which contributed to the attacker's ability to penetrate their network. It was reported in the press that MFA controls were not enabled on the application that the bad guys exploited.

Cyber Frameworks

There are several cyber frameworks that provide strong guidance for managing cyber risk. They can be mapped to the major components of an operational risk framework, including mapping the controls to the RCSA, incorporating threat intelligence into scenarios, and developing risk appetite statements and metrics for articulating the amount of cyber risk an organization is willing to accept (which should be very low). The NIST framework is the one cyber experts in the United States have indicated they favor. The other standard framework that is most often mentioned is ISO 27001,

"Information security, cybersecurity and privacy protection—Information security management systems—Requirements."

NIST 2.0

The NIST framework states in its introduction that although it is designed to be useful regardless of the maturity level of an organization, the implementation of the framework will depend on the unique risk characteristics of each organization, including varying risk appetites and missions. At the same time, NIST addresses the interconnectivity among risks by indicating the framework should be used to "address cybersecurity risks alongside other risks of the enterprise, including those that are financial, privacy, supply chain, reputational, technological, or physical in nature."

NIST's 2.0 Framework includes the following components, with Governance newly added: Govern, Identify, Protect, Detect, Respond, and Recover. Each component can be mapped to a common operational risk framework. It is important to mention, as with any risk framework, that the components are implemented concurrently. Implementing a risk framework is not a linear exercise.

Here is an overview of the core elements of the NIST Framework with mapping to the operational risk framework:

> ***Govern:*** *Function provides outcomes to inform what an organization may do to achieve and prioritize the outcomes of the other five Functions in the context of its mission and stakeholder expectations. Governance activities are critical for incorporating cybersecurity into an organization's broader enterprise risk management (ERM) strategy. Govern addresses an understanding of organizational context; the establishment of cybersecurity strategy and cybersecurity supply chain risk management; roles, responsibilities, and authorities; policy; and the oversight of cybersecurity strategy.*

The govern function incorporates the management of cyber risk across the lines of defense, with every business and function responsible for the management of this critical risk within their domains. The office of the chief information security officer (CISO) is responsible for direct management of the cybersecurity risk management strategy and policy and control documentation, with the CISO personally responsible for communicating the risks, and maturity of the function to the risk committee and the board.

The second line of defense is responsible for incorporating cyber risk management into the operational risk policy and, often, drafting a directive that provides in detail the expectations for strong risk management. The second line of defense is responsible for reviewing and challenging the cyber risk policy and strategy and providing an opinion on if they are designed to mitigate risks within the enterprise. The second line must work with the CISO office to define roles and responsibilities across the lines of defense.

The following chart contains roles and responsibilities for each of the NIST 2.0 elements for first-line CISO office and second-line operational risk. As with all risk types, the third line is responsible for providing assurance that the risk is properly mitigated and for reporting its assessment to the audit committee of the board.

The following are the roles and responsibilities for managing cyber risk across the first-line CISO office and second-line operational risk by NIST 2.0 Framework component:

NIST CSF Function	First-Line CISO Office	Second-Line Operational Risk
Govern	Own and implement cyber policies and procedures. Lead cyber governance forums.	Incorporate cyber into the operational risk policy. Own and implement the second-line cyber standards. Monitor compliance with policy and standard requirements. Define roles and responsibilities across lines of defense. Provide risk oversight and control design challenge. Incorporate cyber topics into risk committees.
Identify	Perform RCSA for cyber topics. Assess for emerging risks and vulnerabilities so that risk profile is fully understood, including consideration of people, systems, processes, third parties, facilities, and data.	Review and challenge CISO RCSA results. Conduct thematic reviews on enterprise cyber exposure and controls. Develop risk appetite statements indicating level of cyber risk organization is willing to accept.
Protect	Implement access controls, encryption, endpoint protection, and secure configurations. Train staff on secure practices.	Review and challenge control design and effectiveness. Monitor compliance with policies and standards. Support policy refinement (e.g., IAM, data protection).
Detect	Ongoing monitoring of threats and vulnerabilities. Perform testing. Report anomalies and security events. Escalate incidents.	Monitor risk appetite metrics and control effectiveness. Review and challenge monitoring routines and testing.
Respond	Execute incident response playbooks. Participate in crisis management and communications. Coordinate with stakeholders.	Oversee response readiness through tabletop exercises. Challenge lessons learned and remediation adequacy.
Recover	Restore systems and data from backups. Reestablish business services. Participate in post-incident reviews.	Assess business continuity and disaster recovery plan adequacy. Review effectiveness of recovery plans. Challenge resilience strategies and improvements.

The CISO office should work with second-line operational risk to define the risk appetite statements and metrics. The cyber risk appetite must be approved by senior management and the board. I have seen different constructs in organizations, with either the CISO office or the second line monitoring and reporting on risk appetite metrics. If it resides with the first line, the second line should review and challenge the comprehensiveness and adequacy of the risk appetite metrics. If the risk appetite metrics cross the yellow threshold (the early warning level), it is a strong practice to open an issue and action plan.

The following are sample risk appetite statements and metrics with conservative example thresholds:

- We have zero tolerance for unauthorized access to or manipulation of sensitive customer or proprietary data. Strong encryption, access controls, and data governance are expected across all systems.

Cyber Risk Area	Risk Appetite Statement	Metric	Green Threshold	Yellow Threshold	Red Threshold
Data Confidentiality and Integrity	Zero tolerance for unauthorized access or manipulation of sensitive data.	Number of unauthorized access incidents per quarter	0	1	1
Data Confidentiality and Integrity	Zero tolerance for unauthorized access or manipulation of sensitive data.	Percentage of sensitive data encrypted at rest and in transit	100%	99%	99%

- We have a low appetite for disruptions to critical systems caused by cyber threats. Systems supporting core business functions must maintain high availability, with recovery capabilities in place.

Cyber Risk Area	Risk Appetite Statement	Metric	Green Threshold	Yellow Threshold	Red Threshold
System Availability and Resilience	Low appetite for disruptions to critical systems caused by cyber threats.	Uptime percentage for critical systems	≥99.9%	≤98%	≤97%
System Availability and Resilience	Low appetite for disruptions to critical systems caused by cyber threats.	Mean time to detect and recover from cyber incidents (MTTR)	≤4 hours	≤5 hours	≤6 hours

- We have a low appetite for known vulnerabilities remaining unremediated beyond acceptable timeframes. Patch management and vulnerability scanning must be consistently applied.

Cyber Risk Area	Risk Appetite Statement	Metric	Green Threshold	Yellow Threshold	Red Threshold
Vulnerability Management	Low appetite for unremediated vulnerabilities beyond acceptable timeframes.	Percentage of critical patches applied within 15 days	≥95%	≤94%	≤93%

- We have a low appetite for cyber risks arising from negligent or malicious insider activity. Continuous user training, monitoring, and behavioral analytics are critical to mitigate this risk.

Cyber Risk Area	Risk Appetite Statement	Metric	Green Threshold	Yellow Threshold	Red Threshold
User Behavior and Insider Threat	Low appetite for cyber risks from negligent or malicious insiders.	Phishing simulation fail rate	≤5%	≤6%	≤7%
User Behavior and Insider Threat	Low appetite for cyber risks from negligent or malicious insiders.	Percentage of employees completing annual cyber awareness training on time	100%	≤98%	≤97%

- We have a low appetite for cyber risk introduced by third-party vendors. We require vendors with access to sensitive systems or data to meet our cyber standards and undergo regular assessments.

Cyber Risk Area	Risk Appetite Statement	Metric	Green Threshold	Yellow Threshold	Red Threshold
Third-Party Cyber Risk	Low appetite for cyber risk introduced by third-party vendors.	Percentage of critical third parties with completed cyber risk assessments	100%	≤99%	≤98%
Third-Party Cyber Risk	Low appetite for cyber risk introduced by third-party vendors.	Number of critical vendors without current SOC 2 or ISO 27001 certifications	0	1	1

Identify: *The organization's current cybersecurity risks are understood. Understanding the organization's assets (e.g., data, hardware, software, systems, facilities, services, people), suppliers, and related cybersecurity risks enables an organization to prioritize its efforts consistent with its risk management strategy and the mission needs identified under Govern. This Function also includes the identification of improvement opportunities for the organization's policies, plans, processes, procedures, and practices that support cybersecurity risk management to inform efforts under all six Functions.*

Each business and function is responsible for incorporating RCSA risks and controls into the assessment for their respective area. Some organizations take a top-down approach on the assessment of risks and controls, since most apply on an enterprise level. Accordingly, the CISO office pushes down to each business and function the enterprise risk and control ratings. The business or function then reviews the top-down ratings and determine if they have unique exposures that may be different than what has been identified at the enterprise level. Proper rationale is required if this is the case. This exercise involves some timing coordination, since the CISO office will need to assess the cyber environment ahead of the kick-off of the RCSA cycle (if the RCSA is on a cyclical approach). If a trigger-based approach is taken, the CISO office will need to update the enterprise view of the RCSA ahead of each business when a trigger occurs.

The RCSA assessment should incorporate reviews of any recent events or near-misses, including peer events, and existing cyber scenarios. If the RCSA residual risk results are higher than the articulated risk appetite (which in many organizations will be low), an issue and action plan should be opened to bring down the level of risk.

Second-line operational risk is responsible for reviewing and challenging the risk assessment results and determining if opened action plans are designed to effectively bring down the level of residual risk.

Scenarios are an effective tool for understanding vulnerabilities, threats, and risks, and the potential underlying control issues that can result in a cyber event. They should be integrated into the RCSA process so that there is a forward-looking view on what could potentially happen.

The following are examples are generic cyber scenarios:

Scenario Title	Description	Root Cause	Severity	Likelihood	Low Loss ($)	Medium Loss ($)	High Loss ($)	Impact
Ransomware Attack	A ransomware attack encrypts payment systems so that they are not accessible and demands a $100 million ransom for the encryption key.	Exploited software vulnerability that lacked current patch	High	Moderate	10,000,000	50,000,000	100,000,000	Disruption of operations, financial losses due to failure to make payments, reputational damage, potential regulatory fines.
Insider Data Theft	A contractor with system access steals sensitive customer data for personal gain and sells the data on the dark web.	Insider threat	High	Low	250,000	500,000	1,000,000	Breach of customer confidentiality, regulatory non-compliance, legal liabilities, reputational damage
Phishing Attack	Employees fall victim to phishing emails, compromising user credentials and potentially installing malware.	Human error in recognizing phishing attempts	Medium	High	250,000	500,000	1,000,000	Compromise of user credentials, unauthorized access, data exfiltration.
Third-Party Vendor Breach	Cybercriminal exploits vulnerabilities in a third-party vendor's system to access sensitive customer information.	Inadequate vendor security measures	High	Moderate	200,000	1,000,000	5,000,000	Data breach, regulatory fines, reputational damage, legal actions
Distributed Denial of Service (DDoS) Attack	Malicious actors flood organization's network with traffic, causing service disruptions.	Botnet-driven traffic overload	High	Low	50,000	250,000	1,000,000	Downtime of online services, loss of revenue, customer dissatisfaction.

Protect: *Safeguards to manage the organization's cybersecurity risks are used. Once assets and risks are identified and prioritized, Protect supports the ability to secure those assets to prevent or lower the likelihood and impact of adverse cybersecurity events, as well as to increase the likelihood and impact of taking advantage of opportunities. Outcomes covered by this Function include identity management, authentication, and access control; awareness and training; data security; platform security (i.e., securing the hardware, software, and services of physical and virtual platforms); and the resilience of technology infrastructure.*

Identifying, implementing, monitoring, and testing controls are central to protecting the enterprise from cyberattacks. This requires a multilayer approach (see the interview with an industry veteran at the end of this chapter), which includes fortified firewalls, strong backup and recovery strategies, security training, and rigorous testing. The inventory of controls should be mapped to a security framework, tested on a risk-based approach, and aligned with control assessments. It is a strong practice to stress the controls through the scenario development process to determine where there could be future vulnerabilities.

The following is a sample list of controls from the Detect portion of the NIST framework that demonstrates the granularity of the framework that can assist with control mapping:

Identity Management, Authentication, and Access Control (PR.AA): Access to physical and logical assets is limited to authorized users, services, and hardware and managed commensurate with the assessed risk of unauthorized access.

- *PR.AA-01: Identities and credentials for authorized users, services, and hardware are managed by the organization*
- *PR.AA-02: Identities are proofed and bound to credentials based on the context of interactions*
- *PR.AA-03: Users, services, and hardware are authenticated*
- *PR.AA-04: Identity assertions are protected, conveyed, and verified*
- *PR.AA-05: Access permissions, entitlements, and authorizations are defined in a policy, managed, enforced, and reviewed, and incorporate the principles of least privilege and separation of duties*
- *PR.AA-06: Physical access to assets is managed, monitored, and enforced commensurate with risk*

Many organizations conduct cyber maturity assessments that provide an indication on where they are on their cyber journey. The NIST documentation indicates that "an organization can use the Tiers to communicate internally as a benchmark for an organization-wide approach to managing cybersecurity risks." The NIST tiers include Tier 1 (partial); Tier 2 (risk informed); Tier 3 (repeatable); Tier 4 (adaptive). The NIST website (https://www.nist.gov/cyberframework/profiles) includes a very detailed spreadsheet that is organized around the six components of the framework that can assist with determining the profile and maturity of a cyber program. It is a strong practice to refresh these assessments regularly and to report the results to the risk committee and the board so that they can monitor overall progress in maturing the program.

Detect: *Possible cybersecurity attacks and compromises are found and analyzed. Detect enables the timely discovery and analysis of anomalies, indicators of compromise, and other potentially adverse events that may indicate that cybersecurity attacks and incidents are occurring. This Function supports successful incident response and recovery activities.*

Continuous monitoring is at the heart of a cyber risk management program. This includes both internal and external monitoring for adverse events. The vendor market is rich with services that provide AI-powered monitoring, which is becoming more sophisticated and accurate (less false positives!) by the day. Monitoring must be enabled to identify threats throughout an organizational network. AI can assist with the correlation of data taken from a variety of sources and overlaying network activity with cyber intelligence from the external environment.

An actual incident occurs when it meets certain predefined criteria, which should be integrated into an organization's event policy and directive.

> ***Respond:*** *Actions regarding a detected cybersecurity incident are taken. Respond supports the ability to contain the effects of cybersecurity incidents. Outcomes within this Function cover incident management, analysis, mitigation, reporting, and communication.*

The response to an event should follow guidelines in the firm's event policy and directive. First, the response should focus on "stopping the bleeding," which may require disconnecting the network from the compromised application or system or from the infected third-party provider. If the event includes significant business interruption, the business continuity plans should be invoked, with prioritization of the most material processes brought back online or if that is not possible, manually executed.

The firm's escalation process must be followed, including notifying senior management, the board and regulators if required (see Chapter 9 for regulatory notification requirements). A playbook should be up-to-date and comprehensive, which must be followed, including a determination if a ransom is to be paid. Issues and action plans should be opened to address any identified control deficiencies, and a root-cause analysis performed.

> ***Recover:*** *Assets and operations affected by a cybersecurity incident are restored. Recover supports the timely restoration of normal operations to reduce the effects of cybersecurity incidents and enable appropriate communication during recovery efforts.*

Once operations are restored, it is a strong practice for second-line operational risk to perform a thematic review of the event and to confirm that the control deficiencies have been addressed and similar vulnerabilities do not exist elsewhere in the organization. A lesson learned workshop should be held once the thematic review is completed to communicate the results and provide an opportunity for raising the organization's awareness of the criticality of embracing and implementing strong cyber hygiene. A post-implementation review, including testing of new or upgraded controls, should occur after the issue and action plan are closed, to determine if the fix is sustainable.

Aligning NIST to an Operational Risk Framework

Industry frameworks, such as NIST 2.0, should be aligned with risk management frameworks, as NIST has stated in its documentation.

The following is a mapping of the NIST 2.0 framework to an operational risk framework:

NIST CSF Component	Governance & Policies & Procedures	Risk Appetite & Key Risk Indicators	Risk & Control Self-Assessment	Loss Data	Scenario Analysis	Issue Management	Monitoring & Reporting	Culture & Awareness
Govern	Establishes and implements cyber policies, directives, procedures, roles and responsibilities, committee governance.	Articulate cyber risk appetite and develop and monitor risk appetite metrics.					Report to risk committee and board on ongoing basis current state of cyber risk and controls, including emerging risks and vulnerabilities.	Promote risk-aware behavior and tone from the top with CEO and senior management communications; conduct cyber training and table-top exercises.
Identify		Identify risks and threats in support of risk appetite thresholds.	Conduct RCSA to identify current state of control environment and current risk levels; incorporate Maturity Assessment results into RCSA.	Events and Near-Misses are escalated, responded to, and remediated.	Develop plausible severe scenarios and incorporate into capital and stress models and RCSA.	Open Issues and Action Plans for identified unmitigated risks.		
Protect	Implement controls that meet standards of governance frameworks (NIST 2.O).		Assess controls through RCSA.		Stress RCSA controls in the development of scenarios.	Address control deficiencies and open issues and action plans.	Report to risk committee and board the results of maturity assessments, control testing, RCSA.	

Detect			Detect anomalies, events, and breaches via monitoring tools.	Open issues and action plans for unmitigated risks associated with detected threats; create new controls or strengthen existing ones.		
Respond	Supports governance via post-incident review and lessons learned.			Coordinate corrective actions during and after incidents.	Escalate incidents and remediation response to senior management, the board and regulators (if required).	
Recover				Conduct post-implementation review on closed issues and action plans.	Report on ongoing status to risk committee and board on remediations and lessons learned.	Reinforce risk management via lessons learned.

Strong Cyber Practices

Cyber risk is one of the existential threats that all organizations face today. It is increasingly difficult to keep up with the bad guys, as they get more and more sophisticated. It is imperative that all organizations have strong controls and guardrails built into their operational risk management programs for managing cyber risk.

Here is an overview of strong industry practices:

Governance: Senior management and the board must fully and completely support the cyber risk management program. This includes providing adequate resources and capacity and to respond when the CISO office or the second line raises issues and concerns. In all risk categories, but especially in this one, issues do not age well, and concerns that are raised through escalation channels and committees should be documented and monitored through to resolution.

It takes a village: Managing cyber risk is complicated and effective risk management requires strong collaboration among the CISO, second-line risk management, the chief technology officer, executive management, and the board.

Interconnected risk management: Cyber must not be managed in a silo. It is closely integrated with other risk types, including fraud, third-party, and resiliency. It should be fully integrated into an organization's operational risk management framework.

Cyber frameworks: Industry frameworks, such as NIST 2.0, should be leveraged to understand what "good" looks like and where an organization is on the maturity scale. An organization should have a clear understanding of where it is in the cyber maturity journey, where it is heading, and how long it will take to get there.

Multilayered approach: It is important to implement a multilayered approach to managing cyber threats and vulnerabilities. The list of controls that are necessary to build adequate defenses is not a "menu of options." Identity management, authentication, access control, training and awareness, platform and application security, cryptography, strong governance, and resilience planning are all critical components of an effective cyber risk management program. An institution can prevent hundreds of attempts every day to breach their network, but the bad guys only need to be successful once and they will find the vulnerabilities.

Third-party oversight: Firms should have strong oversight controls in place of their critical providers and ensure they understand how they are responding in real time to the ever-challenging cyber landscape.

Playbooks: Playbooks should map out procedures if a critical vendor goes down, including step-by-step processes if they are disconnected from a provider's systems and how any manual workarounds would be executed.

Risk assessments: Risk assessments should be updated regularly and evaluate the provider's policies, access controls, monitoring routines, incident response plans, data encryption standards and training and awareness efforts.

Vendor contracts: Contracts should include cybersecurity standards and exit clauses if they are not met.

Testing: Continuous testing should be part of the risk management program, including vulnerability testing, penetration testing that simulates an event, red team testing that emulates a hacker, blue team testing that tests response to an event, and compliance testing against policies, directives, procedures, and frameworks.

Threat monitoring: The internal environment must be continuously monitored for vulnerabilities and threats, along with the external environment to understand where an organization may need to implement new or upgraded controls.

Thematic reviews and lessons learned: A thorough independent review should be undertaken following an event, and lessons learned should be widely shared and communicated.

Cultural awareness: The challenge with cyber risk management is that the bad guys can in theory penetrate a network through one port hole that is created by someone who responds to a phishing attack or other attempt to breach a network. The importance of strong cyber hygiene should be continuously reinforced through senior level messaging, training, and desktop exercises.

Interview with Industry Veteran: Alicja Cade

Alicja's experience managing cyber risk is deep and broad. She is currently employed as a director of financial services in the office of the CISO at Google Cloud. She has previously held senior CISO roles with large global banks and worked as an IT risk and cybersecurity consultant with a Big Four consulting firm in the United Kingdom and the United States. She teaches as an adjunct professor at Columbia University.

1. **Question**

   These are complicated times and especially with so much change in the operating environment. What are some of the qualities, skills and experience an operational risk manager needs today to be effective in managing cyber risk?

   Answer

   I feel strongly that cyber risk should be understood as an operational risk. It is not a black box, but a risk that is fundamental to a company's operations. Financial services regulators are turning their lens on cyber resiliency which is linked to operational resiliency. This has helped companies frame their understanding of cyber risk. Cyber should be understood in the context of how it fits with a company's resilience strategy, and how it is impacted by change in the operating environment, including new technologies, innovation, progress and geopolitical risks.

   Qualities that are needed for managing cyber risk include adaptability, a strategic mindset, and the ability to learn and anticipate emerging risks. A critical skill is the ability to translate cyber risk technicalities into clear business impact and financial terms. Being able to communicate in language that resonates with executive leadership and the board is critical to success.

   I also want to mention the importance of collaboration, including collaboration across functions. It takes a "business village" to run a business and cyber cuts across all business functions. We should always remember that everyone is responsible for cyber risk.

2. **Question**

You have spent a good part of your career in banking organizations before you joined Google. How different is managing cyber risk in a corporate organization from a banking institution?

Answer

Banks operate under a uniquely prescriptive and stringent regulatory environment. This intense oversight prioritizes systemic stability, the protection of customer funds, and the safeguarding of confidential data. Consequently, regulation and compliance are paramount for banks.

In contrast, other sectors generally face less stringent regulatory demands when it comes to risk management. For many corporations, the protection of intellectual property and data takes center stage. However, the nonbank world is incredibly diverse. We're seeing a trend toward increased regulation in Big Tech, with a growing focus on sector-specific risks. For example, when Big Tech firms provide services to regulated entities, they must adhere to third-party risk management requirements.

Regardless of the industry, every organization must view cybersecurity through a customer-centric lens, understanding the direct impact incidents have on their customer base. Both banks and non-banks alike suffer significant reputational damage from cyber events. It's crucial to remember that compliance doesn't automatically equate to security. All organizations need to prioritize robust risk management practices alongside their compliance efforts.

3. **Question**

What are effective practices in the light of evolving threats?

Answer

In today's dynamic cybersecurity landscape, effectively managing evolving threats boils down to two critical strategies: a multilayered defense and an adaptive, intelligence-led approach. While artificial intelligence has certainly scaled up and amplified the severity of attacks, we are still dealing with some traditional threats, such as phishing.

A multilayered approach is essential to respond effectively to both new and old threats. This involves:

- **Layered technical defenses:** Fortifying firewalls and implementing robust security technologies.
- **Strong backups and recovery strategies:** Ensuring business continuity in the event of an incident.
- **Comprehensive security training:** Empowering your workforce to be the first line of defense.
- **Rigorous testing program:** This is paramount. Consistent and thorough testing verifies the effectiveness of your defenses.

Beyond technical layers, organizations must be adaptive. This means implementing a robust, threat-led threat intelligence program that incorporates threat modeling. It's crucial to consider your specific business context and processes. Cybersecurity isn't just about technical applications; it's about understanding where your business holds privileged data and its exposure to third-party counterparties.

A strong program also clearly defines and maps out viable recovery times in the event of an attack. The CISO organization needs to be prepared to respond to various scenarios, including potential reputational consequences. I can't stress enough the importance of testing as a critical element of any risk management program. Stress-testing how bad actors might exploit your company and understanding what an appropriate response would entail are strong practices for resilience.

4. **Question**
What role does the risk function play in evaluating the effectiveness of cyber controls and incident response plans?
Answer
I've seen it play out differently in various organizations. From my perspective, the risk function plays an absolutely critical role in evaluating the effectiveness of both cyber controls and incident response plans.

Think of the risk function, whether it sits in the first or second line of defense, as providing that essential independent oversight and challenge. They're not just checking boxes; they're actively evaluating how effective the entire risk program is. What I've seen work incredibly well is when the risk function acts as a "gelling factor"—bringing together the business side with the technology teams. They're instrumental in setting clear control objectives, defining the organization's risk appetite, and establishing the right metrics to measure success. Beyond that, they constantly monitor trends and themes, giving us a vital early warning system. They're the ones determining if our controls are truly *designed* effectively, helping us dig deep to find the root cause of incidents, and crucially, ensuring that remediation actions don't just fix the obvious, but go further to address the underlying issues that led to the problem.

Where I've witnessed risk functions provide immense value, particularly with incident response plans, is through their proactive approach to testing. They don't just review a document; they put it through its paces. This means developing really challenging scenarios and then orchestrating tabletop exercises or even full-scale simulations. It's an invaluable process because it allows us to analyze the true adequacy of a potential response, identify any glaring gaps—whether it's in our communication protocols, clarity of roles, or resource allocation—and then conduct a thorough "lessons learned" analysis of what worked well and what didn't.

And, if I might add a key principle I've seen in practice, particularly at places like Google: when an incident occurs, there's a strong culture of no blame—so no finger-pointing. Everyone works together with transparency to fix the problem and understand what went wrong. To me, that collaborative and open approach is one of the most fundamental risk management principles an organization can truly live by.

5. **Question**
You have deep experience managing cyber risk from many different perspectives. What challenges have you encountered managing this unique risk over the course of your career?

Answer

There have been plenty of challenges! One of the most persistent challenges has been the sheer pace of change in the threat landscape itself. It's like trying to hit a moving target—as businesses adapt their strategies and operations, the cyber threats evolve right alongside them. Staying ahead, or at least keeping pace, requires constant vigilance and agility.

But perhaps the most significant challenge, and one that often underpins many others, is effective communication. Highly technical cyber teams, while brilliant at what they do, sometimes struggle to translate complex technical concepts into terms that the business, senior management, and especially the board can readily understand. For cyber risk to be managed effectively at an enterprise level, it's absolutely critical that all stakeholders speak a common language and work together. Without that mutual understanding, it's very difficult to align on strategy, allocate resources appropriately, and truly embed cyber risk management across the organization.

This communication challenge becomes acutely important when the CISO interacts with the board. Those 10 minutes on the board agenda are incredibly valuable, and the ability to clearly and concisely communicate the organization's cyber risks and the effectiveness of its controls is paramount. It often involves translating intricate technical vulnerabilities and issues into strategic business implications. Frankly, one of the most exciting developments I've witnessed in my career as a CISO has been seeing this relationship evolve. It's moved from cyber being perceived as a "black box" topic to boards becoming thoroughly engaged, asking insightful and probing questions, and truly understanding their role in overseeing this critical risk.

Challenges include a lot of change in the threat landscape and keeping pace with managing cyber risk through business and strategy changes. Communication is a key challenge, as highly technical cyber teams do not always communicate with the business, senior management, and the board in terms they can understand. It is critical if cyber risk is going to be properly managed on an enterprise level, that all the constituents understand each other and are working together to manage this critical risk.

6. **Question**

What is your approach to managing third-party cyber risk, especially for critical vendors or outsourced technology services?

Answer

That's a crucial question in today's landscape. In my view an effective approach to managing third-party cyber risk, especially for critical vendors, boils down to a few core principles.

First, rigorous due diligence and ongoing supervision are non-negotiable. You need to vet partners thoroughly upfront and then continuously monitor their security posture. Just as important is having a clear exit strategy and offboarding plan—knowing how to safely disentangle if necessary.

Second and beyond initial due diligence, a critical aspect is understanding concentration risk. This isn't merely about vendor count or location; it's about identifying critical dependencies that could create a single point of failure. With cloud, for instance, one hyperscaler spanning multiple zones still represents a concentrated risk if a core service fails. The key is meticulously mapping the nature of services and where fundamental reliance lies, moving beyond simple vendor lists to truly assess the systemic impact on your operational resilience.

Finally, we have to acknowledge the "existential" challenge for any CISO: the complexity of the extended supply chain. Attackers often exploit these open channels—through third and fourth parties—to reach their targets. Given that nearly every organization relies on vendors, industry collaboration becomes essential. We share a common fate, and strengthening controls in one organization ultimately benefits us all by raising the collective security bar.

7. **Question**

There are a lot of people who would like to find a cyber risk role. What advice would you give them in pursuing a career in this area?

Answer

Resilience, problem solving and story-telling are important skills to develop. Be open minded, and don't doubt your rationale for the career choice. Remember that many successful cyber risk experts who do not have technical academic backgrounds yet have grown through their career.

My advice, centers on a few key areas:

Firstly, develop dual fluency. You need to understand the technical intricacies of cyber risk, but equally important is robust business acumen. The real power lies in translating those complex technical vulnerabilities into clear, actionable business insights—what you might call the "jam sandwich" factor. So, if you want to work in this field, become a story-teller and be able to tell the story of how your organization can build resilience in the face of so much change and existential threats.

It truly is a critical combination in organizations of any size. Start-ups with the most brilliant tech people are successful when they understand the business model of their customers and the context they operate in.

Secondly, continuous learning and adaptability are non-negotiable. Embracing continuous learning and adaptability are critical skills because technology in the cyber world is fast changing and what you know today will be obsolete tomorrow. It's important to be curious and stay up-to-date on new technologies and trends. Also, seek out mentorship, develop a peer network, and find your cybersecurity community as the organizations in your industry are fighting for the same cause.

This leads me to the final point: foster collaboration. Seek out mentors, build a strong peer network, and engage with your cybersecurity community. We're all in this together, and fortifying one organization ultimately strengthens the collective defense.

United Healthcare Case Study Courtesy of IBM

IBM **FIRST**
RISK CASE STUDIES

FIRST Report for Loss Event 20676/OpData Id 24597

Short Description

UnitedHealth Group announced in a filing with the US Securities and Exchange Commission (SEC) on February 21, 2024, that its subsidiary, Change Healthcare, had been adversely affected by a cyberattack carried out by unidentified hackers. UnitedHealth said the hacker was able to gain unauthorized access to Change Healthcare's information technology systems that interconnect pharmacies, hospitals, and clinics. The health insurance company also stated that it was working diligently to restore those systems, had hired leading security experts, reported the incident to federal authorities, and notified clients and government agencies. According to press reports, the cyberattack was discovered the same day it caused an outage, but the hacked systems remained inaccessible for at least two days. Some hospitals, pharmacies, and United States military clinics processed prescriptions manually after Change Healthcare disconnected its systems to prevent criminals from stealing patients' personal information. UnitedHealth said the network disruption was limited to Change Healthcare. On April 16, 2024, UnitedHealth issued a press release and filed a report with the SEC, disclosing that in the first quarter of 2024, the company incurred total losses of $872 million connected to the cyberattack.

Organizations

Name	Firm	Country
UnitedHealth Group Incorporated	Change Healthcare Inc.	North America\United States\Minnesota

Details

Loss Amount:	872,000,000
Currency:	USD
Loss Amount Current:	897,065,814
Currency Original:	USD-United States Dollars
Original Currency Amount:	872,000,000
Status:	CLOSED
Geography:	North America\United States\Tennessee
Created Date:	Feb 26, 2024
Revision Date:	Apr 17, 2024

Dates

Start Occurrence: Feb 21, 2024	End Occurrence: Feb 23, 2024	Settlement Date: Apr 16, 2024

Long Description

Event Summary

UnitedHealth Group announced in a filing with the US Securities and Exchange Commission (SEC) on February 21, 2024, that its subsidiary, Change Healthcare, had been adversely affected by a cyberattack carried out by unidentified hackers. UnitedHealth said the hacker was able to gain unauthorized access to Change Healthcare's information technology systems that interconnect pharmacies, hospitals, and clinics. The health insurance company also stated that it was working diligently to restore those systems, had hired leading security experts, reported the incident to federal authorities, and notified clients and government agencies. According to press reports, the cyberattack was discovered the same day it caused an outage, but the hacked systems remained inaccessible for at least two days. Some hospitals, pharmacies, and United States military clinics processed prescriptions manually after Change Healthcare disconnected its systems to prevent criminals from stealing patients' personal information. UnitedHealth said the network disruption was limited to Change Healthcare. On April 16, 2024, UnitedHealth issued a press release and filed a report with the SEC, disclosing that in the first quarter of 2024, the company incurred total losses of $872 million connected to the cyberattack.

Event Details

In 2022, Optum, a subsidiary of Minnetonka, Minnesota-based UnitedHealth Group acquired Change Healthcare, a billing and data systems provider located in Nashville, Tennessee. The merger connected and simplified clinical, administrative, and payment processes that health care providers and payers use to assist patients.

Optum supplies technology services for nearly 67,000 pharmacies in the United States and care to over 129 million retail clients. Change Healthcare, which provides prescription-processing services through Optum, electronically connects over 900,000 physicians, 33,000 pharmacies, and 5,500 hospitals with health insurers. Change Healthcare, which also offers other services that help providers collect money, allows insurance companies to analyze, verify, and pay providers' medical claims.

On February 21, 2024, UnitedHealth filed a report with the US Securities and Exchange Commission (SEC), disclosing that "a suspected nation-state associated cyber security threat actor" had gained unauthorized access to Change Healthcare's information technology systems. The company did not provide further details on the identity or nationality of the hackers, the malware they used to breach the systems, or the number of pharmacies, hospitals, clinics, and individuals adversely affected by the cyberattack. However, media outlets extensively reported on the issue.

Reuters News (February 23, 2024) reported that the American Pharmacists Association (APhA) issued a statement saying that several pharmacies across the US were unable to transmit insurance claims for their patients. Independent pharmacies as well as pharmacy chains, including CVS Health and Walgreens, also stated that the outage adversely impacted their businesses. APhA advised patients to contact their respective pharmacies before visiting them, noting that not all companies were affected. "This situation may take several days to resolve, so in the meantime we would ask the public to please keep in mind the incredible extra stress this situation places on pharmacies and pharmacy personnel," Michael Hogue, chief executive officer (CEO) of APhA, told Reuters News.

The Boston Globe (February 24, 2024) pointed out that not all payments between insurers and providers were stopped during the outage because some companies reverted to paper claims, which take more time and are more expensive to process. CVS Health, which connects with Change Healthcare for pharmacy prescriptions, said the cyberattack slowed down the filling of prescriptions. "In certain cases, we are not able to process insurance claims, which our business continuity plan is addressing to ensure patients continue to have access to their medications," Mike DeAngelis, a spokesperson for CVS, told the Boston Globe.

The Defense Health Agency (DHA), which manages military hospitals and clinics around the world, told the San Antonio Express News (February 23, 2024) that the outage disrupted services managed by military clinics and Tricare, which handles prescriptions for servicemembers. The DHA serves nearly 9.6 million beneficiaries, including active-duty soldiers, reservists, retirees, and dependents. Although the agency had to temporarily stop dispensing routine prescriptions, it continued to fill urgent prescriptions for antibiotics and medications for pain, diabetes, and high blood pressure.

"As soon as safety measures could be assured and to minimize the impact for our patients with other routine and new prescriptions, our pharmacy teams returned to dispensing all prescriptions through a manual process until the system is back online," Elaine Sanchez, a spokesperson for the DHA, told the San Antonio Express News, noting that beneficiaries could still face lengthy delays in filling non-urgent prescriptions. According to the agency, military clinics and hospitals provided outpatient prescriptions through a manual process after Change Healthcare disconnected its systems to prevent hackers from accessing patients' personal information.

The American Hospital Association (AHA) recommended that all health care organizations disrupted or potentially exposed to the cyberattack consider disconnecting from Optum "until it is independently deemed safe to reconnect." In addition, the AHA advised organizations using Optum services to implement related downtime procedures and contingency plans in case the services remained unavailable for an extended period.

Control Failings and Contributory Factors

Insufficient Contingency Planning: Change Healthcare apparently failed to have in place sufficient contingency planning to mitigate the impact of the cyberattack. Pharmacies across the US issued notices that the attack on Change Healthcare was disrupting their ability to process patients' orders.

Lax Security: Information technology systems implemented and maintained by Change Healthcare were apparently vulnerable to hackers, who gained unauthorized access to the IT systems, and disrupted services connected to pharmacies, hospitals, and US military clinics. According to the Times Union (February 24, 2024), an Albany, New York-based newspaper, Change Healthcare should be aware of the rise of malicious software attacks on government entities and health care organizations, with health care facilities at particular risk because of the sensitive hospital data they collect, including Social Security numbers and financial record s.

Corrective Actions and Management Response

On February 21, 2024, in a regulatory filing with the SEC, UnitedHealth stated that "immediately upon detection of this outside threat, the company proactively isolated the impacted systems from other connecting systems in the interest of protecting our partners and patients, to contain, assess and remediate the incident." UnitedHealth also said that although it was "working diligently to restore those systems and resume normal operations as soon as possible," the company was unable to estimate "the duration or extent of the disruption."

UnitedHealth further stated that it had retained leading security experts, reported the incident to federal authorities, and notified clients and US government agencies. "The company believes the network interruption is specific to Change Healthcare systems, and all other systems across the company are operational," UnitedHealth noted.

UnitedHealth set up a customized webpage where clients could access to obtain updated information. "The company has not determined the incident is reasonably likely to materially impact the company's financial condition or results of operations," UnitedHealth added.

On April 16, 2024, UnitedHealth issued a press release and filed an 8-K form with the SEC, disclosing that in the first quarter of 2024, the company suffered total losses of $872 million relating to the cyberattack. UnitedHealth also stated that "first quarter net loss of $1.53 per share is due primarily to currency effects of previously reported Brazil sale and the cyberattack."

The company further said that it made "significant progress in restoring the affected Change Healthcare services while providing financial support to impacted health care providers." According to UnitedHealth, in the first quarter of 2024, "the company provided over $6 billion in advance funding and interest-free loans to support care providers in need."

Lessons Learned

According to the Boston Globe (February 24, 2024), large pharmacy chains, including CVS, would be able to mitigate payment delays caused by the cyberattack. Yet technology consultants told the Boston Globe that smaller pharmacies could run out of cash to cover operations if UnitedHealth was unable to quickly resolve the outage.

Omid Rahmani, a cybersecurity analyst for Fitch Ratings, noted that the nature of critical health care interconnects interdependent organizations with each other through a massive number of interconnected devices. "As a result, when there's an attack against a single node within an organization or against multiple nodes within an organization, that can have a cascading effect of impacting an entire system or an entire interconnected network of providers," Mr. Rahmani told the San Antonio Express News (February 23, 2024), pointing out that it could take months or a year to determine how many individuals were affected by the cyberattack. "It's tough to put a number on it, but in a catastrophic situation, it can have a noticeable impact on care for a large number of people," he added.

Keywords Indexing

Entity Type	FINANCIAL SERVICES\INSURANCE COMPANY
Business Unit Type	OTHER -- (BUSINESS SERVICES)\INSURANCE SERVICES
Service/Product Offering Type	INSURANCE PRODUCTS AND SERVICES\INSURANCE SERVICES\INSURANCE SERVICES (MISC)
Contributory/Control Factors	LACK OF CONTROL\LAX SECURITY STRATEGY FLAW\INSUFFICIENT CONTINGENCY PLANNING
Loss Type:	Known
Loss Impact	DIRECT LOSS\WRITE-DOWN (BIS)\WRITE-DOWNS INDIRECT LOSS\BUSINESS INTERRUPTION - (related to systems and external events) INDIRECT LOSS\EXTRA EXPENSE
Loss Detection Sources	OTHER LOSS DETECTION SOURCES\LOSS SURFACED
Market Focus	INSTITUTIONAL SERVICES
Event Trigger	TECHNOLOGY RISK CLASS\SECURITY\HACKING
Basel Levels I & II	External Fraud\System Security\Hacking damage
Basel Business Line	Others\Insurance (Non-BIS)\Insurance - Life & Health (Non-BIS)
Industry Event	

Rules and Regulations Indexing

Ratings

Ratings Action	Ratings Code	Effective Date	Ratings Watch/Outlook
Affirmed	A	Feb 9, 2023	Rating Outlook Stable
1 Rating found			

Source

2024-April-16: UnitedHealth Group, Press Release, "UnitedHealth Group Reports First Quarter 2024 Results"

2024-April-16: US Securities and Exchange Commission (SEC), UnitedHealth Group Incorporated, 8-K Form, "Current Report"

2024-February-21: US Securities and Exchange Commission (SEC), UnitedHealth Group Incorporated, 8-K Form, "Current Report"

2024-April-16: Minneapolis/St. Paul Business Journal, "UnitedHealth takes $872 million hit from cyberattack, posts first-quarter loss," by Mark Reilly.

2024-April-16: Market Intelligence News, "UnitedHealth Group revenues up despite cyberattack."

2024-February-24: The Boston Globe, "UnitedHealth cyberattack hinders ability to process insurance claims," by Brittany Trang, Tara Bannow, and Bob Herman.

2024-February-24: Times Union, "Cyberattack impacts drug coverage in N.Y.," by Raga Justin.

2024-February-23: San Antonio Express-News, "Cyberattack interferes with prescriptions for soldiers, families in San Antonio and worldwide," by Sig Christenson.

2024-February-23: Reuters News, "Hack against Change Healthcare 'resulting in delays', says American Pharmacists Association," by Sriparna Roy.

2024-February-23: Reuters News, "Moody's says hack against UnitedHealth Group is 'credit negative' for the company," by Raphael Satter and Bhanvi Satija.

2024-February-23: Best's Insurance News, "UnitedHealth Isolates Change Healthcare Systems After Likely Cyberattack," by Renee Kiriluk-Hill.

2024-February-23: The Wall Street Journal Online, "Hospitals and Pharmacies Reeling After Change Healthcare Cyberattack; Healthcare organizations forced to revert to manual procedures after Change Healthcare, part of Optum, disconnects services," by Catherine Stupp and James Rundle.

2024-February-23: Minneapolis/St. Paul Business Journal, "UnitedHealth suspects 'nation-state' affiliate for cyberattack," by Mark Reilly.

2024-February-23: Fox Business, "Pharmacies scramble to serve sick customers as 'nation-state' blamed for ongoing cyberattack outage," by Greg Norman.

2024-February-22: Reuters News, "Pharmacies across US disrupted following hack at Change Healthcare network," by Raphael Satter and Sriparna Roy.

2024-February-22: Fox Business, "Pharmacies nationwide face delays as health-care tech company reports cyberattack," by Timothy Nerozzi.

Claimant

Claimant Name:	
Claimant Type:	

Scaling Data

Scaling Date	Liabilities (USD $M)	Surplus (USD $M)	Total Assets (USD $M)	Gross Premium Written (USD $M)	Net Premium Written (USD $M)
Dec 31, 2022	159,358.00	86,347.00	245,705.00	N/A	N/A

Supporting Material

Revision Comments

04/17/2024: On April 16, 2024, UnitedHealth issued a press release and filed a report with the SEC, disclosing that in the first quarter of 2024, the company lost a total of $872 million connected to the cyberattack; added loss amount.

Copyright Information

Bibliography

Andy Greenberg and Matt Burgess. Change Healthcare Faces Another Ransomware Threat and it Looks Credible. *Wired Magazine*. April 12, 2024. https://www.wired.com/story/change-healthcare-ransomhub-threat/.

BRIEFING EU Legislation in Progress. *EU Cyber Resilience Act*. December 12, 2024. https://www.europarl.europa.eu/RegData/etudes/BRIE/2022/739259/EPRS_BRI(2022)739259_EN.pdf.

Crowdstrike. *2025 Global Threat Report*. https://go.crowdstrike.com/2025-global-threat-report.html.

International Organization for Standardization. *ISO 27001, Information Security, Cybersecurity and Privacy Protection—Information Security Management Systems—Requirements*. Edition 3, 2022. https://www.iso.org/obp/ui/en/#iso:std:iso-iec:27001:ed-3:v1:en.

James Rundle. Hackers Broke into Change Healthcare's Systems Days Before Cyberattack. *The Wall Street Journal*. April 22, 2024. https://www.wsj.com/articles/change-healthcare-hackers-broke-in-nine-days-before-ransomware-attack-7119fdc6?utm_source=chatgpt.com.

National Institute of Standards and Technology. *Cybersecurity Framework 2.0*. February 26, 2024. https://nvlpubs.nist.gov/nistpubs/CSWP/NIST.CSWP.29.pdf.

Office of the Comptroller of the Current. *Cybersecurity and Financial System Resilience Report*. July 2025. https://www.occ.gov/publications-and-resources/publications/cybersecurity-and-financial-system-resilience/files/2025-cybersecurity-report.html.

Risk.net. *Top 10 operational risks for 2025*. March 31, 2025. https://www.risk.net/risk-management/7961268/top-10-operational-risks-for-2025.

Sam Knight. The Disturbing Impact of the Cyberattack at the British Library. *The New Yorker*, December 19, 2023.

Bibliography

Chapter 15

Managing Third-Party Risk

Third-party risks have become ever more critical as companies in all industries turn to outsourcing as a solution for cost and process efficiencies and for leveraging expertise that they may not have in-house. There are some basic imperatives that must be understood and incorporated into a third-party risk management program.

Here are my seven rules for managing third-party risk:

The first rule for managing third-party risk is that the contracting firm still owns the risk. In fact, they own all the risks associated with the process or function they have outsourced, plus third-party risks.

The second rule for managing third-party risk is that the contracting firm must know their vendor thoroughly and understand their financials, control environment, culture, and if they use any fourth parties or subcontractors. Risk assessing, risk rating, and determining concentration of vendors are all critical to the risk management process. This includes location strategy of the vendor and if they are in geographies that are exposed to geopolitical events, social unrest, or natural disasters, such as floods, typhoons, and fires.

The third rule for managing third-party risk is that the contract should incorporate required controls. This includes the inclusion of proper oversight, ongoing risk monitoring, and transparency into how the vendor is managing its critical risks, including cyber and data privacy. In addition, the contracting firm should review carefully the service-level agreements to ensure they are being adhered to during the provision of services.

The fourth rule for managing third-party risk is that active risk management must occur throughout the entire lifecycle of a vendor relationship, from due diligence and onboarding through to contract termination and offboarding.

The fifth rule for managing third-party risk is that it must be risk-based, as every vendor does not pose the same level of risk to an organization. Vendors should be risk rated based on the criticality of the services they provide, which in turn drives the level of oversight and ongoing monitoring. The highest-risk vendors provide services that could impact customers, operations, and the financial condition of the contracting firm, or otherwise create significant risk.

The sixth rule for managing third-party risk is that there should be a contingency plan for potential disruption of service, including disconnecting from the vendor's systems in the event of a cyber event and alternative plans for prioritizing the most material processes (the ones that have systemic impact) in the event of a major system outage.

The seventh rule for managing third-party risk is that the relationship with the vendor matters. A contentious relationship or aggressive squeezing in price will blow back on the contracting firm and can result in a destabilized vendor that will ultimately be unable to deliver.

Third-Party Risk Management Framework

The three major US regulatory agencies came together in 2023 and introduced "Interagency Guidance on Third-party Risk Management" (https://www.occ.gov/news-issuances/bulletins/2023/bulletin-2023-17.html). This helped to consolidate what had previously required connecting the dots among different agency guidance and to establish a solid framework upon which to anchor an appropriate risk management program. The third-party framework should be aligned with the operational risk management framework. The operational risk framework provides the structure for managing third-party risk management, while the regulatory framework is the "double-click" into the specific items that should be assessed and monitored.

The US government framework is both principles-based and risk-based. The method for adopting the framework should be "commensurate with the level of risk and complexity of their respective third-party relationships." The principles-based approach allows for the application of the framework to a variety of financial services firms and according to size and complexity. It also can serve as guidance for nonfinancial firms that are building third-party risk management frameworks and functions or want to compare the maturity of their own organization against an industry standard.

An important consideration when implementing a third-party risk management framework is the risk associated with the services provided by the vendor. As a simple example, providing cloud services carries significant risk. If a cloud vendor has an outage that results in business interruption, there could be significant impact on the firm's ability to deliver services to its clients. This could have systematic impact as well depending on the processes that are impacted. On the other hand, the vendor who cares for the organization's plants will not require the type of oversight and scrutiny as the cloud vendor.

Figure 15.1 Components of the third-party lifecycle

The interagency guidance is structured around the third-party lifecycle, which is designed to manage risk from the planning and vendor selection stage through to contract termination and off-boarding.

Figure 15.1 shows the components of the third-party lifecycle, as articulated in the interagency guidance.

Planning (Including Governance)

Planning incorporates governance and the management of third-party relationships ahead of contracting activities. This includes the execution of a policy, standard, and procedure and the articulation of roles and responsibilities. There are many stakeholders involved in the management of third parties, including each business or function that engages a vendor, the firm's procurement department, and the second-line operational risk management function. In addition, there is interdependencies on managing third-party risk management with the chief technology officer (CTO) and the chief information security officer (CISO) functions, along with the resiliency function. As with many other operational risk types, it takes a village to manage third-party relationships.

First Line of Defense Business Owners and Functional Teams

There are multiple frontline units that are responsible for managing third-party risk, including creating the initial business plan and conducting due diligence, ongoing monitoring, risk assessments, and relationship management.

First Line Role/Function	Key Responsibilities
Business Owners	Create business plan for third-party vendor support and gain support from senior management and impacted stakeholders Define scope of required service Conduct initial vendor due diligence and risk assessment
Vendor Managers/ Relationship Managers	Oversee day-to-day interactions with vendor Risk rate vendor based on criticality Own issues and action plans related to vendor contracts under their remit Assess and monitor vendor controls Conduct risk and control assessments Ensure terms of SLA are met and monitor vendor performance Escalate and resolve performance issues

(*Continued*)

(Continued)

First Line Role/Function	Key Responsibilities
Procurement/Sourcing	Facilitate vendor selection and RFP process Assist with contract negotiation and renewals Establish requirements for onboarding vendors Maintain vendor inventory and spend data
IT/CISO	Assess vendor for information risks and controls Evaluate technical standards for IT and cyber vendors
Business Continuity/ Resilience	Ensure vendors meet continuity requirements Test and validate exit strategies and contingency plans

Second Line of Defense Risk and Compliance Functions

The second-line functions, including risk specialties related to third-party, resilience, and information security, provide oversight, review, and challenge, as well as frameworks to ensure strong risk management.

Second Line Role/Function	Key Responsibilities
Operational Risk Management	Define and maintain TPRM framework and policy or standard Review and challenge first-line risk assessments Facilitate scenario analysis workshops that incorporate third-party and integrate scenarios into stress models Incorporate third-party risks and aggregate metrics into committee and board reports, including ranking top vendors by concentration and criticality
Third-Party Risk Management	Centralize governance and oversight Maintain third-party inventory Ensure lifecycle adherence (planning through termination)
Compliance	Review vendors for regulatory, legal, and reputational risks Conduct due diligence on sanctions, AML, data privacy
Information Risk Management	Set control requirements (e.g., encryption, access controls) Review security assessments and responses Monitor for emerging cyber threats relevant to third parties
Legal/Contract Risk	Negotiate contracts and draft and review legal clauses (e.g., indemnity, liability, termination) Ensure right to audit and regulatory compliance obligations are incorporated into contracts
Operational Risk Committees	Review aggregated vendor performance and concentration data Escalate high-risk vendor issues or exceptions

The first-line businesses and functions, including procurement and the CTO and CISO offices, should work with second-line operational risk to define the risk appetite statements and metrics related to the management of third parties.

The following are sample third-party risk appetite statements and metrics:

- The firm has no appetite for engaging third parties without proper due diligence and assessment of risks and controls.

Risk Appetite Statement	Metric	Green Threshold	Yellow Threshold	Red Threshold
The firm has no appetite for engaging third parties without proper due diligence and assessment of risks and controls	% of third parties onboarded with completed due diligence and risk assessments	≥98%	<96%	<94%

- The firm has no appetite for third-party incidents that result in breach of client confidential information.

Risk Appetite Statement	Metric	Green Threshold	Yellow Threshold	Red Threshold
The firm has no appetite for third-party incidents that result in breach of client confidential information	# of third-party breach of confidential information- related incidents	0	1	1

- The firm has moderate appetite for outsourcing services associated with critical rated processes.

Risk Appetite Statement	Metric	Green Threshold	Yellow Threshold	Red Threshold
The firm has moderate appetite for outsourcing services associated with critical rated processes	% of third parties providing support for critical processes	<95%	<97%	<98%

- The firm has low appetite for vendor breaches of SLAs.

Risk Appetite Statement	Metric	Green Threshold	Yellow Threshold	Red Threshold
The firm has low appetite for vendor breaches of SLAs	% of SLAs in breach of terms	<3%	<5%	<7%

- The firm has no appetite for working with high-risk third parties that lack resiliency risk management policies and frameworks.

Risk Appetite Statement	Metric	Green Threshold	Yellow Threshold	Red Threshold
The firm has no appetite for working with high-risk third parties that lack resiliency risk management policies and frameworks	# of third parties without resiliency policies and frameworks in place	0	1	2

An important step in the Planning stage is to build the business case for engaging a third-party vendor and determining if the costs, risks, and speed to market justify seeking external support. The level of analysis for engaging with a third party must be commensurate with the level of risk involved, as determined by the criticality of the services and processes that are impacted, along with the impact to the customers and the firm's overall financial stability.

The following are considerations that should be incorporated into the business plan for engaging a third party:

Strategy: Does the potential third-party arrangement align with the firm's strategic plan? Will the vendor bring knowledge and subject-matter expertise to the service agreement, that might not exist in-house? Is there a speed to market advantage if the provider is engaged? Is there a downside if the provider is not engaged?

Risks: Can risks associated with the third-party arrangement be managed through the relationship and are they within risk appetite? Will the arrangement bring risks that would be difficult to mitigate? Will there be risks associated with privacy, cyber, and systems integration that require careful assessment to understand risk-reward trade-offs of engaging a third-party?

Cost: Is there a cost advantage to engaging a third party when all variables are considered, including in-house capabilities and ability to execute?

Customer Impact: What is the impact to customers? Will the third party have access to customer data? Will they interact directly with customers? Is there potential for customer harm?

Third-party Oversight: Does the firm have the capacity and skills to manage the third-party relationship and provide proper oversight? Is there a risk that the third party will not be properly monitored and managed?

Contingency: Does the firm have a plan for bringing the support in-house if the third-party relationship is terminated? Are there other vendors that could provide support if needed?

Due Diligence and Third-Party Selection

Conducting a review of a potential third party before signing a contract is critical to understanding the risks that the firm will be taking on. The first rule as mentioned is that the contracting firm may outsource support for processes and services, but it retains the risk in addition to taking on third-party risk. It is imperative that third-party risk is properly assessed and understood so that the contracting firm can gain a level of assurance that they can deliver on their commitments and comply with all laws, regulations, and company policies, without introducing risks that can create undue harm. The level of due diligence should be commensurate with the risk associated with the processes and services that the third party will support.

The goal for conducting due diligence on vendors who pose the most risk to the firm is to ensure ahead of entering the contract phase that they are thoroughly understood as a future partner. There are consortiums and industry groups, such as Shared Assessments (https://sharedassessments.org), that allow firms across the industry to reap benefit from common responses from vendors. This can be helpful in the due diligence phase, as it also allows for sharing of ideas and templates, but the responses ultimately need to be customized when determining the ultimate impact of engaging a third party for one's own organization.

The following are criteria to consider when evaluating a potential third party during the due diligence phase:

Financial: Is the vendor financially viable? Do they have the financial resources to support the service agreement from start to finish? What percentage of revenue would the potential engagement represent for the third party? Do they have private investors who are stable and committed to long-term support? Are they a publicly traded company with a stable stock price? Are their financials audited by an independent firm? Are they able to provide audited financials?

Strategic: Is the service arrangement under review a core competency and strategic priority for the third party? Is there a risk that they will pull away from providing the service in the future through a reorganization or change in strategy?

Regulatory and compliance: Does the third party have a compliance program in place and a chief legal counsel or chief compliance officer who oversees the program? Does the compliance program include reasonable policies and procedures to manage compliance risks? Are there controls in place to manage compliance risks and provide assurance that they comply with applicable laws and regulations? Is the compliance risk culture aligned with the contracting firm's culture? Does the third party test its regulatory and compliance controls?

Risk management: Does the third party have an enterprise risk management framework in place, including policies and procedures, risk assessments, and adequate controls to manage its risks, including privacy and cyber? Does the third party have a chief risk officer or head of enterprise risk who oversee the risk management program? Is the third party's risk culture aligned with the contracting firm's culture? Does the third party's senior management and board demonstrate oversight of the risk management program and ownership of the risks? How does the third party identify and remediate control deficiencies? Does the third party test controls associated with its operational processes?

Experience: Does the third party have the requisite experience to deliver on its commitments? Does it have a track record of implementing similar service agreements with other firms of similar size and complexity? Would the service agreement under review represent the first time the third party delivered on a particular service?

Concentration risk: Is the third party already a critical vendor within the firm, and will a new service-level agreement present concentration risk? Are there other vendors that should be considered for all or a portion of the service agreement, to mitigate exposure to a single third party? What is the trade-off between concentrating services with one vendor who may offer price incentives and understands the firm's operating environment versus engaging an additional vendor?

People: Does the third party have the required skills and capacity to deliver on the service agreement? Are there key people who are overly relied upon for expertise and delivery? Is there a succession plan if a key person leaves the provider in the middle of an engagement? Does the third-party provider conduct background checks on its employees and perform appropriate know-your-employee reviews?

Information security: Does the third party have proper controls in place to protect the contracting firm's and its clients (if relevant) data? Does it have appropriate security controls in place, including authentication, encryption, and access controls? Does it track and monitor risk threats and vulnerabilities? Does it conduct testing, such as penetration testing? Is its information security framework, policy, and controls aligned with the contracting firm's? Does it have a history of information security events and how has it responded?

Resilience: Does the third party have a resilience framework in place, including policies and procedures and a business continuity playbook in the event of a business disruption? Does it test its business continuity plans and perform desktop exercises and preparedness drills? Can the third party articulate how it will respond if it is the victim of a cyber event and how it will protect client data? Can it walk the contracting firm through its business continuity playbook?

Incident reporting: Does the third party have a policy or procedure in place to report incidents to its customers? Does it have escalation protocol in place for such incidents? Does it have a process in place to investigate incidents, determine root cause, and apply lessons learned?

Fourth party and business arrangements: Does the third party contract with fourth parties, and will the fourth parties provide services to the contracting firm? Does the third party perform background checks on its contractors? Does it openly disclose the use of such contractors? Does the third party have reliance on business arrangements that may impact its ability to deliver on its obligations to the contracting firm?

Contract Negotiation

The drafting and negotiation of a contract with a third party is an opportunity to manage supplier risks up front. A firm's legal department will play a critical role in the contract negotiation stage, with particular attention to indemnification, which should be structured to protect the firm from damages caused by the third party's negligence or conduct. This includes violations of laws and regulations. I have experienced this item to be a point of contention between lawyers for the third party and the contracting firm. It is important to understand the risks associated with compromising on indemnification.

Another point of contention that I have experienced is the decision on what party's "paper" or standard contract template will be executed. The third party and the contracting firm usually prefer to use their own templates, as they are designed to provide the highest amount of risk protection for each party. If the third party insists on using their template and it is difficult to negotiate given the type of service they provide, it is important to work with legal and revise provisions that pose risk for the firm. I have experienced circumstances where at the end of the day the vendor is so critical that certain risks must be knowingly accepted. In these instances, it is important to note the exposure and to put controls in place, such as additional monitoring. Some organizations will document this as a formal risk acceptance and monitor accordingly.

The contract, regardless of the template that is used, should clearly define expectations and responsibilities of the third party, including description of how performance disputes will be addressed. It is a strong practice to also execute a service-level agreement (SLA) that clearly articulates expectations for delivery of services, including dates, responsibilities, and performance measures. The detail in the SLA would provide direction if there were disagreements later regarding quality and timing of delivery. I have personally experienced situations where there was nothing in the language of a contract or SLA to assist with differences of perspective on the quality, kind, or timing of delivery of services by the third party. This leads to the type of realization where you ask yourself, "Why didn't I think of this before?"

Third-party risk management practices continue to evolve, which can pose a challenge with vendors that have long standing contracts. It is not always possible to renegotiate these contracts to include additional risk management measures that meet current standards. As a result, it might be necessary to record the risk exposure and execute a formal risk acceptance, with additional controls in place if possible.

The "Interagency Guidance on Third-Party Risk Management" provides a detailed list of considerations when negotiating a contract. Specificity in the contract is important. This includes providing details on third-party access to data, personnel, facilities, customers (if relevant), ownership of intellectual property, resiliency plans for potential business interruption, subcontracting, dispute resolution, and compliance with all relevant rules and regulations. The contract should include access to independent audits, such as SOC reports, and the right to audit. And of course, the contract should be very specific on the topic of renumeration, including if there are additional charges over and above what has been negotiated.

Ongoing Monitoring

Performing ongoing monitoring of the third-party relationship once the contract is in place is essential to the bank's ability to manage third-party risk. The interagency guidance highlights the importance of ongoing monitoring:

- *confirm the quality and sustainability of a third-party's controls and ability to meet contractual obligations;*
- *escalate significant issues or concerns, such as material or repeat audit findings, deterioration in financial condition, security breaches, data loss, service interruptions, compliance lapses, or other indicators of increased risk;*
- *respond to such significant issues or concerns when identified.*

The degree and depth of ongoing monitoring that is undertaken should be commensurate with the amount of inherent risk associated with the third-party service agreement. The highest-risk contract may require quarterly site visits of the third party's operations. Monitoring must include reviews of control documentation, such as RCSA, compliance risk assessment, control testing, and independent audit reports. The interagency guidance suggests that direct testing for the highest risk vendors should be considered. It may be difficult, however, to gain direct access to a third-party's processes and operations. Some organizations hire independent third parties to conduct independent testing as part of their monitoring routines.

Service organization control (SOC) reports should be reviewed during the due diligence stage but also monitored during the course of the contract. These reports represent independent audits of a service provider's control environment. SOC 1 reports focus on internal controls over financial reporting, while SOC 2 reports focus on controls related to security, availability, processing integrity, confidentiality, and privacy.

The baseline risk profile of the third party would have been established during the due diligence phase. Monitoring should focus on changes that potentially present additional risks. This might include changes to the third party's strategy, financial condition, personnel, reliance on subcontractors, risk and compliance programs, reorganizations, and emerging risks that might not have been previously identified.

Termination

Offboarding a third party, whether because of a failure to deliver services or expiration of the contract, should be undertaken with as much care as onboarding. I have experienced organizations that had very strong onboarding controls associated with background checks and system access but were less than rigorous with offboarding controls, including ensuring everyone associated with the third-party relationship had their system access withdrawn, confidential data is destroyed on the third-party's server (if it was allowed to enter their environment in the first place), and all related documentation has been organized and turned over to the firm.

In addition to developing offboarding protocols, which should be documented in a policy or procedures, it is critical to have a playbook for each high-risk vendor detailing contingency plans in the event that they are no longer able to honor their agreement—either through a short-term disruption caused by a cyber event or system outage or a long-term inability to continue providing services due to extreme financial stress, such as a bankruptcy and inability to continue business operations. The playbook should outline how the support will transition in-house or to an alternative vendor. The playbook should also include if there is a disruption that could compromise its network and data, such as a third-party ransomware attack, how the third party will be disconnected from their network for some period, and how a critical process or service will be executed in-house and potentially through manual process.

The following is a mapping of the five third-party lifecycle components to the operational risk framework:

Third-Party Lifecycle Stage	Governance & Policy	Risk Appetite & Indicators	Loss Data	RCSA	Scenario Analysis	Issue Management	Monitoring & Reporting	Culture & Awareness
Planning	Establish governance structure for third-party risk, including roles & responsibilities, policies, and risk committees	Define acceptable risk levels for outsourcing, including criticality tiers and concentration limits						Promote awareness and training for third-party risk management
Due Diligence & Vendor Selection				Assess inherent risks and controls of potential vendors	Develop severe scenarios (e.g., cloud vendor cyberattack) and incorporate into stress models and RCSA			
Contract Negotiation	Ensure legal and risk teams review contracts to embed key controls, rights to audit, SLAs, and exit clauses	Ensure contract terms align with stated risk appetite for critical vendors					Define contract terms that support ongoing monitoring	

(*Continued*)

(Continued)

Third-Party Lifecycle Stage	Governance & Policy	Risk Appetite & Indicators	Loss Data	RCSA	Scenario Analysis	Issue Management	Monitoring & Reporting	Culture & Awareness
Ongoing Monitoring			Capture and classify losses or near-misses due to vendor issues	Update risk assessments based on vendor performance, control test results, SOC reports, and changes to services	Reassess risk scenarios to reflect emerging risks at least annually	Identify, document, and remediate vendor issues, including breach of contract or performance failures	Track SLAs, KRIs, and conduct performance reviews; escalate issues	Maintain awareness through ongoing staff/vendor training and third-party forum
Termination	Execute offboarding in alignment with policy requirements					Address outstanding issues prior to termination, including data return or deletion	Track exit process, communicate with stakeholders, and review post-exit risk impacts	

Interview with Industry Veteran: Jeannie Pumphrey

Jeannie Pumphrey has deep experience with both third-party risk management and supply chain risk management functions. She has led large third-party functions in banking organizations in the first and second lines of defense. She is former military and served in the US Army for eight years as a quartermaster, where she managed supply chain and logistics operations. She credits the time she spent there as providing the foundation for her understanding of critical risks associated with third-party risk and supply chain. She has worked in the third-party space since the discipline was formalized with the first regulatory guidance.

Jeannie shares that there are a number of aspects regarding risk and operations that she leverages in her toolbox that were emphasized in the military. However, when it comes to third-party risk, the primary discipline she relied on is the courage to do what's right even if it is not popular and especially if it's not easy. When managing third parties, Jeannie emphasizes that negative events are bound to occur and the third-party risk manager must take accountability, communicate the risk and remedy, and have the courage to frankly, and with tact, discuss with the third party and internally through the chain of command.

1. **Question**
   What are some of the qualities, skills, and experience an operational risk manager needs today to be effective?
   Answer
   The most critical skill is tenacity, which I cannot overemphasize. As a manager of third-party risk, you are dealing with business partners who are reliant, and therefore protective of their relationships with their providers, and they can be resistant to having a risk person come in and tell them that they need to manage their risks differently. You need to be strong enough to stand up for the company, and your customers, and do the right thing in terms of managing third-party risk. Equally important, is building strong relationships with the business, even when the starting point is somewhat contentious. This is where tenacity becomes important.

   It's equally important to have a risk conscious frame of mind and to look beyond the "smoke" and focus on the true risks. This is why it's important to work across the risk functions, as third-party risk resides in many of the other risk stripes. Collaboration is important with the other ERM functions that have exposure to third-party risk. The assessments need to be done with a level of consistency.

   Finally, I just want to say that it is important to stand up for what you believe is in the best interest of stakeholders and be able to defend your perspective to your business partners.
2. **Question**
   As someone who has managed several large third-party functions, what were some of your challenges in managing the discipline?
   Answer
   As mentioned, relationship building with the business and ERM function is critical. You cannot manage third-party risk in a silo.

It also important to find qualified people with the requisite experience, mind-set and as mentioned, tenacity. You can't just put on a "third-party" hat declare yourself a subject-matter expert without the experience that is necessary to build credibility with the business. Although, as mentioned, the business relationship can sometime start out contentious, one way to develop a strong relationship is to have credibility and know what you are speaking about (because you will be challenged).

3. **Question**
   From your industry perspective, what do you think organizations can do better today in managing third-party risk?
   Answer
   There are so many things related to managing third-party risk from a business perspective and an organizational perspective that I believe we can do better. As mentioned, and I can't say this enough, the relationship with the business is critical. It's important to understand that business units do not always have the risk mindset to manage third-party risk. The third-party risk management organization needs to supply them with the support and tools to manage this risk successfully. It includes training and awareness and more practical tools, like templates that assist with risk assessments.

   A number of organizations are not yet mature in their risk management processes, and they need support in identifying risks and incidents. A proactive risk partner will work with them before they get caught in the tailwinds of an incident and need to fix something.

   I do think there is some needed improvement in business unit support for a third-party risk management function, as it's not a check-the-box exercise. The subject-matter experts understand this risk from different perspectives, which may not be readily apparent to someone who does not spend their days focused on managing it.
4. **Question**
   What governance structures and cross-functional partnerships (e.g., with IT, procurement, legal, compliance) are most important for effective third-party oversight?
   Answer
   Working with enterprise risk management, as mentioned, is critical. It's important to assess third-party risk across all risk stripes to understand it from an enterprise perspective. Each risk manager, including those who work with cyber, business continuity, compliance, and information technology, need to assess third-party risk for their own risk stripe but also work with the third-party team to understand the exposure across the organization. It's the same theme I have been discussing: collaboration, consistency, and partnership across the risk stripes and, as mentioned, lines of defense.
5. **Question**
   What are the key components of a bank's third-party risk management framework, and how do you ensure it aligns with enterprise risk appetite and regulatory expectations? How is risk tiering or criticality determined for vendors?

Answer

The key component is the framework, which is interpreted through a lifecycle. It is a strong industry practice to implement the lifecycle outlined in the latest interagency guidance on third-party risk management titled "Third-Party Relationships: Interagency Guidance on Risk Management." It was released in 2023 and brings together the various guidance that was previously released by three of the largest US regulators.

It's also critical to link a third-party risk program to risk appetite and to work with ERM to make sure it's incorporated into risk statements and metrics.

6. **Question**

Following up on your mention of risk appetite, can you provide a few examples of metrics you have found useful?

Answer

There are three metrics that an organization can start with to capture the primary risks inherent in a third-party risk management program:

1. Number of high and moderate high-risk vendors that are in financial distress, as determined by regular reviews of their financial statements (financial risk).
2. Number of high and moderate high vendors that are colocated with their own operations and your own organization's locations (geographical risk).
3. Number of critical activities performed by a single third-party (concentration risk).

Once these risks are understood, a business may recognize additional, and/or supporting, metrics that could aid the program based on their industry.

7. **Question**

How do you operationalize due diligence, onboarding, and ongoing monitoring for thousands of vendors at scale?

Answer

It's important to assess the risk aspects of the services provided by a vendor and to differentiate between the low-risk and the high-risk services. The same vendor may be providing both, so you can't apply the same risk ratings for a vendor across everything they support and you must look at third-party risk from the operational perspective. There are different risk levels with providing access to a reporting application vs. cloud services. IBM is a good example of a vendor that provides broad services that may have different risk levels.

Technology, if you have access to a GRC system, is an important tool that if set up with workflow, can send out alerts if certain triggers are met. This assists with dynamically assessing a vendor and the services they provide.

I have used third-party consortium-type services in the past that provide standard assessments for vendors, but have found this challenging, as they do not by definition address the risk sensitivities of a specific organization.

8. **Question**

How do you incorporate emerging risks—such as cyber threats, geopolitical instability, and climate concerns—into your third-party risk assessment process?

Answer

I mentioned how I have tracked concentration risk concerns, which is an important risk measure for also incorporating climate risk into a third-party risk assessment. At the center of any risk assessment effort is having good data and especially ready access to a complete inventory of vendors and this includes all vendors. As an example, when Russia invaded Ukraine, I had access to a system that allowed me to pull a list of all the vendors we used in Ukraine, Russia, and surrounding countries. This allowed for an update of the risk rating and exposures of those vendors. I can't stress enough how important it is to have this type of data readily available and to include all vendors, not just the high-risk ones.

9. **Question**

   What lessons have you learned from past third-party regulatory reviews that have influenced how you manage and mature your TPRM program?

   Answer

   The primary lesson is to know your program and be able to defend your program. Defending does not mean to argue or be belligerent, but to be able to demonstrate to regulators that your program is right sized for your organization and addresses third-party risks. Know your program means to really know it, along with all the details, as you will be questioned on them. You need to be able to articulate how your program addresses risk in your organization and follows a risk-based approach and be able to walk regulators through its lifecycle. If you believe in your program, can defend that it addresses applicable risk for your industry and organization, and can articulate (with demonstrations) its details, you will be successful in managing regulatory relationships.

Bibliography

Bank of England. *SS2/21: Outsourcing and Third Party Risk Management.* March 29, 2021. https://www.bankofengland.co.uk/prudential-regulation/publication/2021/march/outsourcing-and-third-party-risk-management-ss.

Financial Conduct Authority. *FG 16/5: Guidance for firms outsourcing to the "cloud" and other third-party IT services.* July 2016. Updated September 2019. https://www.fca.org.uk/publication/finalised-guidance/fg16-5.pdf.

Office of the Comptroller of the Currency. *Comptroller's Handbook: Internal Control.* Washington, DC: OCC, July 2001. https://www.occ.gov/publications-and-resources/publications/comptrollers-handbook/files/internal-control/index-internal-control.html.

Office of the Comptroller of the Currency. *OCC Bulletin* 2023-17: *Third-Party Relationships – Interagency Guidance on Risk Management.* Washington, DC: OCC, June 6, 2023. https://www.occ.gov/news-issuances/bulletins/2023/bulletin-2023-17.html.

Chapter 16

Managing Fraud

The place to start considering risks related to fraud is with words from OpenAI CEO Sam Altman who spoke at a Federal Reserve conference in July 2025:

"A thing that terrifies me is apparently there are still some financial institutions that will accept a voice print as authentication for you to move a lot of money or do something else—you say a challenge phrase, and they just do it," Altman said. "That is a crazy thing to still be doing … AI has fully defeated most of the ways that people authenticate currently, other than passwords."

Sam Altman further added, "Right now, it's a voice call; soon it's going be a video or FaceTime that's indistinguishable from reality" (https://www.cnn.com/2025/07/22/tech/openai-sam-altman-fraud-crisis).

I would argue that AI video capabilities are already here. My heart sank in February 2024 when I read about an event where a person's whole person and not just their voice was impersonated in a video call. It was reported at that time in the business press that a finance worker at an unnamed global organization in Hong Kong transferred HK $200 million (approximately USD $25 million) after receiving instructions during a video call with the company's UK chief financial officer and other members of the staff. The only problem is that this was a scam, perpetrated by fraudsters who used deepfake technology to impersonate the executives.

The employee was originally suspicious about the fund transfer request after he received a message to transfer the funds but was convinced it was above board once he "met" with the firm's senior executives via video because the people on the call looked and sounded like his colleagues. It took the employee a week after the funds were transferred to determine that something might be wrong and confirm the validity of the transaction with the company's headquarters.

It has struck me at the time that we were in the middle of earnings season where CEOs and CFOs around the world were holding press conferences to discuss company financials via video on social media platforms like LinkedIn. It is not too difficult for the bad guys who have the technology wherewithal to use these voice and video images to clone people's voices and images *in real time.*

This is a reminder that firms need to review their protocols for transferring funds and require additional control checks before they send anything significant—say a million dollars—anywhere. In this environment, it is not sufficient to rely on instructions from one senior executive during a phone or video call. Callbacks and verification are critical controls. In this case, a callback to the UK CFO and confirmation from head office before the transfer occurred could have avoided the loss.

I have witnessed significant voice fraud in financial institutions where funds were transferred through deepfake instructions by fraudsters. In many of these cases, controls that required a callback to the number on record were not followed by the employee who initiated the transfer. Some organizations still allow fund transfers based on recognizing the voice on the other end. This is of course an entirely useless control in the world we are living in. We are increasingly managing in a world where a person's physical essence can be misappropriated. On a positive note, Sam Altman advocates a tool called The Orb from Tools for Humanity, which offers "proof" of a human person (https://world.org/orb).

Managing Internal and External Fraud

As expressed by Sam Altman, AI is a significant driver of external fraud. While the world is experimenting on how to harness AI for good, the bad guys are using the technology for nefarious means. This includes creating deepfakes that imitate a bank customer's voice and mislead bank employees into transferring funds into external accounts. Other emerging schemes include conning phone companies into porting over a victim's phone number to their own device, so that they can get past authentication protocols, and business email compromise where an email account that is taken over includes instructions to move funds into accounts that the fraudster controls.

There are risk management controls that provide protection against these types of external frauds, but the controls need to be constantly updated and reviewed, as the fraudsters keep getting better at perpetrating their schemes. A first step in constructing a fraud framework is to have a process for identifying and assessing vulnerabilities, strong policies, and procedures, and assessing the effectiveness of controls. Data analytic tools that track trends are critical to monitoring the environment and, ideally, detecting external frauds before they are consummated.

Internal fraud should also rely on risk assessments, policies and procedures, and monitoring routines. With internal fraud, it is important to have strong reporting and whistleblowing procedures in place so that employees can confidentially report bad behavior when they witness it and to emphasize a culture of doing the right thing through education and training.

Financial institutions have investigation professionals in place that can investigate both external and internal frauds. This function can reside in a legal or compliance department and is responsible for determining if there is any misbehavior or malfeasance on the part of employees. They will work with law enforcement in both internal and external fraud cases, if criminal activity is suspected.

External fraud involves old-fashioned robberies, See Garda World robbery at end of this chapter, theft and fraud, hacking, and theft of information. Internal fraud involves unauthorized activities (see the JPMorgan London Whale case study at the end of this chapter), bribes and kickbacks, embezzlement, and inappropriate transfers of funds out of company or customer accounts.

The OCC provides the following definitions for internal and external fraud:

- ***Internal fraud*** *occurs when a director, an employee, a former employee, or a third party engaged by the bank commits fraud, colludes to commit fraud, or otherwise enables or contributes to fraud.*
- ***External fraud*** *consists of first-party fraud and victim fraud. External fraud is committed by a person or entity that is not a bank employee, a former employee, or a third party engaged by the bank.*
  - ***First-party fraud*** *occurs when an external party, including a bank customer, commits fraud against the bank.*
  - ***Victim fraud*** *occurs when a bank customer or client is the victim of an intentional fraudulent act.*

A lot of mishaps occur in a banking organization that are not internal fraud but rather mismanagement or negligence. At the center of the definition of internal fraud is the concept of intentionality. This is sometimes difficult to sort out and will require a root-cause analysis. If there is collusion between an employee and external party, the event is categorized as an internal fraud in the event database.

The following is the Internal and External branch of the Basel Operational Risk taxonomy that demonstrates types of internal and external fraud:

Event-Type Category (Level 1)	Definition	Categories (Level 2)	Activity Examples (Level 3)
Internal fraud	Losses due to acts of a type intended to defraud, misappropriate property or circumvent regulations, the law or company policy, excluding diversity/discrimination events, which involves at least one internal party	Unauthorized activity	Transactions not reported (intentional) Transaction type unauthorized (with monetary loss) Mismarking of position (intentional)
		Theft and fraud	Fraud/credit fraud/worthless deposits Theft/extortion/embezzlement/robbery Misappropriation of assets Malicious destruction of assets Forgery Check kiting Smuggling Account takeover/impersonation etc Tax non-compliance/evasion (wilful) Bribes/kickbacks Insider trading (not on firm's account)

(*Continued*)

(Continued)

Event-Type Category (Level 1)	Definition	Categories (Level 2)	Activity Examples (Level 3)
External fraud	Losses due to acts of a type intended to defraud, misappropriate property or circumvent the law, by a third party	Theft and fraud	Theft/robbery Forgery Check kiting
		Systems security	Hacking damage Theft of information (with monetary loss)

Source: Bank for International Settlements / https://www.bis.org/basel_framework/chapter/OPE/25.htm / Last accessed by Nov 07, 2025

The following are key considerations in the management of fraud:

Operational risk framework: Fraud is a form of operational risk. Fraud risk management must be aligned to the operational risk framework. This includes mapping from an industry or regulatory fraud framework to the operational risk framework and leveraging standard tools, such as RCSA, control assessment and management, and scenario analysis to determine impact and likelihood of fraud schemes.

Governance: A fraud governance program must include articulation of roles and responsibilities, including who owns the policy, framework, investigations, monitoring, and remediations.

Differences between internal and external fraud: Internal and external fraud are distinctly different beasts that leverage different industry practices and may be managed by different parties within the organization.

Risk thresholds: Establish loss thresholds for tracking external fraud events, which may be aligned with the operational risk loss thresholds (see Chapter 6) or may vary depending on impact to the business.

Risk appetite: The amount of fraud an organization is willing to accept both in terms of individual and aggregate fraud should be aligned to risk appetite statements. A certain amount of fraud in a retail and consumer financial services setting may be accepted as the "cost of doing business."

Incentive structures: Incentive structures can lead to poor conduct and internal fraud if they are designed to drive improper behavior. They should be reviewed regularly from the vantage point of whether they are inadvertently designed to drive undesired outcomes.

Fraud tools: The fraud tool sector is rapidly evolving, with existing vendors offering AI tools to detect fraud and new AI-centric vendors coming online. A red flag that indicates an existing tool may need to be replaced, is a large amount of "false positives" that create noise in monitoring routines and complicate the detection of fraud.

Training and education: Ongoing training, especially in light of developing AI threats, is critical and should emphasize the message that all employees must function as fraud risk managers. It is a strong practice to incorporate fraud events that the organization recently experienced into training and to walk through the event details, the root cause, and remediations during the training session. In addition, the fraud department should work on customer education so that there is an awareness of fraud schemes that are becoming more sophisticated every day.

Monitoring fraud schemes: The external environment should be monitored for new and existing frauds including those related to checks, wire transfers, peer-to-peer payments, social engineering, phishing, account takeover, business email compromise, romance and investment scams, identify theft, and deepfake impersonations.

Vulnerable clients: Special monitoring should occur on the accounts associated with vulnerable clients and especially the elderly who can get caught up in romance and investment scams. Unusual account activity should be monitored and family members who are listed as contacts on the account alerted of unusual activity. Failure to protect vulnerable clients is not only heart-breaking for the clients who are victims of these scams but also creates reputational issues for the financial firm.

Fraud Risk Management Frameworks

There are two fraud risk management frameworks that I have referred to for guidance on establishing and maintaining a strong practices program: the Association of Certified Fraud Examiners (ACFE) and the OCC's guidance from 2019; they set out standard principles that are aligned with each other and a standard operational risk framework.

The OCC's guidance includes acknowledgment that fraud is a form of operational risk and states the following fundamental concept: "Operational risk management weaknesses can result in heightened exposure to fraudulent activities, which can increase a bank's exposure to strategic risks. Failure to maintain an appropriate risk management system could expose the bank to the risk of significant fraud, defalcation (e.g., misappropriation of funds by an employee), and other operational losses" (https://www.occ.treas.gov/news-issuances/bulletins/2019/bulletin-2019-37.html).

The following is a mapping of the ACFE and OCC principles to an operational risk framework:

Operational Risk Framework Elements	ACFE Fraud Risk Management Principles	OCC Fraud Risk Management Principles	Explanation
Governance & Policy & Procedures	Establish a fraud risk management policy as part of organizational governance	Governance	Governance includes board/senior management oversight, tone at the top, policies, and roles and responsibilities

(Continued)

(Continued)

Operational Risk Framework Elements	ACFE Fraud Risk Management Principles	OCC Fraud Risk Management Principles	Explanation
Risk Appetite & Metrics	Establish a fraud risk management policy as part of organizational governance	Risk management	Defines the institution's tolerance for fraud risk and how it fits within the broader non-financial risk appetite; articulate frauds that are "cost of doing business" and monitoring and tracking threshold
Loss Data	Establish a fraud reporting process and coordinated approach to investigation and corrective action, including analyzing and remediating root causes	Fraud response, reporting, and information sharing	Tracks historical fraud losses to inform trend analysis, root-cause analysis, and control enhancement; align with operational risk loss event and incident requirements
RCSA	Perform comprehensive fraud risk assessments; Select, develop, and deploy preventive and detective fraud control activities	Risk management	Incorporates fraud risks into the RCSA process, identifies control gaps, and evaluates control effectiveness
Scenario Analysis	Perform comprehensive fraud risk assessments	Risk management	Uses forward-looking scenarios to estimate fraud exposure under stress or emerging risk conditions
Issue Management	Select, develop, and deploy preventive and detective fraud control activities	Risk management	Captures and remediates fraud incidents, control weaknesses, and emerging risks
Monitoring and Reporting	Monitor the fraud risk management process, report results, and improve the process	Fraud risk measurement and reporting; reviews and audit	Continuous oversight of fraud metrics, red flags, and escalation protocols through KRIs, dashboards, and internal reviews
Culture and Awareness	Establish a fraud risk management policy as part of organizational governance	Governance	Embeds fraud awareness through training, lessons learned, and senior management communication

The ACFE Principles (www.acfe.com)

ACFE Principle One: Establish a Fraud Risk Management Policy as Part of Organizational Governance

> *The organization establishes and communicates a Fraud Risk Management Program that demonstrates the expectations of the board of directors and senior management and their commitment to high integrity and ethical values regarding managing fraud risk.*

The fraud risk management policy must be aligned with the operational risk policy. Some firms include a small section in the operational risk policy on managing fraud and publish a separate and more detailed directive (see Chapter 8). The fraud office in the first line owns the policy in some firms, but the second line is also responsible for publishing requirements for managing fraud across the lines of defense.

Like other risk types, managing fraud takes a village, and collaboration across the lines of defense and businesses and functions. The following is an example of roles and responsibilities across the first and second lines of defense. This includes the first-line business, functions, and fraud department and the second-line operational risk and fraud risk management (which typically reports into the operational risk or compliance departments).

Fraud Management Activity	First Line of Defense (Business, Operations, Support Functions; Fraud Department)	Second Line of Defense (Risk, Compliance, Fraud Risk Management)
Governance & Policy	Define fraud policy and desktop procedures; incorporate fraud topics into business and control committee agendas; comply with fraud risk policies and internal standards	Define fraud governance, policy, standard and frameworks; report on fraud to risk committee and the board
Risk and Control Self-Assessments (RCSA)	Perform fraud-specific RCSA, document controls	Review and Challenge RCSA results, aggregate findings for risk committee and the board
Control Management	Design and implement preventive and detective controls	Provide guidance on control standards and perform control reviews
Fraud Detection & Monitoring	Identify and assess fraud risks in daily operations; monitor transactions for anomalies	Develop fraud KRIs, monitor trends, analyze loss data
Loss Event and Incidents	Business reports suspicious activities to Fraud department; follow escalation protocols	Establish escalation protocols; identify themes and trends; perform thematic reviews
Issue Management & Remediation	Own and remediate identified fraud control weaknesses	Monitor remediation progress, validate that issues are designed to mitigate risks

(*Continued*)

(Continued)

Fraud Management Activity	First Line of Defense (Business, Operations, Support Functions; Fraud Department)	Second Line of Defense (Risk, Compliance, Fraud Risk Management)
Fraud Investigations	Business supports fraud department investigations	Review results of fraud investigations; work with fraud department to conduct lessons learned and look across
Training & Awareness	Ensure appropriate fraud training is completed for respective business and functions	Develop fraud training in partnership with fraud department
Scenario Analysis & Emerging Risks	Participate in scenario workshops and risk forecasting	Facilitate fraud scenario analysis and stress testing
External Fraud Surveillance	Report fraud incidents and work with customers	Liaise with law enforcement, monitor industry fraud trends

ACFE Principle Two: Perform Comprehensive Fraud Risk Assessments

The organization performs comprehensive fraud risk assessments to identify specific fraud schemes and risks, assess their likelihood and significance, evaluate existing fraud control activities, and implement actions to mitigate residual fraud risks.

I have worked with fraud functions to integrate fraud risk assessments into RCSA, as I have done for all operational risk assessments. This required expanding the fraud branch of the operational risk taxonomy so that it could incorporate the specificity of the requirements of a fraud risk assessment. A new lower level in the taxonomy for fraud was created so that it could be incorporated into RCSA. I found this to be a better solution than running a separate fraud risk assessment, which opens up the complaint that there are too many risk assessments in an organization. If this is not possible, it is important to ensure that the risk ratings for RCSA and the fraud risk assessment are aligned.

Regardless of how the fraud risk assessment is conducted, the residual risk rating should be within appetite, as defined by risk appetite statements and metrics. The following are high-level examples of risk appetite statements and metrics:

- We have zero tolerance for internal fraud committed by employees.

Fraud Risk Appetite Statement	Metric	Low Threshold	Medium Threshold	High Threshold
We have zero tolerance for internal fraud committed by employees	Number of confirmed internal fraud incidents	0 incidents	1	2

- We aim to detect and report external fraud within 24 hours of discovery.

Fraud Risk Appetite Statement	Metric	Low Threshold	Medium Threshold	High Threshold
We aim to detect and report external fraud within 24 hours of discovery	Average time to detect and report external fraud	<24 hours	24–48 hours	>48 hours

- We seek to minimize financial loss from fraud events to within our risk tolerance.

Fraud Risk Appetite Statement	Metric	Low Threshold	Medium Threshold	High Threshold
We seek to minimize financial loss from fraud events to within our risk tolerance	Total annual fraud loss as % of revenue over rolling 12 month period	<0.05%	0.05–0.10%	>0.10%

ACFE Principle Three: Select, Develop, and Deploy Preventive and Detective Fraud Control Activities

The organization selects, develops, and deploys preventive and detective fraud control activities to mitigate the risk of fraud events occurring or not being detected in a timely manner.

Controls should be mapped to an organization's risks and processes. The OCC and ACFE provide guidance on the controls that should be in place to manage both internal and external fraud. Monitoring is an important detective control, and there are new solutions that utilize AI to properly monitor for signals that suggest anomalous activity. Behavior analytics are increasingly being deployed as a preventative control to identify signals associated with potential employee improper behavior.

Here are some standard preventative and directive controls to consider:

Governance controls: Policies, standards, procedures owned by first and second lines, and defined roles and responsibilities.

Communication and training: Tone from the top indicating the importance of implementing fraud controls and being vigilant; training focused on implementing controls and identifying improper or anomalous activity.

Customer education: Awareness campaigns aimed at customers, so that they are not unwittingly the victim of frauds and scams.

System controls: Controls integrated into internal, transaction, and customer systems that prevent improper activity among internal, external, and third parties.

Dual controls: Critical activities, such as financial reporting, fund transfers, and payments require an extra set of eyes to ensure the transfer is not only correct, but proper. This includes distinct maker (the person who sets up the transaction) and checker roles (the person who validates the transaction). High-risk transactions and activities should also require supervisory reviews and sign-offs.

Know-your-employee: Background checks for employees and contractors should be performed upon onboarding of new employees and refreshed periodically. Reviews of third-party background checks should be performed as part of the third-party due diligence process (see Chapter 15). It is a strong practice to also perform background checks on employees who will be engaged through third-party service-level agreements.

Mandatory leave: The lessons learned from rogue trading events is that employees who are risk takers or have control over functions that carry substantial risk must step away from their duties for some period of time, and often for two weeks, at least once per calendar year. This includes being disconnected from the network and day-to-day activities and communications. This is designed to uncover any improper behavior that presumably would be transparent if the bad actors no longer had access to the firm's network and systems. I have worked in organizations where mandatory leave was required for the risk management function and in other organizations where it was not.

Behavior analytics: Behavioral analytics is increasingly used to identify potential internal frauds. It creates baseline profiles of employees and monitors for changes and anomalies that might suggest improper behavior. This is accomplished through monitoring system usage, email correspondence, compliance violations, downloads, online usage, and workflow patterns. This is considered a preventative control because the goal of behavioral analytics is to identify potential bad behavior ahead of it occurring through certain signals, which allow for proactive remediation and course correction.

Here are some standard detective controls to consider:

Monitoring: Monitoring is the primary method for detecting internal and external fraud. Monitoring for internal fraud tracks data access and online behavior including file downloads and flags any changes from normal work patterns. Monitoring for external fraud applies real-time machine learning to detect suspicious patterns associated with transactions, customer behavior, devices connected to the network, new IP addresses, failed logins by external parties, and excessive account attempts.

Fraud data: Fraud departments collect a lot of data that they monitor closely. This includes charge-offs, fraud alerts, loss and recovery data, authentication records, logon failed attempts, transaction patterns, unusual employee work patterns, and dark web intelligence.

ACFE Principle Four: Establish a Fraud Reporting Process and Coordinated Approach to Investigation and Corrective Action, Including Analyzing and Remediating Root Causes

The organization establishes a communication process to obtain information about potential fraud and deploys a coordinated approach to investigation and corrective action to address fraud appropriately and in a timely manner.

In my experience, when I reported on operational risk to the risk committees of the board of the organizations I worked in, there was often heightened interest on the topic of external fraud. No senior executive or board member likes to see money being lost from fraud. It is important when reporting on fraud to the senior management and the board that the fraud is put in context including root cause and industry trends. For instance, I have experienced a pattern of controls breaking down among internal staff when external frauds occur. This included transferring funds based on voice recognition and forgoing double-checking by calling the phone number on record. I experienced a large business email compromise event when the business transferred funds based on an email request without calling the client about accounts that made no logical sense in terms of geography and industry. In both instances, the matter became a conduct issue.

Additional considerations to incorporate into senior management and board reporting is seasonality. External fraud often spikes during the last quarter of the year and around the holiday season. This can be presented to senior management and the board in the context of industry trends, as it is helpful to compare one's record with the industry.

Internal fraud reporting often flows through conduct or compliance committees, which include a cross section of senior representatives from the business, functions, compliance, risk management and audit. Significant internal fraud issues are escalated to the risk committee and the board and must be managed with a great deal of discretion. Often when they reach risk committee and the board, they are discussed through a special executive committee with limited attendees. This is especially true of internal frauds that involve senior executives or could result in litigation, regulatory censure, or reputational risk.

Each business should track fraud metrics, trends, and themes for their area and report through their first line risk and control committees (if they exist). Second-line risk management should work with the fraud office on aggregating fraud metrics and reviewing themes and trends and reporting the highlights and any emerging concerns through to risk committee and the board.

Fraud reporting should include trends and themes, root-cause analysis, volume and value of fraud incidents, losses by category, changes from previous reporting period, recoveries, and comparison to industry.

ACFE Principle Five: Monitor the Fraud Risk Management Process, Report Results, and Improve the Process

> *The organization selects, develops, and performs ongoing evaluations to ascertain whether each of the five principles of fraud risk management is present and functioning and communicates Fraud Risk Management Program deficiencies in a timely manner to parties responsible for taking corrective action, including senior management and the board of directors.*

The goal in any risk management program is one of continuous improvement. At the heart of this is a culture where losses are examined for their root cause, lessons learned applied, and a look across conducted to determine if the issue resides elsewhere in the organization. Notable fraud events over a predefined threshold must be tracked in the event loss database and reported through the operational risk reporting process.

Large events must be escalated as soon as possible to senior management following the firm's escalation requirements. Issues and action plans should be opened if control deficiencies are present. If data is compromised in an external fraud, regulators may need to be informed (see Chapter 8).

JPMorgan London Whale Case from ORX: An Example of Internal Fraud

ORX News reference: 5560
ORX Standard: Banking

JPMorgan Chase & Co.	USD 950,000,000.00 | US Dollar
USD 950,000,000.00 | US Dollar	EUR 775,485,000.00 | Euro
BL0202—Global Markets	EL0101—Unauthorized Activity
US—United States	North America
Loss Event	Published in media May 10, 2012

JPMorgan Pays USD $950 Million in Fines and Settlement After "London Whale" Trading Losses of Up to USD $6.25 Billion

JPMorgan Chase suffered trading losses of up to USD $6.25 billion after a large position in credit derivatives held by the firm's London-based chief investment office (CIO) soured. The losses were initially disclosed publicly in April 2012. JPMorgan was subsequently fined a total of USD $1.02 billion in relation to the event, of which US regulators fined the firm USD $800 million. On December 21, 2015, it was reported that JPMorgan has also agreed to pay USD $150 million to resolve a class action lawsuit brought by investors claiming they had been misled about the extent of the trading losses. JPMorgan has therefore paid a total of USD $950 million (EUR 775.5 million) to US regulators and investors.

On September 19, 2013, UK and US authorities fined JPMorgan a total of USD $1.02 billion for its role in the trading losses, including for control and management failings. The UK Financial Conduct Authority (FCA) imposed a GBP 137.6 million fine, the US Securities and Exchange Commission (SEC) imposed a USD $200 million penalty and required the firm to admit wrongdoing, the Office of the Comptroller of the Currency (OCC) imposed a financial penalty of USD $300 million, and the Federal Reserve fined the firm USD $200 million. On October 16, 2013, the Financial Times reported that JPMorgan agreed to pay USD $100 million in a settlement with the Commodity Futures Trading Commission (CFTC) and accepted that its "London Whale" trading incident had had a "manipulative" effect on credit derivatives markets.

Regulators found that traders had mismarked the position of the synthetic credit portfolio by using the most favorable end of the bid-ask spread to mark the position. By March 2012, according to the FCA, traders were deliberately mismarking the portfolio to conceal losses from senior management in the CIO.

The CIO's valuation control group, responsible for valuing the SCP, did not detect the mismarking "in a timely manner" according to the FCA. This represented a material control weakness in JPMorgan's financial reporting as at March 31, 2012. A valuation validation review also failed to uncover the extent of the valuation problems within the firm. Losses were originally estimated to be approximately USD $2 billion before being revised to USD $5.8 billion in Q2 2012.

In addition, according to the FCA, senior management within the bank "gave insufficient weight to inconsistencies raised in the information in its possession," and did not involve key parts of the bank's control framework in its review. For example, compliance in London was not informed of the review until May 10, 2012. The FCA also said that the bank had failed to be open and cooperative with regulatory authorities, for example about the extent of the losses suffered.

According to the bank, the role of the CIO is to invest excess deposits in high-grade securities. The complex trades that led to these losses were part of a hedging strategy intended to insulate the bank from fluctuations in the value of its corporate bonds and loan portfolio.

According to Bloomberg, in late 2011, Bruno Iksil, a trader at the CIO, made JPMorgan considerable profits on a USD $1 billion position on a credit default swap (CDS) index, shorting specific tranches of high-yield US corporate bonds. Iksil's position reportedly generated USD $450 million in profits after Eastman Kodak became insolvent and AMR filed for bankruptcy protection.

As the global economic outlook improved and credit markets eased, the CIO began to hedge this short position by selling large quantities of CDS for investment-grade corporate bonds on an index called CDX.NA.IG.9. However, volatile credit conditions meant the hedge became ineffective. With imperfect correlation between the two legs of the trade and in order to keep the position balanced, the CIO had to continue selling large quantities of long credit protection. In early 2012, because of the volume of CDS being written by the CIO, various market participants started to notice pricing distortions in the index. Media reports of Iksil's trades began to circulate in April 2012 nicknaming the trader the "London Whale" for his massive positions in the market.

Hedge funds reportedly capitalized on these distortions, exacerbating the paper losses JPMorgan's position was accruing. With losses mounting, risk managers reassessed the use of the CIO's newly developed value at risk (VaR) model. This new method of calculating VaR was artificially low. Under the new model, JPMorgan's Q1 2012 VaR was estimated at USD $67 million. Calculated using the CIO's original model, this figure increased to USD $186 million. This discrepancy likely concealed the impending losses from the CIO's complex trades.

According to Bloomberg, by May 2012 JPMorgan was confident that the losses had been capped as 80–90% of the position had been closed. Iksil and fellow CIO traders Achilles Macris and Javier Martin-Artajo left the bank in July 2012, following the May departure of the head of the CIO, Ina Drew. Furthermore, two former traders have been criminally charged in the US with hiding losses linked to Iksil.

An internal review of the losses, published by JPMorgan on January 16, 2013, quoted CEO Jamie Dimon as calling the investment strategy "flawed, complex, poorly reviewed, poorly executed and poorly monitored."

On December 21, 2015, it was reported that JPMorgan Chase & Co had agreed to pay USD $150 million to resolve a securities fraud class action lawsuit that was filed in 2012 by investors suing the bank over the "London Whale" trading scandal. The settlement includes anyone who purchased JPMorgan stock between April 13, 2012, and May 21, 2012, for example US and Swedish pension funds. Investors claimed they were misled about the extent of the losses and that JPMorgan knowingly hid the increased risks. During the one-month period, JPMorgan's share price fell by around 25%, leading to a loss of over USD $40 million of its market value.

According to the *Financial Times*, JPMorgan had made provisions for the settlement in 2015.

The USD $6.2 billion trading loss suffered by JPMorgan is categorized as a market risk loss and is not included in the loss amount for this event. The regulatory fines and investor settlement are operational risk losses.

Updates

September 19, 2013: Loss amount increased from USD $6.2 billion to USD $7.2 billion to reflect regulatory action from UK and US authorities. Paragraph 2 added and headline altered to include details of regulatory action.

October 16, 2013: Loss amount increased from USD $7.2 billion to USD $7.3 billion as a result of CFTC fine.

July 24, 2015: Loss amount changed from USD $7.3 billion to USD $1.02 billion following advice from the ORX Definitions Working Group. This advice sees the trading losses of up to USD $6.25 billion as a market risk loss, but the regulatory fines as an operational risk loss. Details added throughout.

JPMorgan reaches USD $150 million settlement with investors. Digest split between Loss Event 710 and Loss Event 5560 to separate UK and US jurisdictions. Paragraphs 1, 9, 10 & 13 altered, paragraphs 11 & 12 added.

Author: Yvette Lavelle **Published Date:** January 21, 2016 **Last Update:** January 21, 2016

Published In Media	**Occurrence —From**	**Occurrence —To**	**Discovery Date**	**Recognition/ Settlement**
May 10, 2012				
ORX Reference Taxonomy RT0806—Client mistreatment/failure to fulfil duties to customers				
Boundary Risk Other Risk	**Industry Event**			**Scenario** SC0005—Improper Business Practice
Product PD0308—Credit Derivatives	**Process** PC0502—Confirm and Document Transactions			**Event Closed** Yes
ORX Member Yes	**Role of Firm** LS0307—Position Taking (Principal)			**Jurisdiction/ Choice of Law** LS0101—United States of America
Cause 1 CS0204—Management/ Control of Staff	**Cause 2** CS0206—Unauthorized Activity			**Cause 3** CS0403—Inadequate Policy / Procedure
Counterparty LS0212—Not Identifiable	**Environmental Volatility** LS0403—Market Risk			**Provision** No

Garda World Robbery Case Study from ORX: Example of an External Fraud

IBM **FIRST**
RISK CASE STUDIES

FIRST Report for Loss Event 21311/OpData Id 25116

Short Description

On March 31, 2024, news sources reported that a burglary occurred at a GardaWorld Corporation ("GardaWorld") cash storage facility in Sylmar, Los Angeles. According to law enforcement sources, the suspects entered the building through the roof and accessed a secure area where cash was stored. The theft went undetected until the following morning, April 1, when it was discovered by staff. An estimated $30 million was stolen, making it one of the largest cash heists in Los Angeles history.

Organizations

Name	Firm	Country
GardaWorld Corporation	GardaWorld Corporation - No Firm Available	North America\Canada\Quebec

Details

Loss Amount:	30,000,000
Currency:	USD
Loss Amount Current:	30,982,512
Currency Original:	USD-United States Dollars
Original Currency Amount:	30,000,000
Status:	CLOSED
Geography:	North America\United States\California
Created Date:	Jun 23, 2025
Revision Date:	

Dates

Start Occurrence: Mar 31, 2024	End Occurrence: Mar 31, 2024	Settlement Date: Mar 31, 2024

Long Description

Event Summary

On March 31, 2024, news sources reported that a burglary occurred at a GardaWorld Corporation ("GardaWorld") cash storage facility in Sylmar, Los Angeles. According to law enforcement sources, the suspects entered the building through the roof and accessed a secure area where cash was stored. The theft went undetected until the following morning, April 1, when it was discovered by staff. An estimated $30 million was stolen, making it one of the largest cash heists in Los Angeles history.

Event Details

On Easter Sunday, March 31, 2024, news sources reported that a burglary took place at the GardaWorld cash storage facility located in the Sylmar neighborhood of Los Angeles. The perpetrators breached the facility at night, reportedly through the roof without triggering any alarms or alerting security personnel. Once inside, the thieves accessed a secure area, possibly a vault, and stole an estimated $30 million in cash. The break-in was not discovered until the following morning, April 1, when staff arrived and found evidence of the intrusion, including a boarded-up hole and scattered debris near the building. It was reported that the safe showed no signs of a break-in. News sources reported that at least one alarm is confirmed to have been triggered during the heist, but it didn't trigger a call to law enforcement.

According to the police log, the LAPD responded to 13 alarm calls at the building in the year prior to the heist, and all of them were determined to be false alarms. One such alarm occurred just before 11:30 p.m. on March 30, the night before the heist. A patrol car arrived at the warehouse minutes later and deemed it to be a false alarm. Another alarm rang at the building at 4:36 a.m. on Easter, according to the log. Hours later, the log shows, a police car was dispatched to the property, a supervisor was notified and a report was written.

Authorities believe that the circumstances of the burglary suggest the involvement of individuals with insider knowledge of the facility's layout and security systems. The FBI and LAPD are conducting a joint investigation into the incident.

Control Failings and Contributory Factors and Corrective Actions

Lax Security / Inadequate Technology Planning: Despite the officers' presence at the property in the early hours of Easter Sunday—including around the time it is believed the sophisticated burglary was carried out—the criminals remained undetected, according to three law enforcement officials familiar with the investigation of the incident.

The LA Times reported that GardaWorld did not learn of the crime until opening the vault the following day, April 1. It wasn't until then, officials said, that LAPD investigators were notified that a substantial amount of money had been taken.

Failure to Test Products or Systems - During at least one of the responses by a patrol car, GardaWorld was alerted, according to the officials, but the company did not register the intrusion. A longtime security consultant, said the success of the heist appeared to be the result of "a systemic failure." "The physical and the electronic security appear to have had a deficiency that was either not checked by the alarm company, and/or the security command center and/or the security director designated with making sure the system was more than adequate in light of its high-risk environment."

Strategic Flaw - a security consultant observed that "A well-protected facility that houses that kind of money ... normally in those facilities they have two separate alarm systems, they have sensors throughout the facility, cameras on the inside and outside," he said. "No matter how you penetrate the building, a sensor detects that activity and sends an alert. That's why it was such a shock."

Corrective Actions and Management Response

GardaWorld did not respond to requests for comment.

Keywords Indexing

Entity Type	PROFESSIONAL & OTHER SERVICES
Business Unit Type	OTHER -- (BUSINESS SERVICES)\OUTSOURCED FUNCTION
Service/Product Offering Type	RISK MANAGEMENT CATEGORIES\OPERATIONAL RISK MANAGEMENT
Contributory/Control Factors	LACK OF CONTROL\LAX SECURITY MANAGEMENT ACTION/INACTION\WEAK CRISIS MANAGEMENT OMISSIONS\FAILURE TO TEST PRODUCTS OR SYSTEMS STRATEGY FLAW\INADEQUATE TECHNOLOGY PLANNING STRATEGY FLAW\STRATEGIC FLAW
Loss Type:	Estimated
Loss Impact	DIRECT LOSS\WRITE-DOWN (BIS)\WRITE-OFFS
Loss Detection Sources	OTHER LOSS DETECTION SOURCES
Market Focus	RETAIL SERVICES
Event Trigger	EXTERNAL RISK CLASS\EXTERNAL FRAUD\ROBBERY
Basel Levels I & II	External Fraud\Theft and Fraud\Theft/Robbery
Basel Business Line	Others\All Other (Non-BIS)
Industry Event	

Rules and Regulations Indexing

Ratings

Ratings Action	Ratings Code	Effective Date	Ratings Watch/Outlook
Review - No Action	B+	Aug 29, 2023	Rating Outlook Negative
1 Rating found			

Source

2024-April-4: New York Post, "Thieves steal $30 million from vault in Easter heist, leave without a trace—cops have no idea how they did it" by Olvia Land

2024-April-4: ABC News: "What to know about the multimillion-dollar Easter Sunday cash heist in Los Angeles", By LeahSarnoff and Alex Stone

2024-April-16: USC Annenberg Media: "GardaWorld company under scrutiny after $30 million warehouse heist" By Zack Lara, Keira McNamara, and Dash Chaiyasen

2024-April-19: Los Angeles Times, "Police responded to alarm around time of $30-million L.A. heist, but thieves were undetected" by Richard Winton

and Daniel Miller

Claimant

Claimant Name:	
Claimant Type:	

Scaling Data

Scaling Date	Employees	Total Assets(USD $M)	Total Equity(USD $M)	Total Deposits(USD $M)	Net Income(USD $M)
N/A	N/A	N/A	N/A	N/A	N/A

Supporting Material

Revision Comments

Copyright Information

Source(s)

http://blogs.wsj.com/deals/2012/07/13/tracking-the-trade-timeline-on-j-p-morgans-london-whale/

http://online.wsj.com/article/SB10001424052702304070304577396511420792008.html

http://www.bloomberg.com/news/2012-07-24/trading-surges-boosted-whale-positions-beforeaudits.html

http://www.bloomberg.com/news/2012-07-13/jpmorgan-s-london-whale-two-bosses-leave-bank-wsjreports.html

http://dealbook.nytimes.com/2012/06/28/jpmorgan-trading-loss-may-reach-9-billion/

http://files.shareholder.com/downloads/ONE/2115138246x0x605013/81673636-8dc5-4ebb-a253-48a6b84f3b50/JPM_Q3_2012_Earnings_Presentation.pdf

http://www.fsa.gov.uk/library/communication/statements/2013/jp-morgan

http://www.occ.gov/news-issuances/news-releases/2013/nr-occ-2013-7a.pdf

http://www.federalreserve.gov/newsevents/press/enforcement/enf20130114a1.pdf

http://files.shareholder.com/downloads/ONE/2250747141x0x628656/4cb574a0-0bf5-4728-9582-625e4519b5ab/Task_Force_Report.pdf

http://uk.reuters.com/article/2013/01/16/uk-jpmorgan-whale-settlement-idUKBRE90F18120130116

http://www.fca.org.uk/news/jpmorgan-chase-bank-na-fined

http://www.fca.org.uk/your-fca/documents/final-notices/2013/jpmorgan-chase-bank-na

http://www.sec.gov/litigation/admin/2013/34-70458.pdf

http://www.occ.gov/news-issuances/news-releases/2013/nr-occ-2013-140.htm

http://www.federalreserve.gov/newsevents/press/enforcement/enf20130919a.pdfl

http://www.bloomberg.com/news/2012-07-11/dimon-risk-reputation-on-line as-jpmorgan-faces analysts.html

http://www.ft.com/cms/s/0/8663088a-35e6-11e3-b539-00144feab7de.html#axzz2hhyROVOl

http://www.ft.com/cms/s/0/1bb9e27e-a808-11e5-955c-1e1d6de94879.html#axzz3wefQWvlQ

http://uk.reuters.com/article/us-jpmorgan-lawsuit-londonwhale-idUKKBN0U41XZ20151221

Related links

https://news.orx.org/node/4976

Courtesy of O.R.X. (www.orx.org)

Bibliography

Clare Duffy. *OpenAI Sam Altman warns of an AI 'Fraud Crisis.'* CNN, July 22, 2025. https://www.cnn.com/2025/07/22/tech/openai-sam-altman-fraud-crisis.

David L. Cotton, Sandra Johnigan, and Leslye Givarz. *Fraud Risk Management Guide.* COSO (Committee of Sponsoring Organizations of the Treadway Commission) and ACFE (Association of Certified Fraud Examiners), 2nd Edition. March 2023. https://www.acfe.com/fraud-reAsources/fraud-risk-tools---coso/fraud-risk-management-guide.

Heather Chen. CNN. Finance worker pays out $25 million after video call with deepfake "chief financial officer." February 4, 2024. https://www.cnn.com/2024/02/04/asia/deepfake-cfo-scam-hong-kong-intl-hnk/index.html.

Office of the Comptroller of the Currency (OCC). *Federal Bank Regulatory Agencies Seek Comment to Address Payments and Check Fraud.* June 16, 2025. https://www.occ.gov/news-issuances/news-releases/2025/nr-ia-2025-53.html.

Office of the Comptroller of the Currency (OCC). OCC Bulletin 2019-37. *Operational Risk: Fraud Risk Management Principles.* July 24, 2029. https://www.occ.treas.gov/news-issuances/bulletins/2019/bulletin-2019-37.html.

Chapter 17

Managing Business Resilience

Operational resilience is where many of the critical risks—cyber, technology, business continuity, fraud, third-party, global warming, geopolitical—come together. It provides the foundation for ensuring that a firm of any size and in any industry can recover if business is interrupted. And it considers the impact of an interruption of a critical process on the organization's operations. It also includes an analysis of systematic risk on markets and industry. This is a two-headed approach, because although it's important to determine systemic impact, the impact to an individual institution and its critical businesses must also be understood and planned for.

At the core of understanding operational resiliency is the ability of a firm to deliver critical operations during a business disruption. The definitions in the regulatory documents from the Basel Committee, the Financial Conduct Authority, and the European Banking Authority focus their guidance on similar wording. Here is the definition from the US Interagency Guidance on Operational Resilience:

> *Operational resilience is the ability to deliver operations, including critical operations and core business lines, through a disruption from any hazard. It is the outcome of effective operational risk management combined with sufficient financial and operational resources to prepare, adapt, withstand, and recover from disruptions.*
>
> *Source:* https://www.federalreserve.gov/supervisionreg/srletters/SR2024.htm

The Basel Committee defines operational resilience as an "outcome that benefits from the effective management of operational risk." The Basel Committee assumes that "disruptions will occur" and banks must "take into account its overall risk appetite and tolerance for disruption." The committee defines tolerance for disruption "as the level of disruption from any type of operational risk a bank is willing to accept given a range of severe but plausible scenarios."

The Basel Committee defines the drivers broadly: "cyber incidents, technology failures and natural disasters," which could result in widescale systemic disruptions of the financial markets. In essence, being resilient involves a multilayer approach to risk management, including implementing all the core elements of an operational risk framework. This is predicated on the belief that an organization with a robust and comprehensive operational risk program will be resilient in the event of business disruptions, which is a competitive advantage during times of stress.

The following are key considerations in the management of operational resilience:

Operational risk framework: A strong operational risk framework and its implementation allows a firm to withstand disruptions. This includes mapping from the industry and regulatory frameworks to the operational risk framework and leveraging standard tools, such as RCSA, and scenario analysis.

Governance: A resilience governance program must include articulation of roles and responsibilities, including who owns the policy, framework, investigations, monitoring, and remediations.

Core business processes: Core business processes must be identified and prioritized ahead of potential business disruptions. These are processes that if disrupted would have systemic impact on the financial markets in the first order and, in the second order, would impact an organization's revenue, profit, or franchise value. The processes are often already identified through two programs: business continuity and resolution planning. Banks may leverage their recovery and resolution and business continuity plans to identify their critical processes for both operational resilience and RCSA. It is a strong practice, to have one list of prioritized and risk-ranked processes that is used for all risk management programs.

Every organization will need to determine what their core business processes are, and it varies by industry. The following are some examples for a banking organization:

- **Payments and settlements:** ACH, Swift, cross-border transactions, credit and debit card, and merchant services
- **Deposit-taking activities:** ATM, branch, online transactions, and cash vault
- **Loan operations:** Loan origination and underwriting, loan servicing and collections, mortgage, and credit card servicing
- **Trading operations:** Securities trading, trade confirmation and settlement, clearing and settlement of securities trades
- **Regulatory and financial reporting:** Call reports, financial statements, liquidity, funding, stress testing, capital adequacy, money laundering and compliance reporting to regulators
- **Customer support:** Online banking platforms, customer call center, branch operations

Business impact analysis: A business impact analysis is performed to determine the criticality of business functions and processes. This allows for prioritization if there is a business disruption. Rating processes by criticality may not be aligned with the seniority of the people who manage them. For instance, a senior managing director may be responsible for a process that is not as critical to operations, as a less senior operations person.

Business continuity plans: It is imperative that every firm have business continuity plans and playbooks in place. This includes having a plan for resource allocation if people are unavailable and walking through the plans so that if a severe business disruption occurs, everyone on point understands their role. The business continuity plans should include thresholds, often expressed as:

- **Recovery time objective (RTO):** The target time that is set for a resumption of operations after an incident. This is a period that is defined by the business, based on the needs of the enterprise.
- **Recovery point objective (RPO):** The time representing the maximum period of acceptable data loss. The RPO determines the frequency of backup operations necessary to prevent unacceptable levels of data loss.

Scenario analysis: Scenarios assist with visualizing what could happen and how severe a disruption can be. They allow for the consideration of severe but plausible events and validate the efficacy of business continuity plans and playbooks. They should focus on disruption of core business processes.

Tabletop exercises: Tabletop exercises allow for a walkthrough of selected scenarios and test for any gaps in planning for potential disruptions. They should include the actual role-playing and assigned roles and responsibilities so that there is awareness of who does what if a disruption occurs. They allow for a "test-drive" of the continuity plans, and lessons learned should be incorporated into business continuity plans and playbooks.

Risk appetite: An organization should articulate how much disruption it is willing to accept in the face of events that impact its ability to conduct business and to execute core business processes. This can be articulated in terms of RTO and RPO and should incorporate prioritization of core business processes.

Resilience Framework

The Basel principles on operational resilience provide a structure and framework that is reliant on operational risk management strong practices. The principles are aligned with guidance from the US Prudential Regulators, the Financial Conduct Authority, and the European Banking Authority. The principles incorporate the following elements: governance, operational risk management, business continuity planning and testing, mapping interconnections and interdependencies, third-party dependency management, incident management, and information and communication technology (ICT), including cybersecurity.

Governance: Basel Principle 1

> *Banks should utilise their existing governance structure to establish, oversee and implement an effective operational resilience approach that enables them to respond and adapt to, as well as recover and learn from, disruptive events in order to minimise their impact on delivering critical operations through disruption.*

The governance structure must incorporate board oversight and articulated tolerance for potential disruptions, policies and procedures, committees, and defined roles and responsibilities. The operational risk policy, which is owned by the second line of defense operational risk function, may include a high-level paragraph on managing resilience; a directive may provide more detail on the specifics, including references to business continuity, cyber, technology, and incident management, which may have their own policies and directives.

Operational resilience crosses many risk types and encompasses a diverse set of roles and responsibilities. For example, a third-party ransomware event will require remediation and review by the CISO office, the CTO office, third-party risk management, business continuity, a resilience officer if the position exists, the business or function where the event occurred, and second-line operational risk, which provides overall oversight of the remediation, root cause, and lessons learned process. This seems like a lot of people, but large events can be complex and require a diversity of skills and knowledge. It is important to have clearly defined roles and responsibilities that should be documented in a policy or directive.

Here are sample roles and responsibilities for the first line:

First-Line Role	Key Responsibilities for Operational Resilience
Business Unit	Identify critical business processes; map risks and controls to processes; establish risk tolerance and participate in scenario and tabletop exercises.
Process Owner	Owner of end-to-end process; ensure controls are effective; open issues and actions if there are control deficiencies; issue owner of impacted processes if an event occurs or control deficiency is identified; ensure controls associated with critical business processes are resilient.
IT & Cybersecurity Teams	Maintain system resilience (uptime, redundancy, recovery); ensure incident detection, response, and recovery plans align with RTO, RPO.
Facilities & Physical Security	Ensure workplace continuity, safety, and access controls in disruption scenarios.
Third-Party/Vendor Managers	Monitor resilience of critical outsourced services; enforce contractual resilience requirements.
Crisis Management/Incident Response Teams	Lead operational response to disruptions; escalate per playbooks; coordinate restoration of critical services.

Here are sample roles and responsibilities for the second line:

Second-Line Role	Key Responsibilities for Operational Resilience
Operational Risk Management	Develop and maintain operational resilience frameworks, policies and directives; establish methodology for identifying critical business processes; conduct scenario workshops; review and challenge RCSA; integrate into risk appetite.
Business Continuity Risk Management/Resilience Risk Management Oversight	Define and/or review and challenge impact tolerance standards; coordinate and oversee continuity testing; ensure consistency across business units; aggregate results for senior management.
Third-Party Risk Management (TPRM) Oversight	Ensure critical suppliers meet resilience requirements; review SLAs, recovery capabilities, and test evidence.
Cyber Risk Management Oversight	Monitor cyber resilience risk posture; challenge adequacy of detection, response, and recovery capabilities.
Compliance/Regulatory Affairs	Monitor compliance with resilience regulations (e.g., OCC, PRA/FCA, DORA); ensure timely regulatory reporting on disruptions; test for compliance with regulations.

Operational Risk Management: Basel Principle 2

Banks should leverage their respective functions for the management of operational risk to identify external and internal threats and potential failures in people, processes and systems on an ongoing basis, promptly assess the vulnerabilities of critical operations and manage the resulting risks in accordance with their operational resilience approach. Banks should leverage change management capabilities in accordance with the change management processes under the overall management of operational risk as a way to assess potential effects on the delivery of critical operations and on their interconnections and interdependencies.

The following are a recommended application of the operational risk framework in the management of operational resilience. It should be remembered that operational resilience is an outcome of strong operational risk management.

Risk Appetite: An organization should define its risk tolerance for disruption of critical business processes. This includes articulated RTO and RPO and the maximum tolerance for disruption.

The following are sample risk appetite statements for RTO and RPO:

- We maintain a low appetite for failure to meet defined Recovery Time Objective (RTOs) for all critical systems and processes.
- We maintain a low appetite for loss of critical data beyond the defined Recovery Point Objective (RPO) for critical business services and systems.

Statement	Metric	Green	Amber	Red
Recovery Time Objective (RTO) Compliance	% of RTOs met during incidents or tests	96%	90–95%	<90%
Recovery Point Objective (RPO) Compliance	% of RPOs met during incidents or tests	≥96%	90–95%	<90%

Events and incidents: Events that meet quantitative or qualitative thresholds must be entered into operational risk loss databases and remediated as necessary. Incidents should follow escalation protocols, including notification of regulators if required (see Chapter 8).

RCSA: Resilience-related risks and controls should be integrated into RCSA. The RCSA risks and controls should be re-evaluated when an event, incident, or near-miss occurs. Specific risks that could result in a resilience-related outcome include those related to cyber, systems, third-party, or natural disaster events. Testing results from business continuity and cyber programs should be integrated into the control assessment. Assessment of critical business processes should be prioritized for most frequent and in-depth reviews.

Scenario analysis: Scenarios are critical to understanding what could happen and an organization's ability to remain resilient and operational during a disruption. Scenarios should include the drivers for a disruption and dependencies among them, including cyber, systems, third-party, and natural disasters. Resilience scenarios should incorporate outcomes to understand the severity of a potential event.

Issue management: Control deficiencies that are identified through the construction of scenarios, RCSA, or event management must be considered for remediation and the opening of issues and action plans. Assigning owners for the issue and individual action plans are critical and can be challenging in some circumstances when processes cross businesses and functions. Organizations that have assigned owners for critical business processes will find this an easier exercise, as they will already have an "end-to-end process mindset." If this is not the case, someone in an enterprise function will need to step up and assume ownership of the issue. Multiple action plans are often assigned to an individual issue, with the action plan owners able to reside in multiple businesses and functions. Often, an enterprise-wide issue will require this construct. The issue owner is responsible for overseeing the remediations and escalating to senior management when deadlines are missed or unanticipated challenges arise.

Monitoring and reporting: Ongoing monitoring should take an integrated approach with the various elements of the operational risk framework, including reporting to the board on scenarios, RCSA results, any new issues, testing results, and risk appetite levels as measured by metrics and KRIs. In essence, resilience should be embedded in how the major drivers for disruption issues are monitored. Any significant control gaps associated with critical business processes should be highlighted in reporting to risk committees and the board.

Culture and awareness: Resilience should be embedded into the risk management culture of the firm and bolstered by messaging from the top of the house. Risk management training should incorporate resilience as an outcome associated with third-party, cyber, information technology, and damage to physical asset–related risks.

Change management: Change can often lead to unanticipated risk events, including outages during system integration or upgrades (see Chapter 11). Change management protocols should be followed throughout the lifecycle to ensure that business processes can perform as designed during this period. This includes adequate planning, staging of releases, and testing.

Business Continuity Planning and Testing: Basel Principle 3

Banks should have business continuity plans in place and conduct business continuity exercises under a range of severe but plausible scenarios in order to test their ability to deliver critical operations through disruption.

Fostering a resilient operating environment relies heavily on having a strong fit for purpose business continuity risk management program in place. This starts with defining the severe but plausible scenarios that could impact critical business processes and result in significant disruption. The scenarios should be designed to articulate the firm's ability to resume operations following a severe event.

Business continuity controls must be tested periodically to ensure that recovery and resumption objectives and timeframes can be met. A recovery playbook should be reviewed regularly to ensure it incorporates process, organizational, and system changes. Desktop exercises should be performed that allow for a walkthrough of roles and responsibilities if an event occurs, and identified control deficiencies should be remediated through issues and action plans.

The following are sample business continuity scenarios, with example controls, tests, and RTO/RPO:

Scenario	Description	Risks Tested	Relevant Controls	RTO/RPO Targets
Ransomware Attack	A ransomware attack encrypts critical network applications and halts core operations.	Data recovery capability; incident response speed; ransom decision-making (pay ransom or rebuild from backups)	IT disaster recovery playbook; communication plans	RTO ≤2 hours; RPO ≤1 hour
Data Center Outage	A power failure and cooling system malfunction causes a primary data center to go offline for 48 hours.	Failover to backup systems; RTO compliance; application and service dependencies mapping	Infrastructure redundancy; IT recovery; vendor support agreements	RTO ≤4 hours; RPO ≤2 hours

(Continued)

(Continued)

Scenario	Description	Risks Tested	Relevant Controls	RTO/RPO Targets
Pandemic	A severe flu outbreak affects 40% of staff, reducing workforce capacity for multiple weeks.	Cross-training of critical roles; remote work scalability; supply chain resilience	Workforce planning; communication protocols; remote work arrangements	RTO ≤8 hours; RPO ≤4 hours
Third-Party Provider Outage	A critical cloud service provider suffers a ransomware attack, impacting customer-facing applications and compromising customer and organization data.	Protocols for disconnecting from vendor; switching to alternate providers or internal manual processes; customer and regulator communication	Supplier risk management; contract SLAs; dependency mapping	RTO ≤2 hours; RPO ≤1 hours
Natural Disaster	A hurricane causes severe flooding in primary operations center, making it inaccessible for seven days.	Relocation to alternate sites; remote workforce capability; crisis communications	Facilities management; evacuation plans; disaster recovery procedures	RTO ≤6 hours; RPO ≤2 hours

Mapping Interconnections and Interdependencies: Basel Principle 4

> *Once a bank has identified its critical operations, the bank should map the internal and external interconnections and interdependencies that are necessary for the delivery of critical operations consistent with its approach to operational resilience. These plans should incorporate business impact analyses and recovery strategies as well as testing programmes, training and awareness programmes, and communication and crisis management programmes.*

As discussed, operational resilience is a thread that cuts across many of the operational risk type programs, such as cyber, technology, business continuity, fraud, and third-party. It is critical to understand the thread, including how each of these programs could result in a resilience event if a disruption occurs and proper controls are not in place or working as designed. Publishing and reviewing on a regular basis the roles and responsibilities matrixes that incorporate all the relevant functions can assist with understanding the interconnectedness among various functions. Mapping core business processes (see Chapter 11) should include where there are hand-offs between functions so that there is a complete understanding of the impact of a potential disruption.

Third-Party Dependency Management: Basel Principle 5

> *Banks should manage their dependencies on relationships, including those of, but not limited to, third parties or intragroup entities, for the delivery of critical operations.*

Due diligence and ongoing monitoring of third parties should include an assessment of their business continuity plans and their ability to meet their obligations under the terms of a service level agreement in the face of a severe business disruption. The contracting party should have some assurance that the third party's business continuity plans and controls are commensurate with their own. The contracting party should have built into their own plans and playbook, contingencies for operating critical business processes if the third party is unable to meet their obligations. This may include cutting the third party off from their network if a third party is the victim of a ransom attack, executing processes manually if the third party provided system support, or engaging an additional third party for assistance.

Incident Management: Basel Principle 6

> *Banks should develop and implement response and recovery plans to manage incidents that could disrupt the delivery of critical operations in line with the bank's risk appetite and tolerance for disruption. Banks should continuously improve their incident response and recovery plans by incorporating the lessons learned from previous incidents.*

Incident response plans should be built into an organization's business continuity plans and playbooks and be aligned with the requirements of the operational risk event, incident, and near-miss policy and directive (see Chapter 7). This includes defined roles and responsibilities and a communication plan. Most organizations have call trees in place that list the critical people that must be notified if a significant event occurs, that they test regularly. Notification protocols will include regulators if a data breach or cyber event is involved and is a strong practice regardless for notable events. The board and senior management will require immediate notification.

Several organizations that were able to respond quickly to the events of September 11, 2001, noted that they had conducted business disruption exercises on a regular basis, and when they needed to act swiftly in an emergency, they knew what to do. They noted that knowing who was responsible for what was critical in the face of the catastrophic event.

Information and Communication Technology (ICT) Including Cybersecurity: Basel Principle 7

> *Banks should ensure resilient ICT including cyber security that is subject to protection, detection, response and recovery programmes that are regularly tested, incorporate appropriate situational awareness and convey relevant timely information for risk management and decision-making processes to fully support and facilitate the delivery of the bank's critical operations.*

Cybersecurity is increasingly the risk that board members, senior management, and regulators are most concerned about when the assess resilience capabilities. Cyber testing programs should include an organization's ability to recover from a significant cyber event, either directed at its network and systems or through a third party. Business continuity plans, as discussed, should set recovery time and recovery point objectives, along with communication guidelines for all relevant stakeholders, including senior management, impacted employees, the board, and, if necessary, regulators and customers. These plans should be updated regularly as the threat landscape continues to evolve.

A bank should periodically review all components of its business continuity plans and playbook to ensure that contingency strategies and controls remain consistent with current operations, risks, and threats. I would argue that annual reviews are not sufficient in the current climate. These reviews should happen when a new vulnerability scenario emerges, the level of a certain threat increases, risk appetite metrics and KRIs cross certain thresholds, or an event, incident, or near-miss occurs.

Managing Climate Risk

Climate risk and in particular physical risk is increasingly a driver of operational resilience. As global warming increases and we live through year after year of record-breaking temperatures, it is imperative that all organizations have plans in place to prepare for potential weather and natural disaster disruptions. As I write this, a glacier outburst threatened to flood the city of Juno, Alaska, which was under an evacuation order. The Mendenhall glacier in the region was responsible for the flooding, which scientists attribute to climate change. Alaska is warming twice as quickly as the rest of the country according to the Federal National Centers for Environmental Information. Luckily, the city of Juno was spared due to barriers that were previously erected and that funneled the water away from the city in an example of effective resiliency planning.

Recently, we have experienced extraordinary heat and fires in Europe, with Edinburgh, Scotland, under heightened warnings of fire risk. The January 2025 wildfires in Los Angeles destroyed parts of Pasadena, Altadena, Pacific Palisades, Malibu, and Santa Monica. US Southern Coastal states experience devastating flooding from hurricanes regularly, and it may only be a matter of time before the US Northeast experiences another devastating storm like Hurricane Sandy. It has become a common occurrence for the US East Coast to be under air quality alerts as smoke travels down from Canadian wildfires. In the summer of 2023, New York City was plunged into near darkness, or rather a putrid yellowness, from these wildfires.

Operational risk functions have the responsibility of providing the framework and support for management of a firm's response to these dire environmental conditions, regardless of what the political situation is concerning global climate change. A firm's ability to be resilient in the face of environment physical risk is critical and at the most basic level of managing operational risk. Physical disasters such as fires and floods impact a firm's ability to operate on their premises and have devastating impact on the supply chain. Climate risk also has social impacts, such as the connection with pandemics (as native environments are compromised, animals are coming into closer contact with humans and can potentially spread zoonotic disease).

The following are the risks to consider when integrating climate into a resilience program. These can serve as a basis for constructing climate scenarios.

People:

- Employee lives can be disrupted by climate-related events, which can result in loss of access to their systems if they work from home or, in more extreme conditions, relocation from their homes. As an example, companies scrambled to find accommodation for their displaced New Orleans employees during Hurricane Katrina.
- The smoke from wildfires in Europe and Canada during the past few summer seasons drifted through wide swaths of territories and created health and respiratory issues for the impacted populations.
- There have been studies linking climate change to COVID, due to the impact of deforestation on wildlife. As a result, there is the risk of a rise in zoonotic diseases as close contact with wildlife increases, which could impact our people and resources and result in more pandemics, of ever-increasing severity, as mutations occur.
- Extreme heat conditions can impact worker productivity, as we witnessed over the past few summers during prolonged hot weather.

Process:

- Extreme weather events, wildfires, and pandemics impact the ability to transport goods or access critical resources such as raw materials and lead to supply chain disruptions across multiple industries.
- Climate heightens supply chain risks, with reliance on the movement of goods and services through multiple jurisdictions and with many in locations that are vulnerable to natural disasters.
- Physical infrastructure and property are at risk from extreme weather conditions and loss of access to premises resulting from damage to physical assets should be accounted for in business continuity plans.
- Critical processes and the ability to execute business and transactions can be disrupted by severe weather conditions. This can include the unavailability of physical premises or the critical resources to carry out the processes.
- Natural disasters can have impact on a third party's ability to service its clients and fulfill its obligations.
- Natural disasters can impact a financial institution's credit portfolio, if impacted customers are unable to make payments on mortgages and other loans.

Systems and Technology:

- Extreme weather conditions can impact systems and technology, such as data centers and power grids, when they are unavailable due to physical infrastructure damage. This was the case during Hurricane Sandy when the power grid in lower Manhattan was impacted (see case study).

- If power is impacted during a storm, data centers that require cooling can be impacted by HVAC failures.
- Power outages can disrupt online banking, payment systems, ATMs, and customer services.

External:

- Regulatory requirements related to climate change are complex globally, and more so in the United States in the financial services sector, with the recent backlash against ESG investment funds in some states. This has created a split in approach in the United States and European Union, where the later has seen flows into ESG funds hold steady, while some US funds have pulled back.
- A firm impacted by a natural disaster may need to alter certain assumptions made in regulatory filings.
- Climate change has impacted the supply chain, with the Panama Canal reducing container ship traffic at times due to drought and lower than usual water levels.
- Firms that have committed to net zero targets or publish lengthy climate reports should ensure that they can back up their claims with solid data to avoid regulatory and reputational consequences.

Case Study: Hurricane Sandy

Hurricane Sandy struck the US East Coast on October 29, 2012. It resulted in an estimated $74.1 billion in damages and, according to the US National Science Foundation, was the fourth costliest US storm in history, behind Hurricane Katrina in 2005 and Hurricanes Harvey and Maria in 2017. Sandy made landfall three times, in Jamaica on October 24, Cuba on October 25, and Brigantine, New Jersey, on October 29. It had an enormous wind span range and wind speeds exceeding 80 mph, with record storm surges along the coast, which led to catastrophic flooding in New York and New Jersey. The storm disrupted the power grid, transportation, and communications.

After Sandy touched down, Lower Manhattan below 34th Street was plunged into darkness for almost a week when the primary electric power utility on the east side of Manhattan was flooded. As a New York City resident who lived nearby, I heard the power plant on 14th Street near the East River blow, right before downtown Manhattan was plunged into darkness. I was surprised that there was no "failover" system to take over for the utility that became inoperable and, in retrospect, placing a major power utility next to a river is not the best strategy for remaining operational during major storms.

A report by New York City on rebuilding and resiliency following Hurricane Sandy pointed to an "improbable set of factors coming together in exactly the worse way to give rise to the catastrophic impacts of the storm." This included the storm's timing, which coincided with a full moon and a "spring high tide," which was higher than normal in the Atlantic Ocean on October 29. Sandy was massive, with storm force winds that spanned 1,000 miles, which made it three times larger in size than Hurricane Katrina. Rather than going up the East Coast and then heading out to sea as was the usual path for storms, Sandy took an unusual path as it was blocked by a high-pressure system to the north and pushed eastward by a low-pressure system, which eventually sent it westward and headed straight for New Jersey.

The New York City metropolitan area was hit particularly hard, with disruption to businesses that operated in Lower Manhattan. Buildings on or near the waterfront were severely flooded, and the power outage resulted in the shutdown of the city's transportation system. Even street traffic was chaotic, with traffic lights not working. Payment systems, trading operations, and banking services were all interrupted. Even more catastrophic, 43 New Yorkers died during the storm primarily by drowning, and tens of thousands of housing units were impacted.

Hurricane Sandy provided a test for the large financial firms' resiliency capabilities that resided in Lower Manhattan. Some were able to failover to backup sites, while others discovered that they had weaknesses in their ability to do so; some experienced insufficient backup capacity, incomplete data replication, or recovery procedures that simply were not workable in the present circumstances. Some third-party vendors suffered disruptions, due to the location of their operations and data centers. At the same time, there were disruptions in the telecommunications infrastructure, which made it difficult to communicate among data centers. Even firms that had backup centers in geographically diverse locations found communications challenges with their telecommunications providers that relied on an interconnected infrastructure.

The lessons learned from Hurricane Sandy were not dissimilar to those that were experienced 11 years earlier from the events of September 11, 2001. This included the importance of geographic diversity for facilities and data centers. Testing must validate failover capabilities and scenarios and recovery plans must account for disruption of power, transportation, and communications. These were all lessons learned during the earlier event that need to be continuously reinforced as business continuity plans are updated and reviewed.

In a warning that these types of events are no longer 1 in 100-year occurrences, the US National Science Foundation reported that researchers at Stevens Institute of Technology in New Jersey estimated that Jamaica Bay, New York, that experienced catastrophic flooding during Sandy could experience frequent severe flooding in the future. The researchers found that "the historical 100-year flood level would become a nine-year flood level by mid-century (2030–2050) and a one-year flood level by the late twenty-first century (2080–2100)."

Hurricane Sandy, with its complexity of impacts, provides a robust scenario for resiliency planning, which must include consideration of disruption of the infrastructure that we take for granted, along with damage to physical assets.

Bibliography

Basel Committee on Banking Supervision. *Principles for Operational Resilience*. March 2021. https://www.bis.org/bcbs/publ/d516.pdf.

Board of Governors of Federal Reserve. *SR 20-24: Interagency Paper on Sound Practices to Strengthen Operational Resilience*. November 2, 2020. https://www.federalreserve.gov/supervisionreg/srletters/SR2024.htm.

City of New York. Chapter 1: Sandy and its impacts. In *A Stronger, More Resilient New York* (pp. 9–18). NYC Special Initiative for Rebuilding and Resiliency. 2013. https://www.nyc.gov/html/sirr/downloads/pdf/final_report/Ch_1SandyImpactsFINAL_singles.pdf.

European Banking Authority. *Operational Resilience.* https://www.eba.europa.eu/regulation-and-policy/operational-resilience.

Federal Emergency Management Agency. *New York—Hurricane Sandy* (FEMA-4085-DR). 2012. https://www.fema.gov/sites/default/files/2020-09/pda_report_fema_4085_dr_ny.pdf.

Financial Conduct Authority. *Operational Resilience: Insights and Observations for Firms.* May 28, 2024. https://www.fca.org.uk/firms/operational-resilience/insights-observations.

Financial Conduct Authority. *PS21/3 Building Operational Resilience.* March 29, 2021. https://www.fca.org.uk/publications/policy-statements/ps21-3-building-operational-resilience.

Financial Conduct Authority. *Building Operational Resilience: Feedback to CP19/31 and Final Rules.* March 2021. https://www.fca.org.uk/publication/policy/ps21-3-operational-resilience.pdf#page26.

New York State Climate Impacts Assessment. *Preparing for "the Next Sandy": Lessons Learned from Superstorm Sandy's Impact on New York Public Housing and the Red Hook Community.* https://nysclimateimpacts.org/explore-the-assessment/case-studies/superstorm-sandy/.

Official Journal of the European Union. *Regulation (Eu) 2022/2554 of the European Parliament and of the Council of 14 December 2022 on Digital Operational Resilience for the Financial Sector and Amending Regulations (EC) No 1060/2009, (EU) No 648/2012, (EU) No 600/2014, (EU) No 909/2014 and (EU) 2016/1011.* https://eur-lex.europa.eu/legalcontent/EN/TXT/PDF/?uri=CELEX:32022R2554&from=FR.

Office of the Comptroller of the Currency. *Cybersecurity and Financial System Resilience Report.* July 2025. https://www.occ.gov/publications-and-resources/publications/cybersecurity-and-financial-system-resilience/files/pub-2025-cybersecurity-report.pdf?utm_source=chatgpt.com.

Pilita Clark. How the Next Financial Crisis Starts. *Financial Times,* June 26, 2025. https://www.ft.com/content/9e5df375-650d-492e-ba51-fb5a34e6ddd6?utm_source=chatgpt.com.

U.S. National Science Foundation. *Once-in-a-Lifetime Floods to Become Regular Occurrences by End of Century.* December 15, 2020. https://new.nsf.gov/news/once-lifetime-floods-become-regular-occurrences.

Index

Note: Page numbers in *italics* indicates figures and tables.

C

D

E

F